REVISED AND UPDATED
3RD
THIRD EDITION

Healing the hurt within

UNDERSTAND SELF-INJURY AND SELF-HARM, AND HEAL THE EMOTIONAL WOUNDS

Jan Sutton

Foreword by TRACY ALDERMAN,
author of *The Scarred Soul*

howto books

Appendix 6 (pages 439–445)
Short excerpts from this Appendix may be photographed for single
use for non-commercial educational purposes only provided the
source is credited in full. Outside of this use, the material must not be
reproduced for resale, redistribution, or any other purposes (including
but not limited to books, pamphlets, articles, video or audio tapes, and
handouts or slides for lectures or workshops). Permission to reproduce
these materials for these and any other purposes must be obtained in
writing from the Permissions Department of How To Books.

Published by How To Books Ltd
Spring Hill House, Spring Hill Road
Begbroke, Oxford OX5 1RX, United Kingdom
Tel: (01865) 375794. Fax: (01865) 379162
email: info@howtobooks.co.uk
www.howtobooks.co.uk

The right of Jan Sutton to be identified as author of this work has been
asserted by her in accordance with the Copyright, Designs and Patents
Act 1988.

First edition 1999
Second edition 2005
Third edition 2007

British Library Cataloguing in Publication Data
A catalogue record for this book is available from the British Library

ISBN 978 1 84528 226 4

Cover design by Baseline Arts Ltd, Oxford
Produced for How To Books by Deer Park Productions, Tavistock
Typeset by Kestrel Data, Exeter, Devon
Printed and bound by Bell & Bain Ltd, Glasgow

NOTE: The material contained in this book is set out in good faith for
general guidance and no liability can be accepted for loss or expense
incurred as a result of relying in particular circumstances on statements
made in the book. Laws and regulations are complex and liable to
change, and readers should check the current position with the relevant
authorities before making personal arrangements.

Healing the hurt within

howtobooks

Please send for a free copy of the latest catalogue:
How To Books
Spring Hill House, Spring Hill Road,
Begbroke, Oxford OX5 1RX, United Kingdom
info@howtobooks.co.uk
www.howtobooks.co.uk

Contents

. . . .

Illustrations, interviews, case studies and charts

. . . .

Illustrations

Interviews

Case studies

Charts

Acknowledgements and credits

. . . .

This book's creation would not have been possible without the generous help, support, and input from a great many individuals and organisations.

I wish to express my deepest appreciation to all the courageous individuals whose voices appear throughout the book. Their words bring life to the text and their willingness to share their unique personal stories and knowledge of self-injury brings a depth of understanding to a complex subject. I feel truly humbled and honoured by the faith and trust bestowed on me, and to have the singular privilege of being in a position to advance awareness and demystify the many myths and misconceptions commonly held about self-injury.

My heartfelt thanks also go to numerous experts in the field of self-injury, trauma and dissociation for the precious gift of their time, support and valued contributions which add further breadth and richness of understanding to the topics covered in the book – to Tracy Alderman, Karen Marshall, Barent Walsh, George F. Rhoades, Rosemary Bray, Chris Holley, Rachel Horton, and Richard Pacitti. Equally prized are contributions from charitable organisations, namely, Bristol Crisis Service for Women, CIS'*ters,* and Breaking Free. Furthermore, a special thank you to Stephanie Davies and Penumbra for allowing me to summarise the findings of their research into self-harm, and to Cheryl Rainfield, Jenny Stucke, Jo, and Annie for permitting me to include their enlightening and powerful healing tools.

I also wish to extend my sincere gratitude to Tacita and Erin for their steadfast support for my work over many years, for their encouragement to keep going at times when

I was feeling overwhelmed by the enormity of the project, and the massive amount of information received. Beyond that I owe them a great debt of thanks for their insightful contributions to the manuscript, their assistance with proof reading and editing: most of all I value their true friendship, and their strength, for which I have the utmost respect.

Finally, my genuine thanks go to my nearest and dearest for putting up with being neglected while I was a slave to the project. My husband, Gordon, deserves a medal for being such a patient and perfect house husband. He, probably above all others, having lived with me throughout the long hours of writing, as well as the trials and tribulations of bringing this important project to a conclusion, knows precisely how much it means to me.

Credits

The author gratefully acknowledges permission to reprint material from the following sources:

Chapter 4: Media assertions and attitudes to self-injury, the magnitude of the problem and controversies
The safe self-injury initiative
© 2007 Chris Holley and Rachel Horton

Chapter 5: Two research studies examined
Davies S. C. (2002). Self-harm: An examination of Antecedent and Maintenance Factors. Unpublished study. Masters Degree in Forensic Behavioural Science, Liverpool University.
© 2002 Stephanie Caroline Davies.

Penumbra (2001). No Harm in Listening.
© 2001 Penumbra

Chapter 10: Heal thyself
Alternatives to Self-Injury
© Annie

Releasing anger
© Breaking Free
Reprinted from Newsletter Edition Three

Releasing emotions by Jo
© Guernsey Association for Mental Health (MIND)

What to do when you feel like hurting yourself
© Cheryl Rainfield
Talking to your critical voices
© Cheryl Rainfield

Wise and comforting words
© Jenny Stucke

Chapter 12: Guidelines for those working with self-injury and related issues
Alderman, T., and Marshall, K. (2006). 'Working with Self-Injuring Clients', paper presented at the conference 'Understanding Self-Injury and Responding Appropriately'. University of Southampton, Hampshire, UK, 08 April.
© 2006 Tracy Alderman and Karen Marshall.

Bray, R. (1999). Dissociation. In J Sutton *Healing the Hurt Within: Understand and relieve the suffering behind self-destructive behaviour* (pp. 122-127). Oxford: How To Books.
© 1999 Rosemary Bray.

Helpful responses to self-injury
© Bristol Crisis Service for Women (BCSW)

Rhoades, G.F. (1998). 'Therapeutic precautions to help prevent false memory allegations'. In *Trauma & Dissociation (TAD), Trauma & Dissociation Newsletter,* Vol.1, No.1.
© 1998 George F. Rhoades.

Appendix 2
'DSM–IV–TR™ criteria for Posttraumatic Stress Disorder, Depersonalization Disorder and Borderline Personality disorder.' *Diagnostic and Statistical Manual of Mental Disorders,* Fourth Edition, Text Revision. Washington, DC, American Psychiatric Association.
© 2000 American Psychiatric Association.

'TABLE 9.2. Disorders of Extreme Stress Not Otherwise Specified (DESNOS): Proposed Criteria' by van der Kolk, B. A., McFarlane, A.C., & Weisaeth, L (eds.) (1996). *Traumatic Stress: The effects of overwhelming experience on mind, body, and society.* New York: The Guilford Press (p. 203).
© 1996 The Guilford Press.

Appendix 5
CIS'*ters:* Member Code of Contact
© CIS'*ters*

Foreword

· ·

The demand for a third edition of Healing the Hurt Within makes quite a statement about the role of self-injury in our society. There is no debate that self-injury is a behaviour that has become much more visible in society over the past several years. Whether this is just a media created mirage or an actual increase in the number of people hurting themselves still remains to be verified through research. Nonetheless, interest in the field of self-injury continues to grow and the need for quality information on this behaviour is enormous. Those who are hurting themselves, those who are helping self-injurers in a professional capacity, and those who care about people who intentionally hurt themselves are finding themselves at a loss when seeking comprehensive written material that explains, educates, and offers hope regarding these behaviours. Jan Sutton's third edition of *Healing the Hurt Within* is an excellent resource for anyone wanting to know more about this mystifying and often misunderstood behavior.

You'll find that the third edition of *Healing the Hurt Within* is dramatically different from the previous edition. Throughout, the stigma associated with self-injury is reduced and many of the myths and misconceptions regarding the behaviour are clarified and corrected. Jan Sutton explores the reasons why people hurt themselves and the cyclic nature of this act. Noting the impact of trauma on self-injury, this edition of *Healing the Hurt Within* contains a chapter specifically dedicated to this topic. The role of dissociation in relation to self-injury is also explored more fully as well.

Each chapter is loaded with current research, case studies, and helpful ways to understand this complex topic. Throughout the text, Jan weaves quotations, passages, and stories from those who are most familiar with this topic: those who intentionally hurt themselves. These powerful passages will captivate you and give you a glimpse into the world of the self-injurer: from hurting to healing to helping others.

With her vast experience and decades of work as a counsellor, researcher, trainer, and author, Jan creates a truly comprehensive guide to understanding self-injury and providing information designed to help those who are hurting themselves. The third edition of *Healing the Hurt Within* is without question an inclusive and indispensable book about self-injury.

Tracy Alderman, Ph.D.
Author of *The Scarred Soul: Understanding and Ending Self-Inflicted Violence*
Co-Author of *Amongst Ourselves: A Self-Help Guide to Living with Dissociative Identity Disorder*

Preface to the third edition

. . . .

Since publication of the second edition of *Healing the Hurt Within*, much has changed in the self-injury arena. Thus being presented with an invitation from the publishers to write a third edition is appreciated. This new edition has altered radically from its predecessor. While the popular and eye-catching cover remains virtually unaltered from the previous edition, the text has grown from nine to thirteen chapters and includes four new appendices. To reflect advancements in the field, existing chapters have been reworked and further developed, and new topics, testimonies, artwork and case studies have been added. Fresh diagrams have also been incorporated and, to give the book a more reader-friendly appeal, the layout has undergone a face-lift. Additional enlightening contributions from respected experts and voluntary organisations working in the field add a further new dimension to the book. With the intention of guiding the reader to supplementary reliable sources of information, the resources section has been fine-tuned, and the further reading section revised with details of the latest publications on self-injury. Well referenced to original sources, extensively indexed, and presented in a no-frills style, this engaging third edition offers an unrivalled panoramic view of self-injury.

The timescale set for completion of the manuscript for the second edition prevented the inclusion of a significant amount of new data revealed through a qualitative research study undertaken by me via the Internet with 74 females and 8 males with experience of self-injury. Hence, writing this new edition has afforded a welcome opportunity to present a sizeable quantity of new material, and to build on areas previously examined.

Aims of the book

The overall aims of this new edition are to:

- Raise awareness and understanding of self-injury, reduce the stigma and challenge the myths and misconceptions surrounding self-injury.
- Provide comfort, compassion, acceptance, hope and guidance on healing to those who self-injure.
- Guide family members and friends to responding appropriately to a loved one who self-injures and encourage them to address their own needs for support.
- Present workers with a range of useful tools to direct them in their work, empower them to work more confidently with the challenging issue of self-injury, and to underscore the need for self-care and ongoing supervision to avoid the risk of compassion fatigue.

New material

Many people who self-injure feel invisible, insignificant, ignored and voiceless. In keeping with the popular format of earlier editions, considerable space is given to hearing the poignant voices of those with experience of self-injury. Some are harrowing to hear; others are heartening and inspirational and demonstrate clearly that with courage and commitment, the uphill battle to overcome or reduce self-injury can be won. New to this edition are the voices of males struggling with self-injury, and family members and friends concerned about a loved one that self-injures.

Experienced therapists and authors Tracy Alderman and Karen Marshall offer additional sound and practical advice for responding effectively to self-injuring clients. Furthermore, Consultant nurse Chris Holley and her colleague Rachel Horton (RMN) clearly explain the controversial 'safe self-harm' pilot scheme recently implemented at South Staffordshire and Shropshire Healthcare NHS Foundation Trust. Added guidance is also provided for teenagers considering turning to self-injury as a way of coping with their difficulties, and the possible reasons for high self-injury rates in prison are explored.

New appendices include a table of acronyms and colloquialisms, a series of questionnaires used in the Internet research into self-injury, a member code of contact for participating in a survivor-run group, and a reproducible training resource comprising six composite case studies and a set of questions designed to examine reactions to self-injury.

Exploration of the pivotal role self-injury plays in alleviating 'unacceptable tears', unhealthy perfectionism, negative core beliefs, and 'never feeling good enough' adds another fresh element to the book. Ten common myths about self-injury are examined and challenged, the differences between compulsive and impulsive self-injury explored, and sexual self-injury aimed at stimulating sexual arousal is distinguished from self-injury used as a coping mechanism to regulate acute emotional distress. Other newly introduced topics include the association between body modification and self-injury for some people, the distinct needs cutting and burning serve, and the premise that increased stress levels can result in more serious episodes of self-injury.

Reworked and expanded sections

Reworked and expanded sections focus on increasing understanding of the correlation between dissociation and self-injury and highlighting the role of unresolved trauma and posttraumatic stress symptoms in motivating internal self-injury. More attention is drawn to media attitudes and assertions to demonstrate how inaccurate media coverage can fan the flames of misunderstanding, prejudice, stigma, and inaccurate reporting of statistical data on self-injury. Other more developed themes include counselling and therapy, self-help, and the perceived losses of stopping self-injury.

An overview of the differences between editions 2 and 3

In order to compare the main differences between editions 2 and 3, organisation of the two editions is presented below:

Healing the Hurt Within
2nd edition
Chapters

1. Exploring self-harming behaviour
2. Piecing together the puzzle of self-injury
3. Getting to the heart of the matter
4. The cycle of self-injury, the role of dissociation in the cycle, and the eight Cs of self-injury
5. Confusion in terminology and controversy in the media
6. Helping and healing
7. Heal thyself and helpful responses
8. Eating distress
9. Creative works by contributors

Healing the Hurt Within
3rd edition
Chapters

1. Exploring self-injury and self-harm
2. Looking beyond the myths
3. Further insights into self-injury
4. Media assertions and attitudes to self-injury, the magnitude of the problem and controversies
5. Two research studies examined
6. Childhood trauma, negative core beliefs, perfectionism and self-injury
7. The cycle of self-injury and the eight Cs of self-injury
8. Dissociation and self-injury
9. Hurting and healing: true stories
10. Heal thyself
11. Guidance for family and friends, and teens considering self-injury
12. Guidelines for those working with self-injury and related issues
13. Creative works by contributors

Appendices

1. DSM–IV-TR criteria for:
   Posttraumatic Stress Disorder
   Depersonalisation Disorder
   Borderline Personality Disorder
   Disorders of Extreme Stress
   Not Otherwise Specified
   (DESNOS) *Proposed Criteria*
2. Therapeutic precautions to
   help prevent false memory
   allegations
3. Guidelines for treating
   Dissociative Identity Disorder
   (DID), dissociation checklists, &
   diagnostic tools
4. Self-injury monitoring charts
   and two pathways to self-injury
   diagram
5. Self-harm: An examination of
   antecedent and maintenance
   factors: Summary of a 2002
   study of 325 people that self-
   harm

Appendices

1. Table of acronyms and
   colloquialisms
2. DSM–IV-TR criteria for:
   Posttraumatic Stress Disorder
   Depersonalisation Disorder
   Borderline Personality Disorder
   Disorders of Extreme Stress
   Not Otherwise Specified
   (DESNOS) *Proposed Criteria*
3. Questionnaires
4. Self-injury monitoring charts
5. CIS'*ters:* Member Code of
   Contact
6. Case studies: training resource

Information removed and relocated

To accommodate space for the inclusion of new material, it has been
necessary to remove some information from Edition 2. Extracted
subject matter includes Chapter 8 (Eating Distress) (key points now
appear in Chapter 1) and the citations section. Those seeking self-
injury references are encouraged to visit my SIARI (Self-Injury
and Related Issues) website: http//www.siari.co.uk. Other material
removed due to space limitations includes the 1997 Guidelines for
treating Dissociative Identity Disorder (DID) by *The International
Society for the Study of Trauma and Dissociation* (ISSTD) which were
extensively updated in 2005. *See pages* 266–267 for details of accessing
the revised guidelines online. Important material retained from the

appendices of Edition 2 has been incorporated into the main text in Edition 3.

Who will benefit from reading this book?

To date, *Healing the Hurt Within* is the only book on self-injury published in a third edition. It weaves together a rich tapestry of information presenting the truth about self-injury – explaining why it happens and clarifying what it achieves. Importantly, it demonstrates that recovery from self-injury and preventing the external wounds requires *healing the hurt within*. Moreover, it unequivocally demystifies and de-stigmatises self-injury, showing the behaviour exactly for what it is – an effective (albeit unorthodox) coping mechanism for dealing with difficult feelings, emotions, and circumstances – in other words – an insurance policy to safeguard survival, rather than an act designed to end one's life. As one respondent clarifies:

> 'SI [self-injury] is a coping mechanism that has many bad sides, but it works. It is a way to deal with extreme emotional distress, a way to survive.'

Writing this third edition has increased my knowledge and understanding of self-injury. I trust this additional learning is reflected in the book.

It is my sincere hope that it will provide inspiration and help to those who battle with self-injury, and support and guidance to family members and friends striving to help a loved one that self-injures. For those faced with the challenging behaviour of self-injury during the course of their work, my hope is that the book will provide direction on appropriate interventions as well as encouragement to look beyond the wounds and non-verbal language of self-injury. In sum, the book will be of value to anyone wishing to enhance their comprehension about this perplexing and widely misunderstood issue.

Notes

Contributions integrated into this book come from people from different parts of the globe. In the main, for purposes of clarity and consistency, British English spellings have been applied throughout the text.

To avoid stereotyping, wordiness, and awkward phrases, feminine and masculine pronouns are applied interchangeably throughout the text where possible. The terms 'therapy' and 'counselling', also applied interchangeably, essentially refer to the same practice. Further, although the predominantly used term is 'client', the term 'patient' could equally be applied.

Jan Sutton

Cautions, disclaimer, and notes

Cautions

1. Self-injury is a sensitive issue, which can be upsetting to read or think about. While the aim of this book is to offer those of you who use self-injury as a coping strategy, hope, help, and support, it is possible you will feel triggered to self-injure by some of the material, particularly if you are new to studying the topic. Please read with caution and keep yourself safe – put the book down if you begin to feel anxious, vulnerable, or start to lose focus (feel 'detached' or 'spaced out'). If you are in the early stages of healing from self-injury it may be advisable to read the book with support from a friend, loved one, or your therapist or counsellor if you have one.

2. This book contains some strong language as well as sexual content. It is therefore unsuitable for young children.

Disclaimer

Whilst every effort has been made to provide accurate information concerning the subject matter covered in this book, the publisher and author expressly disclaim responsibility in law for negligence or any other cause of action whatsoever. Moreover, inclusion of material does not necessarily imply endorsement of information, nor agreement with the views expressed.

The diagnosis and treatment of psychiatric disorders requires a doctor or qualified mental health professional. The information provided in this book, intended for informational purposes only, should not be used as a substitute for the diagnosis of mental illness – if help is required, the services of a health professional should be sought.

Contributors' personal testimonies, poems, stories and artwork

The personal contributions included in this book have been offered voluntarily and willingly in the hope that it will help readers gain a better understanding of self-injury. Apart from where specifically requested, names have been changed or omitted to protect the contributors' identities.

Chapter 1

Exploring self-injury and self-harm

. . . .

*Self-injury is an expression of acute psychological
distress. It is an act done to oneself, by oneself,
with the intention of helping oneself rather
than killing oneself. Paradoxically, damage is
done to the body in an attempt to preserve
the integrity of the mind.*
—Sutton and Martinson (2003)

Zoe feels depressed, empty, and numb. She lacks the energy to cope with the day ahead of her. The world around her seems fuzzy and unreal, almost as if she is wrapped up in cotton wool, and she cannot think straight. She lights up a cigarette, and starts burning circles on her thigh. When she begins to feel the pain from the burns the haze lifts and she feels different – she can think straight, she feels energised, more alive, more real, and she is ready to face the day.

Arabella is having a flashback. She is seeing vivid images in her mind of traumatic events that she experienced as a young child. She is terrified and feels very small. Her heart is pounding; she is sweating and shaking. She grabs a knife from the kitchen drawer and makes a cut on her left forearm. As soon as she sees her blood flowing, the frightening pictures fade from view. She feels calmer and safe. After carefully dressing her wound and cleaning the knife, she makes herself a hot drink, switches on her favourite record, curls up on the settee and quickly drifts off into a deep and peaceful sleep.

Beyond reason

If read through the eyes of someone who has never self-injured, these fictional scenarios may have caused a furrowed brow of bewilderment. Perhaps the thought of what Zoe and Arabella do to themselves made you flinch, or you found yourself thinking something along the lines of, *'But I just don't get it – that's horrible – how can anyone possibly do that to themselves?'* or *'It's beyond reason, it just doesn't make sense'*. Be assured that if your thinking took a similar route, you are certainly not alone. Self-injury frequently stirs up negative emotions in loved ones, caregivers and society in general. Typical reactions include shock, anger, revulsion, fear, and panic.

Self-injury is widely misunderstood. It is an uncomfortable subject to think about, to talk about, a difficult behaviour to accept, and dealing with the issue presents many challenges to caregivers. The motivations that drive self-injury are diverse, and the behaviour can hold a multitude of different meanings. Further, while those of us who don't self-injure may ponder long and hard trying to make sense of the seemingly senseless, the behaviour usually, though not always, makes perfect sense to those who practise it.

Too familiar

If read through the eyes of someone who self-injures, the scenarios may have felt too close for comfort. Alternatively, you may have felt reassured to know that you are not the only person in the world who self-injures – *many think they are*. Perhaps you don't understand what makes you want to hurt yourself and that's what drew your attention to this book; maybe you feel isolated, desperate, or misunderstood, and are wondering what to do for the best; or perhaps you are seeking ideas on how to stop or reduce the behaviour, or are considering seeking help.

'Sometimes I don't even know why I'm doing it – I just feel an enormous pressure building up, I get restless and edgy and something has to give.'

'I just don't understand why I hurt myself. I wish I did. I've never been abused, I've got a loving mum and dad and a pretty perfect home life. I don't want for anything, am intelligent, yet I feel depressed most of the time, and can't help thinking I'm a waste of space.'

My hope is that this book will bring those of you who self-injure comfort and reassurance that with the right help and support there is a road out of self-injury. Moreover, I remain optimistic that you will acquire some therapeutic tools to help you on your healing pathway. It takes courage and determination to leave self-injury behind, and it would be remiss of me to tell you that letting go of self-injury is an easy process. However, as you will see later in the book people do recover, or they manage to reduce self-injury to a more acceptable level. Often, the hardest step is the first one – admitting to having a problem and reaching out for help.

Choice of terminology

To date, self-injury, which is the primary focus of this book, is not classified as a disorder or syndrome, therefore it does not appear in DSM-IV-TR (APA, 2000), the widely used American *Diagnostic and Statistical Manual of Mental Disorders*. Further, there is no universally agreed term to describe the behaviour, consequently an array of clinical labels and acronyms are applied throughout the literature. The most common are:

- Self–harm (SH)
- Deliberate self–harm (DSH)
- Self–injury (SI)
- Self–mutilation (SM)
- Self–inflicted violence (SIV)
- Self–injurious behaviours (SIBs).

The terms *self-harm* and *deliberate self-harm* are mainly used in the United Kingdom, whereas the terms *self-injury, self-mutilation, self-inflicted violence* and *self-injurious behaviours* are more widely used in America. Other terms employed include *parasuicide, 'cutting', self-cutting, self-wounding, and self-abuse.* The downside of using such a large assortment of terms is, (1) it muddies the waters over what behaviours comprise self-injury, and (2) it hinders establishing the prevalence of the problem.

For further discussion on the perennial problem of terminology see Chapter 4.

Why the term self-injury?

In my dilemma over what term to use in *Healing the Hurt Within,* 2nd edition (Sutton, 2005), the respondents involved with the research for that book were invited to comment on which term they considered most appropriate. The majority regarded 'self-injury' or 'self-injurious behaviours' as the most fitting terms to describe what they do, hence these will be the principal terms used in this new edition. However, the term 'self-harm' will be applied on occasion when material derived from *Healing the Hurt Within,* 1st edition (Sutton, 1999) is used. The term 'self-injurer' will be avoided as this causes offence to some people who use self-injury – the reason being that while self-injury may be one aspect of their behaviour, it does not represent the 'whole' of them. In other words, the term self-injurer dehumanises people, strips them of their identity, and labels them by what they do rather than acknowledging them for the unique human beings they are.

Other writers' work

When referring to other authors' and researchers' work, or quoting directly from research respondents' material, the terms applied will reflect the writer's choice.

Respondents' observations on terms

Below are a few of the comments received from respondents concerning terminology, from which you will note that the term 'self-harm' is considered too broad, and the terms 'self-mutilation' and 'self-inflicted violence' (SIV) are considered unacceptable or misleading:

'I prefer "self-injury" because it is my soul that is in pain and injured, and that is the reason that the injury becomes visible on my body as well. The term "mutilation" dissociates my soul from the matter, and that is a mistake.'

'I don't like the term "self-mutilation". It suggests to me permanent wounds, more severe wounds. The term "self-harm" is something I would consider to include other things, like eating disorders, reckless behaviour. "Self-inflicted violence" I don't like because I don't consider what I do to be violent, the opposite if anything, it is very soothing. "Self-injury" or "self-injurious behaviour" seem to be the most appropriate terms to me.'

'[Self-mutilation] feels sensationalistic. It is also inaccurate and an exaggeration of what most self-injurers do. Self-mutilation seems to fit better with the amputation of limbs or eye enucleation that is sometimes seen in persons in a psychotic state.'

What characterises self-injury?

'SI [self-injury] is a coping mechanism that has many bad sides, but it works. It is a way to deal with extreme emotional distress, a way to survive.'

Although it can be a difficult concept to grasp, self-injury is fundamentally a coping mechanism, frequently born out of trauma or a deep-rooted sense of powerlessness. It could best be described as 'a pain exchange' in that overwhelming, invisible, emotional pain is converted into visible, physical wounds which individuals who use the practice find easier to deal with – put simply, what can be seen can be treated. Usually, following an episode of self-injury, people report feeling calmer, more in control, safe from suicide, and more able to cope and function.

'Once the pain is on the outside, it brings temporary relief to the psychological anguish . . . I can "see" my hurt and give it a tangible reality, unlike the pain that can't be seen on the inside. It brings me relief knowing that yes, I *do* hurt, even if no one else sees it. My "voice" is "heard" on my skin . . . it's there, it's real, and it hurts.'

'Self-injury helps to let out a bit of steam here and there, without totally going to breaking point.'

A safe haven

In general, individuals that self-injure are emotionally fragile, and highly sensitive to rejection. They take things to heart, and their psychological equilibrium can be easily shaken. Self-injury provides a temporary safe haven from the fear of something devastating happening. Basically, the act serves as an effective strategy for 'battening down the emotional hatches' and safeguarding oneself from the likelihood of an overwhelming psychological storm. Albeit unorthodox, self-injury is seen by many as a gift of survival, rather than an act of self-destruction.

'I understand that others will see self-harm as being destructive but for me at the time it was very much a means of survival. Although I agree the physical affect on my body was destructive, the temporary psychological relief was crucial to me, in that moment, for my survival.'

'[After self-injury] there's some sort of peace that descends for a few minutes. All the pain is gone, if only for a moment. The world outside doesn't exist; there are no pressures, no commitments, no failures. It is so weird, as if you have been standing in the middle of a storm, wind pushing from all sides, rain pelting you, thunder rolling and lightning crashing. Suddenly, the storm stops and you realise, for the first time that you were ever in the storm to begin with. The severity of the stillness makes you stand up and take notice. The storm crept up on you so slowly that you hadn't noticed how bad it was until that peace descended. It only lasts for a few minutes, hours if I'm lucky. But it is enough to keep me fighting for a time when I can live outside the storm forever.'

What behaviours does self-injury encompass?

The main focus of this book is on direct acts of self-injury. In particular, the spotlight is placed on two of the most common types identified through research, namely, cutting and burning. However, as you will see from Figure 1.1 (Direct Self-Injury) a wide range of other behaviours are grouped in the same category, some of which to a lesser degree will be mentioned throughout the text.

DIRECT SELF-INJURY (DSI)
Skin cutting, slashing and carving (words, symbols, designs, dates)
Skin burning, scalding and erasing (rubbing off layers of skin)
Compulsive skin-picking (CSP) (also called neurotic excoriation and dermatillomania) and excessive scratching (sufficient to cause bleeding)
Inserting objects into the anus, penis, urethra, uterus or vagina, with the purpose of causing harm (non-sexual intent)
Self-punching, hitting, slapping, biting or bruising
Self-stabbing with sharp objects (pins, needles, compasses, scalpels, nails [finger nails and carpentry type nails])
Head banging
Hair pulling, for example, scalp, eyelashes, eyebrows (trichotillomania)
Interfering with wound healing
Inserting needles under the skin or into veins
Pulling off skin and nails
Swallowing foreign objects
Bone breaking

Fig. 1.1: Direct self-injury (DSI).

Unfamiliar behaviours

While most of the behaviours shown in Figure 1.1 are probably self-explanatory, there are two that you may not be familiar with and perhaps need further clarification.

Compulsive skin-picking (CSP)

Compulsive skin-picking, also referred to as neurotic excoriation and dermatillomania is the practice of consistently picking, squeezing or scratching the skin causing abrasions. One respondent referred to it as 'skin gouging' – this is how she described the practice:

> '. . . by "gouging" I mean compulsively removing (attacking) any real or perceived skin flaws (i.e., pimples, bumps, scars, scabs) by digging it out with fingernails or needles and then bleeding out "the bad stuff" until something in me is satiated. And then going on to the next one. If there's nothing there to "attack" I obsessively/compulsively keep searching until anything will do to trigger this process. At its height, this behaviour created a great deal of constant damage to my skin and I believe, severely affected my immune system as well. I suppose it could fall under "skin-picking" but as the wounds were quite severe in the past, it may also fall under another category.'

DSM-IV-TR lists skin-picking as an Impulse-Control Disorder Not Otherwise Specified (p. 677).

Trichotillomania

According to DSM-IV-TR, one of the essential features of trichotillomania (also referred to as 'TTM' or 'trich') is the 'Recurrent pulling out of one's own hair resulting in noticeable hair loss' (p. 677). Typically, hair is pulled from the scalp, eyebrows and eyelashes, but it may also be pulled from other areas of the body where hair grows. Trichotillomania is also listed in the DSM as an Impulse-Control Disorder Not Otherwise Specified.

What behaviours are not being discussed?

In *Bodies Under Siege: Self-Mutilation and Body Modification in Culture and Psychiatry* (1996: 233) Armando Favazza, a psychiatrist and leading researcher on self-injury classifies the behaviour into three types:

1. Major self-mutilation.
2. Stereotypic self-mutilation.
3. Superficial or moderate self-mutilation.

Our interest is with the latter, thus major and stereotypic self-mutilation will not be addressed. Nevertheless, for those of you who are wondering what behaviours major and stereotypic self-mutilation comprises a brief description is now given.

Major self-mutilation

Favazza uses the term major self-mutilation to describe the least common forms of self-injury that result in significant damage to body tissue or permanent disfigurement. Examples of this type include removal of an eye, castration, and limb amputation. These acts, which are relatively rare, are frequently linked with psychotic states or severe alcohol misuse.

Stereotypic self-mutilation

Favazza uses the term stereotypic self-mutilation to describe repetitive self-injurious behaviours often observed in institutionalised individuals with mental impairments, for instance, autism, Lesch–Nyhan syndrome and Tourette's syndrome. Examples of this type include rhythmic head-banging, eyeball pressing, and finger, lip, tongue or arm biting.

In addition to the aforementioned, other high risk self-injurious acts such as jumping from bridges or high buildings are not addressed.

Culturally accepted self-injury

Deeply embedded culturally permitted practices such as piercing, tattooing, scarification, and cutting of the skin connected with healing, spiritual enlightenment, social order, or as a rite of passage into adulthood is another area not addressed, because the purposes behind these acts hold different meanings to self-injurious practices as discussed in this book.

Note: For those wishing to learn more about culturally sanctioned, major and stereotypic self-injury, Favazza's book *Bodies Under Siege* (1996) comes highly recommended.

Non-direct self-harm (NDSH)

> 'As well as self-harming, I have suffered/am still suffering with an eating disorder. I have alternated between periods of anorexia and bulimia for about 10 years. Also, I do tend to abuse alcohol when I go through "rough patches".'

As seen from the above respondent's testimony, self-injury does not always come alone. Research has consistently shown that self-injury and eating disorders, and self-injury and alcohol misuse are frequent companions. Thus, bearing in mind the close relationship between direct forms of self-injury and some indirect forms of self-harm it is inevitable that a few behaviours shown in Figure 1.2 (Non-direct self-harm) will present themselves during discussion.

What distinguishes DSI from NDSH?

Direct self-injury (DSI) is self-inflicted harm to the body severe enough to cause superficial or moderate wounds and the damage is immediate and *usually* visible. The resulting injuries are not generally life-threatening, and the degree of severity varies from relatively minor wounds that heal reasonably quickly, to more severe wounds that result in permanent scarring. The word *usually* is emphasised because some people injure themselves internally, in which case the damage may not be immediately apparent to the human eye. *Typically,* those who

NON-DIRECT SELF-HARM (NDSH)
Disordered eating: anorexia, bulimia, compulsive overeating
Substance misuse: misusing alcohol, using illegal drugs or misuse of prescribed or non-prescribed medication
Self-poisoning without suicidal intent (overdosing)
Extreme risk-taking (reckless driving, high risk sports)
Gambling
Over exercising/under exercising
Overworking/underworking
Perfectionism
Promiscuity
Self-neglect/always putting other people's needs first
Smoking
Sexual revictimisation
Staying in violent/abusive relationships

Fig. 1.2: Non-direct self-harm (NDSH).

engage in self-injury are fully aware of the fact that they have injured themselves. Emphasis is placed on the word *typically*, however, because some people are not aware of hurting themselves until after the event, as witnessed in the following respondent's testimony: 'Often in the past I don't realise I've done it [self-injured] until it's all over. I have a history of severe dissociation.' What does the respondent mean by dissociation? Essentially, dissociation is an unconscious psychological process in which a sense of detachment between mind and emotions, or mind and body, is experienced. Since dissociation plays a pivotal role in self-injury for some people, it is talked about at various places throughout the book.

Non-direct self-harm (NDSH) is different to DSI because inflicting harm is rarely the aim of NDSH, the damage is not immediately evident or visible, and individuals who engage in non-direct forms may be oblivious to, or in denial of, the long-term physical or psychological consequences of their actions, as in the case of alcohol misuse, smoking, and pill popping for example.

Grey areas examined

What about self-poisoning (overdosing) – surely that is self-injurious? What about the modern trend to adorn one's body with piercings or tattoos – isn't that considered self-injury? Further, what about individuals who intentionally starve themselves, or who binge and purge – don't they count as self-injury? These fuzzy areas are examined next.

Self-injury is not usually carried out with suicidal intent

Self-injury is often misconstrued as a death wish or failed suicide attempt when in all actuality, those who engage in the practice have no desire to die. Indeed, self-injury for many is a life saver, rather than a life taker – in essence it keeps people safe from suicide. Clear evidence of the life-saving function served by self-injury can be seen in the respondents' testimonies that follow:

'Doctors have told me I have a "death wish" but I haven't. I harm myself to enable me to live. I know that if I didn't self-harm at the times I need to, I wouldn't be alive today. Self-harm is the way I cope with the world and my life.'

'I often think about suicide but by self-harming it keeps a lid on things.'

'Often I've used extreme episodes of self-harm to control suicidal thoughts. Self-harm is about surviving terrible pain. Suicide is permanent.'

'Self-injury is NOT a suicide attempt. It is a way of making emotional pain into something physical that you can see and control.'

'[SI] has probably saved me from suicide, strange as it may seem. If I had not had this coping mechanism, this escape, I would probably have killed myself by now.'

'Self-injury is an effective coping mechanism when nothing else works. It allowed me to continue my life without resorting to behaviour that is even more destructive. A little cutting kept me from killing myself, basically.'

'[Self-injury] . . . keeps me alive. Simple as that.'

As noted in the above statements, some individuals who self-injure do experience suicidal thoughts, and sadly on occasions some do commit suicide if life becomes intolerable or if self-injury loses its efficacy as a coping method. However, this tends to be the exception rather than the rule. It needs to be borne in mind nevertheless that self-injury is a risky activity, and accidental death may occur as a result of loss of blood from a severed artery, or from cutting deeper than intended.

Self-poisoning (SP)

Self-poisoning (overdosing) is one of the most common reasons for emergency hospital admission in the United Kingdom. You will note that self-poisoning is included in Figure 1.2 under non-direct self-harm, the reason being that self-injury is now well recognised as a coping mechanism and survival strategy, whereas the intention behind self-poisoning is less clear. For example, say an individual arrives at Accident and Emergency (A&E) following an overdose. Does the treating doctor or nurse know whether the person intended, yet failed to end his or her life? Without further investigation they cannot know for certain. It could be a botched suicide attempt, it could be an accident, it could be a cry for help, or it could be a means of temporarily escaping from emotional turmoil. Depending on the motivation, it could also mean that the patient requires a different treatment regime to the patient presenting with self-injuries.

A further significant difference between self-poisoning and self-injury is that the extent of the damage from self-poisoning is *invisible*, whereas with self-injury (unless the injuries are internal) the extent of the damage is immediately *visible*.

My research suggests that the incentive behind self-poisoning is usually different from the impetus that drives self-injury and respondents' testimonies supporting this theory are given later in the book. However, separating self-poisoning from self-injury is at odds with other researchers in the field, particularly UK researchers, many of whom group self-poisoning and self-injury together under the terms *self-harm* or *deliberate self-harm*. That said, it was reassuring to read recently that London based consultant psychiatrist, Leonard Fagin (Fagin, 2006) shares a similar view to my own – he writes: 'I see self-injury as different from self-poisoning' adding that 'I believe

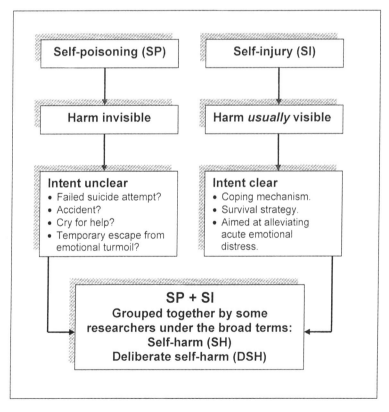

Fig. 1.3: Highlighting the differences between self-poisoning and self-injury and illustrating how the two behaviours are grouped together by some researchers under the broad terms self-harm or deliberate self-harm.

that people who poison themselves have different characteristics from those who injure themselves.' This controversial issue is discussed further in Chapter 4. Figure 1.3 highlights the differences between self-poisoning and self-injury and illustrates how the two behaviours are grouped together by some researchers under the broad terms self-harm or deliberate self-harm.

Self-injury is not usually carried out with sexual intent

The motivation behind *external* sexual self-injury is usually aimed at stimulating sexual arousal and achieving orgasm, rather than the goal being to regulate emotional pain. Two out of eighty-two Internet respondents did, however, mention using sadomasochistic practices to alleviate emotional distress, which suggests that it may occur occasionally but is the exception rather than the norm. The reason emphasis has been placed on *external* is to distinguish the practice from *internal* self-injury which, as demonstrated later, serves a very different function.

Sexual masochism and sexual sadism are classified as paraphilias in DSM-IV-TR, along with hypoxyphilia (more commonly known as autoerotic asphyxiation or sexual hanging) (pp. 572-574). For clarification purposes these are explained briefly below.

- **Sadomasochism (S&M)**
  Sadomasochism is the combination of two words: sadism and masochism. Sadism refers to a person who gains sexual satisfaction and pleasure by inflicting pain and suffering on another person. The term sadism originated from the infamous French author and sadist, the Marquis de Sade (1740-1814). In contrast, masochism refers to a person who gains sexual satisfaction and excitement by enduring pain inflicted by another person. Sadomasochism refers to a person with a penchant for both sadism and masochism.

- **Hypoxyphilia (autoerotic asphyxiation)**
  Hypoxyphilia is a 'dangerous form of Sexual Masochism' which may be carried out 'alone or with a partner' (DSM-IV-TR: 572-573). Characteristically, a ligature is applied round the neck while the individual reaches orgasm. The decrease of blood to the brain is believed to intensify sexual excitement.

Self-injury is not usually carried out with decorative intent

Body modification has become an increasingly popular trend, especially amongst young people, and the question of whether it should be classified as self-injury is a hotly debated issue. As discussed here, body modification refers to piercing; tattoos; branding (creating a permanent design or image on the skin with a hot object – a process not unlike branding cattle), and scarification (similar to tattooing – involves cutting of the dermis [the second layer of skin] to produce permanent marks). Some argue that any form of body modification is self-injury; some make a clear distinction between the two; others (*for example see* Lader 2006) consider the dividing line between the two is thin.

The case against body modification being classified as self-injury

Many consider that body modification is rarely undertaken with the intention of hurting oneself, suggesting that the purpose has more to do with making a fashion statement, expressing individuality, to be accepted by peers, to rebel against conformity, or to enhance the appearance of the body. Moreover, people who choose to get their bodies modified generally do so with the aim of making themselves *look different,* to 'stand out in the crowd', or to improve their self-image, and opt to display their decorations with pride. This contrasts with self-injury which is rooted in shame and *feeling different*, thus, the scars are typically kept hidden. A further clarifying feature proffered is that with body modification the injuries inflicted are done by another person, whereas with self-injury the injuries inflicted are done to oneself.

Examining the thin dividing line

The question of whether the purpose of body modification might share any similarities with the reasons for self-injury has puzzled me for some time, and prompted an invitation to the Internet respondents to express their views on the topic. This produced some important insights, demonstrating clearly that body modification and self-injury are indeed bedfellows for some people. As this subject does not appear to have been widely discussed in the literature, rather than reporting second-hand the opinions articulated, you may be interested to read what the respondents had to say, thus a range of comments are given next:

'I feel that bod-mod [body modification] is simply a way of altering your appearance. I don't feel it has anything to do with SI. I have 6 tattoos and numerous piercings, and the "high" I get from bod-mod is absolutely nothing like the relief I feel from SI.'

'I don't think tattoos and piercing really fall into SI. There are some SI-ers [self-injurers] who have bodmod and they do it for the feeling of SI. They get the same feeling from bodmod as they do from SI. I don't though. I like the way tattoos and piercings look— that's my only reason for it.'

'Sometimes people want to get their bodies altered to become more appealing to themselves or others, to rebel, or to just try out something new and fun. I don't believe it is another form of self-injury because you are not doing it to yourself.'

'I believe that there could be a link between tattoos and body piercings and self-harm. **But** I must emphasise that this doesn't mean that all people with tattoos have a "mental disorder". What I think is that those people who self-harm could possibly also have a number of tattoos and body piercings. The two acts are not the same, for example with tattoos and piercings the individual is not in control and there is no significant sight of blood. However, there could be a sense of achievement or even an internal "high" which could be the link with self-harm.'

'I think one thing that influences people to go for body modification in this way could be partly to do with being individual – making a statement. That is the reason for me anyway. In this form – it is considered to be art and is socially acceptable.'

'I do think that body modification is used by some individuals as socially acceptable forms of self-injury, but I doubt this is true for everyone.'

'I got my belly-button pierced to avoid self-injury.'

'I had a tattoo done when I decided to stop self-injuring. A butterfly on my wrist (where I normally self-injured) – it was supposed to be a symbolic break from self injury – something beautiful to remind me that I was worth more than a bunch of scars. The odd thing was that getting the tattoo done was very much like self-injury. The emotions felt very similar, the dissociation was very similar, the sense of detachment was similar, and the relief was similar. Now I have similar urgings towards getting another tattoo as I did for self-injuring.'

'I haven't been cutting recently. But I have been getting more into tattoos and piercing – at least more than I used to be. I find that the pain and sensations involved play a role in helping me avoid self-injury. I can have "wounds" that are decorative and yet play an important function too. While a piercing or tattoo is healing, I experience a painful sensation and the wound is sore. The knowledge of these wounds, and the feel of them, keeps my body with me. I can feel my body. I know it is there and therefore, that I am there. I have not dissociated for quite a while and I honestly think the tattooing and piercing have played a key part in that. They give me something on my body to focus on. They keep me "real".'

'A tattoo or piercing can offer a huge release of whatever is kept inside you. I am always more peaceful after I get work done on my body. I have also covered some of my bigger, uglier scars [from self-injury] with tattoos. And now they are beautiful.'

'I feel that tattoos and piercing can be a healthy, more socially acceptable, and literally therapeutic way to deal with SI and the "need" for someone to feel pain. I haven't even had an urge to self-injure in a while!'

Reviewing potential links

Figure 1.4 outlines potential links between body modification and self-injury identified from the respondents' testimonies. Important to remember, however, is that a different picture might emerge if a group of people with no experience of self-injury were invited to express their opinions on the subject. The question also remains as to why so many people, young and not so young, are subjecting their bodies to the pain of not just one or two attractive pieces of body art, but to multiple, or head to foot, tattoos and piercings.

BODY MODIFICATION: POTENTIAL LINKS TO SELF-INJURY

May be used as a way of avoiding self-injury

May be used to cover up old scars from self-injury

May be used as a 'healthier' and more socially acceptable method to self-injure

May arouse similar emotions to those experienced from self-injury, for example, an internal high or sense of relief

May induce a sense of detachment similar to that experienced through self-injury by some

May satisfy the need to feel pain, thus reducing feelings of depersonalisation (feeling unconnected, feeling unreal) similar to those experienced through self-injury by some

Urges for body modification may replicate urges for self-injury

Fig. 1.4: Body modification: potential links to self-injury.

Disordered eating

Eating issues is another blurred area, which has been placed under NDSH in Figure 1.2, for the reason that the damage caused through disordered eating usually shows itself longer-term rather than immediately as in the case of direct self-injury. Certainly, there's no question that eating disorders can be life-threatening and do result in loss of life. For example, much adored musician and singer, Karen Carpenter tragically died prematurely from anorexia at the age of 32; another casualty was child singing prodigy Lena Zavaroni who died at age 35, after a twenty two year battle with anorexia. Prior to her death she underwent an operation aimed at helping her to eat, but contracted an infection, sadly from which she wasn't robust enough to recover.

No single cause has been established for the development of eating disorders, and their origins are complex. Research suggests that the following components may have some bearing on the development of an eating disorder:

- Biological factors – an inherited predisposition to an imbalance in serotonin (a brain neurotransmitter involved in a broad variety of tasks such as mood, appetite, hormonal balance).
- Socio-cultural factors – portrayal by the media that thin is beautiful, peers and/or family members' jibes about being overweight.
- Psychological factors – anxiety, depression, low self-esteem, etc.
- Family dynamics – overprotective or controlling parents, high expectations to achieve and succeed, communication problems, a parent's attitude/behaviour towards food.
- Personality traits – perfectionism.

Contributory factors to eating disorders identified from the small sample group findings for *Healing the Hurt Within*, 1st edition (Sutton, 1999. p. 206) included:

- Childhood abuse.
- Body shape not the media norm.
- Repulsed by own body.
- Obsessed by food/appearance/weight/shape.
- Marital conflict.
- Parents' separation.
- Parental pressures.
- Lack of control over one's life.
- Difficulties with boundary setting.
- Stress, depression, low self-esteem, anxiety, panic, self-hate, and lack of self-confidence.
- Feelings of powerlessness and worthlessness.
- Insecurity and rejection.

Functions served by eating disorders were identified as:

- Self-punishment.
- Self-control.
- Comforting, treating/rewarding self.

- Punishing others.
- A distraction from mental anguish.
- Relaxation.
- Produces a 'high'.

These findings echo similarities with some of the motivations and functions served by self-injury. However, a marked difference between eating disorders and self-injury is that whilst those who self-injure tend to recognise that their behaviour is not the norm, those with eating disorders may not perceive their actions as harmful.

Summary

Thus far a range of issues have been addressed. The subjects of terminology, what characterises self-injury, what behaviours self-injury encompasses, and what distinguishes direct self-injury from non-direct self-harm have been examined. Attention has been given to several grey areas, namely: self-poisoning, sexual self-injury, body modification and disordered eating. Also highlighted is that the motivation to self-injure stems from a need to cope with unbearable psychological distress and to regain a sense of emotional stability, further that the act is *usually* carried out without suicidal, sexual or decorative intent.

Defining self-injury

This seems like an appropriate place to introduce you to a definition of self-injury, compiled in collaboration with the Internet respondents, and deemed to be the most accurate from nine draft definitions circulated for debate.

> Self-injury is a *compulsion* or *impulse* to inflict physical wounds on one's own body, motivated by a need to cope with unbearable psychological distress *or* regain a sense of emotional balance. The act is *usually* carried out without suicidal, sexual or decorative intent.
>
> —*Sutton, et al. (2000)*

Compulsive self-injury

With compulsive self-injury, individuals experience a strong urge to inflict injuries on themselves – as one respondent explained, a compulsion is like 'the brain flashing the message "do this, do this, do this, do this . . ."' Characteristically, compulsive self-injury stems from an irresistible craving to perform the act. Fuelled by fear of a disastrous outcome if the act is not carried out, individuals who engage in compulsive self-injury feel they have no other choice. On completion of the act, anxiety or other distressing symptoms experienced before the act are reduced, and a sense of improved well-being ensues. However, invariably, this enhanced feeling of well-being doesn't last, and individuals find themselves repeatedly returning to self-injury to alleviate overwhelming emotional pain, thus getting caught in a vicious circle. Those who self-injure compulsively often become preoccupied with thoughts of hurting themselves even when not actively engaging in the process.

'I see [self-injury] as a compulsion, something I am driven to do, almost beyond my control.'

'I feel compelled to self-harm because it will release the trapped tears and I will feel better.'

'I can't live without the pain. I feel abnormal without it. When I feel bad about myself I have to harm on compulsion.'

Impulsive self-injury

With impulsive self-injury the act is carried out spontaneously, with no previous planning and little thought to aftercare or the consequences. Instead of the 'brain flashing the message "do this, do this, do this, do this . . ."' which can drive a compulsion, an impulsive act is driven by the 'brain flashing the message "**do this**"' says the same respondent. Impulsive self-injury may be carried out occasionally when the need arises, rather then repetitively as is often the case with compulsive self-injury. Self-injury episodes carried out under the influence of alcohol are frequently of an impulsive nature. The following respondents' testimonies clarify their views on whether they consider self-injury is compulsive or impulsive. From their comments you will see that an overlap between the two is not uncommon.

> 'A "compulsion" is like an inner drive, which has a repetitive nature about it, sometimes maybe even ritualistic/planned, whereas, "impulsive" is like a sudden desire/inclination – sometimes even spontaneous. In my opinion self-injury often starts off impulsively, leading to a compulsive nature, or sometimes stays impulsive, where on an infrequent basis the impulse to self-injure will occur, say once or twice over a period of a year or so. With compulsive self-injury it's like the person "learns" to equate self-injury with bad feelings or vice-versa leading into a cycle of self-injury:
>
> **I feel bad -> SI is how I deal with that . . .**
>
> It just progresses until that is the only way to cope - that is the only way you can deal with things.'
>
> 'It's rare that I cut myself on impulse, but when I burn myself with a cigarette that's often the case. I would say my cutting is *deliberate* and *compulsive* whereas my burning is *deliberate* and *impulsive*.'
>
> '[My self-injury] can be both spontaneous or a ritual. But when under the influence of alcohol it is usually spontaneous.'

'For me it differs – sometimes it's impulsive, sometimes more calculated, with much planning and thought. For me, impulsive acts are often more dangerous because I just don't care what I do, as long as I get the **fix,** whilst planned sessions are usually more calm, controlled and with the necessary **clean-up kit.** It depends on many different things too - time of day, environment, stimulus, etc.'

'Sometimes it's a spur of the moment, and I just rush into the bathroom and slash away. But other times, I can plan the act for days, describe it to myself – how deep I will go, how many cuts, where to cut, etc.'

'Whenever I SIed, it was nearly always impulsive. But I do go through a kind of pattern. I'd find my "tool" – which was broken glass (this usually meant having to break a picture frame or a small mirror). I would then find the sharpest edge, and proceed to cut – usually my arm. I would then "nurture" myself, and clean the wounds and take extra care of them. I experience a sense of comfort when doing this.'

'I have definitely engaged in self-injury as an impulsive act from the very beginning, from self-injuring on the bus on the way home from basketball games as a teen, to self-injuring at work, to self-injuring while driving as an adult due to some trigger or another. At these times the act can be construed as an almost knee jerk reaction or an impulsive response, and these are times when anything around me can become my "tool" because I need to self-injure right then and there.'

'There are also times when self-injury is not impulsive, but rather, planned and carefully executed. I have more time; I know it's going to happen, and it may originally be an impulse, but a rather muted one, meaning I can save it for later. At these times, I can take my time and stave it off a bit . . . there's a preferred method and preparation, a deliberate action not fully driven by impulse.'

When asked if their most recent episode of self-injury was planned or unplanned, fifty four percent (54%) of the respondents reported planning the episode in advance, while a slightly lesser percentage, forty six percent (46%) reported that the episode was unplanned.

Repetitive self-mutilation (RSM): Proposed criteria

Favazza (1996: 253-254) argues a case for repetitive self-mutilation (RSM) to be listed in the DSM 'on Axis 1 among the "impulse control disorders not elsewhere classified."' He hypothesises that self-injury 'results from a failure to resist an impulse,' and that those who self-injure 'may brood about harming themselves for hours and even days and may go through a ritualistic sequence of behaviours, such as tracing areas of their skin and compulsively putting their self-harm paraphernalia in a special order.'

Several of the above respondents' testimonies support Favazza's theory that prior to self-injury the act may be dwelled upon for some time, further that a series of rituals may be engaged in beforehand such as careful planning and preparation, with relevant aftercare equipment being purchased in readiness. As confirmed by another respondent: 'I mostly have a ritual, and I'll plan and buy the necessary stuff (gauze, antiseptic) before.' Other rituals may also be involved – these are now discussed.

Self-injury rituals

As well as planning self-injury in advance, spending time preparing, and taking preliminary precautions to reduce the risk of infections, the environment may be set up to lend an air of comfortable familiarity or certain ambiance to the proceedings. Objects for self-injuring (knives, razors), clean towels and aftercare equipment (bandages, steri-strips) may be laid out in a clinical fashion. Curtains may be drawn, lights dimmed, scented candles lit, and some melancholic music might be playing softly in the background.

'When I cut to numb out [shut down emotionally] I spend a lot of time preparing. First, all I can think about is where I'm going to cut myself and what it will feel like. There is a lot of anticipation; also a sense of relief because I've given myself the "green light". I usually have a shower next as I need to feel clean. Then I spread a towel out on the floor of the bathroom and make sure I have another one to hand. I have special towels for this purpose. Then I take out all the dressings and tape for the aftercare and when I have all this around me, then I take my razor blade and start to cut.'

'If I'm at home alone I'll prepare the "tool" and whatever dressings are required afterwards.'

'If the time and place is unsuitable to self-harm, I will plan a time and place. I have a ritual of leaving everything in readiness prior to cutting, e.g. scissors, dressings, etc.'

'I like to "set up my equipment", material to soak blood, plastic to cover bed/carpet, mirror to see what I am doing, new blade, music, cup of tea. Therapeutic activity! Really!'

Self-injury may be performed in a specific room (bedrooms and bathrooms appear to be common), or carried out at a certain time of the day – evenings and night time seem to be particularly common. Factors that may have a bearing on why it happens during these times may include the need for privacy, to avoid the risk of being discovered, anxiety about getting to sleep, fear of the dark or fear of being alone. Insomnia is a problem for many who self-injure. For trauma survivors who self-injure, evenings and night times are frequently a time of heightened anxiety, dread, and hypervigilance (many adult abuse survivors sleep with a light on). Self-injury acts like a sleeping pill – it calms people down and enables them to get to sleep – in other words, it's easier to sleep with physical wounds than with painful traumatic memories, nightmares, night terrors, intrusive thoughts, fear-provoking images or overwhelming feelings. The emotional release from self-injury also appears to make people physically tired. In the following testimonies respondents describe what happens following self-injury. Several, as you will see emphasise the sleep-inducing characteristic of self-injury; others highlight that sometimes people are kinder to themselves following an episode:

'I slept. I gave myself that well-deserved sleep I hardly ever got otherwise.'

'Sometimes I've used band-aids if the bleeding doesn't stop soon enough, usually I just fall asleep and check on where I self-injured to make sure it was starting to heal.'

'I make sure the cuts are clean, and then I usually go to bed. I get very tired after a SI episode.'

'I usually curl up in bed and fall asleep.'

'I usually cut late at night, so I go to sleep after.'

> 'I usually wrap up in a blanket and curl up . . . sometimes
> I rock myself . . . and I lay there and I say to myself its
> alright . . . its alright . . . everything will be okay . . .'

In the following testimonies the respondents are explaining what they did after their most recent episode of self-injury:

> 'I neglect myself very badly sometimes, but after self-
> injuring I am always very kind to myself . . . washing
> and dressing the wounds (I actually think I went a bit
> overboard on the wound dressing, but it felt good looking
> after myself). I think I probably let myself eat something
> nice afterwards, and then slept (I always sleep very well
> after self-injuring; the rest of the time I sleep very poorly,
> mainly because I don't let myself sleep, and actively
> deprive myself of sleep . . . but not after I self-injured).'

> 'I was kind to myself in the sense that, even though I
> thought I had not done enough to punish myself, I didn't
> do any more harm to myself. I allowed myself the comfort
> of sleep, which is a haven from the storm.'

Judith Herman, in her landmark book *Trauma and Recovery* (1992: 109) suggests that: 'Self-injury is perhaps the most spectacular of the pathological soothing mechanisms . . .'

Bearing in mind the respondents' above comments, it certainly seems as if there is a comforting element in the act for some people.

Symmetry, symbols and dates

While self-injury rituals hold important meanings for some people, to others, carving names, symbols, or dates on their skin to remind themselves of significant people, events or tragedies that have occurred in their lives appears to be a noteworthy factor. Order and symmetry also seem to be imperative to some, for example they will make a specific number of cuts, equal the number of cuts on their arms, legs or torso, or cut a series of lines of equivalent length.

> 'I always make combinations that add up to 8 (either 4 + 4 or 3 + 5). Maybe I will do 3 cuts on one arm one night and 5 cuts on the other arm later. I don't know for sure what the significance of the number 8 is. At first, I didn't realise I was doing it. Now, I can see that I do it but I don't count when si-ing [self-injuring]. It just feels right.'
>
> 'I seem to have a very orderly mind and want to keep things so. That has always been very important to me, to match on both sides (don't know why) so, especially when cutting on my legs or chest or stomach, I would cut in twos, one on each leg, or two on each leg, etc. The cuts on my arms, however, are mostly on my left arm as I am right-handed, thus breaking the symmetry.'
>
> 'I carved the word "NO" into my leg to try to get through to myself that I didn't need this.'

Obsessions related to symmetry, exactness and order are frequently associated with Obsessive Compulsive Disorder (OCD). To those who suffer from OCD things that are asymmetrical or imprecise can lead to marked distress.

Elaborating on the meaning of obsessions and compulsions

An obsession is a persistent intrusive thought, idea, impulse or image that enters a person's mind and which causes significant unease or anguish. The individual may endeavour to stifle the obsessive thoughts or to defuse them by taking 'compulsive' action in response to the fixated thoughts, such as arranging things in a certain order, repeatedly checking the cooker to ensure it is switched off, continually checking doors and locks, or repetitively washing one's hands or counting things. Individuals recognise that the thoughts stem from their own mind, but feel driven to perform a compulsive action against their will to relieve the anxiety caused by the thoughts, or to thwart a feared occurrence or situation.

Putting self-injury into context with other self-harming behaviours

> 'Everybody self-harms to an extent – smoking, drinking, over-working . . .'

In many ways self-injury serves a similar function to other harmful behaviours. For example, some people seek solace in alcohol to escape from stress while others chain smoke or comfort eat. Individuals who self-injure turn to their 'tools' as a means of preventing the 'emotional melting pot' from boiling over. Some injure periodically when the pressure gets too great and threatens to overwhelm; others do it on a regular basis to manage tension and stress (whether internally generated or situational).

> '"Normal" people SI too, and they don't consider it that
> . . . our SI is kinda like normal SI gone out of control.
> People punch walls when they're extremely angry, children bang their heads throwing tantrums, people bite their nails when they're stressed, etc. Maybe people could feel closer to our cause if they can relate to it.'

A marked dissimilarity

An essential difference that is noteworthy, however, is that while many people imbibe a few glasses of champagne or similar, or overindulge on food to celebrate a happy occasion such as a wedding or anniversary, some people who use self-injury respond to happy events by hurting themselves, so strong is their belief that they are 'bad' and undeserving of happiness.

Discussion

Self-injury is a phenomenon that society finds hard to understand and accept — it would prefer that it didn't exist. Yet sadly it does exist, moreover, it is much more common than generally realised. If society finds self-injury an uncomfortable issue to deal with, and would prefer to sweep it under the carpet, where does it leave those trapped in the behaviour? Many stay locked in a world of isolation, secrecy, shame, and silence, afraid to speak out lest they be judged and condemned.

Just as society has come to accept that substance misuse, eating disorders, and child abuse are serious problems in our midst, it must open its eyes and heart to the truth about self-injury — that it does exist, that it is a serious problem, and that it causes immeasurable suffering not only to those caught in its clutches, but also to those supporting someone that self-injures.

Self-injury isn't an illness children are born with. It is a behaviour that develops to cope with life's pressures and ills. *Acceptance, awareness, education and empathy* are crucial to enable those suffering in silence to step out of the closet of secrecy and shame, and to receive the help they need and deserve. Furthermore, as a society we have a responsibility to address the issue of why self-injury is becoming so prevalent in our midst.

Key points

- Self-injury is an expression of acute psychological distress.
- Self-injury is a coping mechanism. It transfers emotional pain into physical injuries that people find easier to deal with.
- Self-injury is an insurance policy to safeguard survival, rather than an act designed to end one's life.
- Self-injury is not usually carried out with suicidal, sexual or decorative intent.
- Self-injury is referred to by a plethora of terms which causes confusion.
- Self-injury can be compulsive or impulsive – sometimes there is an overlap.
- Once started, self-injury often develops into a habitual pattern.
- Self-injury involves rituals for some people.
- Symmetry and order are important to some people that self-injure.
- The wounds from self-injury are rarely life-threatening.
- Self-injury does not occur in a vacuum – there are reasons why people self-injure, although they may not always be immediately aware of the reasons.
- Self-injury is symptomatic of an underlying problem. Recovery requires looking beyond the visible injuries and healing the invisible internal wounds.
- Letting go self-injury is not an easy process.

Chapter 2

Looking beyond the myths

. . . .

'SI is not a sign of madness; it is not a failed suicide attempt; it is not mere attention-seeking; it is not selfish, it is not an attempt to manipulate one's friends and family.'

'I just want people to keep in mind that we SI because we are in pain and this is the way we cope with that pain.'

Self-injury is beset by myths and misconceptions. Stereotyping people keeps myths, stigma and prejudice alive. Becoming better informed is vital to reducing prejudice and stigma. In Chapter 1, the misapprehension that self-injury is a suicidal act was examined. In this chapter ten more common myths about self-injury are appraised. To start with though, we look at who is likely to encounter self-injury in their work, as well as discussing the issue of self-injury in prison, wherein rates of self-injury are reported to be high.

Who encounters self-injury?

Self-injury is encountered in a range of environments. It is familiar behaviour to staff working in prisons, young offenders' institutions, secure units, special hospitals and psychiatric hospitals. GPs, psychiatrists, psychologists, psychotherapists and counsellors may also encounter patients or clients that self-injure. In addition, it happens in schools, colleges and universities, and may also be seen in children's homes, housing projects, and alcohol and drug rehabilitation units.

Youth workers, those working with the homeless, and those working in the voluntary sector with rape victims and abuse survivors may also come across the behaviour during the course of their work.

Self-injury in prison

The following testimony from a former repeated offender provides a glimpse into what motivated him to self-injure in prison:

'When I had nothing better to do and 23 hours per day in my cell, I mutilated myself – calling the results, not tattoos but "*agony art*". It was a coping mechanism. If I had not practised this form of self-injury, I might have lashed out physically at either a fellow inmate or one of the screws. However, fear of losing privileges, parole, etc., held me back but the *rage and destructive energy within me had to be released in some direction.*

It was a way of self-expression when there was no one to whom I felt able to confide my inner feelings to. Indeed, I doubt if, at the time, I was even able to identify and verbalise how I was really feeling, because my vocabulary was very limited.'

Research suggests that self-injury is prevalent in prisons, particularly among women inmates. Why is it common in prison? Here are some possible explanations. Besides loss of freedom, incarceration leads to other significant losses such as loss of privacy, dignity, self-respect, income, physical and emotional contact with children, family and friends, and intimate relationships with partners. Control over one's own life becomes a thing of the past, resulting in feelings of powerlessness and frustration. Outward displays of hostility are likely to result in additional punishment, or prolonged isolation. Noise;

poor conditions; overcrowding; bullying; time to dwell on the past, the present, or the future, and lack of stimulating activities can lead to raised stressed levels, depression or other mental health issues. It's also well recognised that traumatic histories feature in the lives of many of those incarcerated.

Strong emotions don't magically disappear, they need a release, and if striking out runs the risk of further pain or punishment, what other choice is there? Hurting oneself may seem like the only other viable solution.

Research also suggests that self-injury is used in prison for secondary gain, for example as a way of manipulating others into being moved to a prison closer to home and family or to the hospital wing.

Writer and broadcaster, Angela Devlin, who visited many women's prisons while researching for her book, *Invisible Women* (1998), gives an example of one such incident – she writes:

> I remember one woman officer telling a prisoner she was an
> attention-seeker. She told me afterwards: "She loves cutting up so
> she can get into the hospital wing." I thought how desperate that
> woman must be to go that far. (p. 277)

Devlin's closing sentence demonstrates sensitivity and a willingness to think 'outside the box' which is essential to understanding self-injury. This takes us conveniently on to the subject of looking beyond the myths.

Myth 1: Self-injury is about getting attention

Unquestionably, self-injury is occasionally used as a way of drawing attention to one's pain and suffering if attempts to express one's anguish falls on deaf ears, words cannot accurately convey what is being felt on the inside or one's emotional needs are not being met. As disclosed by one respondent: 'I think the reason I used self-harm to try and get attention was connected to the fact that neither of my parents ever showed me any physical affection.'

Everyone needs attention and affection to feel nurtured, special, valued, a person of worth – starved of these essential ingredients to healthy emotional development in childhood can lead to feelings of loneliness, isolation, low self-esteem, attachment issues, psychological distress, and a fragile emotional template.

> 'Having missed out on love and affection when I was younger I guess that unconsciously I would go to the A&E (Accident and Emergency) in order to get it from the staff. Getting stitches in my arm and having someone clean it up and then stitch it always makes me feel safe and cosy – like someone is giving me a big hug.'

Moreover, as many people who self-injure go to extraordinary lengths to conceal their wounds from the rest of the world, tarring all those who self-injure with the 'attention seeking' brush not only has the potential to add to a person's distress, it can also serve as a strong deterrent from seeking help for one's injuries.

> 'Self-injury is NOT done for attention getting; most of us hide our wounds from other people. It is done for the release and the relief of the horrible inner pain that we have inside.'

> 'Most of the people I am aware of who self-injure hide their behaviour and are afraid to talk about it. There are even some who are afraid to seek medical care because of the shame involved. Yet, it is seen by many who don't self-injure as a way to get attention. This not only hurts, but it prevents self-injurers from seeking treatment.'

> 'A lot of psychiatrists and nurses think self-harmers are attention seeking, but that is untrue. I'd be too scared of being "labelled" to cut myself so badly that I'd need to go to hospital.'

To shift away from the negative overtones implied by the term 'attention-seeking' one respondent suggested a turn of phrase to 'help-seeking'. From a personal perspective, since self-injury is more about needing attention, rather than actively seeking attention, my preference is the term 'attention-needing'.

Myth 2: Self-injury is a teenage phenomenon

> 'It is NOT only teenagers who SI because of a little stress in their lives. Older people self-injure as well.'

With recent media attention highlighting the issue of self-injury in young people, it is easy to make the assumption that self-injury is an exclusively teenage phenomenon. Figure 2.1 shows the age people started self-injury from the postal survey undertaken for *Healing the Hurt Within,* 1st edition (Sutton, 1999) and the Internet research, from which you see that the highest percentage of respondents from both studies did start self-injuring in their teens. However, the data clearly demonstrates that onset of self-injury in childhood and adult life is also common, thus contradicting the myth that self-injury is a wholly teenage phenomenon.

AGE SELF-INJURY STARTED					
Postal survey			**Internet Research**		
Age of onset	**(N=37)**	**% of sample**	**Age of onset**	**(N=82)**	**% of sample**
Teenager (13-18)	13	35	Teenager (13-19)	41	50
Child (0-12)	12	32.5	Child (0-12)	30	37
Adult (19 +)	12	32.5	Adult (20+)	11	13

Fig. 2.1: Age self-injury started.

Clarifying who self-injures

Self-injury knows no bounds. It affects all strata of society – men and women, all age groups, social classes, ethnicities, religions and educational backgrounds. The bond shared by all is emotional pain.

'Self-injurers are male, female, heterosexual, gay, lesbian, bisexual, young, old, single, married, divorced, with or without solid support systems; and very real, creative, expressive, strong, intelligent, gifted, supportive human beings.'

'We are straight, bi, and gay. We come from all walks of life and can be any age. We are every single race and religion that you can possibly think of. Our common link is this: We are in pain. We self-injure. And we are not freaks.'

'We are from all walks of life. We are straight, gay, black, white, rich, poor, men, women. We don't all dress in black and carry around The Bell Jar. We are just like everyone else except we hurt ourselves to cope.'

Myth 3: Self-injury is a female phenomenon

In the main, research suggests that self-injury is more common among females, and data from both studies supported this theory (2 males [5%], 35 females [95%] – postal survey; 8 males [10%], 74 females [90%] – Internet research). Nonetheless, it is important not to lose sight of the fact that males do self-injure, despite them appearing to be in the minority. Indeed, the Internet research drew my attention to how neglected some males who self-injure feel due to much of the research and other media (books, articles, websites and so forth) focusing principally, or exclusively, on women. Here is what some male respondents had to say on the topic:

> 'Males do it [self-injure] too . . . every book I've read ignores males or treats them like a rare anomaly; both of which I doubt.'
>
> 'Almost everything I read about SI, in magazines, newspapers, online... seems to be aimed at females . . . I mean, from what I read, I get the idea that it's mostly women who SI . . . but, I'm male. And I know there's got to be a decent amount of men out there who SI also.'
>
> 'I think more than anything it just needs to be acknowledged that men self-injure too. Looking around at websites you see lots and lots of "her" and "she" and usually the only time a "him" is mentioned is if they're talking about an abuser, etc.'

Why the possible genders divide?

Common theories about why men are in the minority centres on differences in socialisation. For example, holding the beliefs that 'big boys don't cry', or that 'showing emotions is a sign of weakness' may serve as obstacles to men admitting they have a problem and seeking help for self-injury. Further conjectures are that men resort to more socially tolerated methods to cope with difficult emotions, such as drinking and brawling; by channelling anger and releasing tension through participating in aggressive sports (rugby, football, and boxing). Yelling support or abusive remarks from the terraces at football matches or similar, or risk-taking behaviours such as high-speed driving, may also provide a useful outlet for discharging pent up emotions. The following testimonies from four male respondents provide insight into their thoughts on the subject:

'I think men have a difficult time admitting they have a problem with anything. Society tells us we're supposed to be strong, not show our emotions, not cry, etc. so we hold it in, and it builds up, and has to be released somehow . . . some choose anger, some aggression, or the many other things out there . . . I prefer to write and take it out on my body in various ways.'

'I am a male and I think that men self-injure in more "socially acceptable" ways like drinking and fighting and other things that are typical, though not always condonable, of men and not women.'

'I believe, **if** men have a problem with admitting to SI, it is because of the "macho" social image placed upon them. You know, that we gotta be big and tough otherwise we're fags or something . . .'

'Males maybe think that they can get through this without help and think that seeking counselling makes them a "wuss". I think that there isn't really that many males who self injure . . . It makes me feel pretty left out I guess.'

Closing the emotional floodgates

As borne out by the following testimonies from female respondents, it appears as if males are not alone in their belief that 'crying is not acceptable' or that 'showing emotions is a sign of weakness':

'I can't cry so my arm cries instead.'

'The drops of blood are like a substitute for the tears I cannot cry.'

'The deeper the cut the better I feel. I refuse to relent to pain, it's a sign of weakness, and I was taught never to relent to pain or cry – simply to block it out!'

'[Self-injury was] partly punishing myself for wanting to cry . . . and partly a way to get the sadness out when crying wasn't allowed. And so the blood replaced the tears.'

'I bite my hands when I'm trying not to cry or say something angry. I used to do that when I was a child because I got into trouble for crying. I also did it when I was being abused.'

'I was only 4 or so and I was very upset over something. I was not allowed to be upset over anything so I went outside to cry where no one could see me. I began to hit my head on the side of the house, over and over, while I cried. It helped.'

'I was really upset and crying and then I just started to scratch off the skin on my arm. I stopped crying immediately and felt better.'

'The concentration, the pain (and I did feel the pain the first time), the sight of the blood, the realisation of what I was actually doing calmed me down. I stopped crying. I stopped shaking.'

'Crying was dealt with by isolation until I apologised.'

'I very rarely cried: crying was a sign of weakness by my father's standards. If I did cry, I would be hurt and punished . . .'

Crying is an innate response – it is how babies communicate their needs – their hunger, thirst, discomfort, distress and frustration. It's also a human response to upsetting feelings – to the heartache of sadness and sorrow, the grief of loss and trauma – it takes the sting out of unspent anger and rage, cuts through emotional numbness, lightens the load from pent up emotions, soothes hurt and lifts mood. Crying has a calming effect – it is perfectly normal, healthy, therapeutic, and emotionally healing. An inability to release painful emotions naturally via the conventional channels of talk and tears can lead to unconventional behavioural methods being adopted to cope, one of which, as evidenced from the women's testimonies, is self-injury.

> Tears are the safety valve of the heart when too much pressure is laid on it.
>
> —*Albert Smith*

The women's responses also emphasise how parental or primary caregiver's words and actions towards children, can become an integral part of a person's internal belief system. Being punished for crying or displaying emotional upset as a child can lead to a sense of shame at giving into emotions – it is a sure fire way to dry up the tears reservoir along with a valid reason to close the emotional floodgates to protect oneself from the possibility of further suffering. Not only does this leave people emotionally impoverished and inadequately equipped to verbalise painful childhood experiences, or to work through 'stuck grief' from childhood trauma, it can create issues with trust, and fear that if emotions are expressed, further hurt or rejection might result. The dread of losing control of one's emotions; being at a loss for words; appearing stupid, foolish or weak, or the fear of making oneself vulnerable by opening the emotional floodgates can also serve to keep the barriers firmly closed.

> The sorrow which has no vent in tears may make other organs weep.
>
> —*Henry Maudsley*

Why more women?

If self-injury is more prevalent among women, why is this? Here are some possible explanations for the discrepancy:

- Self-injury often has its roots in trauma, and more women than men experience traumatic events such as sexual assault, rape, or domestic violence.
- Self-injury frequently stems from an inability to express emotions, chiefly strong emotions such as anger, frustration, or resentment. Anger, often bound with fear of conflict, fear of getting hurt, fear of hurting others, or deemed unacceptable to self, is a particularly troublesome emotion for many women that self-injure. Left unexpressed or channelled appropriately, it can become a ticking time bomb, which, when taken out on oneself, is quickly defused. In other words, many women that self-injure implode their anger (turn it inwards), rather than directing it outwards. In contrast, overt displays of anger (physical aggression, fighting, bullying, vandalism, anti-social activities, and criminal behaviour) are more commonly seen in men.

- Women in general find it easier to share their problems and feelings than men do, hence, when it comes to seeking help they may be less resistant to do so than men.
- Depression and self-injury are frequent companions and more women than men suffer from depression. However, whilst this may be true, it is worth bearing in mind that many men suffer from untreated depression, which may hide itself behind the mask of workaholism, substance misuse, or engaging in high-risk activities or aggressive sports.

Myth 4: Self-injury is contagious

'I actually learned about it [self-injury] in a psychiatric unit I was in, and thought to myself that as I was already in pain, why not see if it helps.'

'I was upset and I actually learned about it in the mental hospital I was at, and figured I was already hurting, so maybe this would ease it.'

Self-injury contagion (copycat effect) in institutional environments such as detention and treatment centres has been the subject of various research studies. As yet, though, studies of contagion in schools, colleges, universities and other community based settings are limited (Walsh, 2006, p. 231) and further investigation is needed. However, in a UK cross-sectional survey of 6020 school pupils (Hawton, *et al.*, 2002) the authors concluded that an 'awareness of recent self harm by others suggests a possible modelling effect'. In a similar Australian study by De Leo, D. & Heller, T.S. (2004) of 3757 year 10 and year 11 students from 14 high schools on the Gold Coast, Queensland, the authors came to a likewise conclusion. Due, though, to the broad definition of self-harm used by the study authors, which included self-injury, overdosing, or illegal drug taking, it is unclear exactly which self-harming behaviour the young people are mimicking.

Media portrayal of self-injury contagion among teenagers

> 'Thousands of teenagers across the country are using knives and razors to injure themselves. Nicci Gerrard reports on this alarming new blood cult.' (*The Observer*, May 19, 2002)

The above sub-headline, from an evocatively written article, entitled: *Why are so many teenage girls cutting themselves?* stirred up a hornet's nest among people that self-injure, resulting in a string of complaints to the editor. Many readers felt affronted and upset by the article, particularly the author's reference to self-injury being a 'blood cult'. Some suggested that the article was written to 'grab readers' attention', was 'deliberately sensationalistic' and 'highly contradictory', and was based on fiction, rather than fact. Some charged the author with failing to do her research on the subject, of presenting a misleading and biased picture erring on the side of self-injury being attention seeking or a passing fad and of confusing self-harm with teenage experimentation. One felt strongly that it was 'an appalling piece of journalism'; another didn't mince her words, remarking that the article was 'bull shit'. (SIARI, 2001-2007)

> '[Self-injury is] not like collecting Pokemon cards. In my opinion nobody self-injures just because it's the **"in"** thing to do. There is always a reason, and it's not trivial to the teenager in question who is self-harming.'

Copycat behaviour? Discovered by accident? Just seems to happen?

Two Internet respondents reported copying a friend:

'The first time I injured myself purposely it didn't happen accidentally. I had seen a friend carving things (symbols, etc) in her leg so I tried it. It gradually got to be used for coping.'

'My first experience with SI (self-injury) was foolish and stupid. A friend of mine showed me a few small scars, and I thought "hey, what a great way to fit in" so during a 6th period English class, I took a key to my arm and scratched until I rubbed the skin raw.'

In contrast, a significant number reported discovering self-injury by accident or that it just seemed to happen:

'At eleven years old was the first time . . . it was an accident . . . I cut myself shaving and somehow felt a strange release.'

'The iron was there, I picked it up, burned myself, felt better, and thought, "hey why not do this more often?"'

'My SI happened by me just playing around with a razor. I was very upset about my parents splitting up and I didn't want anyone to know. I remember sitting in my bedroom and putting the razor to my wrist and pushing. It hurt, but felt really good at the same time.'

'It just felt like the most natural thing to do.'

'I must have stumbled upon it by accident. I hadn't heard about it before.'

'I learned about it by donating blood. I was terrified of needles and was donating out of an obligation and the needle felt oddly good.'

'It just seemed to happen, I guess. I didn't know what I thought it would do for me, I just remember thinking that I was angry and sad and I didn't want to hurt (emotionally) any more. I guess I first started doing it out of anger.'

'It basically just happened. I was angry and worked up so I started scratching my skin with a sharp object. I liked the way it felt.'

'It just seemed to happen. I was embarrassed and upset and holding a burning stick. It just made sense. All the pieces seemed to fit together.'

'From what I can remember about starting to SI, I just came about doing it as a reaction to my anger.'

The responses also highlight several other key points: that self-injury provides a release; it makes people feel better, that once started it can become a way of coping, and that several people started as a reaction to their anger. If self-injury is spreading among teenagers, perhaps the most urgent question that needs addressing is why? Further discussion on whether self-injury is on the increase among young people can be found in Chapter 4.

Myth 5: People that self-injure are mentally ill

'You cannot react in a "sane" way to insane circumstances.'

Many who self-injure fear they are going 'crazy' and while the behaviour is known to coexist with other disorders – eating disorders, substance misuse, depression and anxiety, for instance, albeit atypical behaviour, self-injury does not automatically indicate mental illness. Many who self-injure have not learned how to express their feelings in constructive ways. Perfectionism traits, low self-esteem, negative self-judgments, self-loathing, self-invalidation, and self-directed anger have also been positively correlated to self-injury.

'We could have depression, DID [Dissociative Identity Disorder], PTSD [Post-traumatic Stress Disorder], eating disorders, BPD [Borderline Personality Disorder], bipolar disorder [formerly manic depression], or any other type of mental disorder . . . or maybe nothing at all. '

'Self-injury is as bad as any other mental illness; it's not something we can just "get over". We who self-injure are not whiny little babies, for whatever reason, SI is the only coping skill we may have. We're not freaks, and we're not psychos either. We simply need SI for whatever reasons, and we DO need support and love from the people around us to help stop SI.'

'Self-injurers are not scary. We aren't sickos. We are the people next door, the teacher, the mailman. We wait on you in your stores, or you wait on us. We are not all teenagers. We are all ages. We don't necessarily want to hurt ourselves. We aren't all just looking for attention, that's why most of us hide what we've done. We just don't know what else to do with ourselves. Please don't judge. For some, self-injury is all that keeps us alive.'

'Self-injurers are NOT freaks of nature or strange masochistic people. We are simply people who cope in a way that makes others extremely uncomfortable. Once you look to the core of it all, it's not all that different from people who drink or do drugs or retreat completely to try and solve their problems.'

'People who self-injure are not crazy, and self-injury is not necessarily a bad thing – it's a way of handling pain that can't be dealt with any other way. It's a coping mechanism, and a way of surviving when the only other option is suicide. People who SI aren't bad or making up problems. They're doing it to deal with pain. Reacting with anger and horror doesn't help and only hurts. Keeping someone from SI also does further harm – they need to stop on their own, at their own pace.'

'People who self-injure are human beings. We aren't abnormal, we aren't freaks, and we don't corrupt people and try to turn them to self-injury. We just have a different way of handling things because we've never learned another way.'

Self-injury typically indicates that there are unresolved issues that need to be addressed and healed. Crucial, therefore, is to recognise that those who self-injure are doing their best to manage with the only skills they have available at their finger tips.

Myth 6: Those who self-injure suffer from Borderline Personality Disorder

> 'I've been given many labels including obsessive compulsive disorder, impulse control disorder, borderline personality disorder – they are all senseless to me. They just confine me to a set of symptoms – they do not describe my experience.'

Figure 2.2 provides an overview of diagnostic labels assigned to Internet respondents. Many reported receiving several of the diagnoses listed, hence the reason percentages are not included. Borderline personality disorder (BPD), deemed very difficult to treat, is a particularly controversial and unpopular diagnosis. To make a diagnosis of BPD (employing the criteria as set out in DSM-IV-TR, APA 2000), five or more of nine diagnostic criteria have to be met, one of which is 'recurrent suicidal behaviour, gestures, or threats, or self-mutilating behaviour.' (See Appendix 2 for DSM diagnostic criteria for BPD).

> 'All too often, therapists see it [self-injury] as the primary symptom of borderline personality disorder, even if the client doesn't meet the criteria in any other way. And borderlines are still seen as bad news for a therapist.'

> 'I have been warehoused under the BPD classification, which is an area that shrinks have created to put people they don't otherwise know anything about – more or less a trash diagnosis.'

INTERNET RESPONDENTS: DIAGNOSES RECEIVED

Participants who completed survey: N = 52

	Total	
Anxiety Disorders		
Post-traumatic stress disorder (PTSD)	17	
Panic disorder/Generalized anxiety disorder	8	
Obsessive compulsive disorder (OCD)	6	**Overall total = 31**
Mood Disorders	**Total**	
Major Depressive Disorder	19	
Bipolar disorder	7	
Dysthymic disorder	3	**Overall total = 29**
Dissociative Disorders	**Total**	
Dissociative identity disorder (DID)	6	
Depersonalization disorder (DP)	4	
Dissociative Disorders Not Otherwise Specified (DDNOS)	3	**Overall total = 13**
Personality Disorders	**Total**	
Borderline Personality Disorder (BPD)	9	
Histrionic Personality Disorder	1	
Personality Disorder Not Otherwise Specified (with borderline traits)	1	**Overall total = 11**
Psychotic Disorders	**Total**	
Schizoaffective disorder	2	**Overall total = 2**
Disorders usually first diagnosed in infancy, childhood or adolescence	**Total**	
Attention-deficit/hyperactivity disorder	1	
Tourette's disorder	1	**Overall total = 2**
Other	**Total**	
Adjustment disorder	1	
Body dysmorphic disorder (Somatoform disorder)	1	

Fig. 2.2: Internet respondents: diagnoses received.

Dr. Leland Heller, an American family physician, author of the book *Life at the Border: Understanding and Recovering from the Borderline Personality* (1991), and founder of the BiologicalUnhappiness.com website (http://www.biologicalunhappiness.com/) is one among many practitioners who would welcome seeing a change of term. Indeed, in an Internet article entitled *A Possible New Name For Borderline Personality Disorder* (HealthyPlace.com, 1999-2007) he pulls no punches about his views on the term:

> I think it's a horrible, insulting label for a real medical illness.
> The name alone reduces serious research, stigmatizes victims, and
> implies the person is crazy. It denies the medical nature of the
> process, and implies simply a personality problem.

In the same article, Heller explains BPD as 'a malfunction of the limbic system', coining the term 'Dyslimbia' in preference to BPD. To clarify his choice of term he says that 'Dys' indicates 'malfunctioning' and 'limbia' refers to the 'limbic system'. (See Chapter 3 for further information about the limbic system).

Difficult childhoods are reported to feature in the backgrounds of many people diagnosed with BPD, as pointed out by Colin Ross, MD (2000):

> I have never met a borderline who had a childhood that was
> anywhere near normal or happy. I have given dozens of workshops
> in which I have asked whether anyone has ever seen a borderline
> with a normal childhood, and not one out of thousands of
> professionals have ever raised a hand. The "tough" childhood is part
> of the phenomenology of the disorder. (p.207)

You will note from Figure 2.2 that major depressive disorder followed by post-traumatic stress disorder (PTSD) were the two most reported diagnoses. Perhaps this is an indication of a move away from the stigmatising BPD label – let's hope so. Many researchers argue that

BPD is a form of 'Chronic PTSD' (symptoms persist for 3 months or longer). Acclaimed trauma researchers, Judith Herman (1998) and Bessel van der Kolk (1996) for example, make it clear that the diagnostic criteria for PTSD fails to encompass the acute symptoms caused by prolonged, recurrent and chronic trauma. Thus, they have proposed an alternative diagnosis (incorporating the relevant group of symptoms identified) for inclusion in future editions of the *Diagnostic and Statistical Manual of Mental Disorders* published by the American Psychiatric Association. Whereas, Herman coins the term 'Complex PTSD' (CPTSD) for the proposed diagnosis, van der Kolk uses the term Disorders of Extreme Stress Not Otherwise Specified (DESNOS). (See Appendix 2 for DSM-IV-TR criteria for PTSD and BPD, and Disorders of Extreme Stress Not Otherwise Specified (DESNOS): Proposed Criteria).

Myth 7: Those who self-injure are a danger to others

Yet another common myth about self-injury is that individuals who do it are a danger to others, thus it's safer to steer clear of them. This assumption is deeply offensive to some who practice the behaviour and who would never dream of striking out at anyone else. While it may be true that some people put their own lives in jeopardy by their actions, rarely do they appear to pose a risk to other people, as evidenced in the four testimonies below:

> 'I cannot bear to hurt others so I turn my pain inward. I do not want to have large physical displays of anger as my father did. I feel more in control when I take rage out in this manner. Also at times I need to express anger against others but there is not a healthy way to do this or the person is not available to tell him/her how I feel. I take it out on myself as proxy. In my mind I am martyred. I have physical "proof" of the damage I perceive someone else (or myself) to have caused.'

'Even though it [self-injury] is not a good coping mechanism, it **is** a coping mechanism. And, as long as I'm hurting myself, I'm not hurting someone else, right?'

'I do not want to hurt you. I hurt myself to cope with the overwhelming stress and frustration I feel because of my inability to express myself outwardly in an effective manner. I am afraid that if I let the pain out, I will hurt others. For now, this is the only way I can cope with this feeling. If there is one thing you can do to help me, it would be to understand this, to listen when I do try to express myself, and to gently encourage me to express my feelings in a healthy manner so that one day I will no longer rely on self-injury to cope with my feelings.**'**

'I am not crazy. I am not a danger to other people. I do this to survive. I don't understand how people function without doing this. If you want to help me, teach me other ways to survive, show me how to do it. Don't judge me by what you think this behaviour means. Get to know me. Be patient.'

Myth 8: Self-injury is a response to child abuse

It is widely reported that self-injury is a response to child abuse, and whilst this may be partly true, it is not always the case.

Favazza and Conterio's study of 240 women that self-injure (1989: 285) found the following childhood causal factors:

- Childhood abuse (62%)
- Childhood sexual and physical abuse (29%)
- Sexual abuse only (17%)

- Physical abuse only (16%)
- Over half described their childhood as "miserable".

Arnold's survey of 76 women that self-injure (1995:10-11) revealed a number of childhood factors that contribute to self-injury – these included:

- Sexual abuse (49%)
- Neglect (49%)
- Emotional abuse (43%)
- Lack of communication (27%)
- Physical abuse (25%)
- Loss/separation (25%)
- Sick or alcoholic parent (17%)
- Other childhood experiences (19%).

In many cases, the women reported suffering a number of traumatic experiences, 'often including multiple forms of abuse and deprivation'. Adult experiences echoed many of the childhood experiences – the most common being rape, sexual abuse and harassment.

van der Kolk, Perry and Herman (1991:1665-1671) in their study of 28 self-cutters, discovered the following childhood causal factors:

- Significant childhood trauma (79%)
- Major disruptions in parental care (89%)
- Sexual abuse was most strongly associated with all types of self-destructive behaviour.
- '. . . the age at which trauma occurs plays a key role in both the severity and expression of self-destructive behaviour: the earlier the trauma, the more cutting'.

Only one respondent did not report childhood trauma or disrupted care. The authors concluded that: 'Childhood trauma contributes to the initiation of self-destructive behavior, but lack of secure attachments helps maintain it'.

An unpublished Internet study of self-injury (Davies, S. C., 2002) revealed that almost seventy-five percent (75%) of respondents had suffered childhood abuse, and many reported experiencing several forms of abuse and neglect, which mainly occurred in childhood and continued over long periods. Noteworthy too, was that the age when the abuse occurred correlated significantly with the age of onset of self-harm. (See Chapter 5 for a summary of Davies's findings).

Putting things into perspective
Favazza, in the introduction to the book *A Bright Red Scream* (2000) by Marilee Strong, stresses the importance of not making the automatic assumption that self-injury is a response to child abuse – he writes:

> One caveat I would encourage readers to keep in mind is that the childhood physical and sexual abuse so dramatically and accurately described in the book applies to 50 to 60 percent of self-mutilators, which means that a fair number have not been abused. On several occasions I have had to rescue patients from therapists who were frustrated at not being able to find the cause of an individual's self-mutilation and therefore assumed that he or she must have been abused. (p. xiv)

Myth 9: If the wounds are minor the problem's not major

Another conjecture made about self-injury is that the severity of the wounds reflects the extent of the problem. However, what came across clearly from the Internet respondents' testimonies is that the level of harm inflicted can vary from episode to episode, and is dependent on numerous factors, for example, stress and anxiety levels, the degree of anger, despair, self-hate, dissociation, emotional distress experienced, and the trigger severity. Further, the testimonies highlighted that the method used, the area of the body injured, and the duration of self-injury sessions may also vary depending on the degree of emotional suffering or the trigger. Below are a handful of testimonies received on this topic:

'When the level of the stress and anxiety is higher, I'm more likely to injure with greater intensity and anger.'

'If I'm really upset, I cut just a few times, but very deep. If the level of stress is low though, there tends to be far more cuts, but they are minor and usually scar very little or not at all.'

'. . . the severity of the injury depends on how I am feeling. Whenever I am dealing with self-hate from flashbacks or anger . . . I cut and burn deeper.'

'The angrier I am with myself, the more severe and multiple the self-injury.'

'Usually the more upset I am the longer the self-injury session will last and the deeper the cuts will be, generally anyway.'

'If I'm really upset then it's quite bad and deep, but if I'm only a bit stressed it isn't so severe.'

'I have had very uncomfortable anxiety attacks and powerful triggers but I find that I tend to injure more seriously based on my level of despair.'

'The type of emotional discomfort and severity of the emotional discomfort is directly related to the area self-injured, the method of self-injury and the severity of self-injury.'

'SI severity varies according to trigger severity.'

'The most serious SI I ever did, I can't even remember why I did it. Oh yeah, I dissociate a lot, especially when things get very stressful . . . so that also makes it hard to see a correlation.'

'. . . when I feel extremely triggered, anxious or not as "with it" – I guess you would call that dissociated, I would cut much worse then if I had more of a sense of control.'

What needs to be borne in mind from these testimonies is that while individual episodes of self-injury may serve as a useful yardstick for gauging the motivation behind a specific episode, it's important not to lose sight of the bigger picture as self-injury is rarely a one-off occurrence. Further, the degree of emotional suffering should not be judged by the extent of the injuries as everyone's pain threshold is different – in other words, minor wounds may reflect similar levels of internal anguish as more serious wounds. The degree of dissociation experienced at the time of self-injury may also affect the amount of harm done. (See Chapter 8 for further information on dissociation and self-injury).

Myth 10: Those who self-injure are a burden on society

'I guess I have often wished in the material that I have read that they had gone more into detail into the productive lives that many self-injurers lead . . . to make it clear that many self-injurers have very productive lives and yet have coping skills such as self-injury to make it through the day.'

Another assumption made about those who self-injure is that they are a heavy drain on society in terms of NHS time and resources. Whilst it's true that some people who self-injure may be well-known to A&E staff and the psychiatric services, there are a huge number of people who make a determined effort to steer clear of seeking help, thus lining the pockets of the first aid and skin camouflaging manufacturers rather than burdening the NHS with meeting the cost of their treatment. Also extremely important to recognise is that many people who self-injure lead fruitful lives: home making, raising children, running their own businesses, or holding down other responsible jobs – in nursing, teaching, social work, caring for the elderly, to name a few jobs that Internet respondents reported doing. What also became apparent from the Internet respondents' testimonies is that many who self-injure are high academic achievers, or gifted writers and artists. In essence, what came across clearly was that many who self-injure are hardworking people living ordinary lives.

Key points:

- Self-injury happens in a wide range of settings.
- Self-injury is more about attention needing than attention seeking. In the main, the act is carried out in private and the wounds and scars from self-injury are carefully concealed beneath items of clothing, jewellery, bangles, or sweat bands.
- Self-injury occurs in all age groups, and can affect people from all walks of life. It is not an exclusively teenage, all female phenomenon. Men self-injure too. Nor is it a new trend.
- Self-injury serves effectively as an outlet for tears that cannot be shed, for pain and grief that cannot be expressed, as self-punishment for 'being weak' and wanting to cry, to prevent tears from spilling over, or to block out emotional pain.
- Whilst self-injury has been linked to a range of psychiatric disorders, it doesn't automatically indicate that people who self-

injure are mentally ill. Nor is it an automatic sign of Borderline Personality Disorder.

- The question of whether self-injury is becoming contagious among young people needs further investigation.
- People who self-injure rarely seem to present a danger to others.
- Self-injury is not rooted exclusively in child abuse; it has a broad range of predisposing factors.
- Minor wounds don't necessarily signify that an individual's issues are not significant: it's important to look at the overall picture rather than at specific episodes as self-injury is rarely a one-off occurrence.
- Those who self-injure are not always a burden on society. Many lead constructive and fruitful lives.

Chapter 3

Further insights into self-injury

. . . .

'I think it's really important to communicate what the
variety and dynamics and techniques of self-injury
are. It seems really important to me for
caregivers to have some comprehension of the
creativity and diversity of injury.'

'All my ideas of harming myself have come
from me and me alone . . . And, whatever implements
I have used to cut myself have been of my own thoughts.'

Caution: This chapter includes information that those who self-injure, or have self-injured in the past might find potentially 'triggering'. Please make sure you keep safe.

What methods do people use to self-injure? Do cutting and burning serve different purposes? Why the need to see blood? Is there a link between alexithymia and self-injury? What implements do people use to self-injure? Where do people self-injure?

Is there significance to the areas chosen? How long does self-injury last? What do people think of their scars? Is self-injury addictive? Do endorphins play a role in self-injury? These questions are addressed in this chapter, together with a glimpse into the effects of post traumatic stress symptoms on the brain.

Because of my concern that discussing methods and implements used to self-injure could prove distressing to those who practise the act, or might pose a risk by giving people ideas, I decided to seek a number of Internet respondents' views on whether these topics should be included. The general consensus was that to omit the material or 'water it down' would make 'it a book that is lacking in information'. Several respondents thought that inclusion of the material would be helpful to professionals, other caregivers and lay people in general:

> 'I do think it will help professionals and concerned friends or family members to understand what is done and the different methods or tools.'
>
> 'You should probably include the information for the benefit of the helpers who will read the book. It is important that they have the information so that they know what to look for . . .'
>
> 'The subject matter needs to be written, needs to be circulated, and needs to be out there in order for others to understand us...'
>
> 'Personally I think that the **guide** for what to include should be "anything that might help people understand."'

Several agreed that the material could be potentially 'triggering' but considered it should still be included:

> 'I think it should be included. It may be triggering to some self-injurers but it is the responsibility of the self-injurer to keep safe.'
>
> 'I understand how this information could be triggering. I also understand how important it is to discuss the different

ways people SI. I definitely think that you should include the information.'

'It's not all going to be daisies and roses so I think that if someone is reading the book there is a possibility to be triggered but I also think common sense has to come into play. If it's a book on self-injury, there is a chance that it will be "triggery"'.

Other respondents went some way to allaying my foreboding that including the material might give people ideas:

'The way I figure it, and it's just my humble opinion, there isn't anything that someone could tell me to use to hurt myself with that I haven't already thought of.'

'I've become aware of the range of self-injury methods via lists/internet/etc, but it has never really influenced my method of operation or my preferences.'

'I don't think you should exclude the information of items used and such. From my experience, people who self-injure don't need help to find new ways to hurt themselves.'

'. . . my guess would be that most self-injurers who would read a book like yours are probably trying to get better, or at least to understand themselves better, rather than investigating new and improved methods of self-injury.'

What methods do people use to self-injure?

Research has consistently shown that skin cutting is the most common method of self-injury. Figure 3.1 highlights methods used to self-injure compared across three studies.

METHODS USED TO SELF-INJURE COMPARED ACROSS THREE STUDIES					
Favazza & Conterio (1989–USA Study)		Arnold (1995) for Bristol Crisis Service for Women (UK Study)		Sutton (1999) (UK Study)	
Female habitual self-mutilators A study of 240 women who regularly self-injured	%	Women and Self-Injury A survey of 76 women Healing the Hurt Within	%	A study of 37 people who self-harm (35 females and 2 males	%
Cutting	72	Cutting	90	Cutting	92
Burning	35	Inflicting blows	32	Burning	35
Self-hitting or punching	30	Burning/scalding	30	Self-hitting	24
Interfering with wound healing	22	Picking/scratching	12		
Scratching	22	Pulling hair	7		
Hair pulling	10	Biting	5		
Bone breaking	8	Swallowing objects	4		

Fig. 3.1: Methods used to self-injure compared across three studies.

Cutting is rarely the only form of self-injury used

'Self injury is not the exclusive realm of blades, blood, and bandages. There are a variety of methods employed. Some self-injurers have one exclusive action, others use several methods, a few use any available way of causing injury.

I use several methods, and generally each method is for coping with a different set of stresses or overwhelming experiences.'

As evidenced from Figure 3.1, while cutting appears to be peoples' 'preferred method' to self-injure, burning is also fairly common: it is also interesting to note that the percentages on burning from all three studies are very close. This set me thinking about whether cutting and burning might serve difference functions.

Do cutting and burning serve different purposes?

Surprisingly, a literature search for information addressing the question of whether cutting and burning might serve different functions revealed this to be virtually uncharted territory. Thus, in order to ascertain whether there might possibly be a distinction between the two lead once more to inviting the Internet respondents to comment on the subject. They were asked to respond to the following questions: 'If you cut and burn, do they serve different functions for you? Can you explain?' Here are a range of replies received:

> '[Burning is] not as satisfactory as cutting for me.' 'Not particularly . . . burning, though, is easier to explain off as an accident. If I have to go somewhere it's easier to burn, especially since I don't burn myself as severely as I cut.'
>
> 'Cutting is a caress; kind of like a warm yet clinical feeling . . . "Ok, I'm gonna put a cut right there." And you do it. It's almost fun. Burning on the other hand is uncontrolled, violent, and sudden; kind of like getting drunk. It's still serving its purpose, but there's the uncertainty about it that is worrying.'
>
> 'Burning is a more immediate pain, maybe, whereas cutting is more . . . deep.'
>
> 'Cutting is more of a release, an escape. Burning is more of a punishment, self-hatred.'

'They do. Depending on how I feel, sometimes I need blood more than pain, and other times pain more than blood. Burning has never drawn blood for me, so I tend to turn to that method when I just need the pain to snap me back to reality. Cutting, on the other hand, does both, and is usually my method of choice.'

'They don't serve different purposes for me really. Cutting works better because I like to see the blood. But sometimes I like to burn because if the metal I'm using to burn with is hot enough, it seems to melt away the skin and I like watching it.'

'Cutting is a tension breaker whereas burning is "Can I do it?" and "If I can do it, I can make it through anything."'

'They serve the same initial function to me but burning lasts longer and you might say it is the gift that keeps on giving because if I play with the burn area later I get the same relief.'

'Yes, cutting and burning serve different purposes. When I am really angry or feel like I need to suffer . . . I burn. When I am sad or depressed I tend to cut more to release my feelings. I need to see the blood to cleanse myself in a way. When I have flashbacks or self-hate it could go either way . . . cutting or burning.'

'Yes. I burn myself when I want to punish myself. It hurts a lot, even during the self-injury act for me anyway, and so it's more of a physical pain preoccupation. Whereas when I cut, which I normally do, it's to relieve stress, emotions, anger, or to not feel numb, and the preoccupation is more about my thoughts and what's going on inside me, what I feel, what I'm fearing, stuff like that.'

'I don't know about them having different functions, but I prefer to see blood when I'm hurting myself, so I don't like burning too much. But if I don't have anything to cut myself with, I will burn myself.'

'Yes, they do serve different purposes for me. Cutting is usually for when I am so frustrated or overwhelmed, and I am usually dissociated. Burning is very efficient in bringing me 'back' from dissociation. That's about all I use burning for.'

'Burning is a different feeling. It's a "cleaner" sort of pain, if that makes sense. But I can't say it serves a different function than cutting. Ultimately, it's just a question of getting rid of my horrible, horrible feelings.'

'For me, cutting is less severe. I use it in situations of less stress. Burning is much worse for me because I do so much more damage.'

'I used to be more of a burner than a cutter. I sort of felt that I was too lowly to use a knife or another cutting tool. Besides, I liked the welts and scars that burning left. Then one day, fire wasn't available to me so I started using razors and now I pretty much only cut.'

'When I cut, I feel either very destructive or that I need to punish myself for something "stupid" I did (sorry, but can't think of another word). The sight of the blood is a relief . . . almost like letting air out of a balloon that is almost ready to pop. When I burn, I usually feel very numb and I want to feel something. I also will burn when I'm very stressed out. It's like the relaxation technique in which you squeeze your hands really tight and then let go and you can really feel the muscles relax. Burning hurts at first, but when the pain starts to go away, I start to feel relaxed. When I feel really numb, I hold the hot lighter on as long as possible because it feels good to feel.'

'Cutting is my "preferred". Burning has been for when tools were not available, in desperation. Scalding was for when I was very, very angry with myself and wanted more "damage" (and it looked accidental, a big plus for me).'

'I've cut, burned, and hit myself. Yes, they serve different purposes and I'll try to explain. I think I self-injure because of emotions that I can't express – feelings that I can't name. When I get overwhelmed by those feelings, I hurt myself. There are times when the pain of burning is what dissipates those feelings and there are times when feeling the blood flow and seeing it is what brings relief from the intense feelings. I can't tell you what those feelings are because I don't know how to name them but somehow I know which one works for which situation. I'm sure that doesn't make sense but when I get into that overwhelmed state, I just "know" which to do and how much to do to get relief. When I cut, I usually don't feel pain, just the release of the blood. When I burn, I feel the pain and that is what helps. With a cut it is over rather quickly, once cleaned up, it heals, and life moves on. With a burn, the pain and discomfort remains longer and constantly reminds me of itself. I truly don't know how it is that I know but I do. Just like I also know how much cutting is enough to bring relief. Sometimes I will make a cut and it won't be enough and I'll have to do it again until it is enough – there again it is just something that I know. There have been a couple of times when I've gotten out of control but usually I know.'

'Sometimes, if I want more pain, I burn. But if I feel the need to see blood, I cut.'

'This is a bit difficult for me to explain. As far as cutting, it is what I do more often; generally I would reach for a razor regardless of how I am feeling. The burning comes and goes . . . generally when I burn it is more when I am having a bad memory or feeling disgusted by my body.'

'Cutting is for when I need to see the blood running and when a higher pain level is not originally needed. Burning is reserved for when the cutting isn't doing anything and I feel a need for more pain. At these times, I will either burn where I cut or find a new place to burn. Burning is also used when it is not convenient to cut and I need a "quick fix" or if I know that cutting just isn't going to "cut it".'

'Sometimes I find that drawing blood, especially in large amounts, is very important when I self-injure. This was so important to me that I started collecting my blood in jars and bottles once. This went on for months and months. I don't really remember how or why I stopped or what happened to all the blood. I think this is symbolic. There are reasons people choose different methods of self-injury. If people have a wide range of methods available to them, they choose the one that "feels the best" or "works the best" . . . it depends on your motivation.'

'I use whatever is available or most convenient given the situation. For example, cigarettes are easy to use while at work because I am known as an occasional smoker and I don't have to worry about the "blood" factor.'

'We do both at the same time! We heat the knife first. When we have done it separately, the burning has been to punish the body . . . anger at ourselves (feeling directed inwards). The cutting is for release/relief from the inside pressure . . . frustration/overwhelmed (feeling directed outwards).'

Note: The final testimony is from a respondent diagnosed with Dissociative Identity Disorder (DID). Hence, the reason she refers to herself as 'we' and 'ourselves'. This is fairly common practice among people with DID. The subject of dissociation and DID is discussed in various chapters later in the book.

Summary

As can be seen from the testimonies, cutting and burning serve a similar purpose for some, while for others they serve different purposes. The list below provides an overview of possible reasons why people may choose burning over cutting, identified from the responses. However, there does appear to be a degree of overlap in some cases, for example either behaviour may be used to terminate dissociative episodes (feeling numb, unconnected). Also, the choice of method may depend on the trigger and can go either way. This made it difficult to determine whether a clear distinction can always be made. What did come across is that if the sight of blood is important, cutting is more likely to be chosen over burning. Further, to quote a male respondent's interesting observation, perhaps: **'Fire and so** on is more anti-dissociative whereas blades are more anti-emotional.' (Emphasis added).

- Burning provides a more immediate pain than cutting, it hurts more, and the pain and discomfort lasts longer ('it is the gift that keeps on giving'). This suggests that burning may serve the purpose of distracting one's thoughts away from the internal emotional pain for a longer period than cutting.
- There is more uncertainty about burning than cutting, and it is can be a more damaging and dangerous method.
- Burning may be chosen over cutting to cope with exceptionally high levels of stress, when a higher level of pain or more damage is needed, when feeling the need to suffer more or to punish oneself more, or to manage intense feelings of anger or powerful negative feelings of self-hatred or self-disgust towards oneself.
- Burning may be selected over cutting to terminate incapacitating episodes of dissociation (feeling exceptionally numb) or when a quick 'snap back to reality' is needed.
- Burning may be used to prove to oneself that if one can get through the excruciating pain of burning oneself, one can get through the pain of anything.
- Burning may be chosen if a 'quick fix' is needed or if cutting is insufficient to 'cut' through the psychological pain.
- On a practical level, burning may be the method of choice for the sake of convenience – it can be carried out quickly, easily, with relatively little mess. It may also be used as a substitute if a person's 'cutting tools' are not readily to hand, and can be passed off more easily as an accident.

Why the need to see blood?

As mentioned, the sight of blood is important to many people who self-injure. There are several explanations for this. The following respondents' comments (Sutton, 1999, p.121) clarify some of the reasons:

'It feels like a relief, like I am letting the pain out, the bad part of me is being punished.'

'It makes me feel clean, washing away all the impurities that were induced into my body by others when I was a child.'

'If I've got to hurt myself then I'm not satisfied until I see some blood, a little, a lot, when I see it coming out of a wound that's some of the hurt coming out.'

'When I saw the blood I felt nothing, just numbness.'

Alexithymia and self-injury: is there a link?

'I think I self-injure because of emotions that I can't express – feelings that I can't name. When I get overwhelmed by those feelings, I hurt myself . . . 'I can't tell you what those feelings are because I don't know how to name them . . .'

Problems recognising and describing emotional states in words appears to be a common occurrence among people that self-injure. Similar characteristics feature in *alexithymia*. Alexithymia, a term coined by Peter Sifneos in 1973, is derived from the Greek language ("*a* = lack, *lexis* = word, *thymos* = emotion"). Literally it means 'a lack of words for emotions'. Alexithymia, refers to a psychological construct, rather than an illness.

It is important to understand however, that alexithymia does not equate to a deficiency of emotions; rather it means a disengagement from emotions, which in turn hinders the processing of emotions through the language of words. Alexithymia can also have specific consequences. For example, the risk of being repeatedly overwhelmed or swamped with potent yet nameless feelings or memories, or frustration at not being able to communicate to others what one is experiencing internally.

In addition to difficulties recognising and describing emotional states, other characteristics of alexithymia include an externally oriented thinking style, and a limited imaginative capacity (impoverished fantasy life). (Taylor, 1997: 28-31)

Studies of alexithymia

A study by Zlotnick, *et al.* (1996) found a higher degree of alexithymia and dissociative symptoms among people that self-injure than amongst those who didn't. Further, alexithymia has been positively associated with two psychiatric disorders frequently linked to self-injury: post-traumatic stress disorder (PTSD) and borderline personality disorder (BPD) (Zlotnick *et al.*, 2001).

For further information on alexithymia see the useful resources section at the end of this chapter.

What implements do people use to self-injure?

Figure 3.2 (Internet respondents: implements used to self-injure) reveals the wide range of implements that people use to self-injure. As can be seen people can be extremely innovative if the urge to self-injure strikes.

INTERNET RESPONDENTS: IMPLEMENTS USED TO SELF-INJURE					
Razor blades	89%	Knives	81%	Shards of glass	59%
Needles	56%	Scissors	54%	Lighted cigarettes	44%
Cigarette Lighter	43%	Finger Nails	31%	Boiling Water	20%
Nails (carpentry type)	13%	Hammer	13%	Iron	11%
Safety pins	9%	Baseball bat	7%	Hotplate	6%

Fig. 3.2: Internet respondents: implements used to self-injure.

Other implements and methods reported

- Cutting and gouging: Broken crockery, house keys, rings, screws, screwdriver, scalpel, staples, notebook wires, blades of figure skates, tin cans, saws, chisels, cheese grater; pins/bobbi pins, paper clips, zippers, compass, retractable stencil knives, pencil sharpener blades/erasers, broken CDs, nail files, plastic knives, wood splinters, manicure set, box cutter, exacto knives, craft scissors, bits of wire, wire hanger, steel, plaster, wood, anything sharp/broken with edges (e.g. furniture), sharp part of an earring, pointy end of a mascara make-up tool, tweezers, dog lead.

- Burning and scalding: Candle flames and hot wax, blowtorch, curling iron, lighted matches, heated metal, boiling hot showers, hot radiators, hot baking trays, industrial laminating machine, acid/corrosives/chemicals.

- Hitting/knocking/scratching/biting: Thumping walls and dragging knuckles across bricks, banging self, head or knuckles against walls until black and blue; bruising/punching self with fists and hands; throwing self against doors, shutting arms and other parts of body in doors; banging head with hands; hitting self with door wedge, weights, rocks, bricks, concrete blocks and wooden mallet; biting self; erasing skin with sandpaper.

Where do people self-injure?

Research has consistently shown that cutting the arms is the most common form of self-injury, however, as highlighted in Figure 3.3 (Internet respondents: reported areas of the body self-injured) numerous areas of the body may become targets. Percentages have not been included as many respondents reported injuring various parts of the body.

INTERNET RESPONDENTS: REPORTED AREAS OF THE BODY SELF-INJURED	
	(N=55)
Lower arms	48
Upper arms	43
Hands and fingers	43
Wrists	43
Thighs	40
Face/Forehead	35
Lower Leg	34
Belly/Stomach	34
Chest/Breast	29
Shoulder	29
Neck/throat	21
Foot/toes/ankle	21
Hips	19
Scalp and hair	18
Vagina/pubic area/bladder	13
Knee	12
Back	4
Anus	3
Buttocks	3
Penis	1
Lips	1
Back of head	1

Fig. 3.3: Internet respondents: reported areas of the body self-injured.

Is there significance to the areas chosen?

The following testimonies which come from respondents who completed the survey for *Healing the Hurt Within*, 1st edition (Sutton, 1999:37–40) suggest that there is a meaning to why people target specific areas.

Six chose areas of easy access or the most available parts of the body:

'Easy access, near to big veins, hidden, but not completely from others all the time – could be seen by accident.'

'I cut my arms because they are the most available part of my body – plus I can push my arms up as the blade goes down.'

'Simply because my arms were the most accessible part of my body and I'd need to satisfy my urge to cut quickly. Mainly though, because it hurt less and tended not to scar as badly. Also, I wanted to restrict scarring and not ruin my entire body.'

'Outer surface of arm easily accessible – it bleeds more than the inside of my arm.'

'I mostly cut my left forearm because it's easiest to access, the skin is smooth and almost hairless, and I cut that part first when I turned from haphazard damage to actual self-harm 2 years ago.'

'Limbs easier to access, especially forearms and calves.'

Two chose areas that could be seen:

'Because they are the places other people were likely to see. I harm my face, arms, wrists and hands because these areas are the most exposed, so you'll get noticed, you are seeking attention but it's the wrong sort. You're hurting on the inside but you can't tell anyone, so you hurt yourself on the outside. It's saying "look at me I'm hurting", but it's on the inside not the outside.'

'At first I was confused about whether I wanted to die and I thought if I cut my wrists people might take me seriously. Now it is just that those areas are scarred and it doesn't seem to matter any more.'

Two chose areas that couldn't be seen:

'I chose these areas because I knew that I could hide whatever I do from people.'

'I know that I am able to hide these areas most of the time.'

One chose a hated area/area of easy access:

'I used to cut my thighs because it was near my cunt – and I hated my cunt. I used to cut my arms – they were visible and very accessible.'

Another chose an area that caused personal offence:

'I feel this limb (arm) when used can do no right. It causes offence and does only wrong, it has no goodness in it at all and needs to be destroyed.'

Five identified a variety of reasons:

'I don't want other people to see or comment on my wounds, so I cut myself in places I can hide, or in a way I can explain. For example, if I cut my hand or arm, I make up a story about a knife slipping or catching myself on something sharp. Alternatively, I cut my thighs or abdomen in places that won't be seen by others. However, as I cut in order to see how much pain I'm in, I prefer to use my arm as it's easily visible. I would like to cut myself more, but as I receive treatment for other physical conditions, I don't risk comment from doctors about my scars by having them in visible places on my body.'

'I choose areas of my body which are easy to cover up and hopefully where I can do the least damage permanently.'

'My thigh is scarred and private. It looks so ugly it does not matter if I cut. Above my ankle began with an urge to cut somewhere else. I wanted to cut my feet – again – as private – but was afraid that as I felt so bad I could/might get "carried away". Now those places are scarred and it doesn't seem to matter. My arm causes great distress when cut as I do not want to tattoo my whole body with my pain and it leaves me feeling out of control.'

'I'm right-handed so my left arm bears the brunt. My legs were the only option at one stage because my arms were constantly bandaged. Belly – not often – triggered by self-disgust at the size of it and a desire to keep it hidden from the "professionals".'

'My chest because I hate having breasts. My forehead because I feel I should visibly brand myself. My arm because I can see it easily and can choose whether to hide it or not.'

One chose areas associated with sites of sexual abuse:

'I really hate my body. I suppose I've blamed it for being sexually abused.'

Another chose areas associated with sites of abuse, touch and torture:

'Because they are sites of abuse, touches, torture, etc. I choose both sexual and non-sexual parts. I'm unsure why I self-harm the head.'

How long does self-injury last?

Figure 3.4 shows the duration of self-injury as reported by the Internet respondents. The survey for *Healing the Hurt Within*, 1st edition (Sutton, 1999: pp. 35–36) revealed that 27% of the sample group had been self-injuring for over 20 years, 19% for between 10–20 years, 24% for between for 5–10 years, and 30% under five years. Favazza (1996:254) argues that *'In many patients the disorder lasts ten to fifteen years, although isolated episodes of self-mutilative behaviour may persist.'* However, clearly evident from both sets of data is that a significant number of the sample groups had been self-injuring for over 15 years. Further, the data shows that self-injury is plainly not a new phenomenon.

INTERNET RESPONDENTS: REPORTED DURATION OF SELF-INJURY		
	(N=82)	% of sample
1-10 years	49	60
11-20 years	19	23
21-30 years	6	7
Most of lives	4	5
31-40 years	2	2
Under 1 year	2	2

Fig. 3.4: Internet respondents: reported duration of self-injury.

What do people think of their scars?

Self-injury scars hold a myriad of meanings. To some they are an enormous source of shame and embarrassment, and people take great pains to conceal them. Long sleeved tops, blouses or sweaters, and long trousers or jeans may be worn all year round; the wearing of swimsuits or bikinis may be avoided, and camouflage creams may be invested in.

'I hate the scars. I DON'T want them and do everything I can to avoid them. I have found a couple of things on the market that help reduce the scarring a lot, and use them a ton.'

'Actually I really dislike my scars. Possibly because they are so visible, but I just wish I could get rid of them sometimes.'

'I am so ashamed of my scars – to me it signifies weakness, even though in my head it was the only way to cope at the time. It's hard to explain, but it's like I have let the perpetrators win again or something, that I have allowed myself to resort to that behaviour again . . . I hate my scars, I hate what they mean to me, I hate for anyone to see them . . . though my friend has and that was a big step.'

'My scars show my pain, but only to myself. I tend to keep them as concealed as possible. People ask too many questions if they see them. They signify my inner state. They are my voice when my mouth and heart forget how to form the words of how I feel and what I wish for.'

Souvenirs of survival

In contrast, some have a fond relationship with their scars, viewing them as living proof of survival of hard-fought psychological battles, or as evidence that their emotional pain is real. To others, they represent willpower and self-control, a sign of uniqueness (almost like a birthmark), a painful life story etched on the skin, or they serve as a reminder of significant life events such as the loss of a loved one.

'I love my scars, and I think I always will, even the keloid scars that I have on my stomach. Depending on the place and the colour of it, you can tell how angry I was when I made it, and how much it would have hurt if I'd felt it. I think they prove to me that the pain and hurt I felt at those times is REAL, and so when I think I'm overreacting and making it up, I can look at my body and know how much I've had to put up with.'

'My scars mean a lot to me. They show me a story of my life. They show me that I've coped with my pain and have been able to live on. I feel proud of my scars. They are a part of me.'

'Scars show I am a true survivor . . . they show I am strong. Scars tell the story of my life, my abuse, bad things that happened to me . . . Scars are a part of me that I don't want to let go . . . They symbolise my pain and hurt and deep sadness . . . They are a part of me like my liver, and I wear them proudly.'

Is self-injury addictive?

'It's like a drug addiction. First, you need a little, then it builds up and up.'

Fifty-four percent (54%) of the sample group for *Healing the Hurt Within*, 1st edition, (p.149) and eighty-four percent (84%) of the Internet respondents considered self-injury was addictive (see Figure 3.5). In Favazza and Conterio's 1989 study, seventy-one percent (71%) of the sample group reported that their self-injurious behaviour was an addiction. The latter figure compares with the findings of a more recent study (Nixon *et al.*, 2002), in which 33 of 42 self-injuring adolescent patients (78.6%) admitted to a psychiatric hospital over a four month period reported almost daily urges to self-injure.

INTERNET RESPONDENTS: CONSIDERED SELF-INJURY ADDICTIVE		
	(N=81)	% of sample
Yes	68	84
No	7	9
Mixed feelings	6	7

Fig. 3.5: Internet respondents: considered self-injury addictive.

No pain – no gain

Some experts in the field disagree that self-injury is an addiction in the true sense of the word. For example, Conterio and Lader, in *Bodily Harm* (1998:22–26) state that 'self-injury shares certain characteristics with addiction' but argue that it is an 'addictive solution to emotional distress.' In contrast, Turner, in *Secret Scars* (2002:49), a book written from an addictions perspective, asserts, 'The experience of pain becomes addictive. The self-injurer comes to like pain, and she eventually craves it.'

The lure of what comes after

Conterio and Lader's hypothesis about self-injury being an 'addictive solution' makes sense. Perhaps it's not so much a question of getting pleasure from pain (masochism) but more the *lure of what comes after* (the euphoric high, the buzz, the good feeling) that keeps people hooked on the act. Simply put, and as evidenced by the following testimonies, people tolerate or live with A to get to B.

'Self-injury is like a drug because of the euphoric feeling I feel after it. There are times that I want to self-injure just so that I can get that feeling.'

'I'm addicted to the buzz I get after self-harm.'

'It works. That's why it's repeated time and time again. If there was an alternative that worked, I think most people would use that instead. I could see why some people might think it is addictive – but I don't think so. Are you addicted to using your car? It gets you to where you need to be – you keep using it – if there was something better – you'd use that.'

'I would say [self-injury is] just like a drug. It becomes something that you feel like you can't live without. When it works once to "fix" a problem, you will try it again and see that it will work again. Eventually your small cuts aren't enough and you cut more and more. You gain more "tolerance".'

'It's very easy to get blinkered to alternatives to self injury, and to see it as the only way to deal with things. It's like a drug, once you find out how good it makes you feel, how it blocks out the bad stuff, how it is relatively easy to do, then you don't want to give it up.'

Do endorphins play a role in self-injury?

'When I self-injure I want to make the feelings go away. I want the rush after cutting and then the numbness after. I like how it feels. It makes everything go away and I can be at peace for the moment. I want my mind to release everything and I want to just be numb to everything.'

The above testimony provides useful information about the respondent's goals of self-injury. Of particular interest to the current topic is the 'rush' and 'numbness' she says she wants to achieve – these appear to be common reasons for self-injury. One theory is that self-injury stimulates the production of endorphins, which could explain the rush, numbing, and the sense of peace and calm that many people report experiencing following the act.

What are endorphins?

The word endorphin is an abbreviation of two words: endogenous (internally generated) and morphine (a pain-reliever). Endorphins (neurotransmitters, endogenous opioids) occur naturally in the brain and contain analgesic properties similar to morphine. Painkilling drugs, such as morphine (derived from opium) and codeine (produced from morphine), are commonly used in the medical arena to relieve severe pain caused by physical injuries, or to manage chronic pain in ongoing illnesses. Heroin, another semi-synthetic opium derivative (known to be highly addictive) also comes from morphine. Many street drugs mimic or activate endorphins. Put simply, endorphins are the body's natural pain killers. In addition to acting as a pain regulator, endorphins are also thought to suspend fear, increase perception, and have been linked to physiological processes such as appetite control, the release of sex hormones, euphoric feelings (providing a 'rush' similar to adrenaline), and shock. Activities believed to stimulate endorphins include prolonged physical exertion (the 'runner's high'), consuming chocolate and spicy foods (hot chillies), meditation, acupuncture, and a hearty laugh. Thus, as well as relieving pain, endorphins produce an increased sense of well-being (the 'feel good' factor).

If the endorphin theory is correct, and self-injury brings with it rewards such as decreased stress, increased relaxation, and an enhanced sense of well-being, this could perhaps explain why the behaviour continually beckons people.

Recap

Mounting evidence suggests that self-injury can rapidly shift a person's mood from one of dysphoria (an uncomfortable emotional state) to one of euphoria (a feeling of well-being). However, a major missing link in our current understanding of self-injury is that if the act does alter brain chemistry, is it simply via the release of endorphins, or could there be other biological factors at work?

Post-traumatic stress symptoms and brain functioning

Numerous people who self-injure report experiencing post-traumatic symptoms, such as flashbacks, intense emotional arousal or physical reactions on exposure to external or internal reminders of an aspect of the traumatic event, difficulty getting to sleep or staying asleep, and hypervigilance, etc. (See Appendix 2 for DSM-IV-TR diagnostic criteria for PTSD).

In recent years significant progress has been made in understanding the effects of trauma on brain functioning, and the general consensus is that traumatic experiences can have a marked impact. While the full consequences are not yet fully understood, trauma experts, such as international expert, Dr. Bessel van der Kolk, Medical Director of the Trauma Center (http://www.traumacenter.org), are hard at work investigating the effects of trauma on brain structure and development.

The amygdala and the hippocampus, two brain structures housed within the limbic system, 'have been implicated in the processing of emotionally charged memories' posits van der Kolk (1996, p.230), adding that 'A recent series of studies indicates that people with PTSD have decreased hippocampal volume.' (p. 232).

Unfortunately, space does not permit further exploration of this fascinating topic. For those interested in learning more about this topic see suggested further reading sections at the end of the chapter.

Key points

- Cutting appears to be the 'preferred form' of self-injury, but a wide range of other methods are used.
- Cutting and burning serve different functions for some people.
- Seeing the blood holds a significant meaning for some people who self-injure.
- Problems recognising and describing emotional states in words to other people, and discriminating between feelings and the bodily sensations of emotional arousal appear to be common occurrences among people that self-injure. Similar characteristics also feature in *alexithymia.*
- People use a wide range of implements to self-injure, and they can be extremely innovative if the urge to self-injure strikes.
- The arms are the most common target for self-injury, but numerous other areas of the body may be targeted.
- Self-injury may persist over many years: it is clearly not a new phenomenon.
- To some people the scars from self-injury are a source of shame and embarrassment; to others they are a souvenir of survival.
- Many people who practice self-injury describe it as addictive.
- An 'endorphin rush' following the act is reported by many people that self-injure.
- Numerous people who self-injure report experiencing post-traumatic symptoms, such as flashbacks, intense emotional arousal or physical reactions on exposure to external or internal reminders of an aspect of the traumatic event, difficulty getting to sleep or staying asleep, and hypervigilance, etc. The question of whether brain functioning plays a key role in the development of post-traumatic symptoms is currently under investigation by trauma researchers.

Useful resources

Alexithymia
Alexithymia chatsite. Retrieved June, 11, 2007, from,
   http://groups.msn.com/Alexithymiachatsite/
Muller R. J (2000). When a Patient Has No Story To Tell: Alexithymia.
   Psychiatric Times 17(7). Retrieved June, 11, 2007, from,
   http://www.psychiatrictimes.com/p000771.html

Trauma information
David Baldwin's trauma information
   An award winning, firmly-established and informative site that
   provides information on emotional trauma and traumatic stress
   (including PTSD [Post-traumatic stress disorder] and dissociation)
   for clinicians and researchers working in the traumatic-stress field.
   Retrieved June, 11, 2007, from,
   http://www.trauma-pages.com/
The Trauma Center (Founder and Medical Director Dr. van der
Kolk)
   'The Research Department conducts studies on traumatic memory
   and how treatment effects trauma survivors' minds, bodies, and
   brains.' Retrieved June, 11, 2007, from,
   http://www.traumacenter.org/

Suggested further reading

LeDoux, J.E. (1996). *The Emotional Brain*. New York, Simon and
   Schuster.
Levine, P.A. (1997). *Waking the Tiger: Healing Trauma*. Berkeley, CA:
   North Atlantic Books.
Rothchilds, B. (2000). *The Body Remembers: The Psychophysiology of
   Trauma and Trauma Treatment*. New York: W. W. Norton.

van der Kolk, B.A. & Saporta, J. (1991). The biological mechanisms and treatment of intrusion and numbing. *Anxiety Research*; 4:199-212. Retrieved June 16, 200, from, http://www.cirp.org/library/psych/vanderkolk2/

van der Kolk B.A. (2003). The neurobiology of childhood trauma and abuse. *Child and Adolescent Psychiatric Clinics of North America,* 12, 293-317.

Wilkinson, M. (2006*). Coming into Mind: The mind-brain relationship.* Hove, East Sussex; New York: Routledge.

Ziegler, D. (2002). *Traumatic Experience and the Brain: a handbook for understanding and treating those traumatized as children.* Phoenix, AZ: Acacia Publishing Inc.

Chapter 4

Media assertions and attitudes to self-injury, the magnitude of the problem and controversies

· ·

'Most acts of self-harm that result in a young person going to hospital involve overdoses rather than self-injuries.'
—*Hawton and Rodham (2006, p. 11)*

'Self-injury is a neglected area of self-harm research and we know little about its epidemiology, hospital care, and outcome.'
—*Horrocks et al. (2003)*

'The UK is now the self-harm capital of Europe,' claims Anabel Unity Sale in Community Care Magazine (2004). 'It leads to 150,000 attendances at accident and emergency units a year,' states Alexandra Frean (*Times Online*, March, 2005). It's reaching epidemic proportions – more like 170,000 end up in casualty because of it. It's said that 25,000 youngsters are referred to hospital because of it, more young men are doing, it, more young girls are doing it, 'seemingly ordinary, adult women' are increasingly doing it (Mills, *Times Online*, May, 2005) – even kids as 'young as eight' are doing it. (Revill, *The Observer*, June 2005). Celebrities are glamourising it, and encouraging kids to do it . . . so the speculation goes on, and confusion reigns.

Self-harm (self-poisoning and self-injury) are sensitive issues, and presenting accurate information about the behaviour is vital.

The media in particular, play a crucial role in educating the public and shaping and influencing public opinion. As such, they have a responsibility not to mislead or misinform. Indeed, flawed reporting can lead to prejudice, stigma, and misunderstanding.

In this chapter, media assertions and attitudes about self-harm and self-injury go under the microscope, the magnitude of self-injury is discussed, and two controversial issues are addressed. Also examined is the relevance of a change of term recently implemented in the professional arena, and whether researchers and practitioners' use of different terms is responsible for sparking confusion.

Media hype

Self-harm – in particular self-injury – has recently grabbed the attention of all strands of the media, with articles, once rare, now in abundance in teen magazines, national newspapers, professional journals, and health magazines. Books on the subject have flourished; countless websites have sprung up – many authored by individuals with personal experience of self-injury; the topic has featured in television documentaries, dramas, and soaps; films have entered the arena, and the music industry is no exception. Some (yet by no means all) examples are now given.

Television documentaries, dramas, and soaps

- *Jailbirds* (BBC1, April 12, 1999), a fly-on-the-wall documentary showing what life is like for women behind bars, filmed at New Hall Prison, Yorkshire.
- *East: Suffering in Silence* (BBC2, July 17, 2000), which highlighted the growing problem of self-injury among young Asian women in Britain.
- *Hollyoaks* (Channel 4), wherein Lisa, one of the characters (played by Gemma Atkinson), is seen struggling with the problem.
- *Life Isn't All Ha Ha Hee Hee* (BBC 1, May 2005), a compelling drama, in which Sunita, a depressed Asian wife turns to self-injury. (Based on the novel *Life Isn't All Ha Ha Hee Hee* by Meera Syal).

The film industry
- *Girl, Interrupted* (Columbia Pictures, 1999).
- *Secretary* (Lion's Gate, 2002).
- *In My Skin* (Rezo Films [French], 2002).
- *Thirteen* (Fox Searchlight Pictures, 2003).

The music industry: songs referencing self-injury
- Manic Street Preachers' '*Yes*', '*Roses in the Hospital*', '*Die in the Summertime*' and '*Born to End*'.
- The Used's '*I'm a Fake*', '*A Box Full of Sharp Objects*', and '*Let It Bleed*'.
- Papa Roach's '*Scars*' and '*Last Resort*' (American).
- Linkin Park's '*Part of Me*' and '*Crawling*' (their 'Numb' video also shows a girl with scars on her arm) (American).

Books and Internet sites displaying images of self-injury
Internet sites displaying graphic images of wounds and scars have come under hefty criticism because people (including many that self-injure) consider the images are potentially 'triggering', or give encouragement to vulnerable youngsters to experiment with the behaviour. Yet it's not just websites that display pictures – they appear in books, newspapers and magazines – they can even be found on professional websites. Here are some examples:

- Morgan's book, *Death Wishes?* (1979:118-121) contains four pages of pictures of self-injury (mainly limbs), which albeit in black and white, could be classified as 'detailed', and Favazza's book, *Bodies Under Siege* (1996: 159-160) displays a couple of similar pictures.
- An article entitled *The First Cut...* (Carroll, H. *The Daily Mirror Mhealth,* April 15, 2004, p.33) showed a woman displaying badly scarred arms (full colour picture).
- The British Association for Counselling and Psychotherapy (BACP), on the front cover of CPJ (Counselling and Psychotherapy Journal) (2003) displayed a picture of a woman with her face

turned sideways, showing two badly scarred arms (black and white picture).

• While searching the British Medical Journal website for information, I came across two provocative images. Both displayed a pair of arms, with a razor blade in the right hand being held against the left wrist about to be cut. (BMJ 2002; 2005).

Celebrities that self-injure

Numerous celebrities have admitted publicly their struggles with self-injury, or reports have suggested they self-injured. A recent casualty, Dame Kelly Holmes, the thirty five year old track star, publicly disclosed in May 2005, that a year prior to her double gold victory at the Olympic Games in Athens, she had injured herself repeatedly for a period of two-months. Others include actresses Angelina Jolie and Christina Ricci, actor Johnny Depp, 'shock rocker' Marilyn Manson, and Richey Edwards, a former member of the Manic Street Preachers group, who disappeared without trace on 1 February 1995 (Gabrielle, 1999-2007), actress and comedienne Roseanne (Arnold, 1994), and deceased pop diva Dusty Springfield (Valentine & Wickham, 2000).

Young people and self-harm: A National Inquiry

Prompted by concerns over the reported increase in self-harm among young people in the UK, the government launched the first ever inquiry into self-harm among 11-25 year olds at the House of Commons on 30 March 2004. The Mental Health Foundation and Camelot Foundation jointly spearheaded the inquiry.

Aims of the inquiry (2004) included education and awareness raising about self-harm; gaining more understanding about self-harm; making policy recommendations, and initiating practice guidelines and information for individuals and organisations working with young people that self-harm.

The Inquiry definition (2004a) of self-harm included cutting, burning, banging, hair pulling and self-poisoning. It excluded eating disorders, drug and alcohol misuse, and risk taking behaviours such as unsafe sex and dangerous driving.

The two-year inquiry, listened to evidence from over 350 individuals and organisations, paying particular attention to the voices of young people with experience of self-harm. Chair of the Inquiry, Catherine McLoughlin CBE, in the final report entitled *The Truth Hurts: Report of the National Inquiry into Self-harm among Young People* (2006) says this in the foreword:

> This report sets out an agenda for change. There is no shortage
> of things that need to be done. We need to know more about
> the prevalence of self-harm, across the UK as well as in particular
> population groups; we need to commission services where young
> people feel listened to, and respected; we need much better
> evidence of what works, both in relation to preventing self-harm
> and in intervening once the behaviour is underway; we need to
> build a better understanding of why young people self-harm,
> and provide high-quality information for young people, their
> families, and a whole range of agencies and professionals in contact
> with young people. Above all, perhaps, we need to develop the
> confidence of those closest to young people, so that they can hear
> disclosures of self-harm without panic, revulsion or condemnation.
> (p. 3)

The Truth Hurts report can be downloaded for free from the Inquiry website: www.selfharmUK.org (accessed June 12, 2007).

Among other topics, the Inquiry's first interim report (2004b) focused on the prevalence of self-harm in the UK. Citing as its source the National Institute for Clinical Excellence (NICE), *Self-harm scope* document (2002) it states, 'Rates of self-harm in the UK have increased over the past decade and are reported to be among the highest in Europe.'

Horrocks and House report similarly, 'Rates of self-harm in the UK are among the highest in Europe at 400 per 100,000 per year' they report in a paper entitled *Self-poisoning and self-injury in adults.* (2002:509).

Is the UK the self-harm capital of Europe?

Among the highest rates of self-harm in Europe seems to be closer to the truth – not *the* highest, as explicitly claimed by Anabel Unity Sale. Worth keeping in mind too is that significantly more research on self-harm appears to have taken place in the UK compared to other countries, which could have a bearing on the situation. Furthermore, recent media reports suggest that self-injury is a global problem.

The magnitude of the problem

> If you want to inspire confidence, give plenty of statistics. It does
> not matter that they should be accurate, or even intelligible, as long
> as there are enough of them.
>
> —*Lewis Carroll*

Self-injury tends to be a secretive activity carried out behind closed doors and many people attend to their own wounds, so countless episodes go unreported. Hence, an attempt to determine precisely how many people self-injure is beset with difficulties.

Further, many episodes go undetected. For example, those who do seek treatment for their wounds may hoodwink accident and emergency staff into believing their injuries have been inflicted by others or have been caused by an accident.

In the absence of official statistics on self-harm in the UK, evidence of the incidence of self-harm comes mainly from hospital-based studies, psychiatric samples, small community based studies, and school-based studies.

Hospital attendances for self-harm

Alexandra Frean's contention that self-harm 'leads to 150,000 attendances at accident and emergency units a year' is consistent with figures quoted in the National Institute for Clinical Excellence (NICE), *Self-harm scope* document mentioned above. The same figure appears in *Self-harm: The short-term physical and psychological management and secondary prevention of self-harm in primary and secondary care* (2004), the final version of the NICE guidelines. However, as evidenced by the statistics shown in Figure 4.1 (Prevalence estimates for self-harm [self-poisoning and self-injury]), there are considerable inconsistencies in estimates of how many people self-harm.

Aside from the discrepancies, the figures suggest that the backdrop of self-harm has altered enormously over the past eleven years. In fact, comparing the lowest rate (1996, *87,000*) with the highest rate (2005, *170,000*) implies an increase of 93%. What remains uncertain though is how many people from the approximated statistics self-poison and

TERM USED	ESTIMATES OF HOW MANY PEOPLE SELF-HARM PER YEAR	STUDY/SOURCE OF INFORMATION
Deliberate self-harm	170,000	Centre for Suicide Research Website (2005)
Self-harm	160,000	The Samaritans (2000) Based on 1998 figures for England and Wales
Intentional self-harm	150,000	NICE (National Institute for Clinical Excellence (2002)
Deliberate self-harm	140,000	Royal College of Physicians & Royal College of Psychiatrists (2003)
Deliberate self-harm	100,000	Mental Health Foundation (1997)
Parasuicide	87,000	Gunnell, Brooks and Peters (1996)

Fig. 4.1: Prevalence estimates for self-harm (self-poisoning and self-injury).

how many self-injure. Hospital statistics specifically focused on self-injury are hard come by due to much of the research focusing on self-poisoning. However, according to Williams (1997) self-cutters:

> . . . are in the minority, accounting for about 10 per cent of parasuicide episodes. Even so, this means that in the United Kingdom 10,000 episodes of self-cutting come to the attention of accident and emergency departments of hospitals each year. (p. 98)

In a study by Horrocks, Price, House, and Owens (2003), one of the aims of which was to establish prevalence rates of self-injury, the researchers examined statistics on attendances for self-harm at general hospitals in Leeds over an eighteen month period. They discovered that 'about one-fifth of all attendances at A&E departments for self-harm were for self-injury' (21% for self-injury, 82.5% for self-poisoning).

NHS guideline to standardise care for people who self-harm

In 2004, The National Institute for Health and Clinical Excellence (NICE) and the National Collaborating Centre for Mental Health (NCCMH) published a guideline for the NHS in England and Wales, making recommendations on the care of people who self-harm in the first 48 hours after the self-harming incident. The guideline, entitled *Self-harm: the short-term physical and psychological management and secondary prevention of self-harm in primary and secondary care* (National Collaborating Centre for Mental Health, 2004) recommends an extensive list of 'priorities for implementation' (pp. 48-50). These include:

- People who have self-harmed should be treated with the same care, respect, and privacy as any patient. In addition, healthcare professionals should take full account of the likely distress associated with self-harm.
- If a person who has self-harmed has to wait for treatment, he or she should be offered an environment that is safe, supportive and minimises any distress.

- People who have self-harmed should be offered treatment for the physical consequences of self-harm, regardless of their willingness to accept psychosocial assessment or psychiatric treatment.
- Adequate anaesthesia and/or analgesia should be offered to people who have self-injured throughout the process of suturing or other painful treatments.
- When assessing people who self-harm, healthcare professionals should ask service users to explain their feelings and understanding of their own self-harm in their own words.
- Healthcare professionals should involve people who self-harm in all discussions and decision-making about their treatment and subsequent care. To do this, staff should provide people who self-harm with full information about the different treatment options available.
- When physical treatment of self-injury is likely to evoke distressing memories of any previous sexual abuse, for example when repairing harm to the genital area, sedation should be offered in advance.
- Clinical and non-clinical staff who have contact with people who self-harm in any setting should be provided with appropriate training to equip them to understand and care for people who have self-harmed.
- Providing treatment and care for people who have self-harmed is emotionally demanding and requires a high level of communication skills and support. All staff undertaking this work should have regular clinical supervision in which the emotional impact upon staff members can be discussed and understood.

A question of attitude

In the research undertaken for *Healing the Hurt Within*, 1st edition (Sutton, 1999), many respondents reported receiving mixed attitudes when attending A&E for help with their injuries – here are just a few of the testimonies received:

'I was treated unsympathetically. I was told I was wasting their time as my wounds were self-inflicted.'

'I've had various responses – had my wounds dressed, been shouted at, been ignored, been talked with sympathetically.'

'I have had every reaction, from not being medically treated properly and ignored, to being treated kindly and with respect.'

'I got a very dispassionate reaction, no questions, just stitched up and sent home.'

'I am usually treated fairly sympathetically, although the last time I had to be stitched up the doctor doing it suggested sarcastically that the next time I felt frustrated I should try going for a long walk instead.'

Bearing in mind the respondents' experiences, I asked Richard Pacitti, Chief Executive of Mind, Croydon, and member of the Self-Harm Guideline Development Group, if he considered that the new guideline would bring about a change of staff attitudes in A&E to people that self-injure. He replied:

I believe that one of the reasons that people who self-harm sometimes get poor treatment is that some front line staff have misconceptions about self-harm. For this reason, the guidelines make very strong recommendations about the need for training for staff to overcome myths and misunderstandings. My experience is, as someone who provides training about self-harm, that once people have a better understanding of the reasons why people self-harm and the functions it serves for them, their attitudes change. For this reason, I remain positive that the guidelines should lead to people who self-harm being treated with the care, sensitivity, and the respect they need and deserve.

Unhelpful media attitudes to the NICE guidelines

Richard Pacitti also drew my attention to several newspaper articles that appeared following the launch of the guideline. Among them included an article entitled: *This 'epidemic' is all selfishness* (Telegraph.co.uk, August 01, 2004) in which the author Leo McKinstry makes an insensitive, unkind and slanted attack on people who self-harm, asserting that a great deal of self-harming behaviour is 'ruthlessly manipulative'. To further fan the flames he writes:

> [People who self-harm] are so self-important that they think they have the right to clog up the NHS with their undeserving cases . . . . The nurses' attitude is understandable, given that they have to deal with genuine emergencies rather than the antics of a self-centred attention seeker.

Another article entitled: *Cut it out, please* (SocietyGuardian.co.uk, August 03, 2004) written by an NHS doctor (authored under the pseudonym Rachel James) was also scathing – the author writes:

> It is hard not to get frustrated: people who self-harm do have a choice, although it may not seem like it at the time. They could not do it, or they could do it and stay at home to deal with the consequences. Just please don't lacerate yourself, come to hospital and then complain about it. A&E is an emergency service.

Publication of the 'James' article sparked a heated online exchange of views between psychiatrists, doctors, and other professionals – one consultant psychiatrist went so far as suggesting that 'self harming patients be charged £50 for attendance at an A&E ward.' (2004, August 26, James, A.)

With dispassionate attitudes such as these it's hardly surprising that many people who self-injure fear seeking help for their injuries, or steer well clear of A&E. Further, to the unenlightened and uninformed reader the articles present a misinformed and stigmatising portrayal of people that self-injure, destined to fertilise the myths rather than dispel them.

The expected review date for the NICE guidelines is July 2008: it will be interesting to see whether a change for the better in attitudes towards patients that self-injure is reported. From the foregoing, sadly, it looks as if there is still much work to be done in raising awareness and understanding about self-injury.

Note: An unsupported version of the NHS guidelines, a condensed version, a quick reference guide, and a booklet for the public can be downloaded free from The National Institute for Health and Clinical Excellence (NICE) website: http://www.nice.org.uk/

A striking increase in self-harm

If self-harm is on the rise in the UK as the statistics in figure 4.1 suggest, could part of the reason be due to a substantial increase in the number of young men self-harming? For example, the Samaritans (2000) theorise that 'Between 1980 and 1998 rates of self-harm among men aged 15 – 24 almost doubled.' Could another possible explanation be that increased awareness of self-injury has encouraged more people to seek help? Over a decade ago, Favazza (1996) suggested this was already happening – he states:

> The propulsion of self-mutilation into the consciousness of both
> the general public and the mental health establishment has created
> a sense of optimism. Patients are now more willing to seek help,
> and they feel less ashamed of their behaviour. (p. 233)

If Favazza's premise is correct, are we perhaps looking at an 'explosion of admission' in contrast to an 'outbreak of action'? To establish other experts' views on the situation, I invited two American practitioners, both renowned in the field of self-injury, to comment.

Tracy Alderman, author of, *The Scarred Soul* (1997) (personal communication, May 24, 2004) had this to say:

> While I believe that self-injury is on the rise among young people, I also believe that the epidemic numbers of self-injury we're now seeing are due to more and more people admitting to performing self-injurious behaviours. Ten years ago it was difficult to find any information regarding self-injury. Now, information on self-injury is present in books, magazines, movies, television shows and music. People are talking about self-injury more and more. While it is still a secretive behaviour, the vast increase of media attention, and identification of idols who have self-injured, such as Princess Diana, have decreased the stigma attached to the behaviour and allowed young people to be much more willing to admit to others that they too self-injure.

Barent Walsh, co-author with Paul M. Rosen, of *Self-mutilation: Theory, Research and Treatment* (1988), and author of *Treating Self-Injury: A Practical Guide* (2006) (personal communication, June 02, 2004) remarked that:

> I believe we are currently seeing an epidemic of action. I am very busy these days training staff and parents regarding self-injury in middle schools, high schools, and colleges. These settings would have known if children and adolescents were previously self-injuring. There is clearly an explosion of the behaviour in these settings that goes way beyond an increase in more accurate reporting. I wish I had specific statistics to back this up, but I do not.

Recap

Both authors speculate that self-injury is definitely on the increase, especially among young people. Barent Walsh strongly believes that there is an eruption of the behaviour in schools and colleges. Tracy Alderman considers that media spotlight on the issue, a growth of literature on the subject, and high-profile celebrities' public disclosures of self-injury has reduced the stigma, generated more openness, and encouraged more people to admit they have a problem with it, which partially reflects the views of Favazza. Overall, the consensus seems to be that not only are we looking at an 'explosion of admission', we are also looking an 'outbreak of action'? However, as Barent Walsh rightly points out, to support claims that the behaviour is on the increase, concrete statistics are necessary,

Self-injury upstaging self-poisoning

An issue of deep concern is the strong possibility that the public – albeit perhaps not intentionally – are being misled about how many people self-injure in contrast to self-poisoning. For instance, if people read the widely reported statistics that 150,000/170,000 people are receiving hospital treatment for self-harm annually, does it register that the large majority of those cases are due to self-poisoning? Space does not permit inclusion of the many comments received on this issue, but the consensus is that mention the word 'self-harm' and it immediately conjures up images of people cutting themselves. Moreover, because self-injury is 'not the norm', it tends to arouse curiosity – not least from the media, strands of whom sensationalise the issue to the expense of downplaying the extent of overdosing. In some articles featuring 'self-harm', overdoses hardly receive a mention – in some cases no mention whatsoever.

One clear example of self-injury upstaging self-poisoning is evident in a report about Dame Kelly Holmes, which appeared in the Daily Telegraph carrying the headline *'Holmes's self-harm confession highlights "hidden epidemic."'* (Nicole Martin, *The Daily Telegraph*, Monday, May 30, 2005). It quotes the well-publicised assertion that approximately 170,000 people are treated in hospital each year after deliberate self-harm, yet fails to make a single reference to overdosing. Another, carrying the headline 'On a knife edge' in the *TimesOnline* (Simon Mills, 2005, May 08), citing the Samaritans as its source of information, claims 'that 25,000 people a year, mainly women, are admitted to hospital with **self-inflicted injuries**.' [Emphasis added] What sort of image does that conjure up? Overdosing? I doubt it. Cutting? Highly probable. And similar to the previous article, no reference is made to overdosing.

Media misinterpretations of self-harm

The question that urgently needs addressing concerning media interpretations of self-harm is whether journalists, like many lay people, are confused about what exactly is and is not self-harm, which sets the stage for our next topic.

The terminology controversy

Did you notice the various terms used in Figure 4.1 (Prevalence estimates for self-harm)? Now ponder Figure 4.2 (The wide variety of terms used to describe the act of hurting oneself), as this forms the basis for our ensuing discussion on problems with terminology and definitions.

Misunderstandings about what is and is not self-harm arise from different researchers attaching different definitions to the term 'self-harm'. For example, as you read earlier, the Young People and Self-harm National Inquiry included 'self-poisoning' in its definition. Hawton and Rodham in their recent book, *By Their Own Young Hand: Deliberate Self-Harm and Suicidal Ideas in Adolescents* (2006:11) do likewise, defining DSH thus: 'Deliberate self-harm includes any intentional act of self-injury or self-poisoning (overdose), irrespective of the apparent motivation or intention.' Hawton, K. et al. (2002) and De Leo, D. & Heller T.S (2004) include the use of 'recreational' or illegal drugs in their study definitions. The Royal College of Psychiatrists (2004)

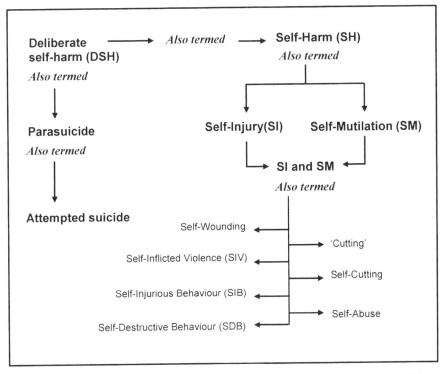

Fig. 4.2: The wide variety of terms used to describe the act of hurting oneself.

stretches their definition of self-harm even further by encompassing 'excessive amounts of alcohol'.

Deliberate self-harm and parasuicide: their historical roots

Employing the term deliberate self-harm to describe self-harm and self-poisoning is standard practice in the UK medical profession, whereas in the Republic of Ireland, the term parasuicide is more common. Where do these terms originate? Their roots go back over a quarter of a century. In *Death Wishes?* (1979) Morgan coined the term *deliberate self-harm* to embrace a wide range of non-fatal self-harming behaviours, defining DSH thus: 'Non-fatal episodes of self-harm may be referred to collectively as problems of self-poisoning and self-injury.' (p.88) Parasuicide is defined by Kreitman *et al.* (1977) as 'a non-fatal act in which an individual deliberately causes self-injury or ingests a substance in excess of any prescribed or generally recognized therapeutic dosage.' (p.3)

Attempted suicide and suicide

To complicate the issue further, the term attempted suicide (regardless of the intention behind the act) is also used to describe non-fatal acts of self-harm – in other words acts of self-poisoning and self-injury. To muddy the waters even more, the term 'deliberate act of self-harm or injury' is being considered as a substitute verdict to 'suicide' in the coroner's court in cases where there is doubt about an individual's intention. (2004, Calthorpe, B., and Choong, S.) This perhaps explains a statement on the University of Oxford Centre for Suicide Research website (1998-2007) asserting that; 'suicide and attempted suicide' are now usually termed 'deliberate-self harm' or 'self-harm' in the UK'.

Looking at Figure 4.2 you will note that I have placed deliberate self-harm, parasuicide and attempted suicide on the left hand side, as essentially they all refer to the same behaviour, and are sometimes used interchangeably.

Focusing on self-injury

Researchers who focus specifically on self-injury are more consistent with their definitions, yet when it comes to terms, there is considerable inconsistency. You will see from the four definitions below that they all emphasise the point that the act is 'without suicidal intent' and all four refer to the behaviour as 'deliberate' or 'intentional'. Many people who self-injure find the modifiers 'deliberate' or 'intentional' objectionable or deem them incorrect. This thorny issue is addressed later on. You may be wondering why I have included so many definitions – the answer is because they put the spotlight on several different terms used to describe the same act, as shown on the right-hand side of Figure 4.2.

Self-mutilation (SM)

'*I define* self-mutilation *as the deliberate destruction or alteration of one's body tissue without suicidal intent.*' (Favazza, 1996: xviii-xix)

Self-injury (SI)

'*We understand self-injury as an act which involves deliberately inflicting pain and/or injury to one's own body, but without suicidal intent.*' (Babiker and Arnold, 1997: 2–3)

Self-inflicted violence (SIV)

'*The term self-inflicted violence is best defined as the intentional harm of one's own body without conscious suicidal intent. In simpler terms, self-inflicted violence (SIV) is the act of physically hurting yourself on purpose.*' (Alderman, 1997: 7)

Self-injurious behaviours (SIBs)

'*We define SIBs as all behaviours involving deliberate infliction of direct physical harm to one's own body without any intent to die as a consequence of the behaviour.*' (Simeon and Favazza, 2001:1)

Self-injury as defined in this book

You will note from the above definitions that the intention behind self-injury is excluded. Embracing this aspect was considered important by the Internet respondents (see Chapter 1). For purposes of clarification and comparison the definition is reproduced again here:

> Self-injury is a *compulsion* or *impulse* to inflict physical wounds on one's own body, motivated by a need to cope with unbearable psychological distress *or* regain a sense of emotional balance. The act is *usually* carried out without suicidal, sexual or decorative intent.
>
> —*Sutton, et al. (2000)*

Classification of self-injury

Favazza (1996) separates self-injury into two groups: *culturally sanctioned self-injury* (further divided into cultural rituals and practices) and *deviant-pathological self-injury* (further divided into major, stereotypic, and moderate/superficial), the latter additionally separated into three subtypes: compulsive, episodic, and repetitive self-injury. More recently, Favazza and Simeon (2001) proposed four main categories of self-injurious behaviours, *stereotypic, major, compulsive and impulsive*. Figure 4.3 (Classifying self-injurious behaviours) provides an overview of the classifications as proposed by Favazza, and Simeon and Favazza.

CLASSIFYING SELF-INJURIOUS BEHAVIOURS

Favazza, *Bodies Under Siege* (1996, pp. 225-260)

Culturally sanctioned self-injury

Divided into:	1.	Cultural rituals
	2.	Cultural practices

Deviant-pathological self-injury

Divided into:	1.	Major	
	2.	Stereotypic	
	3.	Moderate/superficial	*Subtypes* Compulsive Episodic Repetitive

Simeon & Favazza, *Self-Injurious Behaviors* (2001, Chapter 1, pp. 1-28)

Self-Injurious Behaviours

Divided into:	1.	Stereotypic
	2.	Major
	3.	Compulsive
	4.	Impulsive

Fig. 4.3: Classifying self-injurious behaviours.

Compounding the issue

The situation regarding classifying self-injury is not eased by the fact that neither DSM-IV-TR (APA, 2000) nor ICD-10 (WHO, 1992), the two major classification systems for diagnosing mental disorders, recognise self-injury as a separate disorder or syndrome. However, hopefully this situation will change when DSM-V is published, which is anticipated to be in 2010 or later. For proposed terms, see:

1. Favazza (1996: 253-254). Favazza argues a case for repetitive self-mutilation (RSM) to be listed in the DSM 'on Axis 1 among the "impulse control disorders not elsewhere classified."'
2. *Deliberate self-harm syndrome* (1983, Pattison, E. & Kahan, J.) For an adapted version of the classification schema as proposed by Pattison and Kahan, see Walsh and Rosen (1988: 30, Figure 2.1.)
3. *Repetitive superficial or moderate self-mutilation syndrome* (1993, Favazza, A.R. & Rosenthal, R.) The authors recommend classification of the syndrome as an Axis I Impulse Disorder.
4. *Self-injurious Behaviour Syndrome* (2002, Turner, V.J.) Turner proposes classifying the syndrome in DSM as an Impulse-Control Disorder Not Elsewhere Classified. (pp. 58-59)

Why don't researchers agree on a single term?

The answer seems to be because UK researchers have found that self-harm is often synonymous with suicide. For example, in a systematic review of studies from UK and non-UK countries to approximate rates of fatal and non-fatal repetition of self-harm (UK and Ireland [36%]; Scandinavia and Finland [26%]; North America [11%]; Australia and New Zealand [8%] and the rest of Europe [19%]), Owens, Horrocks and House (2002), found that:

- There is a strong association between self-harm and suicide.
- Later suicide arises somewhere in the region of 1 in 200, and 1 in 40 patients that self-harm in the first year of follow up.

- After nine or above years, the figure is approximately 1 in 15 people.

They draw the conclusion that 'Suicide risk among self-harm patients is hundreds of times higher than in the general population.'

Overdosing vs. self-injury

It may be the case that a small number of people attend hospital for both self-injury and self-poisoning. Nevertheless, bearing in mind that those who self-injure are very much in the minority of hospital attendees for self-harm, it would seem a reasonable assumption to make that the large majority of those who later commit suicide come from the group that repeatedly self-poison.

Whilst recognising that self-poisoning and self-injury sometimes serve similar functions (to escape from mental pain, an unspoken plea for help), many people that self-injure make a distinction between the two behaviours – here are two such cases submitted by respondents:

'There was always a clear distinction for me between the cutting and the overdosing. The cutting was far more frequent and was about survival, about coping with the intolerable feelings I was carrying inside. Overdosing meanwhile was about giving up for good, about choosing to stop coping altogether. So actually, as long as I was cutting I knew that I was relatively safe – that I wouldn't die. It was when I stopped cutting that the feelings built up to the point where I simply "wanted out".'

'My reasons for taking the overdose were not the same as my reasons for cutting (which I have always managed to keep under control sufficiently to avoid needing medical attention). I took the overdose because I had hit the end of every resource I could find within myself and I could see no future and no way out. Indeed my reason for cutting has almost always been throwing a lifeline to avoid suicide becoming inevitable. To this end my self poisoning was a different issue to my self-harm even though the root causes may have been connected.'

Recap

To clarify, what the respondents are saying is that:

- Overdosing is about giving up the will to carry on, about loss of hope, about going beyond coping.
- Cutting is an insurance policy for survival; it's about coping, about going on living, about stepping back from suicide. In essence, it is not about wanting to kill oneself or a suicide attempt gone wrong.

It is prudent to remember, however, that self-injury is invariably a sign of acute distress and sadly, occasionally people do kill themselves – at times accidentally by taking things too far – or sometimes because a person's situation becomes so intolerable no other way out can be seen. Any mention of suicidal thoughts therefore needs to be taken seriously and not dismissed as attention seeking, manipulation, or 'crying wolf.'

Is the terminology controversy much ado about nothing?

The controversy over terms is no trivial matter. The terms deliberate self-harm, self-harm, and parasuicide, muddy the waters, causing bewilderment and misunderstandings in their wake. For researchers scouring the academic literature for statistics and information specifically on self-injury it can lead down many blind alleys and waste an inordinate amount of time. For busy journalists it can lead to misreporting the facts. For the public it can lead to believing misrepresented facts presented by the media, and for those in need of help it may lead to the wrong form of treatment. Another respondent also labours the point that self-poisoning and self-injury are two different behaviours – she writes:

> 'They are very different, and lumping SP in with SI can lead to misconceptions about self-injury. There are also very specific, different ways to help and respond to someone who is feeling suicidal or attempting suicide, and someone who is self-injuring or feeling the need to self-injure, and one may not be beneficial for both. In addition, attempted suicide can bring up fear, panic, etc in other people about the person's life, and is not appropriate for self-injury.'

Furthermore, as Walsh and Rosen (1988) emphasised almost twenty years ago: 'This debate over terminology is, of course, no mere quibbling over words. At stake is how SMB [self-mutilative behaviour] should be understood, described, diagnosed, and treated.' (p. 21)

Is self-injury always deliberate?

Whilst some who self-injure agree that the act is 'deliberate' or 'intentional', others find the prefixes offensive. Louise Pembroke, editor of *Self-Harm: Perspectives from Personal Experience* (1996) is one such case – she explains why:

The term "Deliberate Self-Harm" is objectionable. "Deliberate" can imply premeditation and wilfulness. Self-harm is always atypical. Sometimes it can be spontaneous and sudden with little awareness or conscious thought. Conversely, the drive to self-harm maybe powerfully constant and unrelenting with a conscious battle raging. How self-harm occurs and the levels of awareness vary considerably. Self-harm or self-injury does not require qualifying with "**Deliberate**." (pp. 2-3).

NHS self-harm guidelines

With my SIARI website hat on (a registered stakeholder for the NICE self-harm guidelines), I had an opportunity to respond to the *Draft for first Consultation* of the NICE guidelines, mentioned earlier. One of the issues I raised, alongside several other stakeholders, was the significant role of dissociation in the process of self-injury for some people. Another issue, raised by stakeholders and service users, was the Guideline Development Group's choice of term, that being 'Intentional' self-harm. It was rewarding to see in the full guideline published November 2004, that they had dropped the prefix 'intentional'; also to read the following statement:

> Many service users object to these terms, especially those who
> harm themselves during dissociative states, afterwards being
> unaware of any conscious intent to have harmed themselves. Also, it
> can be argued that prefixing the term 'self-harm' with 'intentional'
> would suggest that there may be accidental and non-intentional
> forms of self-harm. Clearly, the non-intentional forms, such as
> those carried out during dissociative states, are covered by the term
> 'self-harm' alone. (p.18)

(For further information on dissociation and self-injury see Chapter 8)

Although these changes may seem inconsequential, a ripple effect appears to be happening. Just recently, I stumbled across a report from The Royal College of Psychiatrists, entitled *Assessment following self-harm in adults* (2004) stating that:

The use of the adjective "deliberate" has not been acceptable to all and some services users fear it might be of itself stigmatising. For this reason we have dropped the term 'deliberate' from the title of this report. (p.7)

Discussion

Walsh and Rosen (1988) present an excellent table spanning fifty years (from 1935 to 1985) of researchers attempts to differentiate self-injury (and associated behaviours) from suicide (pp 16-19). Regrettably, though, it appears as if little attention to resolve the controversy surrounding terminology has occurred since then. Hence, the dividing line between self-injury and suicide remains blurred, causing confusion and misunderstandings both within and outside the field. A major shift forward however, is the abandonment of the qualifiers 'deliberate' by the Royal College of Psychiatrists, and 'intentional' from the NICE self-harm guidelines, demonstrating that change is possible when people are prepared to listen.

By drawing attention to the issue of terminology in this chapter, my hope is that it will generate further discussion between professionals and researchers in the field and lead to eventual resolution of this contentious issue, which has existed for far too long. Perhaps a useful starting point to reduce the confusion would be for researchers to clarify to their target audience exactly what topics they are studying. This is particularly important if the ambiguous terms 'self-harm' or 'parasuicide' are used. It would make life a lot easier and perhaps fewer misunderstandings would arise if articles (academic or otherwise) carried headings such as: Self-harm (includes self-poisoning and self-injury, excludes alcohol and illicit drugs) for example.

'Safe self harm - is it possible?'

This was the title of a debate that took place at the Royal College of Nursing (RCN) Congress in April 2006, the aim of which was to discuss the nurse's role in enabling patients to self-harm safely.

Consultant nurse, Chris Holley, leading the 'safe self harm' pilot scheme introduced at South Staffordshire and Shropshire Healthcare NHS Foundation Trust prior to the congress, opened the debate.

The controversial proposal at RCN Congress that nurses should endorse safe self-injury for some hospital patients whipped up media frenzy, questioning nurses' duty of care to prevent self-harm, and accusations of potentially placing patients at increased risk of suicide. These are a handful of headlines that appeared in the press before and after the debate (some of which err on the side of sensationalism; others present a more objective perspective):

- Hospitals to allow self-harm (Lister, S., TimesOnline, March 22, 2006)
- Hospital allows patients to harm themselves (Daily Mail, March 22, 2006)
- Hospital lets its patients self-harm in pilot scheme (Nicholas, C., Scotsman.com, March 26, 2006)
- Self-harmers to be given clean blades (Templeton, S.K., Sunday Times, February 05, 2006).
- Self harm on the NHS (Myall, S., The People.co.uk, March 26, 2006)
- Nurses want to help self-harm patients (Kirby, J., icBirmingham, April 26, 2006)
- Nurses back supervised self-harm (Triggle, N., BBC News 24, Tuesday, 25 April 2006).

Facts speak louder than words

Chris Holley and her colleague Rachel Horton, in the text that follows, enable us to look beyond the controversial headlines of public journalism, to the authentic picture that activated the initiation of the pioneering safe self-injury initiative, and which resulted in so much media controversy.

The safe self-injury initiative

By Chris Holley and Rachel Horton

At South Staffordshire and Shropshire Healthcare NHS Foundation Trust, mental health professionals have been exploring practice to improve the patient experience. They had recognised that they were nursing patients inconsistently, some of whom had a long history of self-injury, and who would describe their behaviour as making themselves feel safe and human again. The nurses had polarised views about how to care – some felt safe to allow patients who self-injure to continue cutting themselves, as they were aware that the patient would feel relief afterwards. On the other hand, some staff felt that they had a duty to prevent such individuals from harming themselves, having a duty to protect from harm. The result was a poor experience of care for both the patients and staff alike. The staff team tended to split between those who would want to search a patient's room to remove any potentially dangerous implements – and those who would use the 'turning a blind eye approach' whilst a patient self-injured, knowing that they would feel better afterwards.

The Nursing and Midwifery Council (NMC) were consulted for advice as some nurses recognised that they were in an ethical and professional dilemma. Despite the lack of formal guidelines for harm minimisation, the NMC's advice was that whatever method of care was used, it needed to be a **consistent approach** across the whole care team. A Self Harm Consensus Seminar was held in Stafford in January 2005 to gather opinion from experts across the country; and the RCN Institute, along with mental health trusts in Newcastle-upon-Tyne and South Staffordshire, carried out research to explore nurses' attitudes towards patients who self-harm. A self-harm focus group was established to explore a process for improving practice in this area, including developing guidelines for working with self-harm/injury which explores the different functions behind self harm/injury for different patients.

The background

A safe self-injury care plan was eventually agreed to use with a patient who had used self-injury for the past 20 years to manage her difficult and distressing thoughts and feelings. She had been cutting her knees in a controlled way which had not caused her serious harm and was not described as an attempt to end her life; it was to bring her relief. The staff team recognised her cutting as an effective coping mechanism, but struggled with their code of professional conduct. The patient recognised that during previous hospital admissions when she has been unable to cut herself, and therefore being denied the opportunity to utilise her safe and trusted coping strategy, it had resulted in her using alternative/more dangerous forms of self-harm. This had the potential to increase the risk of serious and/or long-term harm – even accidental death.

When not allowed to use the safe coping strategy of cutting herself, the service user became so desperate that she eventually cut herself with whatever she could find – a broken cup . . . or even a piece of (dirty) glass found on a walk in the hospital grounds. Her need to cut was so desperate, at this point, that her cutting was not controlled or safe. She therefore became '*at risk*' because of a nursing protocol which was supposed to ensure (ironically) patient safety.

During a subsequent admission to hospital, in order to improve the service user's experience of in-patient services, a comprehensive assessment was completed which included liaising with other professionals involved in her care; researching case notes – and many discussions with the patient. Her needs were identified and a care plan was negotiated and written in collaboration with the patient which recognised and promoted the need for consistency in practice; sharing responsibility; clear boundary setting and empowerment of the patient. Discussions and agreement of the way forward took place between the patient, nursing, medical and management teams.

The change in practice

The patient was empowered, and involved in defining the team approach, in defining the care plan. She was allowed to cut herself with boundaries in place; she had been checked as having the capacity to make informed decisions about her care, and a very comprehensive specific care plan was developed. The care plan was signed by the patient and by *all* of the professionals involved in her care – something that had not been done before – the contentious nature of the care being provided warranted a totally 'signed up' approach by the team. The care plan, of course, was regularly reviewed, and the result was that the staff team worked confidently and consistently; the patient was happy with her care, without feeling judged.

The care plan included planned 1:1 sessions to explore and encourage the principles of harm reduction; to provide support, and the opportunity to discuss her thoughts and feelings. Staff agreed not to intervene and prevent her from cutting her knees unless she requested this. The lady concerned was used to cutting her knees with glass. Staff agreed not to remove her piece of glass from her room unless she requested this. She had agreed to be responsible for ensuring the glass was kept securely in her room, in a locked drawer, and that she would limit her self-injury to the privacy of her own room – to reduce the risk of distress to other patients on the ward.

The patient agreed to assess her wounds (in the same way that she would do so at home) and dress them independently if she felt that they did not require nursing or medical intervention, and nursing staff agreed to provide her with the necessary equipment to facilitate this – like dressings, antiseptic, etc. She also agreed that she would be responsible for requesting assistance from nursing staff following an act of self-injury if she felt this to be necessary, and nursing staff agreed to assess her wounds and treat them accordingly - or request medical assessment if required.

The patient had stated that she did not wish to receive treatment at the local Accident and Emergency Department agreeing that, in some circumstances, this may not be possible and that medical staff may advise that this is necessary. Therefore, an agreement was made that she would receive medical treatment on the ward, whenever possible. The patient requested that information regarding her self-injury would not be shared with her family without her expressed consent. During this process, she was able to identify factors that would be an indication that she was at an increased risk of more serious harm. She identified that cutting her face was such an indicator and that she would be responsible for informing staff of such risks. At this point, the staff would review her care plan, ensuring that she would be involved with all decisions made regarding any changes.

So what was the impact upon the nursing team delivering this comprehensive care plan?

Honest and open communication between the patient and professionals resulted in an atmosphere of mutual respect and a sharing of renewed attitudes and values. The nursing team were able to openly acknowledge that to witness a patient bleeding from a wound that has been inflicted upon themselves does not *naturally* lend itself to a calm response; some would find it quite traumatic. The team shared their knowledge and skills; communicated more regularly and supported each other better; debriefed and learnt from each incident – and, as a result, are now a stronger team.

Royal College of Nursing debate and the media

As a result of being involved in informing the Royal College of Nursing debate at RCN Congress in April 2006 (this can be viewed on line at www.rcn.org.uk) South Staffordshire and Shropshire Healthcare NHS Foundation Trust has been the subject of much media attention, only *some* of it accurate, receiving – in addition to the media calls ("Are you handing razor blades to your patients?") – many calls from mental health practitioners across the country who have welcomed the promotion of this approach which has been used in silence by numerous practitioners before us. We need to be open/ share information about innovative/new approaches to working with those selected patients who we are aware self injure in order to make them feel safe – in order to improve the patient experience – rather than making it an abusive experience in in-patient settings.

> Harm minimisation is about accepting the need to self-harm as a valid method of survival until survival is possible by other means.
>
> —*Pembroke (2007:166)*

About the authors

Chris Holley, RMN; Cert. Couns.; DN (CPN); M.Sc.

Chris Holley is a Consultant Nurse in Sexual Abuse and Women's Issues employed by South Staffordshire and Shropshire Healthcare NHS Foundation Trust, leading their Sexual Abuse Service. She also has the Lead for women's mental health issues within the Trust. South Staffordshire and Shropshire Healthcare NHS Foundation Trust is also the pilot site for the DH exploratory exercise into the development of guidelines for people who self harm in in-patient settings, and has presented her work internationally.

Rachel Horton is a mental health nurse (RMN) with seven years experience of working in acute in-patient settings, including the perinatal setting. She, together with a service user, compiled the care plan used at South Staffordshire which acknowledged the service user's need to injure herself at times. She has presented her innovative work at conferences locally.

Key points
- Self-injury has become the focus of much media attention, with reports implying that the UK is the self-harm capital of Europe.
- The magnitude of the problem of self-injury is impossible to determine due to the absence of official statistics, inconsistency

over definitions and terms, discrepancies over reported estimates, and because many episodes go unreported or undetected.

- Inaccurate media reporting and judgemental attitudes by the media towards people that self-injure has the potential to increase stigma and prejudice rather than reduce it.
- The UK National Inquiry among young people that self-harm identified that much work still needs to be done to establish the occurrence of self-harm, and to develop knowledge to ascertain appropriate interventions in the prevention of self-harm, and continuance of self-harm once it has become a regular pattern of behaviour.
- Concrete statistics are needed to support claims that self-injury is on the increase among young people.
- Internet sites displaying graphic images of self-injury wounds and scars have become the target of vigorous condemnation.

Chapter 5

Two research studies examined

I n this chapter, the findings of two research studies are summarised. The first, by Penumbra (2001) examines the perceptions and experiences of young people who self-harm. The second, by Stephanie Caroline Davies (2002) examines antecedents and maintenance factors of self-harm.

Penumbra research with young people who self-harm

In January 2001, Penumbra (one of Scotland's leading mental health organisations) published a report on a piece of action research carried out in Edinburgh with young people who self-harm entitled *'No Harm in Listening'*. Presented in this section are the main findings together with testimonies from some of the young people involved with the research.

Summary of the main findings

- There is a significant lack of understanding about self-harm and the issues surrounding it amongst the public and professionals alike.
- Increased awareness is essential to de-stigmatise self-harm, and to develop the work undertaken with individuals who self-harm.
- Services for young people in Edinburgh, and surrounding areas who self-harm are woefully inadequate – more support services need to be developed.
- The views of young people who self-harm concerning the development of service provision, or the suitability of their own

specific treatment and support plans are rarely considered. Young people should be involved and consulted in relation to service reviews and developments.

- Professionals often apply 'labels' to explain self-harming behaviour, yet rarely address the underlying causes. In other words, they treat the symptoms, but overlook the causes.

- Some of the sample group perceived existing services as judgemental and stigmatising of young people who self-harmed.

- When receiving treatment for wounds at A&E, privacy is essential to alleviate the likelihood of increased distress. Efforts to provide a separate room, or 'cordoned' off area should be made. All medical procedures and treatments need explaining to the individual in advance, and any questions he or she may have should be answered.

Testimonies from the young people

About starting self-harm

'There's loads of reasons that you can attribute to why I began self-harming. As far as I see it, it's not as simple as that, like breaking it down to one "event." I just know that I always feel that I'm not successful enough, not fit enough, not slim enough and not earning enough. Try living with that every day.'

'I self-harm because my adoptive dad used to sexually abuse me. That wasn't the worst thing though – the worst thing was that my mum condoned it. How can you get over that?'

About stigma and social exclusion

'Self-harming in general excludes you in a way and puts you in a minority. Different people react in different ways. My friends were terrified of it . . . some friends they turned out to be.'

'Self-harm makes you become socially excluded. People just stare and stare at your arms. They judge you by what you look like. It's not fair. I've had strangers come up to me and call me names in the middle of the street.'

Reasons for self-harm

'Sometimes I know exactly why I self-harm and at other times I don't. It was because of my abuse and because my mum and me were getting beat up all the time. I had also just found out that I was adopted, which didn't help. I self-harm now basically because I don't like myself. I haven't got any self-esteem. Other things have happened as I've got older like getting beat up.'

Stopping self-harm

'I've not self-harmed for about five or six years now. I still have to check myself though, like when I get angry, frustrated or upset. All I have to do is look in the mirror and I catch sight of my scars and I think "Do I really want to add to them? Do I really want to start all of that up again?" There's not a day goes by though when I don't have to think about that, so am I an ex-self-harmer?'

'I'm in the process of trying to give up now. It's not easy because it's the only way I know how to deal with all the pain inside. It's difficult to resist the urge. I'm pretty pleased with myself though, as I've only cut three times in the last six months.'

Reactions of others

'My family don't support me at all. They feel that it's just attention seeking.'

'My friends really treat me as a human being. They don't judge me and they give me support. Some of them don't like me doing it and neither does my ex-boyfriend.'

'The public view self-harmers as an embarrassment to society. We are a sign of dysfunction and lacking in something. We are talked about jokingly, seen as psychopaths. People are scared to look at people who self-harm properly, because one day it could be them, or someone close to them.'

'I hate it when people say we're attention seeking. That's a load of crap coming from people who either don't understand or need excuses. That's their way of labelling self-harm because they don't want to address us or the issues that we're going through.'

Suicide and self-harm

'Suicide is when it's too much and I can't cope any more, I can't think straight and I am so stressed. The thoughts and feelings just build up, build up, and build up and suicide is the only escape. For me, self-harm is a way of getting through as opposed to escaping.'

'Suicide is when you know that you want to die. Self-harm is to make you feel better inside, because when you cut yourself, you feel better inside.'

Self-Harm: An examination of antecedent and maintenance factors

A study by Stephanie Caroline Davies (2002)

This summary of an unpublished study carried out by Stephanie Davies as part of a Masters Degree in Forensic Behavioural Science at Liverpool University, provides important information, as well as reinforcing many of the findings discussed elsewhere in this book.

Aims of the study

The study had two aims (1) to gain greater insight into the antecedents that lead to self-harm and (2) to establish factors that maintain it. Completing a semi-structured questionnaire, primarily consisting of multiple-choice questions with space provided for additional information, three hundred and twenty five respondents, recruited from various self-harm support groups on the Internet, participated in the study. Figure 5.1 provides information about the respondents' self-harm, followed by Figure 5.2 significant events, which suggests that certain life events may trigger and maintain the self-harm response. A written summary of the findings is available following the tables.

PART I: ABOUT THE RESPONDENTS' SELF-HARM			
Age of onset	%	Main method used	%
Childhood	28.0	Cutting	84.6
Teenage	60.6	Burning	3.7
Young adult	8.9	Picking	2.8
Adult	2.2	Scratching	2.8
Areas of body harmed	%	Hitting/bruising	0.6
Arms	55.4	Hair pulling	0.6
Wrists	12.3	Overdosing	1.2
Legs	17.8	Frequency	%
Chest	0.9	Daily	17.2
Stomach	6.5	Weekly	17.2
Face/head	1.2	Monthly	4.0
Genitals	0.6	No pattern	60.0
Internally	1.5	Heard about self-harm before starting	%
Anywhere/most areas	1.5	Yes	37.5
Why areas chosen	%	No	61.8
Can hide it	40.0	How they heard about it	%
Easiest access	23.8	Media	50.5
Unsure	20.0	Friends/family/associates	35.1
Abused there	2.3	Hearing about self-harm influenced decision to start	%
Other	13.8	Yes	14.5
Impulsive or planned	%	No	62.3
Impulsive	34.8	Did not answer	23.1
Planned	5.5	Triggers for self-harm	%
Both/unsure	58.5	Nothing in particular	4.3

	%		
Main feelings immediately following the act	%	Boredom	0.9
Happy/elated/high	2.8	Numb/dissociation	5.2
Relieved/calmer/relaxed	54.6	Intense emotions	22.8
Nothing/Numb	19.1	Anger/frustration	10.2
Guilty/scared/sad	16.7	Depressed/upset	15.4
Most/all of list	1.9	Self-hate/failure	13.2
Experienced a 'high' during the act	%	Rejection	1.5
Strongly agree	8.3	Flashbacks/memories	5.5
Agree	34.2	Arguments	1.2
Unsure	28.0	Family/friends/relationships	2.8
Disagree	23.4	Most/all in list	16.0
Strongly disagree	5.8	**Sought from self-harm**	%
Crave self-harm	%	Blood and the wound	43.1
Strongly agree	36.9	Pain	27.7
Agree	32.0	All factors	13.8
Unsure	13.2	None of factors	6.8
Disagree	11.4	**Care for wounds afterwards**	%
Strongly disagree	5.5	Strongly agree	13.8
Could live without self-harm	%	Agree	25.8
Strongly agree	10.8	Unsure	15.1
Agree	19.1	Disagree	29.2
Unsure	51.7	Strongly disagree	14.2
Disagree	11.1	**Compare wounds with other people that self-harm**	%
Strongly disagree	5.2	Strongly agree	7.4
Do it to get noticed	%	Agree	14.2
Strongly agree	1.8	Unsure	4.9

Agree	5.5	Disagree	18.2
Unsure	11.4	Strongly disagree	52.6
Disagree	30.8		
Strongly disagree	49.5		

Fig. 5.1: Part I: About the respondents' self-harm.

PART II: SIGNIFICANT EVENTS			
Experienced abuse	%	Age abused	%
Sexual	13.6	Childhood	34.1
Physical	3.1	Teenage	20.3
Emotional	29.3	Most of young life	43.3
Neglect/ abandonment	11.1	Adult	2.3
Two or more types of abuse	16.4		
No abuse	25.3		
Lost someone close through death	%	Who died	%
Strongly agree	40.4	Close family/partner	24.5
Agree	21.3	Relatives	49.5
Unsure	4.9	Friends	10.4
Disagree	15.1	Other/various	15.6
Strongly disagree	16.4		
Age of respondents at time of loss			
Childhood (33.5%)	Teens (38.7%)	Adult (14.7%)	Other/various (13.1%)

Witnessed family violence	%	Have/had disabilities/ illnesses/ accidents	%
Strongly agree	27.5	None	80.3
Agree	26.5	Disabled	5.2
Unsure	17.3	Illness	7.1
Disagree	15.7	Car crash/accident	3.4
Strongly disagree	11.1		
Bad home life	**%**	**Reasons for bad home life**	
Strongly agree	27.2	Abuse/violence/ neglect	34.9
Agree	28.8	Arguments/divorce	21.9
Unsure	13.0	Financial/emotional stress	1.4
Disagree	15.5	Illness/mental Illness/alcoholism/ drug abuse	24.0
Strongly disagree	13.3		
		Moved around a lot	3.4
Close to family	**%**	**Reasons not close to family**	**%**
Strongly agree	9.3	Can't open up to them/trust them	24.6
Agree	20.4	They don't understand me/ don't feel accepted	21.2
Unsure	26.3	Was badly treated	20.3
Disagree	20.1	Hate them/they hate me	13.6
Strongly disagree	23.2	Unsure/rather not say	6.8
Happy in childhood	**%**	**Reasons not happy in childhood**	**%**
Strongly agree	1.9	Abuse/rape	29.8
Agree	11.8	Felt different	7.1
Unsure	21.1	Family/parents	23.8
Disagree	29.7	Mental illness	11.9
Strongly disagree	33.7	Many reasons	8.3

Happy in school	%	Reasons not happy in school	%
Strongly agree	7.1	Bullied	46.6
Agree	20.4	Felt different/outcast	25.0
Unsure	13.3	Unpopular	9.5
Disagree	25.1	Other	18.9
Strongly disagree	33.1		
Had happy relationships	%	Reasons for unhappy relationships	%
Strongly agree	9.0	Chose wrong people/got hurt	21.8
Agree	24.8	Abusive/violent/raped	28.7
Unsure	26.9	Couldn't get close/no trust	20.7
Disagree	20.4	Not had a relationship	16.1
Strongly disagree	11.1		
Sexuality identified as	%	Comfortable with sexuality	%
Heterosexual	61.4	Yes	80.8
Bi-sexual	19.6	No	14.8
Homosexual	5.0	Sometimes/unsure	4.4
Unsure	11.8		
Any distinguishing features	%	Disorders/diagnoses they have	%
Overweight	47.8	Depression/manic depression	28.2
Short/tall/look long	11.6	Eating disorder	7.0
'Ugly'	2.9	Personality disorder	8.4
Skin/hair condition	4.3	PTSD	0.9
		Various diagnoses	51.1
Other significant factors	%	Been in hospital	%
Been raped	34.2	Yes	41.9
Been in prison	2.6	No	41.5
Alcoholism/drugs	13.2	Short stay/overnight	16.6
Had an abortion	2.6		

Fig. 5.2: Part II: Significant events.

Summary of the findings

The sample group comprised mainly females, most of whom had started harming in their teens. The principal method used to self-harm was cutting, with burning chosen as a second method. Arms were the most frequently targeted area, followed by the legs. This could possibly be associated with a preference for concealing the wounds from others (which challenges the myth of attention seeking), or/and so the wound can be easily seen and reached. Some respondents stated they chose a particular area due to being 'abused there'. Regrettably, no further clarification was forthcoming, making this a potentially significant area for future study.

Imitative behaviour

The majority of respondents had not heard about self-harm prior to starting; those who had mainly disagreed that hearing about it had influenced their decision to start. Therefore, it would seem that a leaning towards self-harm is not predisposed by having heard about it, and that other factors must play a part in shaping the choice to start.

Relieved and positive

It was clear that the act of self-harm produced positive feelings, which supports the findings of Favazza and Conterio (1989), Arnold (1995), and Sutton (1999). It also lends support to the notion that self-harm serves effectively as a tension-reliever, which in turn may account for continuance of the act.

Craving the high

Looking at whether self-harm could be addictive, many respondents reported experiencing a sense of euphoria (the 'high'), possibly due to the chemical release of endorphins. As the release seems to shares similarities to the sensation when taking drugs, it is probable that self-harm has similar addictive properties. Asked if they craved for self-harm, the majority of respondents agreed they did, thus adding strength to the hypothesis that it has an addictive quality about it.

Not done for attention

Challenging the myth that self-harm is done to gain attention was achieved in two ways. First, a large percentage of respondents disagreed strongly to doing self-harm as a way of being noticed, and secondly, a significant majority claimed they would not compare wounds with others who self-harm.

Recap

In sum, self-harm appears to be an effective strategy for alleviating negative emotions and reducing tension, and seems to have addictive properties. However, contrary to common myth, in the main it does not appear to be imitative behaviour; nor is it adopted as an attention-seeking tactic.

Antecedents

Child abuse and rape

Almost seventy-five percent (75%) of respondents had suffered childhood abuse. Many reported experiencing several forms of abuse and neglect, which mainly occurred in childhood and continued over long periods. Rape was another type of abuse reported, supporting the findings of Greenspan and Samuel (1989). Noteworthy was that the age when the abuse occurred correlated significantly with the age of onset of self-harm. However, although this finding is important, it does not necessarily confirm a causal relationship between the two.

Witnessing violence

When asked if they had witnessed violence, the majority of respondents agreed they had. Results from additional testing to establish whether there could be a link between witnessing violence and having a bad home life showed that the two appeared to be unconnected.

The home environment

Many respondents mentioned familial aspects such as abuse, violence, neglect, divorce, arguments, parental alcoholism, and drug abuse as contributory factors to self-harm. Despite these obvious family difficulties, the majority of respondents seemed unsure if they were close to their family of not.

Bereavement

Almost two thirds of the sample had experienced the death of someone they were close to, and the onset of self-harm correlated strongly with the age the respondents were at the time of the loss. However, again, it would be wrong to assume that bereavement of a loved one is an automatic trigger to self-harm, as it may be merely coincidental not causal.

School

Many respondents disliked school, and many had experienced bullying – this appeared to contribute to a general feeling of unhappiness in their childhood.

Medical problems

There was no strong evidence to suggest that medical problems, such as disabilities, illnesses, or accidents, act as antecedents. However, this could possibly be due to a high proportion of the sample not having experienced these problems.

Summary of antecedents

The findings suggest a strong correlation between self-harm and childhood trauma, particularly child abuse and rape – this lends additional support to the already accumulating evidence in the literature. Losing a loved one at an early age and bullying at school – which can have a profoundly detrimental effect on self-esteem – may also be antecedents to self-harm. Other causal factors such as family relationships (particularly parental relationships), may point to attachment issues, which may merit a firm commitment to future research in this area. Another key area worthy of future research is establishing whether internal self-harm is common among survivors of childhood sexual abuse.

Key points

- There is a significant lack of understanding about self-harm among the public and professionals alike.
- Existing services are perceived as judgemental and stigmatising of young people who self-harm – raised awareness is needed to de-stigmatise the behaviour.
- Services in Edinburgh and surrounding districts for young people that self-harm are scarce.
- There is a tendency to treat the symptoms, rather than address the causes.
- Privacy is vital to reduce possible distress when being treated at A&E, and medical procedures and treatments need to be explained.
- Antecedents identified (both studies): bullying, death of someone close, abuse (several forms – often prolonged and starting in childhood), mother condoning abuse, rape, neglect, violence (witness to, subjected to), divorce, parental arguments, alcoholism and drug abuse, invalidation (never feeling good enough), low self-esteem, and self-dislike.
- Maintaining factors identified: only way known to deal with internal anguish, difficult to resist the urge, way of coping as opposed to suicide, produced positive feelings, feel better inside, similar addictive qualities to drug taking.
- Copycat behaviour questionable – many respondents reported that they had not heard about self-harm prior to starting. Those who had heard of the behaviour mainly disputed that hearing about it had influenced their decision to self-harm.

- Attention seeking behaviour disputed – respondents disagreed to self-harming as a way of being noticed.
- Davies's study (which comprised mainly females) revealed that seventy-five percent (75%) of respondents had suffered childhood abuse, most had started self-harming in their teens, that the principal methods used to self-harm were (1) cutting and (2) burning, that arms were the most frequently targeted area, followed by the legs, and that some chose a particular area due to being 'abused there'.

Chapter 6

Childhood trauma, negative core beliefs, perfectionism and self-injury

· ·

'I was emotionally and physically abused as
a child and self-harm seems to be one of my
coping skills along with my drug and alcohol abuse.'

Supported by respondents' material this chapter provides significant insight into the role of childhood trauma, negative core beliefs and unhealthy perfectionist traits in self-injury. Further, the acrimonious 'false memory debate' is put under the spotlight. We observe first-hand the role of recovered abuse memories in the process of self-injury, and witness the anguish and consequences caused by recovered memories.

Defining trauma

Traumatic events are usually considered to be deeply distressing or psychologically painful experiences that result in harmful long-term effects. Examples include major disasters which result in loss of life or injury, the sudden death or loss of a loved one, rape, sexual abuse, physical abuse, emotional abuse, neglect, domestic violence, abandonment, and bullying.

People react to traumatic events in different ways, depending on a number of factors, such as their psychological make-up, past experiences and access to support. Any event that leaves an individual feeling powerless, vulnerable, unsafe, and unable to cope may be perceived as traumatic. Children exposed to traumatic events such as child abuse are particularly at risk of developing long-term psychological, physical, behavioural, and social problems, or interpersonal problems such as marital or relationship problems.

Child abuse and self-injury

Numerous studies have found a positive correlation between child abuse and self-injury (*see for example:* Favazza & Conterio, 1989; van der Kolk, Perry, & Herman, 1991; Arnold, 1995; Hawton, et al; 2002). Eighty-four (84%) percent of the respondents who completed the survey for *Healing the Hurt Within,* 1st edition (Sutton, 1999) reported childhood trauma/other childhood circumstances as contributory factors to their self-harm. Several reported multiple forms of child abuse (emotional, sexual, physical, neglect and rape).

> 'As a child of 7 years old I was sexually, physically, emotionally abused and raped, while living with my grandparents. I always have felt "dirty, guilty and unworthy". My mother instilled into my memory that I was a "big mistake" and that "I happened", much to her regret. I hate myself and I always feel nothing but self-destruct towards myself and feel I shouldn't be here.'

> 'My father and grandfather were abusing me. I cut because I want the outside to show how I feel on the inside; because I feel I deserve it; because life without abuse is so unfamiliar it's terrifying; because if I don't cut everyone will decide I'm OK now and leave me alone, and I'm not OK.'

'I remember the first time I cut myself. I was 12. My older brother had raped me, and I couldn't find any other way to express my anger.'

'I was very insecure, having had traumatic events in my early childhood, resulting in me being separated from my mum for 3 months. Also when I was older several family members died in a short time (2 years). I have low self-esteem. I was at one time (as an adult) sexually abused, also raped once. I have a much happier life now but I'm still very insecure.'

Defining rape

Figure 6.1 gives a definition of rape provided by the Crown Prosecution Service. Definitions of abuse are provided later in the chapter.

DEFINING RAPE

Rape as defined by the Crown Prosecution Service

The definition of rape has been substantially changed by the Sexual Offences Act 2003 which came into force on 1 May 2004.

Under the previous law as set out in the Sexual Offences Act 1956, the statutory definition of rape is any act of non-consensual intercourse by a man with a person; the victim can be either male or female. Intercourse can be vaginal or anal . . . Consent is given its ordinary meaning, and lack of consent can be inferred from the surrounding circumstances, such as submission through fear.

Offences committed on or after 1 May 2004 will be prosecuted under the Sexual Offences Act 2003. The Act extends the definition of rape to include the penetration by a penis of the vagina, anus or mouth of another person. (pp. 4-5).

http://www.cps.gov.uk/publications/docs/prosecuting_rape.pdf

(Retrieved June 16, 2007)

Fig. 6.1: Crown Prosecution Service definition of rape.

Defining emotional abuse

Emotional abuse is subtle – it comes in various guises and because there are no visible wounds or scars it is difficult to detect. Emotional abuse damages children's self-concept, and leaves them believing that they are unworthy of love and affection. Emotional abuse is invariably present in all types of abuse, and the long-term harm from emotional abuse can be equally, if not more damaging, than other forms of abuse.

'I know I self-harm mainly because I have so much self-hate – I see so much beauty in others, but never myself! Two years ago it came out that I was sexually abused as a child and logically I know this is probably a contributing factor to my self-harm – but I find it hard to accept and admit. Due to the feelings of worthlessness I want it to be my fault!'

Emotional abuse goes beyond the realms of the spoken

Other terms used to describe emotional abuse include verbal abuse, and mental or psychological abuse. Figure 6.2 provides examples of emotional abuse.

EMOTIONAL ABUSE	
Examples	
Being invasive	Ignoring
Belittling through	Innuendos
comments or sarcasm	Isolating
Brow-beating	Intimidating
Bullying	Manipulating
Confinement in dark	Mortifying
places (unlit rooms,	Name-calling
cupboards, closets)	Rejecting
Constantly criticising	Ridiculing
Controlling	Scapegoating
Demeaning	Screaming and raging
Harassing	Silent treatment
Humiliating	Verbally assaulting

Fig. 6.2: Examples of emotional abuse.

Verbal abuse

A torn jacket is soon mended;
but hard words bruise the heart of a child.
—*Henry Wadsworth Longfellow*

Whoever invented the maxim, 'Sticks and stones may break my bones, but words will never hurt me' was mistaken. Constant verbal insults and harsh criticism cut deep, name calling wounds, teasing or spiteful comments hurt. Verbal abuse can stick like glue, leaving deep and long-lasting invisible mental scars that can impact on a child's emotional or social development. Children that live with criticism internalise those beliefs about themselves and often become self-critical. Valerie Sinason (2002) in her excellent book *Attachment, Trauma and Multiplicity* succinctly sums up the damaging consequences of verbal abuse:

What happens when a child has to breathe in mocking words each day? What happens when a parent, an attachment figure utters those words: someone the child needs in order to emotionally survive? Sometimes, that mocking voice gets taken inside and finds a home. It then stays hurting and corroding on the inside when the original source of that cruelty might long ago have disappeared or died. (p. 4)

Clarifying the difference between emotional abuse and neglect

Neglect is another insidious form of abuse. In essence, neglect means a child's basic needs are not met, for example: love, care, nurture, comfort, warmth, a safe environment, food, somebody being there for the child. Figure 6.3 gives a definition of neglect provided by NSPCC.

DEFINING NEGLECT

Neglect is the persistent lack of appropriate care of children, including love, stimulation, safety, nourishment, warmth, education and medical attention. It can have a serious effect on a child's physical, mental and emotional development. For babies and very young children, it can be life-threatening.

NSPCC

http://www.nspcc.org.uk/

(Retrieved June 16, 2007)

Fig. 6.3: NSPCC definition of neglect.

Child without adults

Desertion, devastation, desolation,
the child feels but doesn't know the words,
with the d-d-d of the drumbeat.
And the darkness falls like snow
in the kitchen where she sits.

No tears on the white/yellow food

nor can she grasp the spoon to eat.

With the d-d-d of the drumbeat.

No tears fall, no crying and no, never

no calling out for help.

Where love, comfort, warmth?

Where human voice?

The silence echoes deep

with the d-d-d of the drumbeat.

There's no one there,

she is

alone, alone, alone.

—Nancy

Defining physical abuse

Physical abuse is characterised by inflicting non-accidental injuries, physical punishment, or violence on a child that results in harm or even death. Figure 6.4 gives examples of physical abuse and the range of severity.

PHYSICAL ABUSE	
Forms	*Range of severity*
Beating	Minor bruising
Biting	Scratches
Burning	Grazes
Hair pulling	Cuts
Hitting	Eye injuries
Punching	Fractures
Kicking	Injuries to brain
Scalding	Damage to internal organs
Shaking	
Shoving	**Note:** Signs of fresh wounds or
Slapping	bruises and old scars might be an
Throwing	indication that the child has suffered
Tying up	abuse on more than one occasion.
Torturing	

Fig. 6.4: Examples of physical abuse and the range of severity.

'I self-harm because I was abused sexually, physically, emotionally and spiritually as a child. It somehow helped me cope, and was also a way to vent the self-hate I was given by the abusers, which I turned in onto myself. Self-harm was a way of controlling torture.'

'I know now I self-harm to relieve the pressure I'm under due to my childhood where I was sexually and physically abused for 12 years. Also my Granddad, who was a father figure to me died, and that was a great loss to me.'

Defining sexual abuse

'[Self-injury] stems from 16 years of sexual abuse by my father.'

Sexual abuse 'can be defined as the involvement of a young person who has not reached intellectual and emotional maturity, in any kind of sexual activity imposed upon them by any person who is more powerful by reason of their age or their position of authority, that violate the social taboos of family roles, or that break the law.' (*Breaking Free:* Source, Sutton 1999:61) Figure 6.5 gives a further definition provided by ChildLine.

Child sexual abuse and self-injury

Child abuse provides fertile ground for the development of a range of adverse effects that can impede healthy adult functioning (see Figure 6.6 Child abuse: Potential adverse long-term effects). Self-injury is one, among a plethora of strategies that some (but not all) survivors use to cope.

DEFINING SEXUAL ABUSE

Sexual abuse is . . .

. . . when children are forced or persuaded into sexual acts or situations by others. Children might be encouraged to look at pornography, be harassed by sexual suggestions or comments, be touched sexually or forced to have sex.

—ChildLine

free 24-hour helpline for

children and young people in the UK.

Tel: 0800 1111

What is child abuse?

http://www.childline.org.uk/Childabuse.asp

(Retrieved June 16, 2007)

Fig. 6.5: ChildLine definition of sexual abuse.

'I've recently started to accept the connection between being sexually abused as a child and the feelings that self-harm helps to release.'

'I'd had 12 years of abuse – physical, mental, emotional and sexual (voyeurism) by a psychopathic stepfather, who controlled my life and who I despised. Initially it [self-harm] was to blunt my impotence and feelings of anger.'

CHILD ABUSE Potential adverse long-term effects			
Relationship/Sexual problems	**Physical health issues**	**Behavioural problems/issues**	**Mental health issues**
Attachment and bonding issues (with others/ own children)	Digestive problems	Suicidal thoughts Attempted suicide Completed suicide	Anxiety disorders (panic attacks/ social anxiety)
Fear of men/women	Breathing problems (asthma), hyperventilation (rapid, shallow breathing)	Substance misuse (alcohol/drugs)	Conduct disorders
Sexual anxiety/ dysfunction/ avoidance/ promiscuity	Chronic pain (headaches/back/ shoulders/neck/ stomach/pelvis)	Other addictions, i.e. smoking; gambling, shopping, etc.	Stress Phobias (avoidance of dental/ gynaecological examinations)
Sexuality identity confusion	Pregnancy problems	Self-injury Perfectionism	Depressive disorders
Fear of intimacy Search for intimacy	Infertility problems Failure to attend regular dental treatment, eye examinations	Workaholism	Dissociative symptoms/disorders
Issues with trust touch/authority figures		Risky/compulsive sexual behaviour or avoidance of sexual intimacy, including health screening	Eating disorders Obesity
Relationship with self			Mood disorders
Poor self-concept Low self-esteem Dislike of body/ poor body image		Establishing safe boundaries	Personality disorders: Borderline Personality Disorder Antisocial Personality Disorder
		Revictimisation	
		Criminal behaviour	PTSD symptoms: Flashbacks
		Over/under protective as parent	Nightmares Intrusive memories Sleep disturbance Concentration problems Hypervigilance Exaggerated startle response Heightened emotional arousal Emotional numbness (feeling detached/ lack of emotions)
		Unresolved anger, leading to inappropriate confrontations	
		Inability to stand up for self/becoming overwhelmed with the needs of others	

Fig. 6.6: Child abuse: Potential adverse long-term effects.

The aftermath of child sexual abuse

The following two pictures, The legacy of child abuse by Sian (Figure 6.7), and Child/Woman by Sheelah. (Figure 6.8) demonstrate clearly the aftermath of child abuse.

I don't want this part of me. I won't look at it – I won't touch it except to clean it – if I ignore it maybe it will go away. If I hate it then it won't hurt me – if I feed it, it will stay ugly and nobody else will want to touch it. This part of me makes me feel like shit. I don't want it to be part of me, so I don't listen to it – I want it to go away and never come back – it isn't mine and I don't want it – if I never saw it again I wouldn't care.

If I look at it it makes me feel sick – I hate it – I won't take care of it. Why should I? It's let me down in the past and I don't trust it.

If I could, I'd tell it to '**Fuck off**' – if I could I'd throw it in the waste disposal.

If I'm honest with myself I would say I'm angry with it. It's the reason I feel so bad – it's a waste of space and it's so ugly – **Yukk!!!**

Fig. 6.7: The legacy of child sexual abuse by Sian.

Child/Woman

Fig. 6.8: Child/Woman by Sheelah.

The woman is black and white with a small hand,
symbolising how she feels she must appear/was made
to appear. Clear-cut. However, the little hand expresses
her hidden vulnerability. The child is in colour (see cover
picture for coloured version) with a searching, knowing,
eye. The large hand is severely adult with painted nails,
showing how the hand was used for adult purposes. Her
skin is drawn and aged, the burden of feeling old before
her time. The bow in the pigtail . . . poignant in that it is
the only childlike thing apparent.

Telling but not being believed

Several incest survivors who self-injure as a consequence of their experiences reported disclosing the abuse to a parent or another family member. In one case, a respondent reported that her disclosure to her mother that her father was abusing her had been met with denial and an accusation of 'False Memory Syndrome [FMS]'. FMS is discussed later in the chapter. The same respondent pointed out that 'Somehow my mother's denial had the power to devastate me in a way that recovering of memories hadn't.' Another respondent wrote: 'I believe that the underlying reasons for my self-harm are because I was sexually abused by my father and brother – and because my family don't know whether to believe me.'

The psychological wounds that result from telling about abuse and not being believed cannot be underestimated, especially if the person confided in is a parent or other close relative. Being disbelieved by one's mother, who is typically the child's primary attachment figure, nurturer, and safety anchor, is tantamount to additional trauma – it not only adds fuel to the sense of betrayal the child already feels, it can leave the child feeling ashamed, guilty, helpless, fearful, isolated, and struggling to cope alone without a safety net.

Why don't mothers believe?

There are numerous reasons why mothers choose not to believe. The reasons are mainly rooted in fear – here are a few examples:

- Fear of shame being brought on the family.
- Fear of the family being torn apart.
- Fear of partner going to jail.
- Fear of the financial implications.

Keeping silent about abuse

The following picture by Erin (Figure 6.9) illustrates why she kept silent about the abuse, and how she struggles with issues of trust in the wake of her experience.

The picture represents all the people I feel turned their backs on me when I was being abused. They ignored and denied what was right in front of their eyes. I now find it difficult to trust people and voice my feelings in relation to my abuse.

I'm silent now, because they were when I was little!

© Copyright, 2005 Erin

Fig. 6.9: Picture by Erin.

Why don't children tell?

There are numerous reasons why children don't speak up about child abuse — these include:

- Assuming responsibility for the abuse ('it must have been my fault'; 'I must be a bad girl/boy'; 'there must be something wrong with me') – blaming oneself is a common thread among abuse survivors.
- Not being aware that abuse is wrong ('this must be what all Dads/ Mums do').
- Liked the special status and attention ('Daddy only does it because he loves me').
- Fear of not being believed or the consequences of telling (getting into trouble or getting the perpetrator into trouble).
- Intimidation by the perpetrator ('something bad will happen to you if you tell'; 'you must never tell anyone – it's our special secret'), or enticements to maintain the secret.
- Shame, embarrassment and guilt (e.g. if sexually stimulated or aroused by the abuse).
- Lacking in verbal skills to explain the abuse in words (e.g. if the abuse happened during the child's preverbal years).

The relief of telling

The next picture *'Lifting the secrecy cloud'* by Sheelah (Figure 6.10) exemplifies the relief and sense of empowerment that comes from breaking the secrecy about abuse to a professional or others who are willing to hear.

Lifting the secrecy cloud
By Sheelah

This is a major image for me. At last, I have lifted the secrecy cloud. I had carried that cloud all my life. With help from my counsellor and others, I got it all out. Words came to me 'Such a weight I have been carrying – no child should have to carry such a weight.' Had a cry for her – what a strong child.

Fig. 6.10: Lifting the secrecy cloud by Sheelah.

The controversial debate over recovered abuse memories

The notion that memories of child abuse can be forgotten, and then years later be remembered, sparked a bitter debate among some professionals in the early 1990s. According to Alan W. Scheflin (1999) 'The recovered memory debate has been the most acrimonious, vicious and hurtful internal controversy in the history of modern psychiatry.' Supporters of False Memory Syndrome (FMS), mainly drawn from the ranks of accused parents, question the validity of recovered memories of childhood abuse, arguing that naïve and overzealous therapists are responsible for encouraging or implanting false memories of child abuse in their clients' minds via the use of suggestive techniques. They particularly take issue with hypnosis, yet also question many other therapeutic practices such as:

- Guided imagery
- Creative visualisation
- Suggestive questioning
- Free association
- Dream interpretation
- Deep relaxation
- Recommending survivors' literature
- Survivor support groups
- Looking at childhood photographs
- Bibliography work.

Defining False Memory Syndrome

False Memory Syndrome is defined as
'[A] condition in which a person's identity and interpersonal relationships are centered around a memory of traumatic experience which is objectively false but in which the person strongly believes.'

—*Kihlstrom* (1996)

Those in the opposing camp, mainly researchers who believe in repression and dissociation, and practitioners working in the field of child abuse, argue that it is possible to 'forget' then later remember abuse. Moreover, as Jennifer Freyd, a researcher into memory, and professor of psychology at the University of Oregon, in her milestone book, *Betrayal Trauma: The Logic of Forgetting Childhood* Abuse (1996) hypothesises:

> There are several good reasons why real memories of abuse may arise in the context of therapy. Therapy may provide the first opportunity for a person to feel safe enough to remember the abuse; the therapist may be the first person to ask the client about abuse; and the client may have sought therapy because of memories just beginning to emerge, which are causing emotional crisis without explicit understanding of the source of the crisis. (p. 55)

The False Memory Syndrome Foundation (FMSF, 1998–2007)

Pamela Freyd, Jennifer Freyd's mother, supported by a scientific advisory board of distinguished professionals, established the False Memory Syndrome Foundation (FMSF) in Philadelphia in 1992 (Hacking, 1995:122-123), following an accusation by Jennifer, that her father Peter Freyd had molested her as a child (an accusation vehemently denied by Peter and Pamela). Hacking, a University Professor of Philosophy, and author of *Rewriting the Soul: Multiple Personality and the Sciences of Memory,* writing in provocative manner sums up the aims of the FMSF:

> The foundation is a banding together of parents whose adult children, during therapy, recall hideous scenes of familial child abuse. Its mission is to tell the world that patients in psychotherapy can be brought to seem to remember horrible events of childhood that never happened. Distressed thirty-somethings (and up) believe that they were abused by parents or relatives long ago. But, urges

the foundation, many of the resulting accusations and subsequent family chaos result not from past evils but from false memories engendered by idealogically committed therapists. (p. 121).

The British False Memory Society (BFMS, June 11, 2007)

The British False Memory Society formed in 1993 with similar aims to its counterpart: to raise awareness of the controversial concept of 'recovered memory therapy' and support families of those falsely accused of abuse.

While I contest many of the assertions put forth by the false memory societies, they have at least drawn attention to the fallibility of human memory and the need to tread extremely cautiously when working with clients who recover abuse memories during the process of therapy.

(For information on therapeutic precautions to help prevent false memory syndrome see Chapter 12, Guidelines for those working with self-injury and related issues).

The relationship between recovering memories of abuse and self-injury

The three case studies, interview, and poem that follow highlight the relationship between recovering abuse memories and self-injury, and the terrible dilemma people face when they have unclear memories, and no evidence to corroborate the belief that they have suffered abuse. You will also see that with the right support and help, and against seemingly insurmountable odds, healing from self-injury is possible.

Case study 6.1: Jill (1)

Two Jill's stories are included in this section. To avoid confusion I have referred to them as Jill 1 and Jill 2.

I am 46 years old. I wrote the piece below about two years ago. As I mention in the writing my self-harm had started again and unfortunately escalated to a level where I needed to be in hospital for my own safety. I didn't get well in hospital, in fact I deteriorated. My therapist was aware of a Therapeutic Community and after a period of assessment, I moved in. The experience in the Community has changed my life. I no longer self-harm and through therapy have come to accept what happened to me and move on. I have recently moved out and I am slowly returning to work and rebuilding my life.

All my life I have known something was not right due to quite specific fears I had. I have been in therapy for 18 months so far. After about five months of therapy I started to get images – they made no sense to me but I wrote about them creatively. This carried on for the next eight months or so, after which I began to get more specific images. My self-harm had returned (I had stopped in my late 20s) and I was aware that I wasn't able to 'block' the images/fears.

My therapist was aware for a long time that whenever I got close to anything I would block it (dissociate). I would also avoid eye contact with her so she couldn't wear down my defences. She never once mentioned abuse, using only my word – 'hurt'. I asked her if she believed me, she said yes. I also asked her if she thought I could have imagined it. She replied that this was possible but unlikely because my physiological responses were quite intense.

I am desperate for 'evidence' and I am not sure what I need to help me to accept my images. I have also experienced pains in places where 'the child' has been hurt (in the images). My therapist says my images are memories.

I am at the stage where I cannot ignore the fact that I may have been hurt, however, I am desperately seeking something to disprove it. I have felt as though I am going mad. How can the images seem so real when I have no memory of them happening? Although the images are now much clearer, I think I have always had a sense that something happened to me. I don't want the memories to be true and want to believe in FMS [false memory syndrome] but deep down, I do believe what I 'see'.

I am fighting the process. I am faced with overwhelming emotions

I can't deal with. Cutting helps but it is not as effective as it used to be; it doesn't give me the same relief. Sometimes I think I am aware of flicking in and out of dissociation as I try to block the painful images. It is a very confusing, scary time.

Jill 1: Observations from case study

Did you notice that Jill had always sensed something was wrong, and how she had managed to stop self-harming in her late 20s, but had started again during therapy? Did you absorb that she started getting images in therapy and that over time these images became more specific, or how when things got too close for comfort with her therapist she tried to push them away, and avoided eye contact?

Did you note that her therapist never once mentioned the word abuse, yet acknowledged Jill's belief that she had been 'hurt'? Furthermore, are the physical pains Jill experienced bodily memories? And what about her desperation for evidence that something happened on the one hand, yet on the other, desperation to find something to disprove it – did you pick up on that? Did you also take in the important fact that Jill no longer self-harms? What stuck out most in your mind from reading Jill's case study?

Case study 6.2: Jill (2)

Jill's story illustrates clearly the association between returning abuse memories and self-injury, as well as the agony she went through before help and support was forthcoming. Note too that like her counterpart above, Jill has healed from self-injury.

It is now almost two years since I last self-injured, although I still occasionally experience the urge to do so. As time goes by the urge has become much less intense and no longer dominates my mind. It has though left me with a strong desire to try and help others understand why some people should need to hurt themselves at times.

It is fast becoming recognised that self-injury covers a wide range of ways in which a person may inflict harm on themselves, but I can only tell of what I did to myself and what drove me to do so. Looking back over the years I suppose my many attempted overdoses and drownings could be classed as self-harm in the most general sense, although not intentionally so. Although at the time I wanted to end my life, in retrospect I think it was more to do with escaping or trying to cut off from a life and memories that I was struggling to cope with. In desperation this made me feel that I wanted to die, yet deep down I was so terrified of dying and death that I find it hard to believe that I could have wanted to die. Instead I think I yearned for a state of deep sleep, one from which I might awake into a different world free of my previous fears, panics, anxiety, memories and the awful suffocating black depression.

Throughout my life, at different points, from my late teens to my late forties just a year or two ago, I would turn to those means to escape from a terror I could not understand. Over the years until very recently these attempts to escape were met with mockery, ridicule, cold dismissal and extreme criticism. The general medical view appeared to be that I was 'attention-seeking', and therefore not seriously contemplating or capable of suicide. It still baffles me why anyone could believe that anyone would want the sort of dismissive attention that the general medical profession usually gives you after failed suicide attempts. My over-riding memory after so-called attempts was always deep despair and regret that I had failed to blot out the awfulness of my life. This combined with the shame, self-disgust and guilt that overwhelmed me, makes me wonder now why I still did it over and over again. The urge afterwards was always to run away and hide, something else that took over me frequently in times of anguish.

Yet until four years ago I had not actually hurt myself physically and deliberately by cutting. Then suddenly I began to experience overwhelming urges to cut myself with razors, knives or anything sharp and pointed enough to cause me sufficient pain to block out the inner pain and turmoil that was driving me mad inside.

A flood of recovered memories of years of sexual and emotional abuse by my father, starting from when I was as young as four, was the catalyst for my 'cutting'. Time after time I tried to blot away the 'horridness' inside me which to this day feels as scary as it did then; as well, as then, there seemed to be no relief from it. Until that is the day when I suddenly found that by cutting, scratching, tearing or stabbing with knives, scissors, razors, anything – I could momentarily blot out the hurt inside of me. My cuts dug anywhere but especially in those very private places where the pain and the memory is the worst.

It felt that by concentrating very intensely on creating this other hurt I was able to blot out the deeper and more terrible pain: the relief was only momentary, but so, so welcome. For that very brief time I felt in control and had gained some temporary release from the constant jangling tension, terrifying panic and searing pain inside my head and body.

For more than two years I successfully self-injured in secret and managed to hide my wounds and scars. Then one day I was 'found out' by a very understanding GP who treated me with kindness and patience. Sadly though his best intentions for my care led me to stay on a psychiatric unit where unfortunately the staff responded in a much less empathic way and at times openly critical manner. The system in this unit for dealing with high-risk patients was to place them under constant supervision.

Forcible restraint was their usual answer to any attempt to self-harm and their only method of trying to prevent my urges was to occupy me with constant activities; if all these failed and I succeeded in evading their ever watchful eye to hurt myself, then I would be given a very stern and at times very angry telling off. Somehow though this never deterred me, instead it just seemed to increase my need and determination to hurt myself; it was as if once the urge was there I had to do it come what may.

The turning point came during that spell of hospitalisation when my psychologist ever so gently asked me why I had needed to hurt myself; as she held my hand and listened I was able to slowly tell her. From then on, and with the help of my GP, she devised a pattern whereby I gradually felt able to seek my GP's help at times when the distress was intense and overwhelming. The very first time I summoned the courage to make that call to my GP he responded immediately and was full of praise that I had been able to do so. I still remember how kind he was that day, how he sat and listened without condemning, but really seemed to understand. How reassured and suddenly safe I felt when he offered me a cup of tea in his surgery.

There hasn't always been success since then – at times the urge would totally overwhelm me, but I never lost the support and encouragement of my GP and psychologist. They helped me to recognise the trigger points for these urges. Times when I was feeling panicky or 'out of this world'; when the urge to run was overwhelming; times when the memories of my past abuse were particularly vivid and real and accompanied by my screams of terror; if I was alone, frightened, in pain or desperately needing comfort; when I yearned to cry but couldn't; when I felt totally worthless, unvalued and the future looked bleak; but especially when I felt threatened and in danger. Together we explored where these urges came from and talked of how I could divert the pain away from myself.

A suggestion by my psychologist to keep a diary as a way of me broaching previously unspoken thoughts, feelings and memories, proved to be another major turning point for me. Writing has helped me enormously since; those early jottings down evolved into poems that tumbled out in a torrent of blunt and hurt words.

Then as I wrote more I began to read and started looking for articles about others who had suffered similar abuse to me. One book had a particular impact on me, *Breaking Free: Help for Survivors of Child Sexual Abuse*, by psychologists Carolyn Ainscough and Kay Toon (2000). It made me realise that I was not alone in experiencing all my frightening panics and weird symptoms that I had once thought were just me going mad.

For so much of my life I had felt so lonely and thought that no-one really understood or believed me. Now I had hope and understanding and I finally began to believe that the memories might one day fade a little. But what above all else has helped me was when people, such as my GP and psychologist, asked me what would help me, instead of them telling me what they thought would be best for me.

As the months, then years, went on and people have helped me to be able to ask for help when I most needed it, and as the times increased when I was able to overcome the urges, I gradually came to realise that I was winning through. Of course there are hiccups, times when the memories were triggered again and the urge returned as strong as ever before and I would feel out of control again. But now nearly two years after I last succumbed to the urge and realising that any sensation of needing to hurt myself is very infrequent, I am finally looking to the future with hope. As my memories begin to fade a little I now know that it has helped me to talk when the support was right.

Jill 2: Observations from case study

Did you notice that at times between her late teens and late forties Jill self-harmed in various ways to escape from a feeling of dread that she could not make sense of, yet didn't start cutting until she was flooded with memories of years of sexual and emotional abuse by her father from a very young age? Did you observe how cutting temporarily brought relief from the awful hurt she felt inside, and how she managed to keep the behaviour a secret for two years? What about the accusations from the general medical profession that she was attention seeking and the punitive treatment she experienced while in 'psychiatric care'? Did you note that a caring response from her psychologist was what started to turn things around for her? How her psychologist held her hand and sensitively enquired why she needed to hurt herself? And how with support from the psychologist and validation from her concerned GP, she slowly started to control the urges to self-injure? Furthermore, that by keeping a diary, it enabled her to express the unspoken – her memories, thoughts and emotions, and being asked what she needed, rather than told what was best for her, brought solace and healing? What stuck out most in your mind from reading Jill's case study?

Case study 6.3: Linda

Linda's story highlights yet again how self-injury served as a coping strategy for keeping intolerable memories out of conscious awareness.

One doll and a blanket were my only sources of comfort as a child. There was no love, no laughter, no fun. The only feeling I can remember experiencing was one of fear – fear of my father because of the hell he put me through. Physical beatings, sexual intercourse, oral and anal sex were part of my everyday existence.

Night after night I would lie awake in my bed dreading the sound of those all too familiar footsteps on the stairs. The stench of his stale tobacco and body odour made me want to heave. I prayed the bed would swallow me up and save me from the unbearable pain. As he carried out his despicable and depraved acts he told me he loved me, and what he was doing was OK. I had no reason to disbelieve him – after all he was my Dad.

As if this wasn't enough to endure, he also allowed his friends to abuse me. He totally ignored my desperate pleas for help, encouraging his friends to have oral and anal sex with me. There were many times when I just wished I was dead.

I wasn't allowed to invite any friends to the house in case I told them what he was doing. If I protested he would run a bath of freezing cold water and force me to get into it naked. He would then hold me under the water until I submitted to his perverted desires.

I will never understand why my mother didn't stop him. Often I would scream out in terror, but all she did was stand and watch, or walk away.

When I was six the pain became too much to bear. I hit the wall in my bedroom with my fist. Strangely, this brought a little bit of relief. After that I began hurting myself in various ways. Often I was absent from school due to bruises from the physical abuse my father subjected me to. When I did attend I would deliberately fall off apparatus in the gymnasium; intentionally shut my fingers in doors or fall over in the playground. This brought caring, love and attention, all the things I never received at home.

I grew up feeling very confused and wondering who I really was. When I reached my teens I began drinking heavily, and hurting myself became part of my everyday life. I would cut and burn myself, take tablets and lash out at anyone, and anything.

When I was fifteen my Dad got me pregnant and I gave birth to twins – a boy and a girl. Tragically my little girl died at birth due to a deformity, but my son was a beautiful and healthy baby. I went to stay with friends, and one day, when I had popped out, my father came and took my son away. The anger, guilt, and pain I felt is impossible to describe. It felt as if he had stolen the only precious thing I had ever had in my life, and I have never seen my son again to this day. After this, the emotional pain overwhelmed me and I couldn't stop self-harming. I cut my wrists, drank myself into a stupor and took pills.

I ended up in a psychiatric unit where I received little sympathy or understanding. I could not talk about the traumas I had experienced, and was treated for depression.

On occasions my wounds needed stitching, and I would be admitted to an Accident and Emergency Department. Here too there was lack of sympathy or concern. I was told to stop wasting staff time, or that I was occupying a bed that someone else could be using. Nobody ever attempted to stop my self-harming.

From the hospital I was referred to a hostel. Here I made friends with one of the male residents, only to be raped by him and three of his friends when we were out one evening. This so called friend threatened to kill me if I ever told anyone what he and his friends had done.

As the pain grew and grew inside me, the need to self-harm increased. I began to realise that every time I hurt myself, I was desperately trying to cut out all the bad bits that were buried inside me – most of all I wanted to rid myself of my father.

In 1982 I got married, but the marriage broke down after two years. I felt a complete failure, and this led to me drinking and cutting my wrists again. Consumed with anger and guilt, and completely intoxicated, I directed my rage at my husband by trying to kill him with a knife. However, in my inebriated state, I failed to even scratch him, and instead was pushed down the stairs and ended up in hospital. I was very lucky to survive this traumatic experience.

In 1989 I married again. I have two children, a little boy aged two, and a little girl aged four. The first two years of the marriage were great, but following the birth of my son things started going wrong again. When he was just three months old I tried to suffocate him. Post-natal depression was diagnosed, but I soon realised that it was not this at all – it was the emotional pain I was in due to the traumas I had suffered at the hands of my father and others. For over twenty years all these horrific memories had been pushed into the dark recesses of my mind, but somehow the birth of my son rekindled some of these unbearable and terrifying memories. This made me realise that I had survived the physical pain but the time had come to try and survive the emotional anguish.

I now see a counsellor, but it took me two years to find the right help for me. My counsellor is an abuse survivor, and it's helpful because she understands the feelings that engulf me and lead me to self-harm.

I am still trying to come to terms with, and make sense of the past. I still self-harm as a way of coping and surviving. The thought of my mother's behaviour only adds fuel to the cauldron of seething emotions that have been eating away inside me for so many years. My father died in the seventies, and I hoped that all the pain and suffering he put me through would die with him. Sadly, this hasn't happened yet.

Knowing how difficult it has been for me to get the right help, and how long it has taken, I felt I wanted to help others like myself, so I have started a penfriend network for other people who self-harm. The aim is to fill the gap of loneliness and isolation that I experienced over the years. I also offer a list of resources, which is updated regularly. This is sent to survivors, like myself, so they can access help and support quickly. I would like to see information made more readily available, as I feel certain this would encourage other women to seek the help they need and deserve.

Observations from Linda's case study

Did you notice the indescribable catalogue of childhood and adult traumatic experiences and losses that Linda has suffered? Did you observe that she started self-harming when she was only six, and how it progressed to heavy drinking, swallowing pills, and cutting and burning in her teens? What about the dreadful sense of betrayal from both parents, how must it have felt having no one to turn to, no way of escaping, no one to protect her, no one to care for, or about her? Moreover, what about the accusations of time wasting and feelings of total rejection she felt when she sought medical help for her injuries, and the lack of compassion she experienced while in 'psychiatric care'? Did you spot that the birth of her son reawakened intolerable and petrifying memories that she had managed to keep at bay for over 20 years, or that self-injury was a desperate attempt to 'cut out' the 'badness' she felt inside – the memories, the pain of what her father subjected her to? Furthermore, did you notice how long it took her to get the help she needed? What stuck out most in your mind from reading Linda's case study?

An interview with Sharon

Sharon is forty-five. She lives in the North of England, is married, and has three grown up daughters, all of whom have recently left home. Five years ago, she started recovering traumatic childhood memories – triggered by the stature, smell, and clothing of a man standing behind her at the checkout of a supermarket. In a state of terror, she ran out of the supermarket leaving her shopping on the conveyor belt. This incident not only triggered a flood of horrific memories, it triggered her to self-injure as a way of coping with them. She sought counselling after a year of struggling with the problem on her own.

Sharon always self-injures in private, and only seeks treatment for her wounds if they are severe. Initially, she cut herself on various parts of her body, but lately she has turned to burning. Sharon has been in therapy for four years. She kindly agreed to be interviewed in the hope that it would enable others to see that with the right kind of help and support, it is possible to start letting go of self-injury.

The extract that follows is from a taped transcript of our interview.

JAN: Can you say a little bit about the first time you hurt yourself?

SHARON: The first time I self-injured I had an overwhelming need to cut myself – I searched the house and garage for something to do it with and remembered that I'd recently bought a craft knife to cut my own stencils with. I remember I was a bit scared at first, but then made a small incision at the top of my left arm and the relief was instantaneous. I suppose if I hadn't got any benefit after that first time, I wouldn't have done it again.

JAN: What do you think prompted you to self-injure – had you heard about it?

SHARON: I read a story in a magazine about a woman who self-injured, and I suppose that was what planted the seed. I never admitted to anyone, including myself, that I was copying somebody else. I guess it didn't feel like that the first time I did it. It became solely mine, my way of coping.

JAN: Can you say something about your most recent episode of self-injury . . . was it planned, for example?

SHARON: The last time I self-injured was about six weeks ago, so I have a job to remember exactly whether it was planned or not. Because I had changed from cutting to burning, every time I lit a cigarette there was the potential to self-injure, and there was less need to plan it because there was no mess to clear up.

JAN: Were you aware of any particular event or situation that triggered the need to self-injure?

SHARON: I was feeling scared and overwhelmed by memories of my childhood. I had recently spoken of them to my therapist and wished that I hadn't. There was a feeling that if I burnt myself the thoughts that were racing around in my brain, the resulting feelings would stop, and they did temporarily.

JAN: Can you remember what you were thinking to yourself at the time?

SHARON: Yes – mostly I was thinking things like 'You shouldn't have said anything, you shouldn't have made a fuss; she'll think I'm a horrible person. What if she gives up on me? My Dad would kill me if he knew I'd told – stuff like that.'

JAN: Some people say they use various distraction techniques to try to delay, or stop themselves self-injuring – like going on the Internet, getting out of the house, holding an ice cube, ringing a friend or their therapist, for instance. Were you able to try anything to distract yourself?

SHARON: I think there was a feeling of resignation that I was going to self-injure – like there was an inevitability about it, like I'm not sure I really want to do this but I've got to do it anyway. I did ring my therapist but I had already injured myself. I do think that it helped me not hurt any further though.

JAN: How were you feeling just before you self-injured?

SHARON: Prior to self-injuring, my head was racing with thoughts but the rest of me felt numb, so consequently when I burnt myself the pain was minimal. It was like being two different people – my mind on one side – my body on the other, like the injury I was causing myself was separate from me. I was feeling afraid and overwhelmed prior to self-injuring and the need was to block out the emotional pain and numb out. Although I felt compelled to self-injure, I still felt very much in control of what I was doing.

JAN: How did you know when to stop?

SHARON: On this occasion, as is mostly the case, I stopped when I sensed I'd done enough. I think my body sends its own signal out when I've injured myself enough.

JAN: How did you feel after self-injuring?

SHARON: I was a lot calmer. I still needed to make contact with my therapist but my head was a lot less full. I wasn't shocked by what I had done but there was a sense of satisfaction that I had once again controlled my emotions.

JAN: Was it necessary for you to seek treatment for your injuries?

SHARON: No, not on this occasion. I found the resulting blisters from the burns satisfying, like the build up of fluid was my emotions that could be got rid of by popping them.

JAN: Can you explain what you see as the advantages of self-injury?

SHARON: Self-injury is a sure-fire way of controlling my emotions so they don't overwhelm me. It's something I do to myself, for myself, and it gives me a sense of control.

JAN: Can you see any disadvantages?

SHARON: My self-injury has left me with permanent scars. By relying on it to control my emotions, I have found it difficult to express my emotions in a more healthy way. It is a difficult thing to give up, yet I am trying to do just that.

JAN: Would you like to stop self-injury?

SHARON: More and more now I want to stop self-injuring. I have used it in the past to punish myself, but the need to self-punish is much less now.

JAN: Can you say what you think you would gain by stopping?

SHARON: I would hope to express my emotions more assertively – to feel better about myself. To be free of the compulsion to self-injure – to feel I have a choice about how I express myself.

JAN: What do you think you would lose by stopping?

SHARON: I would have feared losing control. However, this fear isn't nearly as strong now and I don't see it as a loss. I am able to let go of it, the more assertive I become.

JAN: Self-injury is often described as addictive. What are your views about this?

SHARON: I think self-injury, like anything you habitually do can become addictive. Whether it's the chemical high you get when you injure your body, or the sense of control, or the sense of release from emotional pain that results, I think you can become addicted to the effect.

JAN: You mentioned earlier that it is six weeks since you last injured yourself. That's a great achievement. Has anything helped you in particular?

SHARON: Talking to my therapist who listened and believed, and who showed me warmth was wonderful. Making connections between my childhood and my behaviour now, and building up my self-esteem helped enormously. To be able to trust my therapist who was empathic and non-judgemental with my darkest secrets, to feel safe and protected, to not be forced to give up my self-injury until I felt I could, all this is helping me leave self-injury behind. Despite the initial setback, sharing my painful secrets with my therapist, after holding on to them for some 40 years, has helped tremendously. It has left me feeling so much lighter and freer. What has helped more than anything is that after four years of therapy I have finally found my voice.

JAN: Thank you so much for talking with me Sharon. I think what you have said will give hope and inspiration to others – it certainly has to me.

Observations from the interview with Sharon

Did you notice that Sharon started recovering memories of abuse when she was aged 40, that a man she stood next to at a supermarket checkout was responsible for triggering the memories, and that she started self-injuring as a way to cope with the memories? Did you observe that she tried to cope for a year before seeking therapy, or that she has been in therapy for four years? Did you take in that the first time she cut herself brought instant relief from her emotional pain, and how it now serves as a way of controlling her emotions so they don't overwhelm her? What about how she got the idea of self-injury from a magazine story – did that ring alarm bells? Did you detect the reason for her most recent episode of self-injury – being overwhelmed by memories of her childhood, disclosing the memories to her therapist, and fear that her therapist might abandon her? What about the fact that she didn't contact her therapist until after she had cut herself – do you think if she had phoned before, it might have prevented her harming herself? Did you notice the sense of numbness, the minimal pain, and feeling as if she was two different people prior to self-injuring?

You may be wondering why I asked Sharon whether she wanted to stop hurting herself? Some people don't, or are not ready, which is important information for therapists to know. You may also be pondering why I asked her about the gains and losses of self-injury? This can be useful for clients to consider, because with most gains an element of loss is involved. Did you notice Sharon mentions becoming addicted to the effect from self-injury? Lastly, did you pinpoint what helped Sharon stay free of self-injury for six weeks, or notice that she sees learning to articulate her emotions more assertively as an important to factor healing from self-injury? What stuck out most in your mind from Sharon's interview?

The dilemma of suspecting yet not knowing

This touching poem by Sinead illustrates the agony people go through when they have strong suspicions that they have suffered abused, without having clears memories or concrete evidence to support their suspicions.

Little girl

What do you want little girl?
Just stop pestering me.
I won't listen to your lies
They might be true you see.

Liar, liar, pants on fire
That's not how I feel.
Just because you say so
Doesn't make it real.

Cry baby, 'fraidy cat
Stay away from me.
I don't want to feel your pain
Or touch your misery.

Just shut your mouth up little girl,
There's no one you can tell.
Where's your proof little girl?
Well, go on, tell me . . . well?

And if I thought you might be right,
Well, what would that achieve?
I couldn't say with certainty
'I really do believe'.

And if I did, and someone said,
'My God that just can't be!'
How do I explain to them
What I myself can't see?

I'm told that if I reach out
And let me hold your hand,
Maybe, we together
Could try to understand.

That maybe, if I touch you
Then you could touch me too.
And maybe, I could see
That you are me and I am you.

And when you speak of things
That I don't want to hear,
Maybe I should listen
And face up to my fear.

So, I'll try not to hurt you little girl
Go on, scream and yell.
I need for you to be with me
So together we can tell.

Additional support

As demonstrated, recovering memories of child abuse can be acutely distressing for clients and additional support may be required at this very difficult time (extra sessions; permission to telephone, email, or text; a list of supportive people or organisations to contact). As a coping strategy to avoid dealing with the painful memories or in a desperate attempt to dissociate from them (prevent them from entering conscious awareness) self-injury may escalate. Pacing of therapy sessions is critical in this situation – the client needs to stay safe within the boundaries of the 'bearable'.

The final words on the topic of recovering memories come from author and psychotherapist, Phil Mollon (1996) who concisely and eloquently sums up my thoughts:

> I believe it is misleading to suggest (as much of the FMS literature does) that the idea of being abused as a child can be a comforting solution to mental distress. In my experience recovered memories do not make people feel better – at least not initially. Approaching

a traumatic memory may put a person in a state of terror, with disorientation and temporary psychosis. It may provoke extreme self-harm and suicidal acts, especially cutting . . . (p.80)

Not all people that self-injure have been abused

Although well documented in the self-injury and trauma literature that child abuse features in the history of many people self-injure, as mentioned in Chapter 2, child abuse does not signify the only reason. It is also important not to assume that everyone who has suffered child abuse will automatically turn to self-injury as a way of coping. There are numerous other factors involved, for example, the level of support available at the time of the abuse (from the non-abusing parent, grandparents, friends, and teachers, etc.), the degree of secrecy involved around the abuse, the personality of the survivor, and their position in the family. Further, different individuals develop their own unique coping strategies. For instance, in a family where three girls suffered child abuse, one might turn to alcohol to cope; another might turn to self-injury, while one might appear on the surface to have come through the experience unscathed.

An overview of the reasons for self-injury

The reasons why people turn to self-injury are intricate and multi-faceted. Predisposing factors that may trigger the act identified through my work and research include:

- Childhood traumas such as sexual abuse, physical abuse, emotional abuse, rape, torture, neglect, and abandonment.
- Recovered memories of abuse, disclosures of abuse not believed or brushed aside, keeping the abuse a secret.
- Suffering rape as an adult.
- Loss of a primary caregiver through death, divorce, or separation.

- Having emotionally absent parents, feeling unsupported by or 'invisible' to loved ones, or lack of secure attachments.
- Bullying, harassment, abuse of power, a lack of control over one's life, feeling powerless or trapped, exposure to domestic violence (being subjected to, or witness to).
- Growing up in a chaotic/unpredictable family environment, e.g. parent with alcohol or substance misuse problems or mental health problems in a family member.
- Communication deficiencies in the family, e.g. unspoken family rules – 'not allowed' to cry or express feelings and emotions, particularly negative emotions.
- Social marginalisation, stigmatisation, and social exclusion, e.g. being homeless, gay or lesbian, a refugee/asylum seeker, belonging to an ethnic minority, or being labelled with a mental illness.
- Gender identity issues and conflicts.
- Being forced into marriage against one's will.
- Being raised in the care system or by foster parents; being adopted.
- Role reversal in the parent-child relationship (the 'parentified' child), i.e. the child is expected to 'become' the parent in terms of responsibilities, thus requiring the child to act as a buddy, big sister, counsellor, or confidante.
- Self-injury contagion, e.g. copying friends, family members, inpatients in psychiatric care, or inmates in institutional settings such as prisons or young offenders' institutions.
- The stress of coping with imprisonment.
- Low self-esteem because of exposure to traumatic events, stressful life experiences, and/or invalidation, or rooted in fear and insecurity.
- Pressure to achieve (from oneself and/or others), perfectionism, exam stress and sleep deprivation. Not coming up to one's own, one's parents, or society's expectations – never feeling intelligent enough, successful enough, wealthy enough, or good enough.
- Negative core beliefs.

Negative core beliefs and self-injury

As seen clearly throughout this book, and this chapter, many people who self-injure hold deeply embedded negative core beliefs about themselves. Negative core beliefs are flawed beliefs that are swallowed whole (often in childhood) and become interpreted as the 'absolute truth' about oneself. A handful of examples of negative core beliefs noted from the respondents' testimonies include:

- 'I am worthless'
- 'I don't deserve'
- 'I am not good enough'
- 'I was a mistake'
- 'I shouldn't be here'
- 'I am bad'
- 'I am evil'.

These negative core beliefs may lead to establishing a subset of negative self-beliefs such as:

- I am incompetent, inadequate, invisible, a nothing, unlovable, unacceptable.
- I am defective, imperfect, inferior.
- I am different, I don't fit in, I don't belong, there's something wrong with me.
- I don't count, I never get anything right, I can never fix anything, I'll always be the underdog, I'm a loser.

Strongly held beliefs such as these lead to low self-esteem, and feelings of self-dislike, self-hate and self-loathing. They can also lead to acute emotional distress, which in turn can motivate some people to self-injure. To illustrate how low self-esteem, not feeling of worth, and not liking oneself can contribute to self-harm, let us look behind the glamour, and public image of a much loved, much admired, much talked about and sadly missed woman who is known throughout the world.

Case study 6.4: Princess Diana speaks out about self-injury (BBC, 1997)

In 1995, the previously taboo and private subject of self-injury suddenly became a very public issue when, prior to her tragic and untimely death on 31 August 1997, Princess Diana, admitted in her legendary BBC *Panorama* interview that she had hurt her arms and legs. Prompted by interviewer Martin Bashir, she courageously confessed to the world, that 'you have so much pain inside yourself that you try and hurt yourself on the outside because you want help.' Reasons she gave for hurting herself included not liking herself; feeling 'ashamed' because she could not 'cope with the pressures', and not feeling listened to. She also intimated that it was a non-verbal way of communicating her anguish – in other words, a 'silent' cry for help.

Diana also revealed in the interview that, albeit it out of character, she experienced post-natal depression after the birth of William, at which time she was 'openly tearful'; became labelled 'unstable' and 'mentally unbalanced' – tags that regrettably she felt stuck to her 'on and off over the years.' She talked too about suffering for several years from the eating disorder bulimia (bingeing and vomiting) which she described as being 'like a secret disease', and which she considered was due to having low self-esteem and not believing she was a person of worth or value. She described what she got out of her 'eating binges' as a temporary feeling of comfort – 'like having a pair of arms around you', but how this quickly changed into self-disgust 'at the bloatedness of your stomach' accompanied by a need to 'bring it all up again.' It served as an escape mechanism, which worked for her at that time.

Cause and effect

It seems that the strain of endeavouring to present a public image of 'OK-ness' and trying to hold everything together so as not to dishearten the public exacted a high toll on Diana, especially when behind closed doors problems in her marriage were causing stress and anxiety.

What Diana needed

Diana admits that she was crying out for help, perhaps in the only way she knew how, via hurting herself and her eating distress. However, what those around her saw, or chose to see, were the behavioural manifestations of Diana's distress, not the cause of it. They failed to acknowledge the pain caused by the problems in her marriage, of not having time and space to adapt to her numerous roles, of feeling unsupported and longing for human comfort (praise, validation, kind words, a hug or cuddle), some of which she got from an adoring public, but not from those who she most wanted it from.

Diana's motivations for hurting herself echo those of many other people whose words you will read in this book – low self-esteem, not feeling of value, not liking herself, intense emotional pain, feeling unable to cope, shame, and not feeling heard.

Negative self-beliefs and perfectionism

Negative self-beliefs distort self-perception, and can lead to perfectionist thinking, for example, 'if I never make a mistake, if I am always compliant, if I put everyone else's needs before my own, and if I don't say "no" to other people's requests, perhaps people will love and approve of me, or maybe they will stop criticising or judging me.' Perfectionism is a common trait found among people that self-injure and those with eating disorders.

There's nothing wrong with holding high principles, and wanting to perform one's best is natural and healthy. However, when people start berating themselves for making a simple mistake, or make themselves sick with worry by trying to be perfect at all things, or by attempting to be all things to all people, that's stepping into the unhealthy perfectionism arena. Unhealthy perfectionism can exact a high price on physical and emotional wellbeing, as well as taking a toll on self-esteem if high standards set for oneself are not met. Perfectionists often think in black and white terms, either something is right or wrong, flawless or a failure – there's no middle ground or room for shades of grey.

Parents or primary caregivers often set the stage for the direction in which a child's perfectionist tendencies take. For example, children raised in a critical and judgemental environment by parents who overtly or covertly convey the message to a child that he or she is not good enough, where praise and validation is lacking, or where siblings are openly compared with statements such as 'Why can't you be more like your sister?', or 'Why can't you be brainy like your brother?' can set up the beliefs that 'he/she is better than me', 'she/he is more lovable than me', or that 'nothing I ever do is good enough'.

Believing that 'only perfect is good enough' can motivate a constant striving to get things 101% right, or to pushing oneself harder and harder, in the hope that it will bring appreciation, praise, love and acceptance.

In truth, there's no such thing as perfection – it is in the eye of the beholder. To err is to be human and making mistakes makes people real. Sadly, however, to those with deeply ingrained unhealthy perfectionist traits, it rarely or never occurs to them that there is another way of thinking or behaving, and people often need professional help to set them on the path to freedom from detrimental perfectionism.

Changing negative core beliefs and building self-worth

> We can secure other people's approval, if we do right and try hard; but our own is worth a hundred of it.
>
> —*Mark Twain*

The first step to change is becoming aware of negative core beliefs, the second is to challenge and dispute them and to replace them with more realistic beliefs, the final step is to start believing that one is a person of worth, without being dependent on outside approval. Many people find Cognitive Behavioural Therapy (CBT) helpful for recognising and changing flawed self-beliefs, and developing a healthier self-concept.

(See Chapter 12 for a brief description of CBT.)

> No one can make you feel inferior without your consent.
> —*Eleanor Roosevelt*

Case study 6.5: Tacita

In the final case study in this chapter, the consequences of never feeling good enough are clearly evident. Several other beliefs that stem from childhood are also apparent, namely – Don't be disobedient – Don't ask – Don't speak – Don't have an opinion – Don't show emotions – Don't cry – Be strong – Be perfect.

I am the oldest of three children and was raised with a strict Catholic upbringing. I was taught to never be disobedient, never ask for anything or have my own voice or say in any matter, and to be a brave soldier and never cry for anything, even if I was hurt. My father was my world – I lived for him, lived to please him, and always strove to do my best for him; it was expected. I was a straight-A student and played sports but the effort I put out was never good enough for my dad. There was always room for improvement, always that extra push to be an even better player and scholar.

When I was in eighth grade, my parents announced their pending divorce. None of us had a clue it was coming . . . my parents always seemed ok; they weren't affectionate at all towards each other but they did ok. When the announcement was made to us, I could only sit there in shock. My siblings cried but I couldn't. I felt as if I had lost everything, that I was the cause of everything. I felt that it was my fault, that I hadn't been a good enough daughter, a good enough student, or a good enough anything for my parents.

By the end of that summer, things got out of control at home. My parents started fighting all the time in front of us. They would fight over money, dinners, and my siblings and me. Each time they fought, it drove the nail a little deeper into the coffin of emotion and self-hatred that I had buried in my heart. My dad became horrible to live with and I grew to despise him.

Being a 'goody goody' was no longer an option for me and I slowly began to sabotage that reputation. I started smoking cigarettes even though I abhorred the taste and smell of them. At some point in my freshman year I started ed [eating disorder] behaviour but not an ed [eating disorder]. This wasn't for weight control; it was for control over myself, punishment for slowly and painfully becoming a 'nothing', being unable to fix anything. This also gave me a satisfaction that I could do something that no one else around me did.

I also started cutting around this time. The cutting started with my first attempt to kill myself. I remember how good it felt that first time . . . to just slowly cut deeper and deeper and feel the rush of emotion wash out with the blood. After that first time I was so calm, it was incredible. I was even able to go down to the dinner table and act like I hadn't just cut into my arm. I somehow realised that this was a great way to let go of some steam since I never talked about what was going on inside of me and rarely showed negative emotion. I started cutting a lot and carried instruments on my person at all times. Good grades were a thing of the past and I no longer cared about studying or doing my best . . . there was no such thing as 'my best' anymore . . . there was no 'me'.

Dad moved out near the end of my sophomore year and that was the biggest relief and sadness mixed into one big emotion. My bad behaviours continued into my senior year. I was lost in the darkness of self-destruction and hatred and was miserable.

I met my husband at work while I was still a senior in high school. We moved in together a few months after I graduated from high school and got married when I was 20. Things were good during this period . . . I worked two jobs and was happy with my life. Even though there was this somewhat happier period there was also something missing in my marriage . . . trust.

A few months after we got married, I wanted a child; some-one else to love and who would love me back. My first child was born the following summer and I enthusiastically delved into trying to be the best parent for my son along with trying to be the best at my full-time job. By spring, my aspirations of being a wonderful parent faltered and I began realising that I was failing to be a super mom, wife, and exemplary worker; my best was once again not good enough. Something was missing in me and I wasn't quite sure what. I started my first real diet that spring after comments from my husband and others about my higher level of weight and finally began to excel in something . . . weight loss. This became my new obsession . . . losing weight and again doing something that no one else had the power to do. I was failing so miserably in all the other aspects of my life and this was something that I had control over.

I started seeing a therapist (unbeknownst to my husband) and instead of things getting better, they got worse. I couldn't communicate and didn't understand how to talk about what was going on inside. Many of my sessions revolved around the weather instead of dealing with things and I would often take breaks from therapy for months at a time due to frustration with myself and my therapist. Everything from the past had come rushing back and I couldn't stop it. The SI came back with a vengeance on top of a now full-blown eating disorder. SI was a part of my nightly routine and became an addiction much worse than the teen years. I became suicidal and was lost in a haze of self-destruction which warranted a two week psych [psychiatric] hospital stay. Approximately three months after leaving the hospital, I was even worse with the ed behaviour, this time adding laxative abuse to restricting. My husband threatened to leave with my son if I didn't enter another psych hospital, so I did time again on the psych ward, this time for a full month. I gained weight but again never talked to anyone about what was going on . . . I couldn't.

It's been nine years since my last hospitalisation. Currently, I'm not in therapy and am in recovery from the eating disorder though the thoughts and mindset are often still there. SI still plays a rather active role in my life and is a well-guarded secret. It's what's kept me alive and going through many changes in my life and I think it will keep me through many more.

Key points

- Not everyone who has suffered child abuse self-injures, nor has everyone who self-injures suffered child abuse. The reasons why people turn to self-injury are intricate and multi-faceted. There are numerous predisposing factors that motivate self-injury.
- Many people who self-injure hold deeply embedded negative core beliefs about themselves. Perfectionism is also a common trait, which may stem from the belief that nothing I ever do will be good enough. These beliefs can lead to low self-esteem, feelings of self-dislike, self-loathing, self-hate, and worthlessness, which in turn may ignite the need to self-injure.
- Child abuse provides fertile ground for the development of a range of adverse effects that can impede healthy adult functioning.
- Not being believed when abuse is disclosed by a child (particularly if the person confided in is a mother or other close relative) can have a profound psychological impact. Mothers choose not to believe for various reasons.
- Children don't speak out about abuse for a number of reasons.
- Breaking the silence of abuse to someone who is willing to listen and believe is empowering.
- The notion that memories of child abuse can be forgotten, and then years later be remembered, sparked a bitter debate in the early 1990s, and instigated the formation of The False Memory Syndrome Foundation (FMSF), and The British False Memory Society (BFMS).

- Recovering memories of child abuse can be acutely distressing for clients and self-injury may escalate for a period while memories are being processed. Additional support may be needed at this difficult time, and pacing of sessions to enable clients to stay safe within the boundaries of the 'bearable' is critical.

Chapter 7

The cycle of self-injury and the eight Cs of self-injury

··

SI is like the friend
your parents don't want you to
have. You love it because it makes
you feel better and able to cope
with life. It makes you feel
good while at the same time it's
destroying you.

In the first section of this chapter, the cyclical nature of self-injury is discussed as presented in Figure 7.1 (The cycle of self-injury). Each point in the cycle is examined, and the point at which things need to change to break the cycle is identified. The metaphor of a *raging inferno inside* employed to describe the cycle of self-injury was the result of an image that sprung to mind when I was grappling to make sense of self-injury many years ago. Since its first appearance in *Healing the Hurt Within,* 1st edition (Sutton, 1999) the diagram has been updated several times to facilitate my developing understanding of self-injury. Important to bear in mind, however, is that those who self-injure are individuals, thus their pattern of self-injury may not follow one 'typical route'.

In the second part of this chapter, a further diagram is presented (Figure 7.2, eight Cs of self-injury). This encapsulates eight motivations and meanings of self-injury identified through my research.

The Cycle of Self-Injury

Point A: Mental anguish Point B: Emotional engulfment

The individual may be plagued by intrusive or unacceptable thoughts, images, flashbacks, nightmares, 'body memories' (somatic sensations) of traumatic events, or burdened by negative self-beliefs, for example, 'I'm bad, evil, worthless, a waste of space, everything is my fault, I don't deserve.' Trapped inside, the mental anguish begins to cause internal chaos. **A 'fire' starts smouldering.**

The smouldering fire sparks powerful feelings and emotions, which trigger off 'a raging inferno inside'. These powerful feelings and emotions also remain trapped inside. The individual starts to feel frightened, desperate, about to explode, or dissociated ('uncomfortably numb'/feels nothing).

Point F: The grief reaction

The reality of the individual's actions starts to sink in. Shame, guilt, self-disgust or self-hate may rekindle the smouldering embers. Because the underlying issues (the internal chaos) remain locked up inside and unresolved, the cycle continues unless change is effected at Point A.

Point C: Panic stations

The raging inferno gathers momentum. The individual feels out of control, or **too** numb (detached, distant, disconnected), and experiences a compelling urge to self-injure.

Point E: Feel better/different

With the raging inferno under control, the individual temporarily experiences:
- Relief from tension, anxiety, and pent-up emotions such as fear, anger, or frustration
- A feeling of euphoria, numbness or detachment (dissociation)
- A sense of feeling more alive, more real, more grounded in reality − or, if the function was self-punishment − a degree of satisfaction.

Generally, the individual feels calmer, more in control, 'comfortably numb', and can think more clearly. In other words, self-injury appears to reduce the individual's level of emotional and physiological arousal to a tolerable level, and the internal chaos is temporarily soothed. Thus, the physical injuries may seem a small price to pay to escape from the 'raging inferno inside'. Furthermore, following an episode of self-injury, some individuals report sleeping soundly – this is a rare occurrence for many.

Point D: Action stations

The individual self-injures, which extinguishes the raging inferno inside, or alleviates the feelings of alienation.

The act may be carried out in a state of:
- Awareness (the individual feels the pain)
- Partial awareness (the individual feels some pain)
- Non-awareness (the individual feels minimal or no pain [a dissociative state]).

The act may be motivated by:
- A need to release tension or anxiety
- A need to communicate acute emotional distress (to self/others)
- A need to feel pain (self-punish)
- A need to escape from emotional pain (enter a dissociated state)
- A need to end a dissociated state (feeling disconnected from oneself; feeling numb, empty or dead inside; or experiencing oneself or one's surroundings as unreal).
- A need to exert a sense of control over one's body
- A need to ward off suicidal thoughts.

Note: This list is by no means exhaustive.

Fig. 7.1: The cycle of self-injury.

Point A: Mental anguish

The individual may be plagued by intrusive or unacceptable thoughts, images, flashbacks, nightmares, 'body memories' (somatic memories) of traumatic events, or burdened by negative self-beliefs, for example, 'I'm bad, evil, worthless, a waste of space, everything is my fault, I don't deserve.' Trapped inside, the mental anguish begins to cause internal chaos.

> '[Self-Injury is] the only thing that can make me feel better and stop the bad thoughts in my head.'
>
> 'I get overwhelming thoughts of revenge.'
>
> 'I think: "I shouldn't do this", but "I must do this" almost always wins.'
>
> 'I get painful thoughts, repetitive thoughts and I know if I self-harm they will go away for a while.'

Self-view of people who self-injure

Many people that self-injure hold an extremely negative self-view, seeing themselves as intrinsically bad, defective, evil, worthless, or not good enough. Numerous also carry the belief that 'I don't deserve'. Additionally, self-criticism and perfectionism are common traits. A constant barrage of self-wounding and self-devaluing words can easily spark strong emotional arousal.

> 'Self injury "takes the evil out of me". I truly believe there is evil inside of me that needs to get out. I feel poisoned with the pain I have and this coping mechanism is what I've found that works best in taking away the pain.'
>
> 'I feel that I am a bad person and I need to be punished – and have to be punished.'

'Sometimes I have old voices saying I'm worthless, fat, ugly, bad, evil, stuff like that.'

'You stupid bitch. You're so pathetic, so hopeless . . . I'd basically say things like this to myself again and again until something would snap and I'd need to cut myself.'

Trauma triggers

'I experience major nightmares, flashbacks and body memories that don't help my self-harming.'

The following situations were identified by respondents as trauma triggers to self-injury:

- 'When I'm reminded about rape.'
- 'Remembering abuse.'
- 'Memories/flashbacks of abuse.'
- 'Any kind of abuse now.'
- 'When I can't cope with the past, or when it comes back to haunt me.'
- 'Unwanted sexual feelings.'

Flashbacks and 'body memories' (somatic sensations)

As mentioned, many people that self-injure are abuse survivors, and flashbacks (traumatic scenes from the past) and 'body memories' (somatic sensations) frequently plague abuse survivors' lives. Soma refers to the body. Flashbacks and body memories are hard to cope with – they can feel alarmingly real – as if the person has been transported back in time and the abuse is happening all over again (with all its associated feelings, emotions and imagery). They can leave people frozen to the spot, or feeling very small and childlike (as if they are that child again).

Flashbacks and body memories are fleeting states of remembered dissociated traumatic material; they can be triggered by anything that serves as a cue to the traumatic event – a smell, sound, taste, touch, voice, or song, for example, or by one's own thought processes.

They are experienced as traumatic snapshots, which may appear crystal clear or hazy, as a terrifying feeling (panic, dread, terror), or as physical pains or sensations in parts of the body associated with the memory or violation (numb breasts, legs, arms; or pelvic, vaginal, rectal, pain). Frequently flashbacks appear to be accompanied by headaches.

Flashbacks and body memories: the link to internal self-injury

'With the internal self-injury I am very aware of what triggers it . . . it's the flashbacks and not being able to handle them . . . I just want to cut them out of me . . .'

Several female Internet respondents reported injuring themselves internally as a response to severe and/or prolonged child abuse. However, it needs to be borne in mind that there is a huge amount of shame and embarrassment attached to internal self-injury, which is likely to deter people from reporting this particular form, thus it may be significantly underreported. One respondent reported that it's not easy to ask for medical help; another said she steered clear of seeking medical help because she can't cope with internal examinations.

Internal self-injury is used as a strategy for ending distressing flashbacks or body memories, and to make the awful feelings go away. Further, it may be used as a form of self-punishment in response to unwanted sexual thoughts, guilt or shame. Symbolically, it can be understood as an attempt to 'cut the horrific memories out'; 'cut "him" out of me'; 'cut out the bad things that happened there'; 'cut out the "bad" in me', or to cleanse the body and soul from contamination of the abuse.

'[Internal self-injury is] to get rid of the flashbacks/ memories – the whole body ones where I can feel everything . . . I just can't deal with those . . . and he told me if I hurt myself, he will hurt me less . . .'

'Internally I self injure to stop the flashbacks and memories . . . to get rid of the sensations that come with them that someone is sexually abusing me all over again.'

'When I self injure internally I am dissociated most of the time and feel very little . . . I just feel like I want him out – I want the pain to go away . . . but I am not aware of this . . . it's kind of like what do I do . . . you feel so helpless, you feel like you are tied down again and struggling but there is nothing you can do to stop him . . .'

Dissociation (mentioned in the above testimony) is discussed later in this chapter (see main heading *Breaking the cycle of self-injury*). The relationship between dissociation and self-injury is also discussed in Chapter 8 (Dissociation and self-injury), and Chapter 12 (Guidelines for those working with self-injury and related issues).

Dusty Miller, in her insightful book, *Women Who Hurt Themselves: A Book of Hope and Understanding,* presents an interesting concept which she coins 'Trauma Reenactment Syndrome' (TRS). She posits that 'TRS women do to their bodies something that represents what was done to them in childhood.' (1994:9)

Additional informative reading on the topic of 'body memories' are van der Kolk, B.A. (1994) 'The body keeps the score' and Rothschild, B. (2000) 'The body remembers' (see references).

Point B: Emotional engulfment

The smouldering fire sparks powerful feelings and emotions, which trigger off 'a raging inferno inside'. These powerful feelings and emotions also remain trapped inside. The individual starts to feel frightened, desperate, about to explode, or dissociated ('uncomfortably numb'/feels nothing).

> 'Sometimes pressure builds up, a bit like a shaken can of pop. It feels like there is no alternative but to self-injure to release the pressure.'
>
> 'I feel like I don't know what to do anymore. I feel very overwhelmed and hopeless. Like nothing is ever going to get better or the flashbacks and memories will never go away and the abuse even though it is not happening now will never stop . . . sometimes when I cut on my arms or stomach I am angry.'

Point C: Panic stations

The raging inferno gathers momentum. The individual feels out of control, or too numb (detached, distant, disconnected), and experiences a compelling urge to self-injure.

At points B and C individuals are beginning to experience intense psychological arousal and physical reactions, in response to internal or external cues – often described as feeling 'overwhelmed', 'unable to cope', 'out of control' or 'screaming inside'.

Attempts to resist the urge

At point C, individuals may try hard to resist the urge to self-injure, by attempting to interrupt thoughts of hurting themselves:

'Quite often I will pace about trying to resist the compulsion but I become more agitated.'

'I was telling myself that I didn't need to break my 13 weeks SI-free. That I have other ways to cope, I don't need to cut. I went for a walk and climbed trees.'

'I have several techniques that I use to distract myself from self-injuring. If I am at home by myself, I do various physical activities and several writing activities to help me distract. I do have a support system of family, friends, and my therapist, but it is very hard for me to use them.'

Sometimes distraction techniques are successful; sometimes they aren't. Some people may try to delay self-injury, only to discover that when they cannot resist the compulsion any longer, they injure themselves more severely than originally planned.

'I have often thought of distractions . . . the main one available to me is to ring my best friend . . . this doesn't often work . . . I feel undeserving of her affection and caring.'

'I fight urges to self-injure but once I get set on it I don't argue or fight myself anymore.'

'I remember saying to myself don't do it and do it at the same time. I always have a war going inside of my head before I do it. I had made a distraction list in therapy but it didn't even cross my mind at the time.'

'I get the most conflicting arguments going on in my head that make me so confused. Part of me is saying "don't cut because you'll regret it tomorrow – just think of all the scars." Another part says, "You need to cut because you're bad; you have to cut to get rid of all the bad feelings – you need the release." Another one says, "Just think of the people around you – what are they thinking every time you hurt yourself? How can you hurt them like this?" Sometimes I can't stand all the voices in my head that fight each other and then the only way to stop them is to cut – to get it all out of me.'

Point D: Action stations

The individual self-injures, which extinguishes the raging inferno inside, or alleviates the feelings of alienation.

The act may be carried out in a state of:
- Awareness (pain experienced)
- Partial awareness (some pain experienced)
- Non-awareness (minimal or no pain experienced [a dissociative state]).

Some people report feeling pain during self-injury. Others, due to high levels of numbness, or the intensity of psychological arousal, have little or no awareness of pain at the time of, or during, self-injury. However, when the numbness starts to wears off, pain from self-inflicted injuries may be excruciating, especially from burns. Ironically, although many people welcome sight of their own blood from self-injury, some report wincing at the sight of other people's blood, or being a 'wimp' when it comes to hurting themselves accidentally. Important to note too is that the pain from self-injury is reported to be different from pain caused by an accident (the 'ouch' from a paper cut for example), explained perhaps by the fact that in most cases people are aware that the pain is coming so have a degree of control over it.

> 'I don't experience pain during self-injury . . . maybe a little stinging sensation, but I don't consider it pain.'
>
> 'I am actually very squeamish about other people's injuries.'

The act may be motivated by:
- A need to release tension or anxiety
- A need to communicate acute emotional distress (to self/others)
- A need to feel pain (self-punish)
- A need to escape from emotional pain (enter a dissociated state)
- A need to end a dissociated state (feeling disconnected from oneself; feeling numb, empty or dead inside; or experiencing oneself or one's surroundings as unreal).
- A need to exert a sense of control over one's body
- A need to ward off suicidal thoughts.

Point E: Feel better/different

With the raging inferno under control, the individual temporarily experiences:

- Relief from tension, anxiety, and pent-up emotions such as fear, anger, or frustration
- A feeling of euphoria, numbness or detachment (dissociation)
- A sense of feeling more alive, more real, more grounded in reality – or, if the function was self-punishment – a degree of satisfaction.

Generally, the individual feels calmer, more in control, 'comfortably numb', and can think more clearly. In other words, self-injury reduces the individual's level of emotional and physiological arousal to a tolerable level, and the internal chaos is temporarily soothed. Thus, the physical injuries may seem a small price to pay to escape from the 'raging inferno inside'. Furthermore, following an episode of self-injury, some individuals report feeling physically tired and sleeping soundly – this is a rare occurrence for many, as already mentioned in Chapter 1.

Internet respondents' feelings and emotions after self-injury

The Internet respondents reported experiencing a plethora of positive feelings and emotions following self-injury. Commonly reported were feeling relieved; calmer; satisfied; relaxed; at peace; less anxious, angry, frustrated, panicky or tense; elated; ecstatic; happier; triumphant; on a high; stronger; more in control; more rational; more grounded in reality, and more balanced emotionally. A sense of accomplishment, temporary sense of achievement, and a sense of superiority were also reported.

On the downside, some respondents reported feeling remorseful; sad; shaky; upset; uneasy; useless, weak; ashamed; guilty; embarrassed; stupid; scared; self-loathing; angry at themselves or physically cold. Two commented that self-injury resulted in a feeling that justice had been served, or that one's penance had been done.

The positive consequences of the act were noted as:

- Better equipped to cope and face the world
- In better sync with the rest of the world
- Like a weight has been lifted off one's chest
- Like a lid had been put back on one's emotions
- Able to think more clearly and concentrate better
- Able to be more oneself again
- Like the world 'wasn't running helter-skelter'
- Like everything slows down somewhat
- Like being on a huge high.

How long does the relief last?

Having established that self-injury brings relief, it leaves the unanswered question of how long the relief lasts. Here, respondents provide some clues:

> 'It lasts until the stitches come out or a few hours/days with burning.'
>
> '. . . only for a few hours or so.'
>
> 'The relief can last for a week or two, depending on circumstances.'
>
> 'It relieves the pain I'm feeling for about a day or so.'
>
> 'It usually lasts for about 1-3 hours, but sometimes can last for a couple of days.'
>
> 'As long as I am in pain and have open wounds the less likely I am to self-harm.'

The aim of re-opening the wounds is to keep the pain on the outside for as long as possible, thus serving as a distraction from the hurt within.

Point F: The grief reaction

The reality of the individual's actions starts to sink in. Shame, guilt, self-disgust or self-hate may rekindle the smouldering embers. Because the underlying issues (the internal chaos) remain locked up inside and unresolved, the cycle continues unless change is effected at Point A.

> 'The next day I feel guilty and bad about myself and unworthy to to be alive.'

'I feel very ashamed and it reinforces my self-hate.'

'The last time I immediately felt panic and remorse.'

'[I feel] relieved for about ten minutes, then I think "fuck what have I done" so I feel guilty.'

'. . . within a hour or two I realise I've failed again and the shame and guilt thoughts and feelings set in.'

'The relief I felt the first time I did it I can't put into words, but the guilt of doing it soon followed.'

As seen clearly from the above testimonies any positive aspects of self-injury tend to be short-lived, and typically the mental anguish soon returns, thus individuals become trapped in a repetitious cycle of emotional engulfment, self-injuring to feel better ... and so forth. Sian's poem below demonstrates the cyclical nature of self-injury.

> I hurt too much,
> I feel too much,
> I need too much,
> I cut too much,
> I bleed too much,
> I hurt too much.
> —Sian

Breaking the cycle of self-injury

To break the cycle of self-injury, whatever is causing the mental anguish at Point A needs to be addressed. Negative self-beliefs need to be identified and challenged, issues such as shame, guilt and self-blame need working through and letting go of, losses need to be grieved, constructive coping strategies need to be developed to replace self-defeating behavioural patterns, and strengths and self-esteem need enhancing.

Cautious use of prescribed medications, such as selective serotonin reuptake inhibitors (SSRIs), the second generation of antidepressants (for example, Citalopram [Celexa/Cipramil]; Fluoxetine [Prozac]; Paroxetine [Paxil/Seroxat]; Sertraline [Lustral/Zoloft]), or the first generation tricyclic antidepressants (TCAs), (for example, amitriptyline [Elavil]; clomipramine [Anafranil]; Imipramine [Tofranil]) may be indicated to treat any underlying symptoms of depression, to temporarily numb high levels of anxiety, or to alleviate distress from PTSD, or complex PTSD symptoms (for example, flashbacks, nightmares, intrusive memories, feeling detached, difficulty sleeping and concentrating, hypervigilance). Alternatively Lithium, an antipsychotic may be indicated for mood swings, manic episodes or bipolar disorder.

Ultimately though, true healing from self-injury involves coming face-to-face with whatever unresolved internal issues and conflicts are motivating, and maintaining the act. That can be a tall order, as it means 'sitting with the emotional pain'. However, a willingness and commitment to 'stick with it and work through it' can lead to a life-changing and transforming experience for the better, as well as an opportunity to kick self-injury into touch for ever. As stressed by Conterio and Lader, authors of *Bodily Harm* (1998: 171): 'Sadly, there is no real chemical cure for self-injury . . .' thus recovery comes through healing the hurt within.

'No one that has treated me for the last 7 years seems to understand that you need to treat what is behind the self-injury before you can work on the self-injury. There is no way I will be able to stop self-injuring when I am still having awful flashbacks – whole body flashbacks where I can feel everything and you feel so hopeless... They need to treat the PTSD – the after affects of childhood sexual, physical, and emotional abuse . . .'

Healing from dissociation

Braun (1988a, 1988b) defines dissociation as 'the separation of an idea or thought process from the main stream of consciousness'. In the case of childhood traumatic experiences, dissociation is thought to develop as a self-protective, coping 'gift', to prevent children from 'knowing'. Put simply, awareness of the traumatic event or a series of traumatic events are compartmentalised (split-off) from consciousness.

Problems can however arise in later life, and interfere with a person's functioning, if dissociated aspects of the traumatic experience(s) start creeping back into the individual's consciousness. Dissociated pieces of the trauma may return in various forms (a traumatic snapshot [flashback] a snatch of memory [intrusive remembrance] or a wave of paralysing fear [emotions]) that cannot be fully understood.

According to Braun (1988a, 1988b) therapeutic healing from dissociation involves processing the dissociated aspects of the trauma into a cohesive whole, thus enabling the person to integrate the incident into a complete memory, rather than it surfacing in unexplainable and disconcerting fragments. To demonstrate the healing pathway from dissociation Braun (1988a, 1988b) introduced the concept of the BASK model of dissociation. The letters of the acronym signify:

Behaviour (actions related to the event)
Affect (emotions)
Sensation (physical feelings)
Knowledge (amnesia).

Braun stresses that all dimensions of BASK need to be congruent to restructure the dissociative incident and improve mental wellbeing; also that dissociative aspects may occur across all four dimensions or in various configurations. Braun later altered his model to BATS, substituting thought for knowledge, thus making it: Behaviour, Affect, Thought, Sensation. (1988b). A further popular model of dissociation is Peter Levine's SIBAM model (Sensation, Image, Behaviour, Affect,

Meaning). Cited in Rothschild, B. (2000). *The Body Remembers: The Psychophysiology of Trauma and Trauma Treatment*. NY: W.W. Norton Inc. pp.67-70. Based on Levine's SIBAM dissociation model (1992).

Healing from self-injury
Developing self-help strategies to gain control over self-injury can be a useful starting point for individuals, but therapy is strongly indicated if self-injury and/or dissociation are long-standing issues that are severely impeding one's daily functioning. See Chapter 10 (Heal thyself) for self-help strategies, and Chapter 12 (Guidelines for working with self-injury and related issues). Flashbacks are one of the symptoms associated with Post-traumatic Stress Disorder (PTSD). See Appendix 2 for DSM-IV-TR criteria for PTSD.

The eight Cs of self-injury
Key motivations and meanings of self-injury, identified from my research have been clustered into eight categories, as shown in Figure 7.2 (The eight Cs of self-injury).

1. Coping and crisis intervention
Primarily, self-injury is a coping and survival strategy. It enables people to continue functioning when they feel psychologically threatened. Moreover, when the lure of suicide beckons, it serves effectively as a suicide prevention strategy.

'It's a coping mechanism, and a way of surviving when the only other option is suicide.'

'We are doing it because the pain we are feeling is just too intense. We are doing it because we have poor coping skills. We are doing it to survive, not to die.'

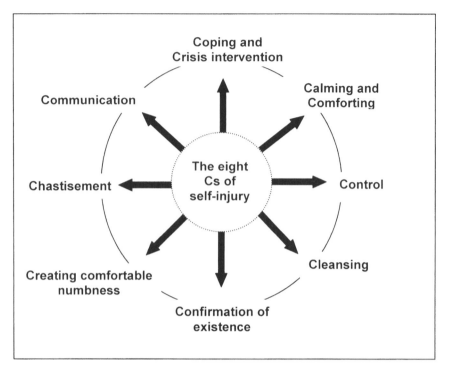

Fig. 7.2: The eight Cs of self-injury.

2. Calming and comforting

Self-injury provides rapid relief from a build up of tension, stress, anxiety, depression, and panic; it soothes emotional pain, and brings about a sense of calm and wellbeing. For some individuals it acts like a sedative, providing them with a good night's sleep. Some people look forward to the opportunity to give themselves some tender love and care after hurting themselves:

'I hope to achieve a sense of equilibrium within myself, and balance with my environment. Too often things are not in balance in one way or another.'

'I know that cutting myself is a very effective way of escaping negative feelings – I don't have to deal with them. It helps me calm down, it makes it easier for me to sleep, it numbs the bad feelings and the self-hatred. It doesn't make me feel good, but it creates a calm, clear feeling as opposed to the panic I feel before the act.'

'I knew it would bring instant relief from the intense emotions I was experiencing. It would also bring instant relief from the headache. I was expecting to numb out for a while, at least long enough to get to sleep. I also knew that I would sleep all night, something I haven't been able to do without the self-injury for over a year now.'

3. Control

Feeling in control of our lives is essential for psychological wellbeing. Many people that self-injure feel they have little control over anything – self-injury gives a sense of control, and sometimes a feeling of strength and empowerment. It provides control over feelings and emotions – anger, frustration, rage, fear, sadness, depression, shame, guilt, helplessness, or hopelessness, crying, screaming; control over suicidal thoughts, a 'busy head', racing thoughts; control over distressing flashbacks, images, memories, intrusive thoughts, and internal voices; control over the level of pain inflicted, how much blood is shed, and where and when injuries are inflicted. In the case of Dissociative Identity Disorder, it can be a way of controlling switching (changing from one personality state to another).

'The purpose of the most recent episode was to release tension, feel more calm and relaxed, more controlled and able to think more clearly and logically. I also injure, at times, as self-punishment and to soothe emotional pain, and to quiet racing thoughts or emotional extremes.'

'When I'm on emotional overload . . . I'm just thinking
that I can't stand it another minute and I deliberately cut
to relieve the tension and overwhelming psychological
pain . . . Ironically, one of the goals for me when I'm
on emotional overload is to numb out for a while which,
combined with the shame I feel, starts the cycle for me all
over again.'

'Self-injury is a sure-fire way of controlling my emotions so
they don't overwhelm me. It's something I do to myself,
for myself, and it gives me a sense of control.'

'I felt out of control definitely, worried, scared, hopeless,
out of my depth, like a child . . . but when I considered
self injury my thoughts changed to anticipation,
expectation of relief.' (Prior to an episode)

'I am usually completely out of control, can't calm down
but have to and know that cutting is the best way to do it.'

'I can't control what others do to me, but I can control
what I do to myself.'

'I can choose/control where and when and how to hurt
myself before anyone else does it to me in a way that I
have no control over.'

'Sometimes I feel in control. I think it depends on the
degree of anger or frustration that I'm feeling. Mostly I
feel like I have no control. It's like this thing has taken
over my body and even if I wanted to I couldn't control it.
I try but my body feels like it has a mind of its own.'

4. Cleansing

People who have experienced sexual abuse or rape invariably feel dirty, violated, contaminated, and ashamed. Self-injury (which may be external, internal or both), can be a symbolic attempt to cleanse one's body and soul from the pollution of abuse, to rid oneself of feelings of guilt and shame, or to literally 'cut out' one's abuser:

> 'I hoped to achieve cleanliness – free from bodily impurities, free from guilt, shame and blame, and also to help me cope with everyday stress.'
>
> 'I feel guilty and full of shame,
> Yes, I have cut again.
> As the blood flows my soul is clean,
> And I can pretend it was all a dream.
> The pain I feel makes me good,
> Makes me feel the way I should.
> I feel clean and pure within,
> I've washed away all my sin.
> I know this sin will build again,
> But for now, it takes away my shame.'
>
> 'As the pain grew and grew inside me, the need to self-harm increased. I began to realise that every time I hurt myself, I was desperately trying to cut out all the bad bits that were buried inside me – most of all I wanted to rid myself of my father.'

5. Confirmation of existence

Self-injury successfully ends debilitating episodes of depersonalisation, derealisation and numbness – put simply it 'kick-starts' the person back into 'aliveness' and serves as an extreme 'grounding' technique.

It helps people stay focused on the present; get back into their bodies, (mind/body reconnection); provides proof that one is alive and real, and evidence that one is capable of feeling something – even if it is pain. It also explains why seeing one's own blood is a blessing to many people – blood is the river of life – blood confirms one's existence:

> 'When I see my blood, it does several things for me. One is that I can tell that I'm alive because I see it flowing from my body. The second thing is that I imagine that it is all the stress and pain coming out and dripping away from me . . .'
>
> 'When I feel numb I cut to try and create feeling – to try and feel alive or at least to feel something.'
> 'Feeling pain is better than feeling nothing at all.'
>
> 'My main goal in self-injury has just been to feel something . . . anything.'

6. Creating comfortable numbness

Conversely, if levels of emotional arousal exceed the individual's capacity to cope, self-injury may serve the purpose of creating a comfortable sense of numbness (entering a dissociative state). In a comfortably numb state individuals experience respite from psychological pain, an escape from reality, a period of peace or calm, or a sense of 'nothingness.'

> 'My goal of self-injuring is to "zone out" and feel absolutely nothing. I get excited when I see my blood running down my leg and then my head sorta detaches itself from my body and I feel like I'm floating.'

'I usually self-injure for the few moments of completely nothingness it gives me, everything focuses on the pain, like punching someone in the stomach to get rid of the pain in their arm. Afterwards it's almost like I feel cleansed, I wonder if this is what meditation is like?'

'It makes everything go away and I can be at peace for the moment. I want my mind to release everything and I want to just be numb to everything.'

'When I cut to numb out, [dissociate] which is more often the case, I feel a sense of warmth, calm and release. It's almost like a sense of achievement – like being wrapped up in cotton wool – all safe and soft. When I hurt myself this way, I am likely to cut deeper and to do more damage, because I don't feel physical pain, or it's minimal. I feel distanced from myself, as if I'm looking in on myself cutting me. I have to rely on sight to monitor the damage. There have been times when I've seen how deep I've cut and I've had to force myself to stop. On a couple of occasions I nearly passed out, but this was because I lost a lot of blood quickly, I think.

This distant feeling comes during cutting and lasts for some time afterwards. If I need to go to Accident & Emergency this distant feeling usually lasts until long after I've been stitched up, so I can remain detached from the experience. I feel on a high, and don't usually "come back" for some time. It's usually a gradual thing - I don't come down with a bump!

It's difficult to explain why I need to numb out. Usually I'm feeling overwhelmed and that I can't cope. Sometimes my head feels so full that there's no room to think straight; no way to do the everyday type things. Sometimes I get a thought in my head that I can't budge, or I'm remembering things from my childhood and I feel sad, lonely, or angry, and because I can't express how I feel I cut to escape - to change the focus - like a time out from my feelings.

Sometimes when I cut to numb out it doesn't work properly and I feel really cheated and out of control. I don't necessarily feel any different in the beginning, but when I start to cut I can't distance myself and so I feel the pain to varying degrees. I am left feeling really frustrated and angry with myself. If I then cut in anger and frustration it hurts, but I do it anyway, and of course I'm still left with the overwhelming feelings that led me to cut in the first place, and I feel like a waste of space.'

7. Chastisement

'I deserve to be punished for being such a bad person' is a strong belief carried by many people that self-injure. Self-blame, shame, perceived wrongdoings, making mistakes, hurting other people's feelings, expressing feelings punished or not allowed in childhood (e.g. anger, crying), having needs, and harsh self-criticism can lead to feelings of self-hate and the belief that self-punishment is justified.

'When I cut to punish myself it usually hurts, but I don't mind this because that's really why I do it – to hurt myself. I am less likely to cut deep because the pain is my regulator, and I'm more aware that it's me that's hurting me. The satisfaction comes from having cut myself despite the pain.'

'I wanted to punish myself and get rid of all the anger inside me. Sometimes before I hurt myself I feel shaky and unreal, as if I've drunk too much coffee. I get horrible thoughts swimming around in my head and I can only get rid of these thoughts and feelings by cutting myself.'

'I self-injure to help me release the stress/tension, to help me get back in my body, sometimes to punish myself, to express my anger, sometimes to help me get to sleep. Other times I self-injure to stop emotions from coming out. Sometimes I self-injure just to see blood to help me know that I am alive that I am real.'

'[I felt] extreme hate, self-loathing, overwhelmed, sad, and upset. I felt the world was incredibly unfair, I felt I wouldn't amount to anything, that I was a waste of space, I wanted to blame somebody, I wanted to blame my abuser, I hated him even stronger than I hated myself, etc.'

8. Communication

Self-injury is a non-verbal form of communication – sometimes to others – sometimes to self. While it may be true that a small number of people do self-injure in the hope of receiving a caring response from others, or as an SOS for help, this tends to be the exception rather than the rule. In any event, as Deb Martinson, author of *The American Self-Harm Clearinghouse* (2002-2007) website points out:

> We all seek attention all the time; wanting attention is not bad or sick. If someone is in so much distress and feels so ignored that the only way he can think of to express his pain is by hurting his body, something is definitely wrong in his life and this isn't the time to be making moral judgements about his behaviour.

Most people that self-injure are aware that their behaviour is not the accepted norm, and would prefer not to self-injure; in fact, many are deeply ashamed of what they do and go to great lengths to conceal their activities. Communicating one's pain on the skin can also be a way of confirming to oneself that the pain felt on the inside is real; or a method of expressing what one is unable to communicate in words, or feelings and emotions that are beyond words.

> 'SI provides very quick relief from feelings that are too overwhelming. Sometimes it's the only way to get rid of built-up tension, a way to punish myself. It makes me feel better and gives me a sure-fire way to ease the discomfort of feeling, not feeling, or not being able to communicate.'

Key points

- Everyone who self-injures is an individual, thus their pattern of self-injury may not follow one typical route.
- Many who self-injure hold negative self-beliefs.
- Trauma triggers (nightmares, flashbacks and body memories [somatic sensations]) can be the catalyst for self-injury episodes.
- Shame and embarrassment may deter the reporting of, or seeking medical help for, internal self-injury.
- The relief from self-injury is usually short-lived.
- Breaking the cycle of self-injury involves facing and working through the issues that are motivating and maintaining the act.
- The motivations and meanings of self-injury are diverse.

Chapter 8

Dissociation and self-injury

· ·

'I feel detached from my emotions and distanced
from myself. It's like my mind is someplace
else – almost as if I am out of my body.'

'I used to dissociate. I can't anymore.
I felt dead. I felt nothing. It was like
watching myself through a movie camera.'

Research suggests that some children repeatedly exposed to severe trauma – for example, sexual, physical and/or emotional abuse – develop the gift of 'dissociation' (a creative survival strategy that enables children to switch off psychologically from the traumatic experience). Over time, however, dissociation can develop into a conditioned response to any stressful situations. Thus what served effectively as a problem-solving strategy in childhood can become a debilitating condition that may seriously impede healthy adult functioning.

What exactly are dissociative disorders?

According to DSM-IV-TR (APA, 2000: 519), 'the essential feature of the Dissociative Disorders is a disruption in the usually integrated functions of consciousness, memory, identity, or perception of the environment.' Put simply, dissociation is a psychological mechanism that allows the mind or body to split off or compartmentalise traumatic memories or unsettling thoughts from normal consciousness.

DSM-IV-TR lists five dissociative disorders, as shown in Figure 8.1.

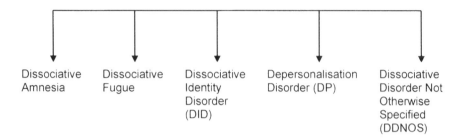

Fig. 8.1: The five dissociative disorder listed in DSM-IV-TR (pp. 519-533).

1. **Dissociative Amnesia** – distinguished by a persistent loss of memory of significant personal information, typically of a traumatic or stressful nature, that is too all embracing to be explained by normal absent-mindedness.

2. **Dissociative Fugue** – defined by an abrupt, non-scheduled journey away from one's home or usual place of work, accompanied by a loss of memory of one's past, confusion over one's identity, or assuming a new identity.

3. **Dissociative Identity Disorder** (DID – formerly Multiple Personality Disorder) is the most extreme form of dissociation. It is characterised by two or more separate identities or personality states that recurrently take control of the individual's behaviour, accompanied by a loss of memory of significant personal information that is too all-embracing to be explained by normal absent-mindedness.

4. **Depersonalisation Disorder** – defined by an unrelenting or frequent feeling of disconnection/detachment from oneself (mind-body split), during which reality testing remains intact. Depersonalisation is sometimes accompanied by derealisation (a sense that the external world feels strange or unreal).

5. **Dissociative Disorder Not Otherwise Specified (DDNOS)**. This term is used to classify disorders where dissociative symptoms are a predominant feature, but do not meet the criteria for any specific Dissociative Disorder.
Paraphrased from DSM-IV-TR criteria (APA, 2000: 519–533)

Dissociation is not a new theory. It was described by Pierre Janet (French physician and psychologist) in the early 1900s, and later by Sigmund Freud. Etzel Cardeña (1994) gives this concise definition of dissociation:

> In its broadest sense, 'dissociation' (Janet's désagrégation) simply means that two or more mental processes or contents are not associated or integrated. (p. 15)

Mollon (1996) explains dissociation thus:

> It begins with the child's self-hypnotic assertion 'I am not here; this is not happening to me; I am not in this body'. (p. 15)

Dissociation in relation to self-injury

It is becoming increasingly recognised that dissociative processes such as depersonalisation, derealisation and dissociative trance-states can frequently underpin self-injury, and numerous self-injury experts have noted a link between depersonalisation, derealisation and self-injury (*see* Conterio and Lader, 1998:176; Babiker and Arnold, 1997:78; Favazza, 1996:274; Walsh and Rosen, 1988:185). Many who self-injure report, (1) feeling 'emotionally numb', 'detached from themselves' or 'dead inside' prior to the act; (2) feeling little or no physical pain during the act, and (3) feeling more alive, more real, and more grounded following the act. Herman, in *Trauma and Recovery* (1994), while discussing dissociation and self-injury within the framework of major childhood trauma, identifies that:

Survivors who self-mutilate consistently describe a profound dissociative state preceding the act. Depersonalisation, derealisation, and anesthesia are accompanied by a feeling of unbearable agitation and a compulsion to attack the body. The initial injuries often produce no pain at all. (p. 109)

Experiences of physical pain

Physical pain from self-injury varies in intensity. The findings from the survey carried out for *Healing the Hurt Within*, 1st edition (Sutton, 1999) revealed that 59% of the respondents experienced no awareness of pain, 18% experienced an awareness of pain, and 23% experienced pain in varying degrees. In Favazza and Conterio's 1989 study of 240 females who self-injure, 29% reported feeling no pain, 38% reported feeling little pain, 23% reported feeling moderate pain, and 10% reported feeling great pain. (p. 286) These findings support the theory that dissociation plays a significant role in the process of self-injury for a considerable number of people.

Depersonalisation

According to Conterio and Lader (1998:176) depersonalisation interferes with peoples' awareness of pain. In essence, it produces a temporary altered state of consciousness, resulting in a disturbance in one's perception of self, for example, a sense that one's body is non-existent or as if one's body and mind are separate. People who experience depersonalisation 'have disconcerting feelings of being detached from their bodies and mental processes,' says Favazza (1996: 247). Moreover, episodes of depersonalisation are reported to be extremely unpleasant and frightening, and self-injury appears to serve as an effective strategy for terminating distressing depersonalisation experiences.

Derealisation

Derealisation is listed in DSM-IV-TR as an associated feature of depersonalisation disorder. With derealisation one's perception of the environment may be experienced as 'strange or unreal', or 'the individual may perceive an uncanny alteration in the size or shape of objects (macropsia or micropsia) and people may seem unfamiliar or mechanical.' (p. 530)

Respondents' experiences of depersonalisation and derealisation

The respondents' testimonies that follow, in which they are describing how they felt prior to, during and after self-injury, highlight episodes of depersonalisation and derealisation:

'I feel worlds away when I self-injure almost like I am not there . . .'

'I usually feel like the rest of the world has disappeared and it is only me and the knife. I concentrate so hard on what I am doing, and the wonderful feeling I will have after I am done, that I notice nothing else. In other words – a marching band could be going by me and I would never know they were there.'

'Cutting feels like I'm watching from somewhere else although it is my hands doing the cutting.'

'It sometimes feels like I am stuck halfway in the transporter on the Star Trek Enterprise. I am out of focus, out of touch, sounds are muffled, and every sense is not quite "there". Other times I feel all my senses are very sharp – sharper than the rest of the worlds, while they muddle through in a slow motion haze. In both instances, SI would be an attempt to reset, to equalise the tempo.'

'It's kind of like sometimes you know the world is going on around you, but you can't make out the words – it's a language you don't understand. You did at one point, but you just don't anymore, and the harder you fight to make sense of it all, the less it makes sense. You see things, but they are so far away – and you can't touch them because they are just too far. Cutting brings things back to where they should be.'

'It was like being in someone else's head, watching them burn their hands. I think that if it wasn't like that I wouldn't be able to self-injure … the thought of someone burning or cutting themselves seems almost ridiculous – how could anyone, logically do that to themselves! I am thankful that I was able to experience the detachment; otherwise, I probably wouldn't be able to do it.'

'It's like I'm in the world, but not of it. Like I am watching myself from a great distance. I can see what I am about to do, but the majority of the time feel powerless to do anything about it.'

'It felt as if I was standing beside myself, looking at another person's body, another person's arm. And the body that was about to be harmed was not mine. It was just a thing.'

'Things felt unreal. The thoughts were racing in my head. I felt dizzy and invisible; like I was just watching what was going on around me, but I wasn't really there.'

'I didn't feel real – I never feel sure that I exist.'

'I often feel dead inside and out . . . like there is nothing inside my body – no feelings or emotions. I am just an empty shell. When I feel like this there is a huge numbness that takes over my whole body. I can't feel anything and often will cut to try and get some feeling or emotion or just to try and feel the physical pain. It usually doesn't work.'

'It's like another part of me takes over and is aware of what they're doing and the extent of the damage to be done.'

'Sometimes I scream at myself to stop, but I can't. Sometimes I feel like it isn't really me.'

'I feel distanced from myself, as if I'm looking in on myself cutting me, I don't feel physical pain, or it's minimal.'

'I felt angry first [before self-injuring] then after I almost went into a daze and felt nothing. I was calm – at peace. I was far removed from myself, my environment, everything.'

'Sometimes it's as if my mind has been elsewhere.'

'It's as if I am viewing someone else's pain and blood.'

'I am not exactly sure how I felt specifically this time. I do know that during previous times, I have felt spacey, not part of myself, and detached . . . this feeling is hard for me to explain. It is almost as if it is not "me" . . . it feels like something else has taken over and I no longer control it . . . it feels as if "I" am not really present during the time.'

ICD-10 classification of depersonalisation and derealisation

ICD-10, Classification of Mental and Behavioural Disorders, (WHO, 1992), the other major diagnostic system used extensively in Europe, classifies depersonalisation and derealisation syndrome as a neurotic disorder rather than a dissociative disorder. It also notes that the syndrome can happen in 'obsessive–compulsive disorder' (OCD), 'phobic disorder', or 'depressive illnesses'. Additionally, *ICD-10* suggests that basic features of the syndrome 'may occur in mentally healthy individuals in states of fatigue, sensory deprivation, [or] hallucinogen intoxication.' (pp. 171–172)

Post-traumatic Stress Disorder

Feelings of detachment or estrangement from others are also listed among the diagnostic criteria for PTSD in DSM-IV-TR (see Appendix 2 of this book for DSM-IV-TR criteria for PTSD). Interesting to note, however, is that according to George F. Rhoades (1998-2007), a specialist in anger management, trauma and dissociation, discussion has been taking place 'within the diagnostic community of possibly having Post-traumatic Stress Disorder listed as a dissociative disorder and thus removed from the DSM-IV category of Anxiety Disorders.'

Self-injury: an antidote to depersonalisation and derealisation

The following respondent's insightful testimony demonstrates the role of depersonalisation and derealisation in the process of self-injury as well as accentuating how self-injury serves as an effective antidote:

'Sometimes before I self-injure I feel dissociated. The world looks like a diorama or a movie set. Objects, environment and people seem two dimensional, like cardboard cut outs on a stage. Sometimes I barely even recognise what things are. Objects appear to be randomly placed about a room. Light becomes over bright or dims.

My sense of touch is disturbed, sensations echo which is confusing. For example, I can be lying in bed and every part of my body that is touching something else, pyjamas, sheets, pillow, bed, etc., is tingling and echoing – I'm not sure what I'm touching because I can't feel the outlines of whatever it is. I find that I can't do up the buttons on my clothing, unless I look directly at them. I've noticed this happens when I am under stress, particularly if I feel guilty about something. Sometimes I see the world from over my shoulder, or slightly above myself. I watch myself doing things like typing without being aware that I am directing my body to do so. I have also had that sensation while self-injuring. I watch myself in an internal stupor as my body tears itself up, engages in bizarre rituals (like bottling or displaying blood and flesh) without me really knowing why. This is the emotional state I am in when I self-injure to "get back to reality", to remedy dissociation.'

The significance of the blood

The sight of one's own blood holds significant meaning for many people who self-injure. For those experiencing episodes of depersonalisation and/or depersonalisation it provides confirmation that one is real, alive, does exist – as illustrated in the following testimonies:

'Seeing my blood has a big significance to me. It makes me feel real. Makes me feel alive.'

'I feel relief when the blood flows: it shows me I'm alive and it shows that the emotional pain I feel is real.'

'Blood is so red - it proves that I am alive.'

'[Self-injury] . . . reminds me I exist and am alive.'

'I love the sight of my blood as I feel it's letting out the bad bits and it proves that I am alive even when I feel I'm not.'

Dissociative trance

Several respondents reported experiencing a dissociative trance-like state prior to self-injury which is similar to a hypnotic state. Dissociative trance states are characterised by a transient altered state of consciousness, being oblivious to one's surroundings (feeling a million miles away), feeling detached from other people, feeling as if time has slowed down, or losing track of time (staring off into space). Trance-like states, whether induced by choice or unconscious, tend to impair reality testing. Here are four respondents' descriptions of trance-like states in the context of self-injury:

'Usually when the need to hurt myself was greatest, I would find myself in a place where time would seem to slow down and I would stare blankly at things, feeling tense and confused.'

'It's almost like you're in a trance or something, and your body just takes you and does what you have to do to make it all better. It isn't like dissociating where you lose time, but kind of like that in the way that you aren't actually making your own moves.'

'I go into a "trance" where I can watch what is going on, I see what is happening, I experience the cutting and the bleeding, but I feel no pain and I cannot stop the actions. No matter the severity of the cutting, I feel no pain. Hours later, at the site of the injury, I feel no pain. It is as if it never happened – great gaping wounds yet no pain – going into shock from loss of blood, yet no pain. No physical pain from the injury and no emotional or mental pain because I have temporarily released it all by cutting.'

'It's like a trance. Like I'm in a fog, or high on drugs-dreamy feeling. I make myself go into this state before I cut, it helps make the whole world go away and all the thoughts and worries and fears and anger and sadness while I'm cutting. This is the best part of it to me, besides watching the blood.'

According to DSM-IV-TR (pp. 532–533) 'Dissociative trance involves narrowing of awareness of immediate surroundings or stereotyped behaviors or movements that are experienced as being beyond one's control.' Dissociative trance disorder is classified in the DSM as a Dissociative Disorder Not Otherwise Specified (DDNOS).

Self-injury: an effective tool to cope with dissociation

For purposes of clarity, probably one of the best explanations of the relationship between dissociation and self-injury comes from Ruta Mazelis (1998) author of *The Cutting Edge: A Newsletter for People Living with Self-Inflicted Violence:*

> Whereas SIV [self-inflicted violence] is used as a coping mechanism to manage excruciating emotional states, it can also serve to alter feelings of profound numbness or deadness ... SIV seems to be an effective tool for managing dissociation in both directions – to facilitate it when emotions are overwhelming, as well as to diminish it when one feels too disconnected from oneself and the world.

Two common pathways to self-Injury

Figure 8.2 (Two common pathways to self-injury), tracks the process of self-injury from two perspectives – from a position of emotional overload, and a position of emotional shutdown. For DSM-IV-TR criteria for depersonalisation disorder see Appendix 2.

Dissociative Identity Disorder (DID)

Dissociation presents itself in varying degrees – from mild to severe. At the mild end of the spectrum are forms most of us have engaged in such as daydreaming, 'losing ourselves' in a good book or film, 'switching off' from a boring lecture, or 'tuning out' from the kids bickering. At the severe end of the spectrum is dissociative identity disorder (DID), more typically known in lay society as Multiple Personality Disorder (MPD). According to DSM-IV-TR, DID is 'characterised by identity fragmentation rather than a proliferation of separate personalities.' (p.519) In addition to identity disturbance, other dissociative symptoms such as amnesia, depersonalisation, and derealisation are frequently experienced.

A controversial diagnosis

DID is the subject of much heated debate and vilification. Many professionals argue that the disorder does not exist, an opinion formed partly on the basis that dissociative clients are easily hypnotisable, hence their symptoms are 'iatrogenic' – in layperson's terms, a result of therapist suggestion or 'false' memories implanted by over-zealous or inexperienced therapists. Doubters also express concerns over the possibility of an incorrect diagnosis being made. While the debate is one readers might want to explore further, our purpose here is to look at the relationship between DID and self-injury.

Dissociative identity disorder and self-injury

Six Internet respondents reported being diagnosed with Dissociative Identity Disorder. Here, two explain the relationship between DID and self-injury:

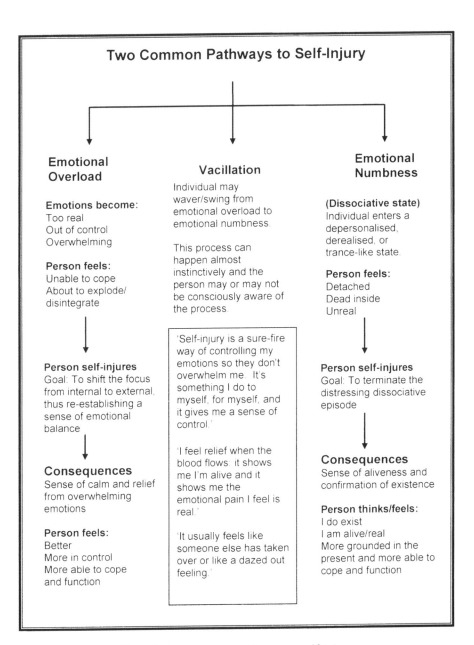

Fig. 8.2: Two common pathways to self-injury.

'A DID client can have many entities that self-harm. The basis for DID is a fragmentation of self as a result of devastating childhood trauma. There can be few or many fragmentations, alters, or parts. Each part is dealing with his/her own issues and those individual issues may include the need to self-harm. So the self-harm is on many levels with many different parts of the system, each individual part of the system capable of "taking over" the system, living in the forefront and engaging in his/her own behaviour, be it self-harm, childish games, reckless behaviour, etc. Each part must be dealt with individually, including each individual's self-harm tendencies and practices.'

'I feel detached from myself. I have DID [Dissociative Identity Disorder] and there is an alter . . . sometimes when I consciously self-injure she will come out and take over and finish the job. I will not know what damage had been done until I wake up the next day. I become so detached that it is like I become in a trance-like-state, and it is like I am watching someone else doing the cutting.'

A picture paints a thousand words

The following two pieces of artwork, Figure 8.3 (Untitled by Sheelah) and Figure 8.4 (S.elves Portrait by Sheelah) provide a unique glimpse into the complex inner world of dissociation.

Fig. 8.3: Untitled by Sheelah.

Fig. 8.4: S.elves Portrait by Sheelah.

Statistics on dissociation and self-injury

From the eighty two Internet respondents, forty-six (56%) reported being in a dissociative state prior to their most recent episode of self-injury, twelve (15%) said that it happened rarely, sometimes, or they had dissociated in the past, and twenty (24%), said they had not been. A study by Saxe *et al.* (2002) to establish the prevalence of self-destructive behaviours in a group of psychiatric inpatients with dissociative disorders compared to a group of patients displaying few dissociative symptoms, found that eighty-six percent (86%) of patients with dissociative disorders injured themselves. This data adds weight to the evidence that dissociative phenomena are common among people that self-injure.

Dissociation: A psychological safety device

A simple way of understanding dissociation is to view it as a psychological power cut. For example, if a person's emotional system is on overload from negative emotions, self-wounding words, intrusive thoughts, memories, images, or bodily sensations, to keep the system safe the psychological earth trip kicks in and shuts the system down.

Essentially a self-protective strategy, born out of denial, dissociation can become problematic if the emotional system fails to shut down effectively – in other words, if the negative emotions, self-wounding words, intrusive thoughts, memories, images, or bodily sensations, start filtering through into conscious awareness and interfering with an individual's ability to function in everyday life. It's often at the point where the life-saving erected dissociative barricades start crumbling that people seek therapy.

The following case study illustrates an example of disintegrating dissociative barriers, as well as showing how self-injury becomes an alternative coping strategy to escape from what is going on in the respondent's mind.

Case study 8.1: Stephanie

Depersonalisation: a sense of nothingness

As a child

It's difficult to explain, but I developed an ability to detach from myself and my surroundings. It wasn't a conscious thing. It was like I was slowly breathing down, which gave me a tingly feeling – like I was going inward (a bit like meditation). It felt as if I was under water – there was no sound, or as if I was in the air, floating above everything and everyone and looking down. I felt invisible – I could see other people but they couldn't see me. It was a pleasant sensation, a nice place to be – it felt safe, familiar and comforting.

Sometimes it felt as if I was climbing a ladder into the 'attic of my mind' where I could shut the door, not feel, and remove myself from my environment. It was a fail safe way of coping.

As an adult

I try to achieve that same familiar feeling of numbness but it won't work. It's like I can't turn the switch off any more, and a voice in my head intervenes: 'You shouldn't do it'. When my breathing slows down alarm bells start ringing! I start getting angry with myself then, and feel a strong need to switch off from what's going on in my head. Cutting myself takes me to that familiar and safe place where I feel a sense of nothingness.

Dissociation and what it achieves

Dissociation is thought to develop in childhood as a response to severe and repeated trauma. It guarantees survival by enabling the child to detach psychologically from the trauma – *to not know, not remember, not feel, not sense, and not integrate the experience.*

In the case of child sexual abuse (CSA), children often detach their mind from what is happening to their bodies by projecting themselves into the wall, on to the ceiling, or up in the sky, for example. This process is clearly portrayed in the following piece of artwork (Figure 8.5: Depersonalisation experiences by Sheelah).

Fig. 8.5: Depersonalisation experiences by Sheelah.

Dangerously unconnect_ed

Figure 8.6: Dangerously Unconnec_ted by Erin, also demonstrates the role of dissociation in self-injury. A key explaining her diagram, and an extract from an interview in which Erin elaborates on her diagram follows the drawing.

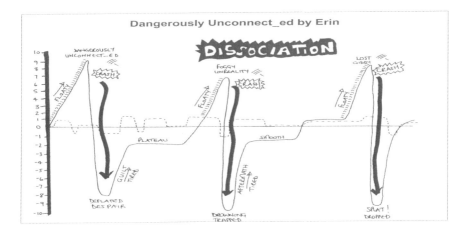

Fig. 8.6: Dangerously Unconnec_ted by Erin

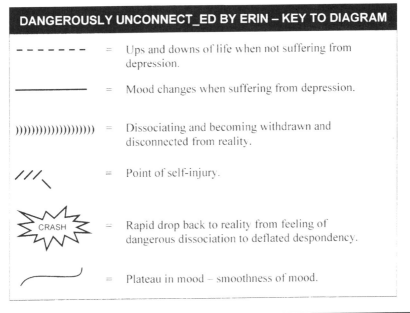

DANGEROUSLY UNCONNECT_ED BY ERIN – KEY TO DIAGRAM

– – – – – – –	=	Ups and downs of life when not suffering from depression.
————————	=	Mood changes when suffering from depression.
)))))))))))))))))))))	=	Dissociating and becoming withdrawn and disconnected from reality.
///\	=	Point of self-injury.
CRASH	=	Rapid drop back to reality from feeling of dangerous dissociation to deflated despondency.
⌐‿⌐	=	Plateau in mood – smoothness of mood.

-8 -9 -10	= Depression, withdrawal, not caring, sleepy, feeling of no hope, trapped, never getting better.
10 9 8	= Floaty, unconnection, unreality, giddy, spaced, bouncy.

'Truancy of the mind'

Extract from an interview with Erin in which she describes her diagram

JAN: Can you elaborate on your diagram? For example, you say that the dotted line - - - - - - represents the ups and downs in life when not suffering from depression. Are you referring to yourself here or to people in general?

ERIN: To people in general. It represents the ups and downs in life when some people might get happy or sad or may even consider themselves to be depressed. It shows that their lives can plateau, that they can feel the changes in mood, but not necessarily huge big jumps and swings about. If it was flat like the straight line through the centre, then I suppose people would be boring and wouldn't have any mood changes etc. at all.

JAN: Thanks ... that makes sense ... now can we look at what happens when you feel 'floaty' ... can you describe how floaty feels?

ERIN: Unconnect_ed, unreal, not touching, not feeling, generally a little dazed, hazy, unsteady, unstable, shaky, wobbly, sickly, sometimes giddy, day dreamy, foggy, thoughtful, lost, heightened senses, nervous, numb.

JAN: I'm not clear what you mean by 'not touching' ...

ERIN: OK ... I'll try to explain. If you grab your left arm with your right hand can you feel your left arm?

JAN: Yes.

ERIN: Well, when I touch my arm I feel the initial contact ... but then it feels as if there is nothing there ... I can't feel my arm with my hand ... I think that's why I don't feel any pain when I cut ...

JAN: So it's as if you experience a sense of depersonalisation – like you feel detached from yourself ... like your mind has separated from your body ...

ERIN: That's it exactly . . . I call it 'truancy of the mind'.

JAN: I think I'm beginning to get a clearer picture. So going back to your diagram, it appears as if the higher the 'floaty' level . . . the greater the intensity of anxiety and disconcerting feelings of disconnection from reality . . . and perhaps the more pressing the need for action . . .

ERIN: That's right. When I reach the point of feeling 'dangerously unconnect_ed', I get scared of doing serious damage to myself, and possibly others (for example by driving in this state), highly anxious, scared that others might see that I am weak, fearful of everything, desperate and nervous. I feel a sense of impending doom, sad, upset, sometimes low . . . as if something bad will happen, and that I will constantly feel this way unless I do something to end it.

JAN: So, it's when you reach the point of feeling 'dangerously unconnect_ed' that you self-injure?

ERIN: Yes.

JAN: Can you explain how self-injury changes things?

ERIN: Cutting allows me to feel . . . it allows my senses to become less heightened, I feel less numb . . . it reminds me I am alive by showing me that I bleed and I bruise, and later that I hurt too . . . it makes me take some action, i.e. planning, cleaning up, hiding etc. It brings me back to earth, stops me floating around in the sky, stops me daydreaming, requires me to concentrate, and prevents further floatyness.

JAN: To clarify then, self-injury takes you from a place of feeling unreal, detached, numb, dead inside – in other words disabling dissociation, and grounds you almost instantly back into reality – effectively shifting you from a place of dissociation to a place of association (mind and body reconnection). Does that sound about right?

ERIN: Yes, that's it in a nutshell. Feeling floaty, unreal and unconnect_ ed is not a nice feeling . . . it's very scary, especially when it escalates rapidly and feels like it will never end . . . like I will be continually floating on a high forever. Self-injury immediately stops the 'floaty' feeling . . . it can also save me from the risk of causing worse harm, for example, seriously considering suicide . . .

JAN: That's really useful to know . . . however, there's one thing that's still puzzling me. If we look at your diagram again, the middle 'floaty point' doesn't go as high as the first – it stops on the scale at about 7. This leaves me wondering whether a floaty feeling, once it starts, can be stopped.

ERIN: It can sometimes be stopped, or sometimes it can be put on 'pause' . . . in other words, put off indefinitely. For me, to stop the feelings it needs to be caught early and resolved, maybe by talking about what is happening with someone else, writing something down, or by forcing myself to concentrate on something else. When it's on pause, it is only stopped by telling myself something to pacify the floatyness for example, 'I can't cut in this environment', 'I've not got the right tools with me to self-injure.'

JAN: So you seem to be saying that if you become aware that dissociation is causing a problem, and can take appropriate action before it gets out of control, it can alleviate the need to self-injure? But, if dissociation is rapidly escalating to the point where it feels uncontrollable, self-injury can only be put on hold?

ERIN: Sometimes this is possible but not always. Sometimes the dissociation just overwhelms me and then yes . . . sometimes self-injury can be put on hold but this is very difficult and uncomfortable to live with . . . it's always waiting, and when the self-injury does happen, it's usually more severe . . .

JAN: Thank you for explaining the role of dissociation in the process of self-injury from your own experience – I found it very insightful and am sure other people will think likewise.

Working with dissociative clients

Working alongside dissociative individuals on their healing pathway can be a rewarding, yet challenging journey. In this section, three respondents diagnosed with dissociative identity disorder give guidance on one thing they consider it would be helpful for therapists to know about DID.

The Delacroix

'We as a system refer to ourselves as the Delacroix (which I believe is French for the tower/fortress – it has a sort of dark connotation to it). We refer to ourselves as "x" eDelacroix (meaning "x" of the fortress).'

> 'If I could tell all therapists one thing about DID (multiplicity), it would be that it is not a disorder. Multiplicity is not in and of itself a problem. It is just the way we are, and some of us would prefer to stay that way. It is each individual's issues with the past, it is the troubles with interpersonal relations (just like in any organisation). Multiples have many gifts, many advantages that therapists tend to overlook in their effort to 'fix' what is not even broken. If in the course of fixing what is broken we integrate, then great, but again, don't focus on the multiplicity, focus on the issues.'

Flute

Flute refers to her system as 'The tunnel'.

> 'I guess I would like my therapist to know that there are many specific parts of me, they were all created for a purpose, much like a many-pocketed coat, each pocket has a purpose and holds a specific item. That just because of the multiplicity of us, we are not any different and do

not want to be treated any differently than a single would want to be treated. However, there are times when there are different alters in for therapy or memory work or to work on problems, and those alters must be respected. **Never** demand that the main alter return, let the alter forward have his/her time. You see, I don't consider myself the host, I think there is a very damaged child somewhere in the system who is the host child but she is too damaged to emerge. I think I'm just another alter performing a task, albeit for many years, but just doing my job. I don't know if the host child will ever surface, or if she will stay buried in the depths of the tunnel forever. So, the therapist should treat whoever presents in the therapy session, even if it is not on the therapist's agenda.'

Cass

'We are a DID system which has the body name of Cass.'

'If there was one thing, it would be to ask them to **listen**. Listen because the fact that a client is sitting in front of you willing to talk is a huge, huge thing – one which most therapists and doctors do not remotely appreciate. You have no idea what it costs someone with DID to do that . . .

Listen because you do not know. You **cannot** know. You as a therapist are what us DIDs call mono – minds or singletons. DIDs are multi. As a mono, you cannot presume to understand what multi is like. You may know some theories about DID, you may be highly qualified in your field, but you are coming from a different base line, a different start point, a different life. DID is a person – not a theory . . . How **can** you know if you don't listen?

Many doctors have the attitude 'I am the doctor, therefore I know.' To treat someone who has been so severely abused in this way is just repeating the abuse. Someone has trusted enough to come for help – no one comes for fun – they are usually desperate. Patients are not lesser life forms than doctors, and they deserve to be treated with respect. As a doctor and fellow human, you should be willing to answer questions, to take time, to not put money before the needs of the patient.

Assessment is very traumatic. You are asking questions, touching, looking, poking at things that have **literally broken someone's mind** – do you not think that hurts? Your mind is not broken, therefore it can be safely said that you have absolutely no comprehension of the pain. Yet some bulldoze in, give no warning, insist on answers, rush the process, don't allow the patient to speak, some don't even do a proper assessment – no independent testing – just their personal judgement – then get rid of you as fast as they can, like a piece of rubbish. Not caring that they have re-traumatised, not caring that they have terrified, not caring that they have shredded someone's dignity and deepened the despair.

Someone with an equivalent physical injury would not be treated that way.

Other therapists put the person first; they are respectful, gentle, not rushed. They create safety and calm, they are sensitive to the particular needs of DID clients. They leave you as a patient, feeling valued, respected, somehow comforted and most importantly – with hope.

Listen because it is the only thing that will help you. A DID can tell you what is happening on the inside, explain the workings of their unique system to you - but they cannot if you cannot be trusted to hear.

Don't make everything complicated either, it really is as simple as **listen to the patient**. Then act accordingly, adjust if you have to, it really isn't a big deal . . .'

Further information about dissociation and dissociative identity disorder in relation to self-injury is provided in Chapter 12 (Guidelines for those working with self-injury and related issues).

Training in dissociation

Training in dissociation is a scarce commodity. The main training organisation in the United Kingdom is the UK Society for the Study of Dissociation (UKSSD). UKSSD is a component society of The International Society for the Study of Trauma and Dissociation (ISSTD).

As a non profit professional society the aims of the UKSSD are to:

- Promote research and training in the identification and treatment of dissociative disorders
- Provide professional and public education about dissociative disorders
- Support national communication and cooperation among clinicians and investigators working in the field of dissociation
- Promote the development of local groups for study, education and referral.
  http://www.ukssd.org/

Dissociation screening and diagnostic tools

The following screening and diagnostic instruments are widely used by clinicians working in the field of dissociation to measure dissociative symptoms or diagnose disorders. A word of caution. They are included here for educational purposes and should not be administered without adequate training or guidance from an experienced practitioner. All links are active at the time of writing. (April 27, 2007)

- **The Dissociative Experiences Scale (DES)**
  A widely used 28-item self-report questionnaire developed by Eve Bernstein Carlson, Ph.D. and Frank W. Putnam, M.D (1986). Measures the frequency of dissociative experiences and is available in over 20 languages. The DES is quick to complete and easy to score.
  Further information about the DES is available on Dr Colin Ross's site
  http://www.rossinst.com/des.htm

- **Adolescent Dissociative Experiences Scale (A-DES)**
  A version of the DES developed specifically for use with adolescents (approximate age 10-21 years) by Judith Armstrong, Frank W. Putnam, and Eve Bernstein Carlson – currently available in English only.
  The DES and A-DES are available from The Sidran Institute
  http://www.sidran.org/catalog/des.html

- **The Dissociative Disorders Interview Schedule (DDIS) DSM-IV Version**
  132-item highly structured interview, developed by Dr Colin Ross, which takes approximately 30-45 minutes to administer. It evaluates DSM-IV diagnoses of somatisation disorder, borderline personality disorder, and major depressive disorder, as well as all the dissociative disorders.
  The DDIS is available on Dr Ross's website (with permission to copy)
  http://www.rossinst.com/dddquest.htm
  It is also included in: Ross, C.A. (1997). *Dissociative Identity Disorder: Diagnosis, Clinical Features, and Treatment of Multiple Personality*. 2nd Ed. New York: John Wiley & Sons, Inc. (pp. 383-402)

- **The Structured Clinical Interview for DSM-IV Dissociative Disorders (SCID-D)**
  A semi-structured diagnostic interview designed and developed by Marlene Steinberg, M.D (1994) that enables trained clinicians to assess the severity the dissociative disorders based on DSM-IV criteria – dissociative amnesia, dissociative fugue, depersonalisation disorder, dissociative identity disorder and dissociative disorder not otherwise specified (DDNOS) (See references)

- **Steinberg Depersonalization Questionnaire**
  A 15-item questionnaire that identifies symptoms of depersonalisation (mild, moderate or severe). Available online with scoring facility. Reprinted from *The Stranger in the Mirror – Dissociation: The Hidden Epidemic*, by Marlene Steinberg and Maxine Schnall (2000).
  http://www.strangerinthemirror.com/questionnaire.html

- **Somatoform Questionnaire (SDQ-20 and SDQ-5)**
  The 20-item *Somatoform Dissociation Questionnaire* (SDQ-20; Nijenhuis, Spinhoven, Van Dyck, Van der Hart, & Vanderlinden, 1996) evaluates the severity of somatoform dissociation. The five item SDQ-5 is a screening instrument for DSM-IV dissociative disorders. For further information, see webpage: http://www.enijenhuis.nl/index.html

Key points

- Dissociation is a creative survival strategy that enables children to switch off psychologically from traumatic events.
- Dissociative processes such as depersonalisation, derealisation and dissociative trance-states are common among those who self-injure.
- Physical pain from self-injury varies in intensity.
- Dissociation can interfere with an individual's ability to function in everyday life.

- Self-injury serves as an effective antidote to dissociative episodes.
- Training in dissociation is a scarce commodity.

Further useful resources

All links active at time of preparation (May 23, 2007)

Available from The International Society for the Study of Dissociation (ISSTD), formerly ISSD (International Society for the Study Dissociation)

- Guidelines for Treating Dissociative Identity Disorder in Adults (2005)
  http://www.isst-d.org/education/treatmentguidelines-index.htm#adults
- Guidelines for the Evaluation and Treatment of Dissociative Symptoms in Children and Adolescents (2003)
  http://www.isst-d.org/education/ChildGuidelines-ISSTD-2003.pdf

Available from The Sidran Institute: *Traumatic Stress Education & Advocacy*

- Dissociative Disorders Glossary
  http://www.sidran.org/

First Person Plural

- UK Survivor-led Association for Dissociative Survivors of Abuse & Trauma and their allies. FPP is a small registered charity led by abuse survivors with first hand experience of complex dissociative distress.
  http://www.firstpersonplural.org.uk

Chapter 9

Hurting and healing:
True stories

··

For each unique case of self-injury,
there is an equally unique pain that lies behind it.
—Mitchell and Morse (1998, p. 126)

'It is liberating, to be able to kick SI to the
curb and say, "I don't need you."'

In this chapter, eight informative case studies are presented, seven by women and one by a man. Two show that self-injury is still active in the respondents' lives; the remainder demonstrate that healing has been achieved. Each case study is summarised to draw out specific themes, and reiterate important learning components. The chapter concludes with two heartening testimonies and an overview of key points identified from all eight case studies.

Hurting stories

Case study 9.1: Juliet

I have been self-harming on and off for about five years. It was something I 'learnt' while in hospital with anorexia. I resented not having control over food any more and hated the fact that I was getting larger instead of disappearing. Initially I began to cut myself on my chest, arms and thighs. The cutting was fuelled by the repulsion I felt at my body and was directed particularly at areas giving me femininity. I was being forced to become an adult woman again and it frightened me. The self-harm lessened for a year or so as the anorexia came back but then worsened again as I recovered from anorexia. It began to be closely linked with bingeing and other times when I felt very low or isolated. When my parents found out they were horrified and refused to talk about it. It was something that couldn't be happening in our family and as such I felt terrible about it.

There have been whole months where I haven't self-harmed, at other times it can be two or three times a week. It helps by providing a release for me – I can't cry so my arm cries instead. I feel much more able to cope immediately afterwards, however within an hour or two I realise I've failed again and the shame and guilt thoughts and feelings set in.

Sometimes I don't even know why I'm doing it – I just feel an enormous pressure building up, I get restless and edgy and something has to give. Other times it is linked directly to bingeing or desperation. Either way, I usually know a couple of hours beforehand that I will self-harm and that it's just a case of how long I can put it off for. Part of me thinks that it doesn't matter what I do to myself because it doesn't affect anyone else (no one else knows about it) and I don't like myself anyway. Another part of me knows that it isn't a constructive way to cope and that I need to stop if only for practical reasons. I find it very addictive though and difficult to stop because it is so effective in releasing the unbearable hurt I feel at the time.

On one occasion I needed treatment for my arm when the self-harm was particularly bad about 18 months ago. Never again. *I was seen by the triage nurse then deliberately kept waiting for four hours while others arriving afterwards were treated first.* Eventually, the psychiatrist I saw let me go on the condition that I came back for an appointment the next day. When I came back he told me I had to come into hospital or be sectioned so I had no choice. *It was one of the worst places I could imagine – I was woken in the night several times by various patients wandering into my room, one of whom was chanting.* I discharged myself first thing on Monday morning. *The one amusing thing was the label the psychiatrist had given me - a 'disorder of impulse control.' Maybe I'm being cynical but I suspect it was more for his benefit than mine since nobody explained anything about it to me.*

I found very *little support* available to me in either understanding or trying to stop self-harming. I believe, however, it is much more common than generally realised. There is a huge stigma associated with it – admitting to such a problem is in many people's views tantamount to admitting madness. *I have encountered reactions such as shock, hostility, disgust and have been ignored because of it.* I believe that self-harm is not seen as a high priority in the medical world because it is 'self-inflicted' and often seen as a cry for attention, when in fact sufferers can go to great lengths to keep such behaviour a secret. In my situation, no one knows about it except my GP.

I have been on anti-depressants for five years and have recently started having counselling once a week which I am financing myself since at least locally there is no suitable free or NHS counsellor. It is strange but in a nice way – trust is a big issue for me but I hope this will develop. It's very healing to have a person there for me who accepts me unconditionally and I'm finding it is taking some adjusting to! We look at various issues such as expressing emotions, relationships and anything which I think is important to talk about.

What helps most is for those trying to help looking beyond self-harm to the person themselves - valuing them as they are and for who they are. However, I would like to see more help available for people who self-harm and to see health-care professionals better educated about it.

Attitudes must change in society too because criticism and condemnation only add to the shame and guilt felt already by the sufferer. With understanding, acceptance and love, the isolation felt by the individual lessens and with continued support I believe the need for self-harming patterns of behaviour can be left behind for good as new, constructive ways of coping are learnt.

Summary of Juliet's story

Motivation to self-harm	Significant points
• 'The cutting was fuelled by the repulsion I felt at my body and was directed particularly at areas giving me femininity.'	*'I have been self-harming on and off for about five years. It was something I 'learnt' while in hospital with anorexia.'*
• 'Sometimes I don't even know why I'm doing it – I just feel an enormous pressure building up, I get restless and edgy and something has to give.'	*'The self-harm lessened for a year or so as the anorexia came back but then worsened again as I recovered from anorexia.'*
Function served by self-harm	*'I have encountered reactions such as shock, hostility, disgust and have been ignored because of it.'*
• 'It helps by providing a release for me – I can't cry so my arm cries instead.'	*'What helps most is for those trying to help looking beyond self-harm to the person themselves - valuing them as they are and for who they are.'*
• 'I feel much more able to cope immediately afterwards, however within an hour or two I realise I've failed again and the shame and guilt thoughts and feelings set in.'	

Fig. 9.1: Summary of Juliet's story.

Case study 9.2: Caroline

For weeks, months, years, tension has been building up inside until I felt as if I was screaming silently, all the time. I slammed doors, crashed saucepans, and cried tears of rage to express my anger. One more insensitive remark by the husband I no longer loved caused the anger to boil over. Alone, in my car, I reached for a sharp object. I dragged the corner of an audio cassette box down my forearm repeatedly until the flesh yielded. As I watched the blood flow, I felt tremendous relief. At last, I could see the emotional pain and know how great it was.

Relief turned to shock: surely only mad people damaged themselves intentionally? I hid the marks, but looked at them often so I could see the reality of my anguish. Despite the heat of summer, I

244 HEALING THE HURT WITHIN

wore long sleeves to prevent others from seeing the healing wounds, which were for my eyes only. I was 35 years old and had kept my emotions under tight control all my life, always putting on a brave face when I felt like crying.

As time passed, I continued to cut myself with furious, silent slashes when I felt angry or upset. Years of quiet hostility had taught me the futility of directing the anger at my husband. Instead, I turned it on myself, using whatever sharp object was to hand – kitchen knife, scissors, razor blade. Once, when he broke a treasured dish of mine, I sat on the floor surrounded by the pieces and cut my arm with shards of china. Mostly, I use a particular pair of sharp pointed scissors with which I can cut easily and painlessly.

I suppose there is a pattern to my self-harm. I feel emotion welling up inside until it reaches a point when I know I must injure myself, and I cannot rest until I have done so. I am always alone and, at that moment, I can feel quite calm. I usually cut, although I have burned myself and hit myself with something, like a rolling pin, as those injuries are easier to explain away. Cutting is painless at the moment I do it, but I find burning and hitting too painful to do often. I do not cut myself deeply enough to require treatment, as I cannot risk my secret being discovered by doctors.

I cover the cuts with a dressing and sit quietly to appreciate the calmness. Sometimes, several weeks will pass before I need to cut again, but at others the relief is short-lived.

My biggest fear is that other people will see my wounds, so I have to maintain enough control to cut in places where they won't be seen or in such a way that I can explain them. People must think I am very clumsy, living in a home with many sharp corners and that I am slow to heal. Often, I reopen the wounds to make them stay visible to me as long as possible. I have scars that will never fade completely, leaving me permanent reminders of my distress. Most of them have been hidden by clothing or the wrist splints I wear because of arthritis. Sometimes my scars have been commented on and I never know how to respond. While my tales of tin cans are unconvincing, I doubt many would understand the truth. Occasionally, I have had to stop myself from self-injuring because of a forthcoming appointment with a doctor or osteopath about my arthritis, but the panic I feel inside makes me wonder if it's worthwhile. I resent being unable to do what I want to my own body. Although I long to be comforted, I do not self-harm in order to gain attention.

I conquered my fear of being labelled 'insane' and talked about my self-harm to the counsellor I was already seeing. *I am grateful that she did not judge or tell me to stop, but simply accepted that I needed to injure myself.* She encouraged me to paint, and I found it a good way to express my hurt and anger without damaging myself. I have also written some poetry and understand my self-harm better as a result. Both methods have, at times, been easier for me than talking about self-harm.

My husband remains blissfully (and remarkably) unaware of my self-harm, but a couple of close friends know. One of them gave me the address of the Bristol Crisis Service for Women. Their magazine '*SHOUT*' [no longer published] *showed me I was neither crazy or unique, and I have benefited greatly from sharing my experiences with other women who self-harm.* Sadly, hearing what has happened to others has shown me I have been right to steer clear of needing medical attention. Self-harm seems to be greatly misunderstood, and I hope I shall not need treatment in the future.

I have also received invaluable support from the Samaritans. They have provided a listening ear on many occasions when there has been no one else to turn to. A couple of times, a phone call has prevented me from self-harming when I have known I could not risk needing to explain fresh wounds to someone.

I self-harm in less obvious ways too, such as starving myself, drinking salt water to induce vomiting and even denying myself pleasures as diverse as days out, parties, books and affection. These are ways to punish my undeserving self, whereas cutting is about being able to see my mental anguish.

Although I do not see an end to my self-harm at present I am not concerned, as it doesn't endanger my life or anyone else's, and appears to be strangely comforting. For a few minutes after cutting, I am kinder to myself than at any other time. If, in the future, I no longer need to self-harm, I know I have only to look at my body to remind myself I have survived great emotional pain.

Summary of Caroline's story

Started self-harming as an adult.	Significant points
Self-harming behaviours: • Starving, vomiting, and denying self any pleasures. • Cutting, burning, self-hitting.	*'I was 35 years old and had kept my emotions under tight control all my life, always putting on a brave face when I felt like crying.'*
Motivation to self-harm • Build up of tension over many years. 'I felt as if I was screaming silently, all the time.' • 'I suppose there is a pattern to my self-harm. I feel emotion welling up inside until it reaches a point when I know I must injure myself, and I cannot rest until I have done so.'	*'I self-harm in less obvious ways too, such as starving myself . . .'* *'Despite the heat of summer, I wore long sleeves to prevent others from seeing the healing wounds . . .'* *'My biggest fear is that other people will see my wounds, so I have to maintain enough control to cut in places where they won't be seen or in such a way that I can explain them.'*
Functions served by self-harm • 'As I watched the blood flow, I felt tremendous relief. At last, I could see the emotional pain and know how great it was.' • Starving self, denying self any pleasures, etc. ' . . . are ways to punish my undeserving self, whereas cutting is about being able to see my mental anguish.' • 'For a few minutes after cutting, I am kinder to myself than at any other time.'	*'Often, I reopen the wounds to make them stay visible to me as long as possible.'* *'I conquered my fear of being labelled 'insane' and talked about my self-harm to the counsellor I was already seeing. I am grateful that she did not judge or tell me to stop, but simply accepted that I needed to injure myself.'*

Fig. 9.2: Summary of Caroline's story.

Healing stories

Case study 9.3: Paige

I'm not sure where cutting fits in my life today. I don't want to do it anymore. I want it to be in my past. I want control over it instead of the other way around. I've gone about 26 months without cutting (my longest ever) and I've gained a lot of control over it. I never want to do it again, but the fight can be so hard. I don't know what makes it the hardest – anxiety, boredom, depression, mania, or mixed states. So much can be temporarily fixed by cutting and sometimes all I want is that one moment break, even though I know I'll feel much worse when I'm done. I have more things I can do now to try and take the edge off. I can exercise, draw, write, play music, listen to music, call someone, e-mail someone, read, watch television, lay with the puppy, and sleep. I was just going to write that sometimes it's not enough, but for 26 months it **has** been enough. Being on good medication for baseline stability also helps.

I used to try to do some of these things in the past and they weren't enough. I would cut, sometimes quite often. I don't really know what changed for me that I'm able to effectively redirect myself. It's a good change. Maybe I care more about myself, both my physical body and my life? Maybe I feel like I have self-worth? Not too sure about this. I guess that's more searching I will have to do and answers I have yet to find.

Summary of Paige's story

Significant points

- *'I've gone about 26 months without cutting (my longest ever) and I've gained a lot of control over it.'*
- *'I have more things I can do now to try and take the edge off.'*
- *'Maybe I care more about myself, both my physical body and my life? Maybe I feel like I have self-worth?'*

Fig. 9.3: Summary of Paige's story.

Case study 9.4: Amy

It is now nearly thirty years since I stopped self harming. I have been in therapy for the last ten years on and off. This is an attempt to try to come to terms with the shame and self-disgust that are the inevitable companions of this behaviour. Therapy is working. I think I'm getting there but it is, at times, a traumatic and painful process. It can also be enlightening, freeing and exciting. It has involved giving up old beliefs and assumptions and putting in place new images of myself and others. The trust needed from both myself and my therapist is enormous.

I started consciously self-harming when I was about 8 years old. I was away at boarding school. I didn't mind, it was preferable to being at home. Somehow, somewhere I discovered that physical injury evinced a caring response in adults – something I hadn't been able to discover at home where illness or injury resulted in anger and abuse from my mother.

Aged 8, I took a rounders bat in my right hand and hit my left arm repeatedly causing extensive bruising. The school matron bandaged my arm and seemed to believe the story I told her. After one or two more incidents I saw the school doctor who was angry. I was left feeling humiliated. If my parents were informed they never mentioned it.

Aged 13, I developed an eating disorder. I would starve myself for long periods, become ill, eat, starve. It became a way of life. No one ever addressed the problem directly. Various bribes were offered if I put on weight but these were, of course, useless. Throughout my teens at school I was aware of a deep seated unhappiness which resulted in self-loathing. I dreaded the school holidays but could not share this with anyone. I came from a privileged background. We were a 'loving' middle class family where the ethos was established through self-discipline, a concern for others, high moral values and the Protestant work ethic. How could I be unhappy unless there was something fundamentally wrong with me?

Aged 18, I went to work as a student nurse at a children's hospital.

After 18 months of just about coping I went into hospital for a tonsillectomy. At last I was somewhere where I was cared for and I gave up the fight. I knew I couldn't face life outside again but I had no way of explaining it to anyone because I did not know it myself at the time. It is only with hindsight that I can tell this story. At the time it just felt like a nightmare.

When the time came for me to be released from hospital grew nearer I injured my throat repeatedly to make it bleed and to stop it healing. I knew I couldn't cope with life on the outside anymore. It was frightening and made me panic. Eventually, after about four weeks I was sent home and referred to a psychiatrist. Again nobody mentioned self-harming. I was diagnosed as depressed. Within four weeks I had had a complete nervous breakdown and was admitted, under protest, to a psychiatric hospital.

I was completely unable to express the pain I felt. I had no language for it. I knew somewhere deep inside me that I wasn't insane or ill, I was just unhappy. I started to cut and burn myself repeatedly. Despite close supervision I managed to procure matches and razor blades. I think this must have given me some sense of control or power. The tension would build up and I would slash my arms or burn my hands and for a brief period the physical pain overrode the emotional. It was a respite. The nurses were kind, caring and tried to understand. The doctors at first just stitched me up silently and then grew angry and refused any treatment except ECT (Electroconvulsive therapy) and drugs. I did not care. I had few resources left. I did not have to take any responsibility for myself in hospital. I refused to see my parents. Without having to see them I could just about manage. I accepted that I was bad, worthless.

After about three months in hospital I was released. Heavily drugged and confused I somehow put some sort of life together. No one in my family ever acknowledged that I had been in hospital or that I had self-harmed. People in our family did not do that sort of thing.

Aged 21, I met my future husband. I disowned my previous self and launched myself into the role of wife and mother. Excessive busyness kept the pain under control for nearly twenty years. I got a degree, took a job as a teacher, worked as a volunteer for the Macmillan Nurses. Then I became ill and was hospitalised and all the old feelings re-emerged. It was time to discover what this was all about.

In therapy I learnt to look at the blackness and discovered a very unhappy small child. Hospitalised repeatedly for my first two years, I had none of the sense of self or security so essential for a healthy personality. I believe my mother grew to hate me. Love and hate are close allies. I was everything she did not want in a daughter. Difficult, defiant and very lively. These behaviours resulted in physical abuse. Crying was dealt with by isolation until I apologised. I became a very confused, lonely child, although by some miracle I was still able to form relationships and had many friends.

I carried this inner child with me. She was not completely crushed. She screamed and yelled to be heard and the pain was caused by my inability or unwillingness to do so. I am slowly learning to do this. I am proud of my child for surviving. The methods she found to tell me and others she was alive and kicking were extreme but no amount of anger, drugs or ECT could kill her off. It was only when she was recognised, respected, cared for that she could begin to heal.

A turning point in the healing process came when my mother died two years ago. I was eventually able to express all my complex feelings for her. I was able to gather information about her early life that helped me understand why she behaved as she did. I don't feel a need to blame or forgive just to accept and go forward. This journey of self-discovery will never end but it has eased the pain and opened up new visions.

Summary of Amy's story

Identified progression route of self-harm	Significant points
	'I accepted that I was bad, worthless.'
Self-harm in childhood	
• Age 8 Hit arm repeatedly causing extensive bruising	*'Crying was dealt with by isolation until I apologised.'*
Self-harm in teens	*'I was completely unable to express the pain I felt. I had no language for it.'*
• Age 13 Eating disorder	
• Cutting and burning	*'Excessive busyness kept the pain under control for nearly twenty years.'*
Motivation to self-harm	
• Build-up of tension	*'It is now nearly thirty years since I stopped self harming.'*
Function served by self-harm	**Amy is now a**
• It provided a brief respite from the emotional pain	**professional counsellor**

Fig. 9.4: Summary of Amy's story.

Case study 9.5: Emma

From what I remember, I began self-harming when I started secondary school at age 11. I would isolate myself and avoid food when I could. Looking back now, I know I had no understanding of what I was doing; it was just how I lived. The self-harm carried on and no one seemed to notice. By age 14, I started scratching myself. I wanted someone to see; someone to stop me but no one did. Some people did see but didn't know what they saw or that I was asking for help. From then on, the self-injury became secretive and I didn't want anyone to know or see what I could do to myself. I was ashamed and scared but also felt alive. I felt that this was something I could do, something I was good at, and it belonged only to me.

The self-injury continued all through my GCSE years and allowed me to function through depression, lack of identity, and a very low self-worth. I could separate myself from the surrounding chaos I felt and keep going. I did well in my GCSE's despite my scars becoming numerous and my free time being taken over by self-injury.

By age 16, I was cutting and would go through phases of cutting daily to maybe a couple of times a week. This would go hand in hand with not eating as much as I should have and isolating myself from those around me. By age 17, I was using razors and my arms were covered in cuts every day. I was now self-injuring to get through the next day. It was an addiction for me, a coping mechanism, a major part of my identity; it seemed it controlled me.

At 17, I sought help from a teacher at school. This was a massive step and I guess the beginning of my fight with self-injury. This is the point where I realised it needed to stop. It was not helping me to function anymore, and it was getting in the way of the rest of my life. My A-levels went badly grade-wise, but I saw a number of mental health professionals during those two years, one of which I was able to trust. I did not realise at the time that she had an important impact on my self-injury.

I managed to get into university and continued self-injuring there. Moving away from home meant there was no one to monitor my eating, and no one to worry about seeing my scars. Consequently, for two years my self-injury got out of control. My recollections of university are mostly about cutting my forearms, or making certain scars. I would constantly pressure myself to stop; setting myself targets – so many cuts a day or no razors – I would always fail. By this time, I was on antidepressants and waiting for my first outpatient appointment with a psychiatrist. Life was all over the place.

After self-harming for nine years, I accepted that it had become part of me and my life and was something I couldn't stop; that it would always be there and I had to minimise its effects, but that would be the best it could ever be.

Once I made that conscious decision, I began to look at myself more rather than focusing on my self-injury; it was now that I was able to heal. Within six months of accepting that the self-injury was never going anywhere, I was cutting less. Within a year, it had stopped. It has now been five years since I cut myself.

It has been an extremely hard road and I sometimes wonder how I made it. I know I had to let go of focusing on my self-injury and focus on myself. I know I also had to let go of the control self-injury gave me. There is one member of my family who knew what I was doing to myself, but I never felt judged no matter what I put that person through – quite the opposite in fact, this person helped me learn that I was a worthwhile individual.

Since being able to look at myself, I have been able to restore healthy relationships in my family, and have been able to move on with my life – I like life now. I'm a deep person; I think too much and I analyse more than I need to, but I have fun the rest of the time and things seems to balance out. I am covered in scars but that's okay . . . at least I'm able to live now without causing more.

Summary of Emma's story

Identified progression route of self-harm	Significant points
Self-harm in childhood • Age 11 Avoiding food *Self-harm in teens* • Age 14 Scratching herself • Age 16 Cutting **Motivation to self-harm** • Depression, lack of identity, and very low self-worth **Functions served by self-harm** • To separate herself from the surrounding chaos and keep going • 'I felt that this was something I could do, something I was good at, and it belonged only to me.'	*'At 17 I sought help from a teacher at school. This was a massive step and I guess the beginning of my fight with self-injury.'* *'Within six months of accepting that the self-injury was never going anywhere, I was cutting less. Within a year, it had stopped. It has now been five years since I cut myself.'* *'I know I had to let go of focusing on my self-injury and focus on myself. I know I also had to let go of the control self-injury gave me.'* *'I am covered in scars but that's okay . . . at least I'm able to live now without causing more.'*

Fig. 9.5: Summary of Emma's story.

Case study 9.6: Julian

I'm not sure if I remember exactly when I became a self-injurer, I believe I was around twenty-two years old. I don't look back and see my self-injury as a time when I fell from emotional stability into turmoil. I had always had a lot of personal issues and depression, though I hadn't always identified those things in myself; you only experience being yourself, so you have nothing to compare with.

Usually when the need to hurt myself was greatest, I would find myself in a place where time would seem to slow down and I would stare blankly at things, feeling tense and confused. The most certain way to get out of this state was to hurt myself, and I remember resenting that because I didn't feel in control.

To help myself stop I joined an online chat room and read some things. I learned some techniques, like holding ice cubes while thinking of a time and place where I felt safe. Some tricks I discovered for myself: music would help when time seemed to slow, and the scent of sandalwood oil could sometimes snap me out of things. At times when I failed and had to have the peace I knew self-harm would bring, I tried not to use my failure as another way of undermining my confidence. A lapse needs to be only a lapse.

Keeping faith in yourself is important. I always had an 'inner critic' who would at any moment throw vicious names into my stream of thoughts. During a more enlightened moment, I recognised this inner critic and even named him, using a silly name to help belittle him. I found it an especially useful skill: when undermining words would enter my head, I would ask (sometimes out loud) what that part of my brain was accomplishing while the rest of me was trying so hard to get on with my life. It sounds strange, but I believe it was a significant step in "choosing whose side I was on" and believing in myself.

Self-injury phases came and went. To begin with, I tried to distance myself from the notion [of self-injury] whenever it wasn't an immediate presence, but I think this was a mistake. Something changed in me when I became a self-injurer, and simply forgetting about it was not going to change things back. When a self-injuring phase came upon me, I would find myself as unable to deal with it as when I first started. So I stopped running away from it, and let myself feel less afraid of identifying myself as a self-injurer. Even this can help; sometimes we need physical evidence to validate our feelings, and just as you can learn to use a fading scar as a substitute for a cut, even the memories of self-injury can help you know that your feelings are real. Fighting the urge to self-injure takes a lot of energy, but it's never wasted. Even when you fail, every extra five minutes of enduring the urges before giving in is important.

In the end, I fought urges by gaining more understanding of why I wanted to self-harm. In my case, my brain had learned a trick of denying emotions when they were unacceptable to me. Rather like the question of a tree falling where nobody can hear it, I had decided that if something hurt me and I was the only one to know it, then perhaps it had never happened after all. I realised that when somebody close to me acted in a way that was hurtful, I tended to 'forget about it' and act like it had never happened. The emotions would form a confusing conflict inside me, a collection of ongoing negative stimuli with the labels cut off. A few times during urges, a friend was there to ask me what had happened, and each time, I said that nothing had. She knew me better and persisted. After talking, she would uncover something which logically had obviously triggered me, but I would be unaware of it. After thinking it through more I would find my urges easing; I think that triggers by their nature are an emotional blind spot for me. Even something trivial, if not acknowledged and processed, can provide a strong trigger because there's been no chance for my brain to dismiss, forgive, or explain it on a rational level.

I've been asked by a few self-injurers what it was that stopped me from getting urges to hurt myself, and the answer is that I never did. Self-injuring thoughts and urges are something I've learned to be happy with as a part of me. I would go as far as to say I would feel lost without them, because they are now a part of the spectrum of emotional signals that I get. I have learned to recognise them as a secret signal that there is an emotion I have blocked or not accepted. Once I look for it and consider the things that might have triggered me, I'm able to go back and respond more rationally to the original stimulus. That's when the urge to hurt calms. It's not intuitive, thus, it is sometimes hard for me to remember when in the panic of a serious urge, but with enough practice, it has become more natural.

I am now a 30-year-old recovered self-injurer, by which I mean nothing more official than the fact that four years have passed since I last performed an act of self-injury. I don't worry about the self-injury returning though, because as an impulse, it never really left and I know that I won't let myself lose the skills I need to be who I am. As fate would have it, I married another recovered self-injurer. We talk about it sometimes, and it can feel strange and distant, but at the same time it feels no odder than a lot of other bits of growth and learning you go through in life.

Summary of Julian's story

Started self-harming as an adult.	Significant points
Motivation to self-harm	*'To help myself stop I joined an online chat room and read some things. I learned some techniques, like holding ice cubes while thinking of a time and place where I felt safe.'*
• 'Usually when the need to hurt myself was greatest, I would find myself in a place where time would seem to slow down and I would stare blankly at things, feeling tense and confused.'	*'Fighting the urge to self-injure takes a lot of energy, but it's never wasted. Even when you fail, every extra five minutes of enduring the urges before giving in is important.'*
Function served by self-harm	*'A lapse needs to be only a lapse.'*
• '. . . sometimes we need physical evidence to validate our feelings, and just as you can learn to use a fading scar as a substitute for a cut, even the memories of self-injury can help you know that your feelings are real.'	*'I have learned to recognise them [self-injury thoughts and urges] as a secret signal that there is an emotion I have blocked or not accepted'.*
	'. . . four years have passed since I last performed an act of self-injury.'

Fig. 9.6: Summary of Julian's story.

Case study 9.7: Morven

It's hard to imagine where I was just a few years ago. It seems so far away, yet it still feels close in so many ways too. I guess it just strikes a few nervous chords within me when I remember and think about where I was back then...

In short, I hated myself. Actually, I loathed myself. I couldn't possibly understand how anyone could love or care for me and didn't trust anyone who told me they did. It was a lonely existence. I felt abandoned. I was afraid that no one would understand what I had experienced and how it affected me. I was always confused. I felt tormented, angry, and hurt. I hated the thought of not knowing how I was going to feel from one day to the next. I felt guilty for hurting, guilty for hurting those I loved, and for being angry and feeling hatred towards those who had hurt me, but still loved. I felt misunderstood, and analysed and personalised everything – every small thing that went wrong was my fault. I felt empty at times – or it seemed as if I was trying to feel empty, to prevent myself from feeling anything else. Nothing gave me pleasure, but I was an expert at masking that.

Self-harm was my retreat; a way of suppressing and retracting into a world of my own – a world I could control – my way of easing the guilt and the hurt that was within. It was also my way of punishing myself too – punishing myself for the person that I was, and for the things that had happened. For a time self-harm would make me feel human again, but soon the cycle of guilt returned to haunt me.

It's been over four years now since I self-harmed. I wish I could explain how I managed to stop the cycle, and bottle it, so everyone could use the formula. It hasn't been a smooth ride, and admittedly, I have times even now when I want to turn to the razor blades again just once more, but I don't. Why? Because I believe that 'once a self-harmer, always one' and once is never enough.

The thought of letting go of something that seemed so intrinsic in my life was a terrifying one. It took many months to achieve. For some it takes years – but for us all, it is a constant battle. I promised I would quit for friends, but soon realised that in order to really quit I needed to make the conscious effort to quit for myself.

When coming out of any addiction, you are counselled to give up everything that is associated with it. This phrase springs to mind, 'What holds my attention, holds me'. And so I did. I quit all those associations concerned with self-injury. It was hard (and it's not for everyone), but I knew it was something I had to do. Through taking these small, yet huge steps, I was able to re-evaluate where I was, what my priorities were, and who I wanted to be.

Throughout my relatively short life, I have continued to ask questions such as 'Why do bad things happen to good people?' and 'Why do people have to live through other peoples' actions?' Along with those small steps, I also realised that maybe we have to learn about unanswerable questions and inconsolable answers. Many people think they have the answers and perhaps they have some, but many haven't ever had to ask the questions and that makes all the difference. I guess I began to acknowledge that what actually makes quitting difficult is the process of confronting and solving those issues that underpin the action of self-harm. In some cases it's not necessarily the issues or experiences in question, but more the feelings they invoke, and the pain they involve that needs to be acknowledged. Fear is a strong emotion. It caused me to ignore, try to forget, pretend that things never happened, never existed. I tried for most of my life to escape my past, when in reality, what I really needed to do was suffer through it. I needed to confront the past and my fears head on. When I decided to quit self-harming, I also began to face my fears and truths of the past. I began to get stronger, and with this newfound strength, strived even harder to maintain my commitment to not self-harm.

Over time, I am now able to look at the past without so much fear and say to myself, 'Yes, it happened, they affected me, but now I have moved on.' I can say that I have actually gained from all my experiences and in some way, I hope to be able to touch others through them. I now look at the future with optimism and know I actually have one – that I can look to the future and be happy. I am happy.

Over the past four years I have continued to develop my career and have gained confidence in who I am and what I can be. I now have positive goals to further my career even further. Set-backs, whether on a personal level or professionally do not affect me the way they used to – sometimes I still feel the urge to self-harm, but I have never succumbed. I have also found the beauty of loving someone and being loved and accepting that love and acknowledging they love me for who I am. Sometimes that knowledge overwhelms me, but most of the time I feel happy and at peace. So now, I not only do not self-harm (though admittedly it is a hard battle at times) for myself, but also for my long-term partner and for my future children and beyond every other reason for not self-harming they have made all the difference.

Summary of Morven's story

Motivation to self-harm	Significant points
• 'Self-harm was my retreat; a way of suppressing and retracting into a world of my own – a world I could control – my way of easing the guilt and the hurt that was within. It was also my way of punishing myself too – punishing myself for the person that I was, and for the things that had happened.'	'. . . I hated myself. Actually, I loathed myself. I couldn't possibly understand how anyone could love or care for me and didn't trust anyone who told me they did.' 'I promised I would quit for friends, but soon realised that in order to really quit I needed to make the conscious effort to quit for myself.' 'I guess I began to acknowledge that what actually makes quitting difficult is the process of confronting and solving those issues that underpin the action of self-harm.'
Function served by self-harm	
• 'For a time self-harm would make me feel human again, but soon the cycle of guilt returned to haunt me.' • Morven lives in Scotland. She is 30. Having gained several degrees, she has become a respected professional in her field of expertise.	'When I decided to quit self-harming, I also began to face my fears and truths of the past.' 'It's been over four years now since I self-harmed.' 'I now look at the future with optimism and know I actually have one – that I can look to the future and be happy. I am happy.'

Fig. 9.7: Summary of Morven's story.

Case study 9.8: Kate

The statement below is from an email Kate sent me in September 2004
'I'm still doing really well; no depression, no self-injury, a good set of supportive friends and I'm just about to finish my degree and get a job (fingers-crossed!). I'm pleased to say everything finally seems to be going right for me.'

Warmed by her words and achievement, I invited Kate to write a piece about what turned things around for her. These are her words:

It's difficult to say what happened, I think probably a number of things contributed to me stopping self-injuring and turning things around.

Well, one day I actually made a conscious decision not to self-injure. Oh and it was **so** difficult, but I just didn't allow it to be an option. At first, I spent a lot of time finding distractions, things that would just take my mind off self-injuring for a while until the desire passed: taking long walks, painting, writing, making jewellery and restoring vintage dolls (I've even made a little money with the last two!). Distractions are good, but ultimately they're not a fix, I think there has to be a more fundamental change; a change in thinking, so that the first thing you think when you feel bad isn't 'self-injury', but something else, something more healthy.

I found just being able to recognise the emotions I have has been important. That sounds so simple, but I think before I was lumping things together and everything made me feel either 'good' or 'bad'. Now, I've come to know the sorts of situations and emotions that trigger me – anger, stress and frustration – and I just stop myself. I recognise what's going on in my head and that's part of the problem dealt with. I've learned to recognise when I'm about to drift off and out of control.

Also, I stopped trying to cope on my own. I made the most of support groups, I moved in with my parents and just let them look after me so I didn't have to worry about running a home and all the responsibilities that go with that and I accepted that I wasn't well enough to work. I took advantage of all the help that friends and family were offering, and focused on staying alive and getting better.

I haven't self-injured in over four years, but I am still a member of a support group and I think that has been very important to me – to know that there is support available to me if I ever need it and to know that I'm really not alone in this.

Now, although things aren't perfect they are pretty good . . . and I am no longer scared of wearing short sleeves.

Summary of Kate's story

> ## Significant points
>
> - '. . . one day I actually made a conscious decision not to self-injure.'
>
> - '. . . I stopped trying to cope on my own.'
>
> - 'Distractions are good, but ultimately they're not a fix, I think there has to be a more fundamental change; a change in thinking, so that the first thing you think when you feel bad isn't 'self-injury', but something else, something more healthy.'
>
> - 'I haven't self-injured in over four years.'
>
> - 'I found just being able to recognise the emotions I have has been important.'
>
> - 'I've learned to recognise when I'm about to drift off and out of control.'
>
> - 'I am no longer scared of wearing short sleeves.'

Fig. 9.8: Summary of Kate's story.

Life after self-injury by Rae

Life after SI is one where SI no longer has control over you. Yes, there is a feeling of loss of control and a loss of identity when you first stop injuring yourself, but that is temporary. When SI is removed from your life, you are forced to find other means of self-control and other means of identifying who you are. The issues don't go away, but you find better ways of dealing with them. It is liberating, to be able to kick SI to the curb and say, 'I don't need you.' My life after SI is one where I am stronger, prouder, healthier. SI has no control over me.

> 'Whoever comes out of an experience like self-harm, becomes a special person with special qualities. It is a long hard battle. It's a battle that no one else ever can see because it happens within. And it is a battle *you can win.*'

Key points

- Self-harm was a behaviour Juliet learned in hospital while being treated for anorexia.
- A link between disordered eating and self-injury is evident in four case studies: Juliet's, Caroline's, Amy's, and Emma's.
- A progression route from self-harming behaviour in their childhood to self-injuring in their teens is apparent in Amy's and Emma's case studies.
- Caroline and Julian started self-injuring as adults.
- A negative self-concept (self-dislike, self-loathing, self-hate) was evident in several case studies.
- Motivations to self-harm included repulsion of one's body, tension building up, emotions welling up, screaming silently inside, anxiety, depression, lack of identity, very low self-worth, being in a 'trance-like' state, confusion, to gain self-control, to ease guilt and hurt, to self-punish, unable to express the emotional pain.
- Functions served by self-harm included providing a release for anger, more able to cope immediately afterwards, punishing undeserving self (disordered eating etc.), being able to see one's mental anguish (cutting), brief interval from emotional pain, to keep functioning, physical validation of one's feelings, and to make one feel human again.

- Time stopped self-injury: Amy (almost 30 years); Emma (5 years); Morven and Kate (over 4 years); Julian (4 years); Paige (26 months approx.).

What helps those wanting to recover?
- Having a counsellor that does not judge you or tell you to stop self-injury.
- Looking beyond the injuries and appreciating the person as she/he is for who he/she is.

What helps recovery?
- Making a conscious decision not to self-injure.
- Making the conscious effort to quit for yourself – not for others.
- Accepting that self-injury is going nowhere.
- Focusing on yourself, rather than self-injury.
- Letting go of the control self-injury has over you.
- Developing a range of alternative coping strategies to resist the urge.
- Caring more about yourself.
- Therapy.
- Getting support.
- Joining an online chat room.
- Educating yourself about self-injury.
- Recognising that a slip need only be a slip – not a failure.
- Awareness that self-injury thoughts and urges might be an indication of an emotion being blocked or ostracised.
- Being able to identify your emotions.
- Being able to recognise times when you are dissociating (drifting off/going into a trance-like state/staring blankly into space).
- Changing your thinking so that when you feel bad, self-injury isn't the automatic route to feeling better.
- Confronting and solving the issues that underlie the need to self-harm.

Chapter 10

Heal thyself

· ·

Change is not made without inconvenience,
even from worse to better.
—Richard Hooker

The self-help strategies offered in this chapter are aimed at distracting your thoughts away from self-injury, reducing the intensity of your emotional arousal to a more manageable level, and coping with internal critical voices that may trigger the urge to self-injure.

Changing deeply ingrained behaviour patterns is not easy – imagine how you would manage if you were asked to write a letter or essay with your left hand when you are naturally right-handed or vice versa? Any changes, no matter how small, can feel strange or uncomfortable at first, and it's not unusual to slip back into old familiar ways, especially in the early stages of attempting to modify established behaviour patterns, or at times of stress. Moreover, because we are all different, strategies that prove helpful to one person, might not work for another. Often, it's a case of having a go and finding out what works for you, and discarding what doesn't. The important thing is not to give yourself a hard time if a particular technique doesn't work, or if you stumble at the first hurdle – just go back to the drawing board and try another strategy. Keep in mind too that 'Rome wasn't built in a day'; also that 'success often breeds success'.

The collection of helping hints included here come from people who are at various stages in their recovery – **they are not a substitute for professional help**. If the suggestions or exercises feel too daunting, perhaps it might be worth considering seeking the support of a friend to help you with them, or asking your therapist, if you have one, to support you while you test some out. The final helping hint comes from members of a survivor-run group – they might be useful to anyone thinking about joining a support group.

Healing hint 1

The first healing activity comes from Cheryl Rainfield,[1] a survivor of incest and ritual abuse, who used self-harm to cope for many years. Cheryl lives in Toronto, Canada. A commitment to healing has been a very important part of her life, and one of the key things that helped her to stop self-harming was to begin to care about herself enough to realise that she didn't deserve to be hurt. Other things that helped were discovering the reasons why she hurt herself; therapy; and creating positive messages for herself. 'Eventually, with enough repetition, the positive messages actually sink in,' she says.

Cheryl runs a popular website offering hope, healing, and compassion to others, especially women, survivors, and people who self-harm (for further information see references at the end of the chapter). In this article, the first of two contributed by Cheryl, she provides guidance on things to do when you experience the urge to hurt yourself.

What to do when you feel like hurting yourself
By Cheryl Rainfield

Self-harm is something that usually happens alone, and in secret. Those of us who hurt ourselves or used to hurt ourselves may do so for one or more of the following reasons:

- To relieve great emotional pain and distress
- To avoid, distract from, or suppress overwhelming emotion
- To try to feel better
- To stop a painful memory or thought
- To punish ourselves

- To re-enact childhood abuse or the messages our abusers taught us
- To try to connect to ourselves
- To keep from committing suicide
- To release or express anger that we're afraid to express to others
- To silently cry out for help
- To show ourselves how bad the pain is that we feel inside.

There may be other reasons that cause people to hurt themselves, but ultimately, whatever the motivation, hurting ourselves does just that – it hurts us. Self-harm may bring a temporary relief, but it ends up traumatising us, even if we think it doesn't at the time.

As a survivor of abuse, I used to cut for most of the reasons I've mentioned above – and also because I was taught to use cutting to keep myself silent and to keep from remembering. Within ritual abuse, my abusers also encouraged me to hurt myself because they thought it would help discredit me in the event that I began to talk about the abuse I was remembering, and because they wanted to keep me in emotional turmoil so that I would be less able to heal. Self-harm helped me survive during the abuse and for some years later; it kept me alive. But it also hurt me. Parts of me felt traumatised when I hurt myself, as if those parts were re-experiencing the abuse I endured. And while I haven't cut for many years, I know that method of coping is still something parts of me think they can fall back on if things get too bad and I really 'need' it. I have scars on my body that I can't erase, and when I wear short-sleeved shirts, I often experience negative reactions, condescension, intrusive and judgmental comments, blatant curiosity, and rudeness from people who see my arm. This can be painful to deal with and can also bring up old shame. Sometimes I wish I could just erase the scars – but they are a part of my history.

Self-harm is hard to go through. There is the emotional overload before the self-harm, and then the shame, self-hatred, and anger at ourselves afterward, and sometimes added depression or despair. And there is always the secrecy, the triggers, and the loaded emotions that SI can bring up for survivors of abuse. Then there's the actual physical pain that results from self-harm, and the emotional pain that comes from having cared so little about ourselves that we could hurt ourselves so badly. Self-harm hurts . . . on every level.

So, what can you do if you want to stop hurting yourself?

First, realise that this is a process. If you've been hurting yourself for a while, most likely you won't be able to stop overnight. It takes time to stop self-harming. It's important to see each little victory you make along the way, no matter how small it may seem, and to recognise the skills you're building that will eventually help you to stop self-harming.

Second – and this was key in helping me to stop hurting myself – you have to care enough about yourself to stop self-harming. You have to be able to love yourself – even just a little bit. You have to see yourself as valuable, to truly know that you don't deserve to be hurt, not by anyone.

It can also really help to have a therapist who can help you explore the reasons you self-harm and support you as you try to find new ways to cope. A good therapist can be invaluable, and can help you get where you want to go faster than you might on your own.

It can be healing to talk to someone about your self-harm – when you are ready and able to. This is especially important for survivors of abuse; many survivors were forced to keep the abuse a secret, and to feel shame about it. Self-harm shouldn't have to carry the same emotional weight. Talking about your self-harm with someone you trust can break the silence, shame, and guilt around self-harm, and prevent those feelings from reinforcing the self-harm. It's a good idea to start slowly and to choose someone you trust to tell. You may also want to prepare what you have to say ahead of time.

Discovering what triggers your self-harm is one of the most effective and important parts of learning to stop hurting yourself. Try to see the pattern. There may be a number of patterns. For instance, do you feel like hurting yourself every time you've gotten into an argument with your parents or your lover? Do you feel like self-harming when you think you've messed something up? Do you self-harm when you're feeling really hurt, angry, or depressed? Do you self-harm to try to punish yourself, silence yourself, or distract from your feelings? Do you self-harm when a memory of abuse comes up that you don't feel like you can deal with? Write a separate list for each trigger.

Next, ask yourself how you felt when you got triggered, and how you felt just before you hurt yourself. Were you feeling furious? Threatened? Incredibly sad? Were you feeling unlovable, unworthy, like you didn't deserve anything good? Were you feeling overwhelmed, depressed, or self-hating? Write down what you were feeling on your list. If you hear words or phrases that go along with the feeling, write them down too.

If you can, take this even deeper. Try to remember the first time you felt this way. When was it? What was happening then? Does it relate to something that happened a long time ago? Making that connection may help you to understand why you hurt yourself.

You may want to figure out what you really need or what you were trying to get by self-harming. For example, did you need to receive comfort, to express emotion, or to gain relief from emotional pain? Write any identified needs down and then write out as many things as you can think of that will help you to:

- Get out the emotion
- Distract yourself
- Soothe or calm yourself
- Reach out to someone
- Do something fun
- Give yourself positive messages.

Those of us who self-harm often hold a lot of self-hate, self-criticism, and anger turned inwards. We also often have low self-esteem. For those reasons, it is especially important to give yourself as many real, positive messages and reassurances as you can – and to receive them. You may want to write a list of positive messages that you need to hear and keep that list close by for when you need it. Or you may just want to list things in the 'give yourself positive messages section' of your trigger list.

Sometimes the list will work and sometimes it won't. If you get through the whole list and still feel like hurting yourself, go back to the beginning and start again. Below are two examples (Figure 10.1 Example 1: Self-injury trigger and alternatives monitoring chart) and (Figure 10.2 Example 2: Self-injury trigger and alternatives monitoring chart).

Remember that learning not to self-harm is a process; it takes time. Maybe the first time you try not to hurt yourself, it will only work for ten minutes. That's okay; that's progress! You postponed hurting yourself for ten minutes. Give yourself praise for that. It really is something; you're building your skills. Next time, maybe it will work for thirty minutes, and then forty, and then an hour. Soon it will be days, then weeks, and eventually you won't need to self-harm at all. Every bit of progress is important, and it helps to recognise the progress you're making. It all counts!

All these techniques are tools that can help you stop self-harming. But don't expect yourself to stop self-harming overnight – that's pretty impossible. Rather, you're looking to gradually reduce the self-harm by:

- Bringing in alternative methods of recognising your feelings and triggers, and of dealing with them
- Building up your options
- Increasing your ability to recognise when you're feeling triggered
- Learning to treat yourself with caring and compassion, and to respond to yourself in healing ways when you are feeling distressed.

Example 1

Trigger event/ situation:	I have a fight with someone. I raise my voice.	
Feeling:	I feel angry at someone else. Then I feel angry at myself, and scared. It scares me when I'm angry. I don't want to be like my Dad.	
Link to past experience: Can I see a connection?	My Dad used to yell at me.	
Goal of self-injury: What was I trying to get?	Reassurance, knowing I'm not like my Dad. Relief from my anger. Punishment. Stopping myself from being angry at someone else.	
How to get what I need:	Ask my therapist/parent/friend/lover for reassurance. Look at the ways that I'm different from my Dad, the way I don't take my anger out on people. Give myself permission to be angry with my father, and with what he did to me. Learn that it's okay to feel angry. Learn how to control and contain my anger. Learn how to safely express my anger. Take a course in meditation, tai chi, yoga. Keep doing things on this list.	
Alternatives to self-injury: What I can do instead.	Get out the emotion:	Go for a run. Punch a pillow. Scream into a pillow. Throw a ball against the wall. Tear up a phone book. Throw raw eggs into the bathtub. Dance out the emotion. Write out how I'm feeling. Throw a sticky toy against the wall. Listen to a tape of a thunderstorm and yell along with it. Write a letter to my father without mailing it.
	Distract myself:	Listen to loud music with my headphones. Go for a bike ride. Take the dog for a run. Watch a movie. Play a video game. Sing at the top of my voice. Throw some paint on a canvas or paper. Crunch a hard candy between my teeth.
	Soothe and calm:	Listen to some soothing music. Pat my cat or dog. Make a warm drink. Reassure myself, tell myself everything will be okay and that I'm a good person. Find a way to smell something that makes me feel good – a cinnamon stick, an orange.
	Reach out to someone:	Call my therapist. Call a friend. Call a crisis line. Go online to a chat room about self-harm (or abuse, or whatever has greatly affected you) and talk to someone there.

cont'd . . .

	Do something fun:	
	Positive Messages:	It's okay to feel angry; what's important is how someone uses their anger. I'm not like my Dad; I'm healing. I have a right to my feelings. I'm very strong to even try not to hurt myself. I deserve to feel happy. I deserve to have good things in my life.
	Start at the beginning again if I need to.	

Fig. 10.1: Example 1. Self-injury trigger and alternatives monitoring chart.

Example 2	
Trigger event/ situation:	I'm with my friends, and they're all talking to each other, but not to me. I feel left out.
Feeling:	I'm afraid I don't belong. I'm afraid I'm not equal, or that they don't really like me. I feel sad, alone, vulnerable, unlovable, unloved. I feel like hurting myself.
Link to past experience: Can I see a connection?	My mother often told me that no one would love me.
Goal of self-injury: What was I trying to get?	To see my pain, to know how badly I felt. Comfort. Reassurance. Distraction from how badly I felt.
How to get what I need:	Write out how I feel – write in my diary, write poetry, draw a picture. Tell someone I trust how I've been feeling. Ask my therapist/parent/ friend/lover for reassurance. Ask for a hug. Ask a friend to go out for a walk with me or just to listen to me. Go to a movie.

Alternatives to self-injury: What I do instead.	Get out the emotion:	Cry, if I need to. Tell a friend how I feel and what happened to me. Play sad music and sing along with feeling. Scribble out my feelings. Scream into a pillow. Go for a walk. Write some poetry. Write out how I feel.
	Distract myself:	Read a good book. Watch a movie or TV show. Call up a friend. Go on the internet. Play a game. Play with my pet. Do an art or craft project.
	Soothe and calm:	Make a warm drink. Spray some lavender in the room. Hold my teddy bear. Listen to fun or soothing music. Go for a walk and look at nature, notice the details. Have a warm bath or shower. Go to sit by the water and listen to the waves. Listen to a tape of the waves. Pat my cat or dog.
	Reach out to someone:	Call my therapist. Call my friend. Go on a message board. Email a friend. Write a letter to a friend. Call a crisis line. Go out in the street and just smile at someone.
	Do something fun:	Blow some soap bubbles. Buy myself a treat. Read a comic. Watch a cartoon. Put on the silliest clothes I can. Play with my cat or dog. Get a pack of gum and blow the biggest bubbles I can.
	Positive messages:	It's okay to feel sad. I'm a good person. I'm a likeable person. My friends love me. I'm compassionate, caring, intelligent, and kind; I'm a person that I would like if I met myself. I deserve to feel happy. I am loveable and strong.
	Start at the beginning again if I need to.	

Fig. 10.2: Example 2. Self-injury trigger and alternatives monitoring chart.

Eventually, these tools should help you to no longer need to self-harm.

It can also help to give yourself positive reinforcement every time you want to self-harm but don't, or every time you stave off self-harm just a little bit longer. You may want to give yourself a little treat, allow yourself to have some fun, or do something that feels good – and really notice the steps you're making. It all counts!

Know that you are not alone. Many other people have gone through what you're going through – and many people are, right now. Sometimes it helps just to know that.

And please know that you deserve not to be hurt. You deserve to be happy, to have fun, and to feel all your feelings. And you deserve to love yourself.

(See Appendix 4 for a blank sample of a self-injury trigger and alternatives monitoring chart).

Text copyright © Cheryl Rainfield.
Used with permission
Chart design copyright © Jan Sutton

Healing hint 2

Annie,[2] a 22-year-old graduate student from the United States, offers this list of alternatives to self-injury that she found personally helpful.

Alternatives to self-injury
By Annie

- **Carry safe things** in your pockets as well as razor blades, knives, a lighter, or whatever you use to self-injure . . . anything that feels right to you; maybe a picture of someone you trust, those little stress-relieving squeezing things, maybe those 'silly slammers' even. Anything that feels comfortable and safe.

- **Find something to do to keep both your hands and your brain occupied**. You know those puzzles where you have to rearrange the tiles into a whole picture? A fellow self-injurer told me about that one, and I tried it, and I think it works for me. I also have a game where the buttons light up and you have to match the order that was given to you. The idea of being in control of something can help me get through the urges and shaky times.

- **Writing and journaling** is something I always recommend. If you are into writing, I would suggest short stories, essays, or poetry. Even free-writing is helpful. Sit down with a pen and paper, and write whatever comes in to your mind. For those of you who have trouble writing, set a timer for about ten or 20 minutes and force yourself to write. Write about how you are feeling, just let loose. You may look back at it later, and then again, you may not. But still, it is a terrific release for all those mixed emotions.

- **Making collages** by going through old magazines and newspapers helped me a lot. I'm not very good at drawing, so I would make collages. Sometimes I would dedicate a notebook to just collages, and sometimes I would take my journals and decorate the front. This helps you take all your emotions and make something constructive out of it. I really like the collages I have made.

- **Calling friends and talking to them** was something I must have done millions of times over. Sometimes I don't bring up the fact that I am having urges; I just listen to them or talk about work, my boyfriend, etc. By talking to another human being, you can remind yourself that you are not alone and that someone cares about you. It is also helpful to make a list of phone numbers of people you can trust. Post it somewhere where you will see it when having a crisis. I have three or four lists tacked around my house.

- **Remind yourself where you are.** This is similar to keeping in reality when experiencing a flashback. Once again, get out that piece of paper and a pen and write down everything you see around you, what you are touching, and so on; for example:

1. I am sitting on my bed
2. My legs are touching my blanket
3. The walls are blue
4. My ceiling is white
5. The time is 9:00pm, etc.

- **Other lists that can help** are brainstorming ideas of things you like to do. I generally call this *My List of 10 things I like to do . . .* What you do is you get out that old familiar pen and paper, and write down 10 healthy things you like to do. For example, I would write down 1) read a book, 2) take a bath, 3) watch TV, 4) play piano, 5) go to the movies, 6) pet my cat, etc. until you have a list of ten things. When you are in a crisis, take out this list, and go through from 1 to 10 until your urge has been minimised or is no longer there. Of course, I couldn't do things like going to the movies every time I had an urge, so I would have to skip it. If you get to 10 and find you still need to harm yourself, go back to 1 and start all over.

- **If you cut to see the blood**, you can use a red washable marker and draw on yourself where you want to harm yourself (a lot of people do this). Some people find this triggering though, and cut themselves over the lines. If you find yourself cutting over the lines, then this particular method is not for you. However, if you cut to feel pain, try putting a rubber band around your wrist or ankle and snap it when you want to self-injure. This method is very convenient because you can wear the rubber band around your wrist wherever you go and can even quietly snap yourself on the bus or in a classroom if you need to.

- **When the urge has passed**, if you are capable, it is also helpful to go back and try to figure out what triggered your urge. By doing this, you can recognise sooner what the trigger is and how you feel when the trigger is starting to affect you, and then you can stop the urge before it comes.

Copyright © Annie
Used with permission

Healing hint 3

In this second inspirational article from Cheryl, she addresses another crucial aspect to healing the hurt within; recognising and challenging self-criticism.

Talking to your critical voices
By Cheryl Rainfield

Negative or critical voices can interfere with you feeling good about yourself – or feeling good at all. Sometimes they become so loud that they are all you can hear – and you miss out on your beauty, your growth, and all the wonderful things you're doing. Women, especially, are frequently barraged with negative messages from advertisements, television, and magazines. It's hard to have a healthy self-image and not become self-critical, hearing those messages so often. And if you grew up with critical or negative parents or are a survivor of abuse, you have an additional, painful layer of negative messages to deal with. You may have heard horrible things said about you so often that you came to believe them, or you may still have those messages running through your head like a tape player – so softly that you hardly hear them, or so loudly they blot everything else out. At times, those critical voices may overwhelm you or make you feel like there is no escape. But there is a way to lessen the intensity of those critical voices and to find some relief.

1. **Notice the critical messages**
   To help quiet self-criticism, you need to be able to recognise that it is happening. You may be putting yourself down or criticising

yourself without even noticing that this is what you are doing, or you might think that by putting yourself down, you're being reasonable, objective, or humble. But criticising yourself doesn't help you – it just feeds more negative and self-harming thinking and can hurt your self-esteem and self-image.

So how do you pay attention?

Try to sit quietly for a while, and listen to your thoughts – those in the foreground, as well as those in the background. What do you hear? You may find that writing out your thoughts can help you to hear them more clearly. Listen especially for phrases that include 'I'm too', 'I never', 'I always', 'I should/shouldn't', 'I can't', and 'I'm just', as well as the more obvious critical messages, put-downs, and insults.

If you're having trouble hearing the critical messages, you may want to think of the last time you were feeling depressed, ashamed, or angry with yourself, and see if anything comes up. If you really can't hear your own critical messages, ask a friend or lover to point out when you're criticising yourself. However, you probably criticise yourself less frequently out loud than you do in your own head, so this is just a starting point.

2. Acknowledge your critical voices

Try to listen to your critical voices and find out exactly what they're saying. The more we ignore something, the stronger it gets. It helps to acknowledge those critical voices and to let them know you've heard them. Allow those critical messages to be there for a few minutes, and really hear them. Hearing exactly what your critical messages are saying can often help you to see how untrue they are, or how close they are to things you were told as a child.

3. Look at the patterns

Try to notice every time a new onslaught of self-critical messages begins inside you. Write down what was happening just before they started and what you were feeling at the time. Try to get more than the surface feeling; if you were feeling angry or impatient with yourself, what feeling was beneath that? Fear? Sadness?

Notice what the trigger was – the incident or feeling that started off your self-criticism. Did you make a 'mistake' and verbally slap yourself or laugh at yourself before anyone else could? Did someone else say something that made you think they were putting you down? Did someone laugh at you when you were feeling vulnerable? Write that down.

Try to become familiar with your triggers – with what sets off that criticism inside you. Then try to recognise that trigger as soon as it happens, or as soon after it has happened as you can. When you see that pattern occurring – a trigger setting off critical messages inside you – try to step back and see yourself with compassion, the way a friend would. Remind yourself that you're feeling particularly vulnerable, or hurt, or scared, and that you don't need to be so harsh on yourself.

4. Trace the messages back to their root

Look at the messages you hear in your head. Are any of them familiar? Did anyone tell you any of those messages when you were a child? Do they sound like your mother – or your father? Maybe they sound like a babysitter, a classmate, a teacher. Try to figure out when you first started 'thinking' those phrases. Sometimes knowing where those messages come from can decrease their intensity. (For example, 'Ah ha – that's something my mother used to say to me. But she's not right! I don't need to carry her voice in my head any more.')

5. Have a conversation with the critical voices

It might help to do this by writing it out so you can see it more clearly. Ask those critical voices what they need, and why they're telling you such negative things about yourself. Ask them what they're afraid of, and why they need to criticise you so much. Just let the answers rise to the surface and be there. Now is the time to listen. If you're feeling stuck, try this exercise: ask your critical parts what they're afraid of. Then, for two minutes, write whatever comes into your head as quickly as you can, without stopping. You may be surprised at how much comes up.

Try not to judge your critical voices. It may help to realise that critical voices are often created out of desperation and duress – such as a little child blaming herself instead of the adults who were hurting her, because it was safer to think that way. Behind all those negative messages and criticism is often a lot of vulnerability, insecurity, and fear. If you can get in touch with that vulnerability and understand where it's coming from, you may find that the need to criticise yourself greatly diminishes.

6. **Reassure the critical voices**

If you have discovered that those critical voices feel insecure, vulnerable, or are afraid of something, try to reassure those parts inside you. If you can meet the needs of those parts, the need to criticise yourself will decrease.

7. **Recognise the strength inside you**

Critical voices are often created as a means of self-protection – as a way to cope or survive. If you are a survivor of abuse and trauma, those critical voices may be the parts who absorbed all the negative messages and allowed other parts of you to remain playful, hopeful, or loving. You may also have tried to protect yourself by turning the critical messages on yourself instead of blaming the adults around you who hurt you. Or you may have used critical messages to try to suppress your inner beauty and uniqueness, in an attempt to fit in more or become what you thought people wanted.

But you don't have to be smaller than you are. And hurting yourself doesn't stop others from hurting you. Acknowledge the strength and help that those critical voices may initially have given you, and realise that you no longer need to use them the same way.

8. **Give the critical messages a new job**

Those critical messages may have helped you survive – but now it's time for something new; something that helps you now.

Give those critical voices a new job they can do instead of the one they originally took on. Talk to those critical voices and thank them for the job that they did by protecting or helping you when you needed them to. Gently let them know that that job no longer helps you – but that you have a new job that you really need help with. A new job that only they can do: protecting you from others' criticism and negativity; alerting you when people aren't trustworthy and helping you to trust your intuition; or whatever job you can think of that is meaningful and will truly help you.

The job you offer the critical voices has to be important; it can't just be some willy nilly thing or those voices won't take you seriously. And this job has to be something positive, something that is vital to feeling good, and something that you couldn't do alone.

Your critical voices might not take you up on your offer the first time you talk to them. But if you let them know that they're the only ones you think are strong enough to do it, or tenacious enough, or that they're the ones who can do it best – and if you thank them in a real way for trying to protect you in the past, and let them know that this is the best way to protect you now, then those parts will, almost assuredly, come around. Then you'll have a strong team on your side – because critical messages are very strong, but loving messages are even stronger.

9. **Replace those messages with new, loving ones**

Criticising yourself probably served a purpose when you were a child; maybe it even helped you cope or survive. You may have thought that if you criticised yourself first, it wouldn't hurt so much when other people criticised you. Or you may have thought it would make others criticise you less if you were the one to do it. Or maybe you thought that the negative person in your life would like you more, or accept you, if you criticised yourself or reflected back to them what they said. You may have had no choice but to absorb some of the things that were constantly being said about you. Whatever the reason you learned to criticise yourself, know that it doesn't help you now; it hurts you. And you don't deserve to be hurt. So try to give yourself new, loving messages. Make up some new messages for yourself – and remind yourself of them as often as you can.

This is a great job for those critical voices. Ask them to do this for you. You need their help – and they can be powerful allies. Here's how you (or they) can do it:

- Every time you hear yourself start to criticise yourself, take a moment to notice that, and then give yourself a new, loving message. It can help to write out those loving messages, and put them anywhere that you'll find them. You can also ask a friend or lover to help feed those loving messages back to you. You may need to hear those messages from others for a while before you're able to start giving them to yourself – but sometimes the most powerful messages come from yourself, so try to give them to yourself, as well. You can even make a tape or audio file of loving messages and put them on a CD, your computer, or your mp3 player and listen to them as often as you can.

10. Release the critical messages

Try to release those critical and negative messages. You don't deserve to be emotionally hammered. You deserve kindness, respect, and love – especially from yourself. Realise that playing critical messages over and over inside your head is a form of hurting yourself – and try to find the compassion for yourself to let go of those negative thoughts.

Some people like to make a ritual out of it – a tangible act that helps them to let it go, such as writing out the messages and burning or tearing them up. Others like to visualise something that helps them to let it go, such as seeing the negative messages as red light (or whatever colour you choose), and then pushing that light out of their body. Try one of these suggestions or come up with one of your own; whatever method works best for you.

11. Be compassionate with yourself

More than anyone else in the world, you deserve your own compassion. You are the one who is with you always. And you are the one who, ultimately, can hurt yourself or heal yourself the most.

Withholding compassion from yourself doesn't help you – and it doesn't help the people you love. The more compassion and love you're able to give yourself, the more you're able to give others – both from your heart and from your example.

You deserve your compassion and love. You truly do. You won't make yourself into a 'better' person by criticising yourself or being harsh with yourself. You won't make people love you more by emotionally beating yourself up. But when you give yourself compassion, you allow yourself to be more of who you are – and in that blossoming, you encourage others to do the same. You may also find that you can give and receive love more easily – and that you feel better, happier, and more alive. Know that you are beautiful and just right for how you need to be, the way you are.

12. Forgive yourself

Whatever you think you've done wrong, whatever you judge yourself for, you probably judge yourself far more harshly than anyone else ever would. Let go of that judgement. Forgive yourself for everything that you judge yourself for. We all make mistakes, every one of us. We all have times that we can't live up to our ideals. Ideals are good things – when we remember that they are what we're trying to reach, through practice and growth – and that we may not always be able to reach those goals.

Let yourself know that you are doing your best – and in truly and wholeheartedly forgiving yourself, those critical voices will lose some of their power, and you will find that you are more beautiful than you thought.

Letting go of critical messages can be hard to do – but criticising yourself just continues the negativity that others taught you or forced onto you. It's not the route to feeling good; giving yourself love and compassion is.

With patience and focus, you can find a way to lessen your self-critical messages, increase your loving messages, and eventually replace your old messages with new ones. You can make new patterns and habits so that what becomes second nature is for you to praise yourself, to love yourself, and to have compassion for yourself. Every little step you take helps you, and shows the strength you have inside you.

So next time you hear your critical messages, take a moment to breathe, and then let those messages go. Recognise the beauty in your soul – and give yourself the loving messages you need.

Copyright © Cheryl Rainfield
Used with permission

Summary

To recap, these are Cheryl's twelve steps to recognising and challenging self-criticism:

1. Notice the critical messages
2. Acknowledge your critical voices
3. Look at the patterns
4. Trace the messages back to their root
5. Have a conversation with the critical voices
6. Reassure the critical voices
7. Recognise the strength inside you
8. Give the critical messages a new job
9. Replace those messages with new, loving ones

10. Release the critical messages
11. Be compassionate with yourself
12. Forgive yourself.

Healing hint 4

These hints on releasing anger come from Breaking Free,[3] a UK based charity that primarily supports women survivors of childhood sexual abuse. However, whether or not you are an abuse survivor, you might find some of the tips helpful if expressing anger is an issue for you.

Releasing anger
By Breaking Free
Exploring attitudes towards expression of anger

Anger is a perfectly natural response towards our abuse/abusers. We were probably not able to experience, express and act on our outrage when we were being abused. For some of us, we may not even have known that we had a right to feel outraged at those around us. Rather then be angry at the person or people who abused us, we probably did some denying and twisting of our anger, and, for some of us, we may still even do that now.

One way survivors cut themselves off from their anger is to become immersed in the perspective of the abuser, so that they lose connection with themselves and their own feelings.

But if we are unable to focus our rage at those who abused us, it will go somewhere else. Many survivors turn it on themselves, leading to depression and self-destruction. We may have wanted to hurt or kill ourselves. We may feel that we are bad, criticise ourselves unrelentingly, and devalue ourselves. We may have tried to stuff our anger down with food, drown it with alcohol, stifle it with drugs or made ourselves ill.

Having been taught to blame ourselves, we stay angry at the child within – the child who was vulnerable, who was injured and hurt, who was unable to protect herself, who needed affection and attention, who experienced sexual arousal or orgasm.

- **But this child did nothing wrong. She does not deserve our anger**

  Many survivors have also turned their anger against partners, family, friends, colleagues and children, lashing out at those who (usually) mean us no harm. We may have found ourselves pushing our child against the wall or punching our partner when we got mad.

- **It is time to redirect our anger where it belongs and appropriately at those who violated us**

  We must release ourselves from the responsibility of what was done to us and place the responsibility – and **our anger** – clearly on our abusers.

- **But this is not easy for those of us who fear our anger**

  Many of us may be afraid of getting angry because our past experiences with anger may have been negative. As one survivor put it, '*I don't get the difference between anger and violence yet. When I hear loud noises, I think they are coming after me.*'

  In our families, we may have witnessed anger that was destructive and out of control, often with people getting hurt. But our own anger need not be either. We can channel our anger in ways that we feel good about and respect. Even women with no history of violence are often afraid that if they allow themselves to feel anger, they're liable to hurt or kill someone. It is extremely rare for women to violently act out their anger towards the people who abused them as children. And for women with no history of violence, the fear that they might hurt someone with their anger is usually unrealistic.

- **Anger is a feeling, and feelings do not violate anyone**

  It's important to make the distinction between the experience of feeling angry and the expression of that anger. When we acknowledge our anger, then we have the freedom to choose if and how we want to express it. Anger does not have to be an uncontrolled, uncontrollable phenomenon. As we individually welcome our anger and become familiar with it, we can direct it to meet our needs – like an experienced rider controlling a powerful horse.

Another aspect of anger that is often misunderstood, and this keeps women from releasing their [dammed-up] emotions, is the relationship between anger and love. Anger and love are not incompatible. Most of us have been angry at one time or another, with everyone we love and live closely with. Yet when you've been abused by someone close to you, with whom you shared good experiences, it can be difficult to admit anger for fear that it will eradicate the positive aspects of that relationship or of your childhood.

But getting angry doesn't negate anything you want to retain of your history. What's good can still remain in your memory as something from which you benefited. We forfeit nothing of our past by getting angry, except our illusion of our abusers as innocent.

Often survivors are afraid of getting angry because they think it will consume them. They sense that their anger is deep and fear that if they tap it, they'll become submerged in anger forever, becoming bitter and hostile.

- **But anger obsesses only when it is repressed and misplaced**
When you meet your anger openly – naming it, knowing it, directing it appropriately – you are liberated.

  Can you take the step of acknowledging that anger can he positive and healthy and are you willing to acknowledge and express the anger that you feel towards the right people – 'those who abused'?

- **Positive expressions of anger**
  - Speaking out.

- Writing letters (either to send or purely to get feelings out on paper).
- Pounding cushions or the bed with a tennis racquet.
- Breaking old dishes.
- Screaming (get friends/supporters to scream with you).
- Creating an anger ritual (burning letters to abuser).
- Taking a course in Judo, martial arts.
- Organising a Survivors' march.
- Painting – paint anger out in sessions.
- Role playing with counsellor what you would like to say to your abuser.

Copyright © Breaking Free.
Reprinted from Newsletter Edition Three
Used with permission

Healing hint 5

The do's and don'ts of anger

The reason why so many people who self-injure struggle with anger can be simply explained – by prefacing the word *anger* with the letter **D** we have found the answer – *anger signals* **Danger**. Anger may be associated with violent scenes witnessed in childhood; the expression of anger may have resulted in punishment; or met with disapproval so became an emotion to avoid at all costs. Healing the hurt within involves resolving the anger within – anger managed effectively does not have to be dangerous. In fact, channelled constructively, it fuels people with vital energy to solve their problems.

Do:

A	Acknowledge your anger
N	Nip it in the bud
G	Get help for your anger if necessary
E	Express your anger constructively
R	Release it and let it go.

Don't:

A   Avoid it

N   Numb it out with alcohol, food, self-injury

G   Grin and grit your teeth

E   Explode

R   Rationalise it – make excuses for it, explain it away.

Remember

- 'Anger supplies the arms.' —*Virgil*
- 'Holding on to anger is like grasping a hot coal with the intent of throwing it at someone else; you are the one getting burned.' —*Buddha*
- 'Always write angry letters to your enemies. Never mail them.' —*James Fallows*

A word of caution about anger

If you harbour a lot of deeply buried anger, or have not been used to expressing anger, you may find it beneficial to seek therapy to learn how to handle your anger more effectively.

Healing hint 6

Healing hints 6 comes from Jo[4] – it too provides insight into the subject of releasing emotions. The information is included in a leaflet Jo wrote on self-harm for *Guernsey Association for Mental Health – MIND*.

Releasing emotions

By Jo

- Do you ever feel like screaming?
- Do you ever feel as though your life is going out of control?
- Do you hate yourself?
- Have you ever been abused and blame yourself for what has happened?

If you have answered 'yes' to any of the above, what follows may be of some help to you. I hope it is. I have been a 'self-harmer' for about 16 years and I have found ways of coping with these feelings, which may be of help to others with a similar problem.

- Do you ever feel like screaming?
  - at the people who care for you?
  - at people passing in the street?
  - at the cat or dog?

Screaming is a natural way of releasing tension: but it isn't acceptable to scream in the middle of the supermarket or other public place. I often feel like screaming when life feels unfair and I have been hurt.

I try to talk to someone before reaching this point so as to avoid bottling up everything inside myself. Even if all that can be said to a colleague at work is 'I'm having a bit of an off day today', this will help release some of the tension.

Exercise can sometimes calm me down, and a brisk walk for ten to fifteen minutes will dampen down my need to scream. *Writing down the things that are making you want to scream at that moment can also bring release.* If all else fails, find a quiet spot and have a good scream, or go and thump a pillow, or tear up some cardboard boxes. The worst thing that can happen are flying feathers or bits of card to clear up.

Do you ever feel as though your life is going out of control?

Sometimes it feels as though someone else is driving and you don't know how to stop. It can seem like a fairground ride that gets faster and faster so that you feel confused, dizzy, and sick.

So take time out and find a few minutes to relax, and breathe deeply. Say to yourself: 'this is my life, I am in control: I will be OK and things will get better'.

Nothing lasts for ever. Especially at night, it can seem as though it will never end, particularly if your heart is breaking and you just can't cry anymore.

Try to talk to someone. If you have no friends or family, or if the problem involves one of them, ring the Samaritans. They are there 24 hours a day and are always ready to listen. Often, just the knowledge that someone is there stops the world spinning so fast.

So give yourself time. This can be a great healer. The hurt that is so deep inside you and breaking you apart will ease. *Treat yourself kindly,* and give yourself time to unwind with a magazine and a cup of tea and a biscuit. If there is no one to talk to you could try writing things down. List the things that are causing your life to run out of control and this may help you to see possible solutions. *And don't be afraid to ask for help.* Many people are prepared to help if they are asked and know the problem. To harm yourself is the easy way out, since the pain you inflict on yourself masks the pain you feel inside. But in turn, this causes grief and a sense of rejection in your family and friends. *Is this what you really want?*

Do you hate yourself?

This is easy to do; to blame yourself for all that is wrong in your life and for things that haven't worked out, and for the times you have been hurt. Self-harm is easy. Because you hate yourself it is easy to punish your body, and this becomes a vicious circle. So your body becomes scarred, and you can dislike yourself even more.

It is important to love yourself. Try to find the good things which others see in you and concentrate on these. *Everybody has good points.* It may be that you are friendly and helpful; perhaps you have a special talent for drawing or for baking cakes.

Try to build up these good points and let yourself receive praise. Allow others to love you and be your friends. When you are feeling low it is very easy to push others away and say 'I want to be alone'. *This is when you need other people's support and friendship most.* It is an uphill struggle to learn to love yourself, and may be possible only after months or even years of hate, *but it is possible. Try to think of one positive thought about yourself every day.*

Have you ever been abused and blame yourself for what has happened?

Abuse can take many forms: physical, emotional and sexual; and it can occur at many and different times in your life. It may be that you will need counselling in order to come to terms with the abuse you've suffered. I am not qualified to give advice, though I have been abused myself. This is a hard thing to come to terms with. *The first step is to stop blaming yourself for what happened.* If you have been abused it is easy to feel that you are worthless. *Yet everyone is special and unique including you.*

Self-harm may only aggravate the situation, so why hurt yourself? Surely you have been hurt enough already! Sometimes this can be a cry for help, but it often goes unanswered in the frustration of the situation. *Self-harm can be anger which should be directed at the abuser but which is turned in on yourself.* Please seek counselling or other help and advice before self-harming.

Summary

In summary, then, there are many reasons for self-harm and I have only covered a few. The most common reaction from others to my harming myself is anger, and that I am wasting their time. It is much better to say to someone, *'I need help with this situation or problem; please help me.'* People are much more likely to listen and help than if you self-harm. Apart from this, I have had two operations to correct damage I have inflicted on myself. So I say to anyone tempted to self-harm:

'Please don't!
Whatever the problem there is a way through it.
The scars of self-harm are there for life.'

Healing hint 7

The following wise and comforting words for survivors of childhood sexual abuse comes from Jenny Stucke,[5] who runs Directory and Book Services.

Wise and comforting words
By Jenny Stucke

When you have been sexually abused as a child, you may lose all sense of self-worth. It can be hard to believe anyone could love you, to feel that anyone does, no matter what they say or do. It can be difficult to take care of your body, which you might hate and blame. You may not even want to live.

The legacy of childhood sexual abuse can be devastating, making itself felt years later, and seeming insurmountable at times. Adults who were sexually abused as children often find they have a host of difficulties: Depression, illness, eating disorders, problems with sex and intimacy, or drug and alcohol abuse. They may find themselves in dangerous situations again and again, as if some basic safety skills are missing. Or be driven to hurt themselves, cut themselves, finding some relief from the intolerable pain in making it visible.

Children are about ten times more likely to be abused in their own homes, schools and clubs, than by a stranger. The abuser is most likely to be someone known and trusted by the child, needed, even loved.

In these circumstances, the only way a child can survive is to blame him or herself. 'I must have brought it on myself. I must be dirty and bad for him to hurt me like that.' Incredible as it may seem, this is easier to live with than the enormity of the betrayal that actually occurred. As children, we instinctively know that our survival depends on these bigger people. So we protect them to save ourselves, but in doing so take on an awful and unjust burden of self-blame.

There are often elements of sexual abuse which feel physically pleasurable, adding to the feelings of confusion, guilt and shame. It might be the hugging, the attention, the treats, or the genital stimulation. All these things are pleasurable; it's normal to find them pleasurable. That the abuser used these good things to hurt us, as part of something despicable, is not our fault. There is no blame, no culpability that can be attached to the victim of the abuse.

Adults who were sexually abused as children may go for years without telling anyone about what happened to them. They may have been threatened with awful consequences if they did tell. They may believe the adults around them need to be protected from such knowledge, or be sure that they would be blamed, or accused of lying. In many cases, children do try to tell, verbally or otherwise, but no one can hear them or believe them. *Is it any wonder they then stay silent?*

A particular life event, like having a child or losing a loved one, can spark a flashback years later. Or the childhood abuse may be mentioned in seeking help for another problem. The ways of being that protected us as children can be destructive to what we want from our adult lives. Not feeling anything is one way of surviving the abuse, but there comes a time when we want to feel. To feel joy, love, anger; to live. Sometimes it just becomes too much of a strain to carry on trying to act 'normal', feeling all the time that you don't fit in. Many people will try everything else first, and only when it is unavoidable will they look at their experience of sexual abuse. It is a difficult and brave step.

There is help available. It is still sometimes hard to find, but there are more trained counsellors, more self-help groups, more good books, each year. For people who already feel so isolated and different, it's easy to think: 'Yes, but they don't apply to me'.

Don't talk yourself out of what you need and deserve to have

If you are reading this as someone who has been sexually abused, you have already started your healing. You have courage, and will need encouragement. The healing process may involve looking more closely at what happened, remembering more of what was done to you and how you felt. It involves work and commitment, grief and anger. But it ends the isolation and secrecy. It gradually cuts away the lies that became part of us and can cripple us with self-hate. It teaches us to trust and love ourselves, and to interact with others more safely and more satisfyingly.

Whatever leads you to finally seek help, know that it is worth it; that you are worth it

Copyright © 1997 Jenny Stucke
Directory And Book Services (DABS)
Used with permission

Healing hint 8: Kate

Finding effective distractions and alternatives has been very useful . . . writing down things that worry me and putting them away until I can deal with them, worrying about things only when I absolutely have to, then dealing with them the best I can. Talking about the abuse I experienced in the past – just letting it out, and having other people tell me that it is okay for me to feel upset about these things – validation about feelings I've had for so many years and not been able to talk about.

I've started writing stories about my experiences, as if they happened to someone else, then looking at the things my character did from an impartial standpoint and seeing that I coped the best I could and that I wasn't really to blame for a lot of things I had been carrying around on my shoulders for many years.

I've also started writing poetry. It's not very good but it's a way of expressing emotions rather than just bottling them up.

Healing hint 9: A collection of self-help tips

'Writing is medicine. It is an appropriate antidote to injury. It is an appropriate companion for any difficult change.'

—*Julia Cameron*[6]

Gaining relief through writing

- 'Write down what you think and feel no matter what it is, and keep it safe as it's a part of you. If possible, share what you have written with someone you trust.'
- 'I have written a lot about my feelings and experiences which has provided an alternative release.'
- 'Writing down your feelings or writing imaginary letters to people who have upset or angered you can help.'
- 'A lot of writing helps. I wrote posters with specific messages, which I hung on my bedroom wall at the hospital.'
- 'Write poetry.'

Keep a journal or diary

- 'Try to set aside half an hour a day to write down your thoughts and feelings. Go with the flow. Write whatever comes into your head. Don't censure or edit your writing. At the end of the week, read through your journal. Note whether any particular thoughts, feelings or themes have emerged. Getting your thoughts and feelings out on paper is therapeutic – it can help you see things more clearly and put things into perspective, so keep your journal going. If you are in counselling or therapy, or in a trusting relationship, it might help to share any common thoughts, feelings or themes identified.'
- 'I often write down what I feel in my diary but this is often when I have cut myself. However, sometimes after I have written in my diary my tense feelings lessen and I don't feel I need to cut myself.'
- 'Writing a mood diary has helped me become visible and makes my feelings visible to myself and my counsellor.'

Expressing feelings through drawing and artwork

- 'Drawing how I feel, using shapes, colours, diagrams – also drawing into the picture some hope or an "escape route"(other than a razor). This has really helped me.'

- 'Painting has been a big help – painting the anger, frustration or pain has sometimes removed the need to self-harm.'

Talking is healing

- 'I find it hard to trust people and it is not always easy to talk, but it is better to talk than cut.'
- 'Talk to a friend who doesn't get frightened by what you do.'
- 'Don't block things out, or suppress your feelings. Find someone you trust and feel comfortable to share you feelings with. It helps to get all your thoughts and feelings out in the open. Owning your feelings is freedom. Denying your feelings is pain. They are yours and are not right or wrong – they just are. Responsibility comes with how you behave in response to them.'

Be kind to yourself

- 'After harming myself it sunk in what I'd done and I used to abuse myself mentally. Now, if I do harm myself I do something nice for myself afterwards.'
- 'I will reward myself e.g. buying something nice, if I go over a certain period of time without self-harming.'
- 'Be kind to yourself. I treat myself to a candle-lit aromatherapy bath if I'm feeling low; it's harder to hurt myself if I'm trying to love myself.'

Focus on the positive

- 'Every time I think of harming myself, I envisage all the good things I've had in my life. I think of something that makes me feel good. I think of the good/bad points of my self-harm – I think I am worth more than this – I think – who's this gonna hurt more – me or them.'
- 'I am trying to stop now, and have gone a couple of weeks without self-injury. I found one wonderful way that is so encouraging and helps so much. I've tried many different ways before and none of them worked. This one does. I keep a calendar and put a smiley face

sticker on every day that I don't cut. In the past I have found that it is very discouraging to just keep count of how many days you've gone without cutting because if you slip over, you have to start all over again. But by using these stickers, I can look at all the stickers on the days I didn't self-injure compared to the few days that I did self-injure and it gives me so much encouragement. Instead of saying "Well, I made it 2 weeks and then screwed it up." I can say, "I did good . . . I only cut once in 2 weeks." It has worked great for me and I recommend it to anyone else who wants to stop.'

- 'Make notes of any compliments people pay you. Put them in a box and when you get the urge to self-injure look in the box to remind yourself of the nice things people have said about you.'

Create a place of safety
- 'Construct a sanctuary in your mind – imagine how you would like it to look – the colour, the texture, the smell, the furnishings, and the entrance. This is your safe haven – nobody and nothing can hurt you here – you are completely in control. When you are having a difficult time, or thinking about self-injury, sit quietly, close your eyes, and imagine you are in your refuge. This might take time to achieve but it can work, and some people find it a very comforting exercise.'

Get moving
- 'Go for a long run, or a brisk walk.'
- 'Put some loud music on and jig about or dance around the floor.'

To alleviate numbness
If you self-injure to ease feelings of numbness try squeezing an ice cube in your hand until it melts, or chew something with a strong flavour (raw onion, raw ginger root, a chilli pepper, or piece of lemon). Alternatively, as mentioned earlier, place a rubber band around your wrist and ping it to break the feeling of numbness.

Healing hint 10

Tips for reducing stress

- Gain insight into stress and what causes it – healthy levels of stress can lead to success, whereas unhealthy levels of stress can lead to distress.
- Learn the art of relaxation and tension reduction.
- Listen to your inner critic – that voice in your head that tells you what you should, ought, must, or have got to do. Try challenging the inner critic with less stressful words such as could, will, would like to . . .
- Learn to say 'No' without feeling guilty.
- Eliminate cant's from your vocabulary – they put obstacles in your way. Much less stressful to tell yourself 'I can if I choose to'.
- Learn to express your anger constructively. Bottling anger and other negative emotions such as shame and guilt can lead to stress and depression.
- Learn to give and accept compliments – what you give out you get back.
- Learn to manage your time wisely – too much activity can lead to over-stimulation and exhaustion.
- Set yourself realistic goals. Achieving goals can provide a great sense of self-satisfaction as well as increasing self-confidence and self-esteem.
- Enrol on an assertiveness course.

(See questionnaire 7 [Self-esteem/stress/assertiveness levels] in Appendix 2 to assess your current levels of stress and assertiveness).

Healing hint 11: CIS'*ters*

CIS'*ters*[7] is a well respected charity based in Hampshire – they have been operating since 1995. They run a telephone helpline, and provide support, workshops and groups for adult females who experienced sexual abuse as children, by a member of their immediate or extended family. Non incest survivors are also welcome. In addition, they organise regular conferences, as well as providing training to the statutory and voluntary sector on child abuse issues. To establish the advantages and disadvantages of belonging to a survivor run group, some of their members kindly agreed to be interviewed.

Belonging to a survivor run group: Identifying the advantages and disadvantages

Advantages
1. 'You know that you won't be judged.'
2. 'Not having to try to be what you are not – able to be yourself.'
3. 'A safe place/right place to talk.'
4. 'Half the time people know what you are thinking, no matter what you are saying.'
5. 'Others really understand where you are coming from and how you are feeling, because they have had similar experiences.'
6. 'Being able to discuss memories and feelings with others.'
7. 'Knowing others who have been through "bad times" and have reached a better place.'
8. 'A sense of belonging.'
9. 'Not feeling isolated.'
10. 'Support from others and supporting others.'
11. 'Being able to share experiences (i.e. impact of the abuse).'
12. 'Making friends with people you can trust.'
13. 'Don't feel stupid.'
14. 'Group is always there.'
15. 'Workshops put on for members.'

Disadvantages
1. 'Not being in the same place as other group members on their healing journey. For example, may arrive at a meeting feeling sort of ok, but could leave feeling "wobbly" if triggered by some of the things others are saying.'

2. 'Not feeling OK to explain to friends and family about group meetings (as it is confidential) hence, there is more secrecy. '

3. 'My paranoia was so great when I started attending the group that I thought it had been just for me and that everyone else was just actors on a stage.'

4. 'Sometimes you can get a feeling that "more" is expected of you especially if those around you seem to be making faster progress – even if the facilitators say it is ok to go at your own pace, you still think you should be doing more.'

Worthy of note from the members' comments is that the advantages far outweigh the disadvantages. To conclude, the founder member Gillian, offers this advice to anyone considering setting up a survivor run group:

> Providing the group is well organised, and group members remain
> focused on the aims of the group, a survivor run group can be
> a forum of creativity. An identified list of topics that members
> want to discuss can also be useful. New group members should
> be helped to settle in as they will feel nervous and the setting of
> group rules for membership/attendance can facilitate this, and an
> understanding of what support is available outside of the meeting.
> It is hugely important that adequate supervision is available to
> the group's facilitators to ensure they are able to maintain the safe
> setting for group meetings, and the boundaries within it.

(To view a copy of CIS'ters 'Member code of contact' see Appendix 5).

A final word of caution

The Internet is replete with ideas for fighting the immediate urge to self-injure, distracting one's thoughts away from self-injury, and keeping one's hands busy.

Techniques frequently suggested to suppress the urge include some of those mentioned in this chapter, such as placing a rubber band on one's wrist or finger and snapping it (to 'snap' oneself back into the present), or holding an ice cube against one's skin to provide an alternative focus. While these techniques are very helpful to some people, others argue that they are merely replacing self-injury with other painful behaviours – so please make sure you feel comfortable with any strategies you decide to try. Ultimately, freedom from self-injury involves finding your own unique healing pathway.

Key points

- Self-injury may bring temporary respite from emotional pain, but longer term it can pile distress on distress.
- Letting go of self-injury is hard work and it takes time – being ready to stop means valuing yourself, caring about yourself, and believing that you deserve a better life.
- Chalking up your achievements, no matter how small, can help build the confidence and strength you need to keep your eye firmly focused on the goal of stopping.
- Talking about self-injury is healing – it breaks the silence, the shame, the guilt and the isolation.
- Recognising your triggers, identifying and staying with difficult feelings, learning to spot and challenge negative self-talk and self-criticism, and developing alternative coping strategies to replace self-injury are all stepping stones that can help you get off the treadmill of hurting yourself.
- To quote the words of singer Tori Amos, 'Healing takes courage, and we all have courage, even if we have to dig a little to find it.'

References

1. Cheryl Rainfield's Website, LoveYourself: joy-filled affirmations to inspire, encourage and comfort (2001).
Retrieved May 06, 2007, from http://www.cherylrainfield.com/
Cheryl's site offers online affirmation cards showing women and girls of many shapes, sizes, races, and ages, with encouraging and comforting messages designed to build self-esteem. She says, 'The messages are all

things I've needed to hear myself, as a survivor and as someone who has had great self-hate, or that I know other survivors have needed to hear.' Her site also offers articles on self-care, self-love, and healing; articles specifically for survivors of incest and ritual abuse; an online game of affirmation concentration; hand-drawn e-cards; a free affirmation card screensaver; book reviews of teen fiction (she also writes teen fiction); articles on writing; healing links and resources; and a game section.

2. Annie's website: SASI: Survivors of Abuse and Self-Injury (1999). Retrieved January 21, 2005, from: http://www.waghq.com/sasi/ & http://www.waghq.com/sasi/urges.htm

3. Breaking Free, Marshall House, 124 Middleton Road, Morden, Surrey SM4 6RW
    Support for women survivors of childhood sexual abuse
    Email: support@breakingfreecharity.org.uk
    Website: http://www.breakingfreecharity.org.uk/

4. Jo, Releasing emotions, Copyright © Guernsey Association for Mental Health – MIND

5. Jenny Stucke, Directory and Book Services (DABS), 4 New Hill, Conisbrough, Doncaster, DN12 3HA, Tel/fax: (01709) 860023 Email: books@dabsbooks.co.uk
    Website: http://www.dabsbooks.co.uk
    Specialist, confidential mail-order service for people who've been abused, and those who live or work with us.

6. Cameron, J. (1998). *The Right to Write: An Invitation and Initiation into the Writing Life. New York:* Tarcher/Putnam (p. 31)

7. *CIS'ters*, c/o PO Box 119, Eastleigh, Hampshire SO50 9ZF
    Helpline: (02380) 3380080 – Saturdays 10am – 12 noon
    Description: Provides support for adult females who were sexually abused as children by a member of their immediate or extended family, a quarterly newsletter; group meetings (including workshops for survivors) and training for people working with survivors.

Chapter 11

Guidance for family, friends, and teens considering self-injury

· ·

'It killed me when my mom would blame herself,
I hated that I was hurting her.'

'Reacting with anger and horror doesn't
help and only hurts.'

Discovering that someone you care about is self-injuring can be distressing and knowing how best to help and provide effective support is not easy. This chapter offers guidance to family members on strategies that may help, and direction on what to avoid. It also addresses the important issue of self-care. Further, it provides suggestions on helping a friend who self-injures. Finally, guidance is given to teenagers who might be considering self-injury as a way of coping with their difficulties. The useful resources section at the end of the chapter provides pointers to information that in addition to being of potential interest to family and friends, might possibly be helpful to students, teachers, school staff, and health care professionals.

Guidance for family members

As previously mentioned self-injury generally has a profound effect on family members and can arouse strong emotions. Sometimes an attitude of 'take no notice – she's only doing it for attention', or 'it's no big deal, or it's just a passing phase – she'll soon grow out of it' is adopted, which only adds fuel to the fire. It's unlikely that anyone who takes this attitude will pick this book up, which is a shame because self-injury is a serious issue and people don't do it for the fun of it. Another way that people cope with the knowledge that someone they care about is self-injuring is by denying its existence – they adopt the attitude 'what I don't see can't hurt me', or 'I know that you are doing it but I don't want to hear about it'. This stance may stem from feelings of fear, helplessness or powerlessness. My hope is that this book might find its way into the hands of people who hold this attitude, because loved ones need support and understanding to help them recover. On the contrary, discovering that someone you care about is self-injuring throws many people into a state of turmoil, confusion, or fear, and worrying thoughts start going round and round in their minds – thoughts such as 'what if she really is trying to kill herself?', 'what if he does it again?', 'what if I say the wrong thing?', 'it must be my fault . . .', 'what on earth can I do to help?' My hunch is that if you are reading this chapter, you fit into this category and are probably struggling to know what to do for the best to help your loved one. First, be assured you are not alone. The following comments from family members explain how they felt on discovering that their nearest and dearest were hurting themselves:

- 'I felt very sad and like it was my fault. I felt helpless.'
- 'I was shocked, horrified and terrified. It took me completely by surprise.'
- '[I was] upset. I didn't quite understand how somebody could hurt themselves . . . but I knew to take it very seriously.'
- 'I could not understand why our seemingly well adjusted girl, would hurt herself. She did not show any of the traditional signs of depression or emotional maladjustment.'
- '[I felt] terribly frightened as I was not aware at the time it was an injuring phenomenon, which in itself is serious, but really thought she was trying to commit suicide.'

Perhaps you can identify with some of these feelings.

How to react and safety issues

If you discover your daughter, son, partner, or a parent is self-injuring (parents self-injure too) first and foremost, try to remain calm – even though you are unlikely to feel calm. Try to understand that your loved one is hurting emotionally and that this is his or her only way of expressing that hurt. It's also important to recognise that even though the wounds are self-inflicted, he or she is likely to be in a state of shock if the incident is recent. Pressing for explanations, or giving your loved one the third degree immediately following a self-injury episode is unwise as he or she may not be in the right place mentally to be able to explain, or might not be aware of what triggered the episode. Getting angry, shouting, or being judgemental, is also likely to exacerbate the situation rather than defuse it. Priority to wound care is a must – if the wounds are fairly minor and clean, provide a sterile gauze bandage or plaster, and a dose of 'tender love and care'. If the wounds are deeper, or won't stop bleeding, they probably need stitching and should be seen sooner rather than later by a health care professional. Don't hesitate to call an ambulance if necessary, or seek advice from your GP if you are uncertain about the best course of action to take.

Focus on the person

Strive to be accepting and open-minded. Let your loved one know that you are there for her or him, give reassurance of your unconditional love, and make it clear that you won't abandon him or her by offering your ongoing support. Provide an ear to listen, a shoulder to cry on and a hand to hold. Assure your beloved that it's okay to talk about what motivated the need to self-injure when he or she is ready, or feels able to do so. Offer to assist with seeking professional help, for example arranging to see a GP, counsellor or therapist, but don't force the issue, and avoid taking control – many who self-injure struggle with control issues. Try not to take it as a personal affront if your loved one feels unable to talk to you about what is going on in his or her life that is driving the need to self-injure. There is a great deal of shame and guilt attached to self-injury and it could be that she or he may feel embarrassed or uncomfortable talking to you. It's not unusual for people to find it easier to talk to someone who is not emotionally involved in the situation. Here are some additional tips from family members supporting a loved one that self-injures, some of which reiterate points mentioned above:

- 'Take time to listen. Try to be calm. I think it's important that the person can feel comfortable talking about what's happening, or else it will just make them feel even more "bottled up".'
- 'Be more loving. Love can't solve everything, but it makes dealing with things much easier.'
- 'Give them lots of love. Help them get any assistance or therapy they may need. Try not to be judgemental of the manner in which they are trying to cope. Pray a lot.'

Things to avoid

Avoid blaming and shaming

It's perfectly natural to want someone you care about to stop self-injuring. However, in a desperate bid to avert the behaviour, caregivers sometimes resort to unhelpful strategies. One such approach is using blaming and shaming tactics. For example, by saying things like, 'can't you see that what you are doing is tearing the family apart – surely you must realise you are being selfish,' or 'you've got everything going for you – a good husband, two lovely kids, an interesting job, a beautiful home – you need to grow up and take a grip on yourself'. Taking this critical and condemnatory, 'pull yourself together' attitude won't work. If your loved one could pull himself or herself together, self-injury wouldn't be an issue. Taking such an attitude will merely reinforce the belief held by many who self-injure that 'nobody will ever understand how bad I truly feel'. Indeed, as one respondent stresses, using blaming and shaming tactics may prove detrimental:

'It is my SI that helps me to get a grip. When I am denied this strategy, I am in a more dangerous position than SI is itself. "Pulling yourself together" is not easy either; where do you even start when your life is in a thousand pieces?'

Avoid issuing ultimatums

Don't give ultimatums, for example, 'stop or else...' as they rarely work, and may drive the behaviour underground. As stated earlier, self-injury has a highly addictive quality about it, and if a person experiences the urge to self-injure they will invariably find a way.

'I would urge people who are friends or family of someone who self-injures not to condemn them for their actions, but to support them to understand why they feel the need to do this.'

Avoid confiscating your loved one's 'coping tools'

It hurts knowing that someone you care about is self-injuring, and a common response is to remove temptation from harm's way. While confiscating your loved one's 'coping tools' may seem like a good idea, and one that may be implemented with your loved one's best interests at heart, again it can do more harm than good. When the urge to self-injure strikes, those who engage in the practice can be incredibly creative – they can turn almost anything into a 'self-injury' tool at times of desperation, and may resort to unhygienic methods to hurt themselves, with the potential of putting their lives at risk.

The desire to prevent a person from self-injuring, which albeit is a basic instinct, often stems from our own needs, rather than the needs of the person who self-injures.

Just listen

As one family member pointed out above it's important to 'take time to listen'. This is excellent advice as most people who self-injure have a strong need to feel heard. Good listening is an art; it involves listening without interrupting, without passing judgements and without giving advice. In my view, this poem by an unknown author sums us the essence of *how **not** to listen*.

Listen

When I ask you to listen to me
and you start giving advice
you have not done what I asked.

When I ask you to listen to me
and you begin to tell me why I shouldn't feel that way
you are trampling on my feelings.

When I ask you to listen to me
and you feel you have to do something
to solve my problems,
you have failed me, strange as that may seem.

Listen! All I ask is that you listen
not talk or do – just hear me.

—Author unknown

You may think that you achieve little by listening, yet never underestimate the value of good listening. With someone who self-injures a few minutes spent listening might just take the edge off the person's urge to run upstairs, lock their bedroom door, and grab their survival kit. Be patient. With adequate love and support and when your loved one is ready, the need to self-injure may reduce or stop.

An effective strategy for helping

You cannot take away the psychological pain from someone who self-injures. Nor can you 'rescue' them by taking their problem from them. What the person needs least is criticism or condemnation, and the chances are that removing their 'psychological prop' won't make them stop. So what can you do?

- What you can do is show Concern.
- What you can do is convey Acceptance of the fact that although you don't approve of self-injury, you do understand that it is helping them to cope in the best way they currently know how.
- What you can do is show Respect for their courage and determination to survive.
- What you can do is communicate Empathy, by listening without becoming judge and jury; by trying to put yourself in their shoes in an effort to understand what it feels like to be in those shoes; by being there for them, and by trusting them to find solutions that feel right for them.

In summation, the best way you can help someone that self-injures is by showing that you CARE.

What can you do to support yourself?

You probably don't need it spelling out that supporting a loved one who is self-injuring can be a painful, emotionally draining, and possibly, at times, frustrating experience. However, perhaps it might be worth spelling out that as a caregiver you have taken on an important role, and you need to take good care of yourself. What you can try to do – though easier said than done – is to stay Calm, even when you don't feel calm. What you can do is Accept your limitations, and give yourself permission to Reach out for help for yourself if necessary. What you can do is Educate yourself on the topic of self-injury (and well done for making a start by reading this book).

In sum, to enable you to support your loved one effectively you need to take CARE of yourself and your own needs as well.

Dealing with your own feelings

Be honest with yourself about how your loved one's self-injury is affecting you. It's perfectly normal to feel hurt, devastated, heartbroken, shocked, angry, sad, frightened, guilty, responsible, hopeless or powerless. If you are struggling to cope with strong emotions or feel in need of support yourself, might it be worth talking things through with a counsellor or therapist?

Further information for family members

Below are some insights from family members on what they consider their loved ones self-injury communicates:

- 'I think it communicates that she is feeling enormous amounts of pain, but doesn't know how else to express herself.'
- 'Pain that she doesn't know how to express in a more "acceptable" manner.'
- 'Extreme dissatisfaction with either herself or the world in general.'
- 'Frustration, a feeling of powerlessness.'
- 'Apparently something deep inside is hurting and this is the only way she can get relief.'

And finally, family members respond to the questions: Has your loved ones self-injury changed the relationship between you? How?

- 'Yes, very much so. I take care to try to be much, much nicer and more polite to her, and more openly affectionate . . .'
- 'I think I am more aware, more mindful of our relationship.'
- 'We are more aware of issues going on in her life. We have begun to study "cutting" as a family.'
- 'It has made us even more aware of how precious all of our daughters are to us and perhaps makes us try harder to be more understanding of their problems.'

Read on

The next section is aimed at helping a friend who self-injures. However, there are some tips that family members might also find useful, so please keep reading – remember nothing ventured, nothing lost.

Helping a friend who self-injures

It can be difficult for an outside observer to understand the non-verbal language of self-injury, and broaching the subject with someone you suspect of engaging in the practice is tough, especially if there is a strong emotional tie between you. Nevertheless, it is important to resist any temptation to pretend the problem might not exist and remain silent. Ultimately, you may be doing your friend an enormous favour by bringing the subject out in the open. The sooner the problem is addressed, the greater the chance of nipping self-injury in the bud.

Approaching the subject

Give thought to your timing. Approach the subject when you are somewhere quiet with your friend and you have plenty of time together to talk without interruptions. Alternatively, you could put the ball in your friend's court by saying something like:

'There's something important I would like to discuss with you. When would be a convenient time?'

Choose your words cautiously

Approach the topic tentatively, sensitively, and avoid being too intrusive. Say something along the lines of, 'It's really difficult for me to say this, and I could be wrong, but I've noticed some scars on your arms recently and can't help wondering if you have been hurting yourself . . .'

Be prepared for denial

In divulging your belief to your friend that he or she is self-injuring, you are taking a risk with no guarantee of a positive reaction to your disclosure. It may go one of two ways. On the one hand, your friend could feel vulnerable, ashamed, or embarrassed at what might be a tightly guarded secret being exposed. She or he may react by denying the truth or by blaming the injuries on an over-zealous cat or accident. Conversely, knowing the truth is out and that he or she is no longer alone with such a painful secret could bring a huge sigh of relief.

Don't take things to heart

If you are convinced that your suspicions are correct, yet your friend denies or 'bends' the truth, try not to take it personally. The shock of having one's protective coat of armour pierced often leads to a defensive reaction or a need to shield oneself more strongly from the possibility of further pain.

Offer the gift of listening

Allow time and space for the dust to settle. It could be that your friend will welcome the opportunity to talk once he or she has had time to reflect on your disclosure. Reassure your friend that you are willing to be there in the future by saying something like, 'What I've said might have come as a bit of a surprise to you, and perhaps you would prefer to leave the matter there for the time being. However, I want you to know how much I appreciate our friendship and that I am here to listen if it would help to talk at another time.'

Set clear limits

If your friend does own up to self-injury, beware promising more than you can provide. Realistic gifts of help come packaged as support, a shoulder to cry on, an empathic ear to listen, encouragement to seek professional help, and information gathering. Promising to keep your friend's self-injury a secret between you can place you in a precarious position, and no such assurance should be made without careful thought to the potential consequences. For example, what if you become concerned because your friend's self-injury is getting more frequent or more serious – would keeping the secret be in the best interest of your friend? It's much better to be honest and clear at the start about what you can realistically offer, rather than risk your friend feeling betrayed or let down by you later.

Don'ts and Do's: A Summary

- *Don't* avoid the issue of self-injury. *Do* give your friend permission to talk about it if he or she is willing.
- *Don't* blurt out your suspicion at an inappropriate time or in an unsuitable place. *Do* plan the time and place carefully.
- *Don't* condemn, chastise, or criticise your friend. *Do* show caring, concern, and compassion.
- *Don't* risk drowning in tricky waters by pledging to keep your friend's self-injury an absolute secret. *Do* protect yourself and your friendship by being genuine about how far you are prepared to go.
- *Don't* give up at the first hurdle. If your friend seems reluctant to discuss the issue initially, *do* make it clear that your offer of support remains open.
- *Don't* pressure your friend to stop self-injury. *Do* accept that the behaviour is playing an important function in your friend's life and that he or she may not be ready to stop or may need to learn healthier coping skills before being able to let go of self-injury.
- *Don't* focus entirely on the wounds and scars; the surface symptoms. *Do* recognise that your friend's outward behaviour is a manifestation of internal anguish.
- *Don't* put pressure on yourself by trying to resolve your friend's problems. *Do* encourage your friend to seek professional help from a doctor, therapist, or counsellor.
- *Don't* ignore your own needs. Being a good friend to someone in emotional turmoil can be stressful. *Do* take care of yourself and do seek support for yourself if necessary.

And finally, **do** consider these wise words from Ralph Waldo Emerson (1803-1882):

'The only way to have a friend is to be one . . .
A friend is a person with whom I may be sincere.
Before him I may think aloud.'

The value of true friendship

This extract is from a conversation between a woman who disclosed self-injuring to a friend (the only friend that knows about her self-injury). She is asking her friend whether she did the right thing telling her, and seeking her opinion on how knowing affected her. It demonstrates clearly what can be achieved with courage, honesty and open communication.

MD to friend: After telling you about my SI, how did it make you feel? What did it make you think?

Friend: Looking back it may seem strange that hearing about SI [self-injury] didn't startle me or affect me in any great way. I felt quite impressed at the courage it took to tell me – and I was glad I was considered a good enough friend, the type of person who could be confided in. I felt a bond grow right there and then. A part few others knew. I felt an immediate responsibility – it wasn't overwhelming or heavy, I just had more knowledge. It was my obligation to be aware, to be there when needed. I didn't think any less of you as a person – maybe I even felt more. Suddenly you were this strong women who needed my help. I wanted you to know that it wasn't horrible or abnormal or strange. It was just a way of communicating. I did, however, want you to stop. I wanted to do all in my power to try and ensure you self-injured as little as possible.

MD to friend: What do you think my SI behaviour communicates?

Friend: A lack of esteem. An inability to talk about problems; a need to cover them up; a need to look strong and independent. It shows a deeply hurt soul. A troubled part. A punishment of self. It's a controlling method. A silent release that burdens no one, except yourself. I said first that it showed a lack of self-esteem, yet I think it goes further than that – almost to self-loathing and disgust.

MD to friend: Do you think I was right to tell you?

Friend: Definitely. Our friendship is deeper now, stronger. I can 'be there' and try to understand. I think talking about it is essential – essential to understanding that you aren't considered weird or anything because of your SI. It's a part of you, but the more that I know, the more help and love there is.

MD to friend: Do you think your knowledge of my SI has changed our relationship? If so, in what way?

Friend: Some relationships can go on for years without really forcing people to share private things about themselves. I think that it's only through this sharing, this daring to look at each others weaknesses that we truly get to know others and ourselves. You could do things or think thoughts for years and think they're unique to you, that you are weird or disgusting or whatever, yet half the population could be prone to the same behaviour. Our friendship is stronger. It is open to communication. Past can be discussed as easily (well, not easily – but openly!) as present. Secrets are spilled from both sides and the joint healing begins.

MD (concluding remarks): I always thought that I was such a burden on my friend, that I was contaminating her in some way with everything . . . I know not everyone is this understanding and I know that I am very privileged to meet someone like her.

Thoughts of self-injury: guidance for teenagers

If you are having thoughts about self-injury, try to think before you act, and consider asking for help. This is no time to 'put on a brave face' and pretend things are fine, or to attempt handling the situation on your own. No person is an island. We all need someone to lean on at difficult times in our lives, and admitting we need help is nothing to be ashamed of, nor is it a sign of moral weakness. On the contrary, it takes strength and courage to say 'No, actually I am not fine, and I need help'.

Considering hurting yourself is a sign that something is seriously amiss in your life and that you are struggling to cope with the situation. Self-injury might seem like a viable solution to cope with the emotional pain you are suffering and it may indeed serve as a temporary distraction from what is really hurting you. Yet the relief gained through self-injury isn't permanent – it is sometimes just passing, often merely fleeting, and when the pain from the external wounds decreases and no longer becomes the focus of your attention, chances are your mind will once more start dwelling on the deeper issues that are driving you to hurt yourself. Further, left unresolved, these troubling concerns can lead to an increase in the frequency or intensity of self-injury and the possibility of becoming addicted to the act, as well as a growing number of scars to hide and a mounting sense of shame, isolation, alienation, or disconcerting feelings of being 'different'.

Self-injury is not a cure-all

Self-injury simply places a sticking plaster over the real issues that are worrying you, and once embarked upon it is likely to exacerbate your problems rather than reduce or eliminate them. So try hard to avoid becoming ensnared in the clutches of self-injury – it can be a long and difficult road back.

Food for thought

- Consider the permanent damage you could cause to your body.
- Think how you might feel on a scorching hot summer's day when the lure of sunbathing on the beach or taking a dip in the sea appeals, or on those balmy evenings when replacing uncomfortable long-sleeved blouses and trousers with sleeveless tops and shorts attracts. Embarrassment, fear of being discovered, a need to cover one's tracks, or having to explain away wounds and scars can all serve as strong deterrents from stripping off in hot weather or throwing caution to the wind and joining in the fun.
- Consider how self-injury could alienate you from your friends and loved ones – how sleepovers with your peers could become a missed pleasure for fear of awkward questions, or how forming intimate relationships might become a no go area due to fear of rejection at revealing your scars.
- Think about the discomfort of having to explain your injuries to a doctor or nurse at Accident & Emergency if your wounds require stitching, or if a blood test or other medical procedure becomes necessary.
- Weigh up the advantages of self-injury against the disadvantages, not just in the immediate moment, but also longer-term.

Better out than in

The pull of self-injury can be a strong one. If it is tugging hard at you, please talk to someone you feel you can trust – a friend, family member, your family doctor, or another health professional. Silence is not always 'golden' as sometimes claimed, and just acknowledging the fact that you are 'not fine' can bring an enormous sense of relief. Moreover, whilst talking things through may initially produce rivers of grief, important to remember is that crying is ultimately curing – cutting is not.

If coping alone is all too familiar and anxiety rears its ugly head at the very thought of discussing your concerns face-to-face, or confusion reigns deeming it difficult to explain in words what exactly is worrying you, try writing your concerns down on paper. Make a note of what is causing you to consider self-injury as a way of coping, and how you arrived at this point. Writing allows space to speak the unspoken. Additionally, it can bring clarity to bewildering and chaotic thoughts, as well as providing liberation from powerful feelings and emotions.

From a busy health professional's perspective, presenting with a written list of concerns, symptoms, and questions to ask can ensure best use of the time available. It can also be a valuable tool for professionals in enabling them to steer you in the direction of the best form of treatment. Presenting with a list also has benefits for you in that it avoids the risk of leaving the consultation thinking 'if only I'd said . . .' or 'I wish I had told him/her about . . .'

Finally

Please do your utmost not to turn to self-injury as a way of switching off from your emotional pain, or as a means of switching on to feeling more alive, more real, or more connected. In the heat of the moment, it might seem like the answer, but be assured it's not. Prevention is definitely better than cure, and with the right help and support, venturing down the damaging, dark, and despairing tunnel of self-injury is avoidable. To quote the wise words of one respondent:

> 'To harm yourself is the easy way out, since the pain you inflict on yourself masks the pain you feel inside. But in turn, this causes grief and a sense of rejection in your family and friends. *Is this what you really want?'*

Some parting words of wisdom

These astute and poignant words from another respondent are worth their weight in gold to anyone supporting someone who self-injures:

'Listen. Don't judge or pigeonhole. There are several excellent books and websites addressing the behaviour; use those resources to be a better support person. Don't freak out; that's what puts the walls back up that we were peeking around with great trepidation. Self-injury is best described as a coping mechanism. You will find that self-injury shares similar co-morbid illnesses and behaviours as those of alcoholism, drug abuse, and sexual promiscuity to name a few. Realise that many of us fear hurting others with our pain, which is why we turn it back onto ourselves. We don't have well-developed, healthy coping mechanisms for stressors in our lives. If we reach out, we want to heal. But it takes time, and the unknown scares us. Do not threaten us with ultimatums if we don't stop the behaviour cold turkey. Self-injury is not the disease; it's a symptom. Self-injury is the part you see on the outside. The real issue is what lies beneath the surface. And beneath that surface is not just pain, but beauty.'

Key points

- Strong feelings are a natural reaction to discovering a loved one is self-injuring.
- It's important to remain calm, and to avoid getting angry or being judgemental when faced with the knowledge that a loved one is self-injuring.
- People who self-injure need reassurance that they are loved unconditionally despite of their actions.
- Issuing ultimatums, veiled threats, and confiscating a person's 'coping tools' can prove counterproductive.
- Offering the gift of listening and support are priceless to someone who self-injures.

- Supporting someone who self-injures in whatever capacity can be stressful and taxing. It's essential not to ignore your own needs – **you are important too.**
- Talking to a trusted person is crucial if you are having thoughts about hurting yourself.

Useful resources

LifeSIGNS: Self-Injury Guidance and Network Support

http://www.selfharm.org/

LifeSIGNS, a popular, professionally presented, well-established and well-organised site, offers wide-ranging information on self-injury, including self-help strategies for those who self-injure and guidance for others. Of particular interest to those who self-injure are instructions for carrying out a self-help activity aimed at suppressing the urge to self-injure, called the '15 Minute Rule'. Fact sheets for those who self-injure, for students, for friends and family, for teachers, and for health care professionals, are also available at the time or writing. Other useful documents include creating a school self-injury policy, and first aid for self-injury.

The 2006 book, *By Their Own Young Hand: Deliberate Self-harm and Suicidal Ideas in Adolescents*, written by Keith Hawton and Karen Rodham, with Emma Evans, published by Jessica Kingsley Publishers, contains a useful appendix entitled **Self-harm: Guidelines for School Staff** (see Appendix III: 202-223).

Chapter 12

Guidelines for those working with self-injury and related issues

. . . .

'In order to help those who self-injure,
therapists must understand what role this powerful
coping mechanism plays in their clients' lives.'
—Deb Martinson (1996-2007)

C ontrary to common myth, people that self-injure rarely get pleasure from pain. They hurt themselves to bring relief from unresolved psychological pain. Therefore, merely paying attention to the surface injuries *(the behaviour)* is like sticking a plaster over the real wounds *(the internal anguish).* It temporarily brings relief or distraction from the inside hurt, but for lasting recovery the psychological wounds need to be addressed and healed.

This chapter provides guidelines for those working with self-injury and related issues (dissociation, recovered memories) whether in a professional or voluntary capacity. Contributions come from Bristol Crisis Service for Women (BCSW), and experienced practitioners Tracy Alderman and Karen Marshall, Rosemary Bray, and George F. Rhoades. Two case studies, along with respondents' testimonies are included to highlight particular topics being discussed. To accommodate the contributors' choice of terms 'therapy' and 'counselling' are used interchangeably, but essentially they mean the same.

Helpful responses to self-injury
Bristol Crisis Service for Women (BCSW)

Short Term
- Show that you see and care about the person in pain behind the self-injury.

- Show concern for the injuries themselves. Whatever 'front' she may put on, a person who has injured herself is usually deeply distressed, ashamed, and vulnerable. You have an opportunity to offer compassion and respect – something different from what she may be used to receiving.

- Make it clear that self-injury is alright to talk about and can be understood. If you feel upset by the injuries, it may be best to be honest about this, while being clear that you can deal with your own feelings and don't blame her for them.

- Convey your respect for the person's efforts to survive, even though this involves hurting herself. She has done the best she could.

- Acknowledge how frightening it may be to think of living without self-injury. Reassure the person that you will not try to 'steal' her way of coping. (Also reassure yourself you are not responsible for what she does to herself.)

Longer-term
- Help the person make sense of her self-injury, e.g. ask when the self-injury started, and what was happening then. Explore how it has helped the person to survive in the past and now. Retrace with her the steps leading up to self-injury – the events, thoughts and feelings which lead to it.

- Gently encourage the person to use the urge to self-injure as a signal – of important but buried experiences, feelings and needs.

When she feels ready, help her learn to express these things in other ways, such as through talking, writing, drawing, shouting, hitting something, etc.

- Support the person in beginning to take steps to keep herself safe and to reduce her self-injury – if she wishes to. Examples of very valuable steps might be: taking fewer risks (e.g. washing implements used to cut, avoiding drinking if she thinks she is likely to self-injure); taking better care of injuries; reducing severity or frequency of injuries even a little. In all cases more choice and control are being exercised.

- Don't see stopping self-injury as the only or most important goal. A person may make great progress in many ways and still need self-injury as a coping method for some time. Self-injury may also worsen for a while when difficult issues or feelings are being explored, or when old patterns are being changed. It may take a long time for a person to be ready to give up self-injury. Encourage her and yourself by acknowledging each small step as a major achievement.

© 1998 Bristol Crisis Service for Women (BCSW)
Used with permission

(See the resources section for further information about BCSW)

Working with self-injuring clients

Tracy Alderman, Ph.D., & Karen Marshall, LCSW

What is helpful?

View self-injury as a coping skill

Self-injury is a coping skill that people use to help them manage a variety of negative and overwhelming feelings. It is important to give clients the opportunity to determine why they self-injure. Once they can identify the reasons that they self-injure they can start to create other coping skills that are less harmful. The goal of treatment is to address the underlying issues that are served by the coping skill of self-injury. Self-injury is one way that people maintain control so it is important that treatment give as many options for the person remaining in control as possible. It's always useful to keep your own coping skills in mind when working with those who harm themselves. Imagine if we weren't allowed to utilise our most effective means of coping any more. In many cases, this is exactly what happens with people who hurt themselves. It's our challenge to help them find other ways to express themselves and to cope while allowing them control of all of their means of distress management, including self-injury.

Assess for and talk about self-injury

Sometimes therapists and caregivers are afraid to raise the issue of self-injury, believing that talking about it might give the client ideas. But, without talking about self-injury and asking clients if they engage in these behaviors, chances are you won't learn of any self-injurious behaviors until much later on in the therapeutic process, if ever. Asking about self-injury opens the door for the client to talk about it, if not at that particular moment, then later on. Once the self-injurious behaviors are revealed, you can begin taking a thorough assessment which will be key to helping your client decrease these behaviors. It is important to know your own reactions to self-injury and to be honest with your clients about your reactions. People that self-injure are extremely perceptive and will read your reactions. If you do not tell the person that self-injures what you are really feeling and try to act as if it doesn't bother you when it really does, you will end up losing trust with the client.

Maintain clear boundaries and be consistent

Many people who self-injure have difficulty trusting others. For various reasons, many have learned to be vigilant and expect others to disappoint them in a variety of ways. People that self-injure also do not believe that they deserve to be treated well. Therapists and caregivers need to maintain clear boundaries and be consistent with self-injuring clients in order to develop a trusting relationship. If a therapist is inconsistent, taking an emergency phone call one night, but not the next, the client will feel as if they are being rejected and will likely want to self-injure. However, if the therapist maintains clear and consistent boundaries of never taking such calls, and the client is informed of this at the beginning of the therapeutic process, it alleviates any potential confusion and resulting behaviors.

Encourage proactive reinforcement of positive behaviors (*while minimising secondary reinforcement of self-injury*)

Too many times therapists, caregivers, teachers, healthcare staff, and parents respond to self-injury with an outpouring of attention. Hospitals often provide those who self-injure with their own personal staff person to watch them, talk with them, and follow them for a day to ensure that there are no more episodes of self-injury. Typically, all of this attention serves to reinforce the self-injurious behavior. What is more helpful is offering attention (or some other desired reinforcement) prior to an act of self-injury. For example, a therapist could easily set up a plan with a client to speak by telephone for five minutes three times a week. This would be reinforcing neutral or positive behaviors from the client as opposed to speaking after the client harms him/herself, which reinforces self-injurious behaviors.

General information to keep in mind when working with people that self-injure

It is important to help people that self-injure understand that they are entitled to and should expect to be treated well. In order for people to heal and to begin to utilise other coping skills they need to learn how to nurture themselves and allow themselves to feel good and have fun. It is critical that caregivers and therapists understand the level of distress that someone who is hurting themselves is feeling.

What is not helpful?

'No self-harm' contracts

'No self-harm' contracts only set up an individual to fail. If your clients were able to not harm themselves they wouldn't be seeing you for help with this issue. When they reach this critical point of wanting to hurt themselves having choice and control is helpful – contracts such as this take away choice and control. Instead, work with a client to develop options of what they could do prior to self-injuring. When the client is able to implement some of these options then having a contract that asks a client to do three or ten things prior to self-injuring seems to work fairly well. This still allows choice, control, and the overall decision to self-injure while reminding the client of other coping skills that could be utilised during that difficult moment.

Hospitalisation

For the same reason that 'No self-harm' contracts generally are contraindicated, so is hospitalisation. Hospitalisation typically takes away the control of the clients, leaving them in a setting in which they are virtually powerless. In many cases, clients will increase their self-injurious acts while they are hospitalised or immediately upon release. Of course if a client is suicidal and/or is self-injuring to the point of being a serious danger to himself or herself, hospitalisation may be necessary. But generally, hospitalisation for most people who self-harm is not recommended.

Helping therapists and others who offer care to those who self-injure

As rewarding as working with clients who self-injure can be, it is often no easy task. The reactions, both psychological and physiological, that we, as caregivers, may have can be quite intense. The stories of suffering and trauma that our clients relate seep into our memories and our hearts like a wave onto the beach, no matter how hard we have packed the sand. Much like the physical scars of our clients, we may develop our own internal, and hopefully transitory, wounds via vicarious traumatisation. Vicarious traumatisation, also known as compassion fatigue, and secondary stress disorder, refers to the transformation of the caregiver's inner experience due to the work done with someone who has survived traumatic life events. Typically, those who self-injure have survived some form of trauma. Because the nature of therapy and of being a care provider is so intimate, vicarious traumatisation is a real risk. The effects of vicarious traumatisation can be far reaching, impacting professional and personal functioning. The following list illustrates some of the effects this secondary stress may have.

Impact on personal functioning:

Diminished Concentration
Confusion / Disorientation
Preoccupation / Dissociation
Hypervigilance
Racing Thoughts
Depression / Sadness
Impatience / Irritability / Anger
Anxiety / Fearfulness / Stress
Questioning meaning of life
Withdrawal / Isolation / Loneliness
Somatic Reactions
Losing Items / Forgetfulness
Apathy / Numbness
Physical Symptoms
Poor Immune Functioning
Lack of Purpose in Life
Hopelessness / Helplessness
Distrust or Mistrust of Others
Overly Needy of Others
Guilt
Preoccupation on Clients
Use of Negative Coping Skills

Impact on professional functioning:

Lack of Motivation
Increase of Mistakes
Increased Absences and Tardiness
Negative Attitude
Avoidance of Work Related Tasks
Avoidance of Coworkers / Isolation
Irresponsibility
Inattentiveness
Impatience
Poor Communication With Others
Conflict
Exhaustion
Poor Decision Making

When we feel frustrated with clients it's important that we step back and examine the issues. If we do not re-evaluate what is occurring in the relationship with our clients we will get frustrated and begin to feel resentful and/or burned out. Often we as therapists and caregivers can be invested in our clients not harming as a way to see that the work we do with our clients is making a difference. If we are too invested in getting our clients to not harm themselves before they are ready to stop then we will burn out because we will feel like we failed. Instead, learning to accept the client's pace and goals instead of our own is essential in any type of therapeutic work.

When working with self-injuring clients, it's essential for therapists and caregivers to routinely check for our own levels of mental and physical health. We need to stay connected with ourselves to ensure that we are maintaining a balance of work, rest and recreation. We can't be of much use to anyone else if we, ourselves, are in a state of need.

The following ideas may inspire you to take better care of your own needs.

Ways to care for yourself:

Eat regularly
Eat healthy
Exercise
Get regular medical care for prevention
Get medical care when needed
Take time off when sick
Get massages
Swim, walk, run, play sports or do some other physical activity that is fun
Get enough sleep
Take vacations, day trips or mini-vacations
Turn off the telephone
Make time for self-reflection
Go to your own psychotherapy
Write in a journal

Read for fun
Start a new hobby
Decrease stress in your life
Practice relaxation exercises
Ask others to do things for you
Spend time with friends
Watch movies
Praise yourself
Allow yourself to feel
Find things that make you laugh
Play
Find what gives you comfort
Take breaks during the day
Set limits with others
Balance work, family, play and rest

© 2006 Tracy Alderman and Karen Marshall
Used with permission

Defining vicarious traumatisation (VT)

As pointed out by Tracy Alderman and Karen Marshall, stepping in and out of the terrain of clients' traumatic experiences (incest;

abuse; torture; rape; neglect, etc.) can have a considerable impact on therapists, placing them at risk of vicarious traumatisation. Pearlman and Saakvitne (1995:31) define VT thus: 'Vicarious traumatisation refers to the cumulative transformative effect upon the trauma therapist of working with survivors of traumatic life events' further clarifying that: *'Vicarious traumatisation is the transformation in the inner experience of the therapist that comes about as a result of empathic engagement with clients' trauma material.'*

There's no blueprint for working with people that self-injure

There are no 'quick fix' solutions or magical cures for self-injury. From a counsellor's perspective, working alongside clients that self-injure, and dealing with the issue presents many challenges. To understand the complex meanings behind the act, we need to look beyond the etchings on the body to the individual. We need to step sensitively inside the client's world, treading carefully, compassionately and respectfully in an attempt to grasp their struggles; we need to show admiration for their remarkable self-preservation instinct. No one therapeutic approach can meet the needs of every client – a large repertoire of skills, techniques and flexibility is the key to a successful therapeutic outcome. Typically, counselling with people that self-injure is long-term.

> 'The unhelpful therapies that I endured were usually a result of a therapist who thought they "knew" what it was I needed. Therapists need to have more faith in the client. There was no one sure fix for me, because my personal trauma and the underlying cause for my pain were different, as is everyone else's. It is impossible to take some single approach and use it the same way on any two patients, because everyone is different. If the therapist tries to do that, then they will fail. If for no other reason than that the client knows the therapist doesn't really care.'

What is counselling?

There are innumerable counselling approaches, which can be confusing to the layperson.

In general terms, counselling is an empowering process. It provides you with the time and space to talk in confidence with someone who is trained to listen, who will not judge you or tell you what to do, who will support you to explore your difficulties and help you find possible solutions that feel right for you. Through the counselling process thoughts are clarified, difficult feelings and emotions are identified, expressed and soothed, and new ways of being are tried out and evaluated.

Some approaches focus primarily on here-and-now issues; others focus on unresolved childhood issues that are impacting on one's ability to cope with life in the present. Whatever the approach, however, the relationship between counsellor and client is considered to be the lynchpin to a successful outcome.

Change doesn't happen overnight. It can sometimes be a slow, difficult, and arduous journey, and a firm commitment by both client and counsellor to the process is vital for therapy to result in a positively transforming experience for the client. **An overview of five therapeutic approaches used to treat clients that self-injure is presented later in this chapter.**

Stopping self-injury is not easy

The thought of giving up self-injury – which for many people seems intrinsic to their survival, can be petrifying, and making a firm commitment to stopping is a difficult and courageous step to take. Like the alcoholic striving for sobriety, the road to recovery is rarely smooth, and slips and relapses often happen along the way. Again, similar to recovery from alcohol addiction, quitting rarely works if the individual is coerced into giving up self-injury by others - *the choice to stop must be a personal decision,* and alternative coping strategies need to be firmly in place before a reduction or cessation in self-injury can be expected. Any attempt to take control may drive the client away.

Facing the unknown

As well as providing opportunities for personal growth, all transitions, even for the better, involve loss and a degree of uncertainty. Change means leaving something behind that is known and familiar. Hence, continuing to walk the tightrope of self-injury may be seen as preferable to the scary prospect of letting go of the behaviour.

> 'It takes tremendous willpower to stop self-harming. Tremendous. Taking charge of emotions, sitting with them, living with them, knowing that the emotions and feelings won't kill me. That's a difficult lesson to learn, and hard to maintain.'

Respondents' views on stopping self-injury

Figure 12.1 provides a summary of the Internet respondents' views on stopping self-injury, from which you will note that ten percent (10%) had already/almost stopped, fifty percent (50%) expressed a wish to stop, while thirty nine percent (39%) had no desire to stop or expressed mixed feelings about stopping.

VIEWS ON STOPPING	(N=82)	% of sample
Desire to stop	41	50
No desire to stop	17	20
Ambivalent feelings about stopping	16	19
Already stopped/90% recovered	8	10

Fig. 12.1: Internet respondents' views on stopping self-injury.

Why the reluctance to stop?

Considering stopping self-injury can raise all manner of anxieties, for example: How will I cope? What will I do instead? What if I lose control? What if I fail? Figure 12.2 encapsulates the identified losses of stopping self-injury reported by the Internet respondents, which are by no means insignificant and perhaps explain why some people are hesitant to stop.

IDENTIFIED LOSSES OF STOPPING SELF-INJURY	
Loss of a key coping mechanism	Loss of a piece of oneself/a part of one's life
Loss of a sense of control	Loss of a release for difficult feelings
Loss of a 'reliable friend'	Loss of a calming strategy
Loss of one's mind – sanity – life	Loss of a security blanket and a sense of safety
Loss of a method for self-care	Loss of a quick fix
Loss of a way to communicate	Loss of an escape route when desperate
Loss of the known and familiar	Loss of freedom to do what one needs to do and wants to do

Fig. 12.2: Internet respondents' identified losses of stopping self-injury.

Contracting

Contracting should include agreement on goals, boundaries of confidentiality, liaison with other professionals involved in the client's care, fees (if applicable), frequency and length of sessions, out of session crisis support, holiday arrangements, cancellations, anticipated duration, treatment approach, homework activities, and so forth. It needs to be emphasised that therapy is not an easy journey and there are no quick fix solutions. If the client is experiencing flashbacks, advice should be given on how to cope with these (see resources at the end of this chapter), and a strong therapeutic alliance and support network outside the therapeutic environmental need to be in place before any trauma work is undertaken.

Trust and safety with childhood trauma survivors that self-injure

Childhood trauma can have a profound effect on a client's ability to trust, and whilst clients may yearn desperately for connection with a trusted person, fear and anxiety may get in the way of forming a healthy attachment with the therapist. Feelings of betrayal, abandonment, and rejection are familiar to many trauma survivors, hence the therapist's efforts to establish a safe and trusting alliance may be sabotaged – albeit unwittingly – because the client may have no markers to measure the meaning of trust.

Trust doesn't come cheap when working with trauma survivors who self-injure – it has to be earned. It can take months, sometimes years, to build a relationship of trust. Creating a warm, nurturing, confidential, and safe environment, and building a strong therapeutic alliance can give the client courage and confidence to address the underlying issues.

'If there is no relationship, the communication breaks down, the trust is lost and the problems continue. It all starts with trust. Once you have that, then, the communication begins . . . then the true therapy and behavioural changes can begin.'

'No theory or techniques will work if the relationship is not there. A client needs to trust a counsellor before any work can begin.'

More on 'no self-injury' contracts

As Tracy Alderman and Karen Marshall stressed earlier, "'No self-harm' contracts only set up an individual to fail." Further, as Tracy

Alderman also emphasises in her popular book, *The Scarred Soul* (1997:204) 'contracts are generally made to meet the needs or fears of the therapist, rather than the client.'

Counsellors faced with a client that self-injures sometimes feel a need to 'do' rather than 'be' and may consider imposing a no self-injury contract as a condition of counselling. The client – who could have been waiting months for an appointment – rather than risk losing the opportunity of help and support, may agree to the contract, even though he or she disagrees with it, or knows in his or her heart that it will not be possible to stick to it.

Contracts should be used cautiously with people that self-injure. Unless mutually agreed between client and counsellor, they rarely work, and can lead to shame and dishonesty on the part of the client. This in turn, can have a negative impact on the therapeutic relationship.

One respondent explains how she and her counsellor resolved an issue regarding a 'no self-injury' contract:

> 'My therapist tried to make a contract with me. The only effect a "no self-injury" contract had was that I continued to self-injure . . . but just never told her. In the end, this came out, and the contract was negotiated to an "if I self-injure I have to tell you" contract. This worked much better.'

Next, four respondents give their views on why they consider 'no self-injury' contracts are ill advised.

> 'I think it is a mistake to consider the cessation of self-injury as a cure. The issues are still there to be dealt with, the method of coping has ceased. It's a bit like an alcoholic who has stopped drinking. Ongoing support is still necessary. Plus the individual needs to create a whole new

identity, another social circle and a new way of behaving. And the issues have to be dealt with. With trauma survivors, I think this is especially important because often the self-injury has worked as a numbing agent to keep the individual from re-experiencing the trauma. Once that numbness is gone, once the focus is no longer on self-injury the trauma presents itself in full. That experience may be shattering while the method to cope with it is no longer available or no longer works.'

'I don't think contracts are an answer. What's the point of taking away a person's way of coping if there isn't something to fill the void? I self-injured several times to stop myself committing suicide – it worries me what would have happened if I had made a contract not to self-injure (or suicide) with someone I have put so much trust and faith in. I think it might be more helpful to put in place a set of steps which should take place before self-injury, e.g. calling the therapist. Or some sort of agreement about the degree of self-injury if there is a risk of serious injury.'

'I think contracts can be quite damaging in a way. Self-harm is something someone has relied on, a protective mechanism, a way of coping – to down specific boundaries is a frightening prospect. In my own experience, I found it incredibly hard and in fact went deeper "underground" about it by being more secretive. "Contracts" where there no hard and fast rules I think are more beneficial. A therapist can state that they would prefer it not to happen because of "x" reasons – a therapist needs to empower their clients not to do it, but the reasons have to valid and non-restricting. Then again, it certainly does depend on the client. If that's what works, so be it.'

'I was put on a contract to stop self-harming whilst living in supported accommodation. It made me want to self-harm more and I'd do it in secret as often as I could. Basically, the frequency and severity both escalated dramatically. I felt it was taken out of my control and this had the effect of only adding to my problems.'

Silences

In the early stages of therapy, silences can feel uncomfortable or threatening to clients, and encouragement to talk is essential. This is particularly important in the case of trauma survivors, who may have lived in a prison of silence and secrets for years. Likewise, adults raised in an atmosphere of 'kids should be seen and not heard' may struggle with long silences.

Childhood abuse and neglect leave special scars with regard to issues of trust, and the silent counsellor may be perceived as punishing, authoritarian, all powerful, remote – even abusive.

'For [therapists] 1 & 2, I was not ready and didn't know how to talk to someone about what was going on. Unfortunately, both therapists preferred to have me talk so much of the time was spent in silence. When I was ready to try again, [therapist number] 3 was very unprofessional in many ways and inattentive.'

Considering the appropriateness of touch

Touch can convey a powerful message of unconditional acceptance, if used sparingly and appropriately. However, it is crucial to check out the client's views about being touched. With a distressed client, a simple question such as: *'What would you like me to do?'* can guide the counsellor to responding appropriately.

'The first thing she [the counsellor] asked me was could I show her my arm. There was no accusation, no disgust, just compassion. And when she actually touched my arm I was so relieved she didn't find me repulsive or dirty, and I felt safe.'

'I wish to get a hug from them, or a pat on the back sometimes. The no contact at all thing I think stops the therapist from connecting a trusting relationship. There have been many times when I wished I had had a hug from my therapist, or anyone, after a therapy session.'

For survivors of child abuse, touch can be a particularly difficult issue – some are not comfortable with any form of touch as it can open the doorway to unresolved wounds, or re-activate painful memories – **so please tread cautiously**.

Case study 12.1: Jill (1)

Written October 2001

My skin is a visible and physical barrier to me. I like to think I control who comes close, who has contact, and who doesn't. But not everyone seeks my permission. Those who know me never touch me; they understand the rules. But others just assume it is OK. They touch and hug – I hate it!

I get an intense physical feeling; I feel myself wanting to repel them, to push them far away. Yet I am weak and scared. I don't say no, **I should say no**. When I fail to stop people I feel contaminated and violated. The line has been crossed, my line – my protective barrier which keeps me in and others out. Touching leaves me feeling uncomfortable, invaded, and full of self-hate.

I control and operate the barrier. It is up to me what I let out and whom I let in. It has not always been this way; some enter uninvited.

They hurt me, cause me pain, and reject me. I should have stopped them; I feel ashamed.

Cutting breaks the barrier; I control this. It's my way of releasing tension, letting out some of the badness, and feeling cleansed.

My body is scarred. The scars are a reminder of my pain; they make my pain real. The scars are unattractive, ugly. That's good; no one will want me and no one will hurt me.

Most of my scars are only visible to me. I hate my scars; they cause me to lie.

I would like to feel free to cut wherever I wanted to, but I am wary. I mustn't be found out. It feels dangerous. I end up making superficial cuts in 'safe' areas, cuts I can treat. There are places I really want to cut, places that are bad but I am scared.

I want to change. I need to understand why I feel this way, why touching is so frightening. I want to be able to say **no** to someone who touches me so I feel in control. I should have said no.

My body yearns to be held, to feel safe, loved and accepted – but this is scary!

If I think about touch and 'listen' to my body I feel my heart racing, my breathing quickening in pace, I'm shaking – I have to block it to stop the panic.

I want to wrap my arms around me, to protect me, to feel safe, to keep people away. I feel confused, I see nothing – I'm safe. If I cannot see someone they cannot hurt me. I want to curl up and hide.

I see the hurt in others when I reject them; it's not their fault, it's mine. I am caught up in a cycle that I am struggling to break free from.

Every time I don't say no I feel a rush of self-hate, fear, and panic. I then cut to make the feelings go away. Sometimes I feel I am punishing myself by cutting, punishing myself for not saying no when I should have.

Cutting offers immediate relief but all too soon I'm back with the negative feelings. I am trapped, too scared to break free.

Children are safe – I can freely give and accept their love and touch. Their touch is innocent, unconditional, SAFE.

Trauma-focused work

In the early stages of therapy, clients rarely have the coping skills to tolerate trauma-focused work; therefore, exploration of traumatic material should be discouraged. Pressure to do such work too early carries the risk of retraumatisation, escalations of self-injury, or premature termination of treatment by the client. If the client's self-injury escalates, the pace of the work may need slowing down – the client needs to stay safe within the boundaries of the 'bearable'.

Escalations may be a sign that the client is struggling to cope with an overload of intrusive thoughts, feelings, body memories, flashbacks or panic attacks.

> 'I never thought that "talking" or "opening up" could be so painful . . . I am still working with my psychologist and am finding it hard going. I am suffering a lot from flashbacks, panic attacks and anxiety attacks which were not as pronounced before. The self-injury is also increasing as a measure of helping me cope at this difficult time with all my thoughts, emotions and feelings which are causing a lot of pain.'

Treatment interventions

Research on the effectiveness of treatment methods for self-injury is sparse, and evidence to suggest that any one particular therapeutic approach is more beneficial than another is lacking. Important though is that counsellors should avoid becoming so firmly ensconced in one approach that it blinkers their vision of what others have to offer.

Emotional expression

Bearing in mind that many people who self-injure have difficulty identifying and verbalising their thoughts, feelings and emotions in words, expressive therapies, for example, art therapy, poetry, movement, psychodrama, or music are worth considering as a useful adjunct to other therapeutic interventions, especially in the early stages.

An overview of five therapeutic approaches used to treat clients that self-injure

Psychodynamic counselling

Essentially a 'talking cure', aimed at relieving symptoms and gaining insight, psychodynamic counselling evolved out of Sigmund Freud's original theory of psychoanalysis. The psychodynamic approach focuses largely on identifying unconscious processes of the mind (outside of the client's awareness) and making the unconscious conscious (bringing unconscious conflicts into the client's awareness), thus enabling the client to develop insight into how the past influences his or her actions in the present and to discover more effective ways of coping with present day reality.

Techniques used by psychodynamic counsellors to promote insight and reveal the unconscious include free association (encouraging clients so say whatever comes to mind no matter how insignificant it might seem), interpretation (tentatively offering the client possible explanations for their difficulties), dream interpretation, overcoming resistance (sensitively challenging, yet respecting any defense mechanisms the client may be using to keep anxiety provoking urges, impulses, thoughts, emotions, and memories at bay), and working through the transference (drawing the client's attention to unconscious reactions/patterns of relating to the counsellor that derive from a significant person in the client's past or present, such as a parent).

Psychodynamic counsellors are also guided by various conventions, including the principle of abstinence, which means they disclose very little about themselves and rarely respond to client's questions (for example questions about whether they are married, how many children they have, where they are going for their holiday, etc.). To the client, this can sometimes be interpreted as the counsellor being remote, aloof, distant, and perhaps even deficient in compassion, whereas maintaining a position of abstinence is intended to keep the client's best interests at heart, to prevent the focus shifting from client to counsellor, and to avoid information about the counsellor intruding into the therapeutic space and relationship.

Psychodynamic counsellors hold the view that long-standing unresolved conflicts are rooted in childhood experiences. This approach can be particularly useful for individuals wishing to gain self-awareness, or to those with prolonged psychological or emotional issues arising from childhood trauma.

Person-centred therapy

Person-centred therapy, a humanistic approach, is based on the philosophy of the American psychologist Carl Rogers (1902-1987). In contrast to psychodynamic therapy, which concentrates on bringing to awareness what was previously unaware, person-centred therapy focuses more on 'here-and-now' issues. Initially Roger's referred to his approach as 'non-directive', but later changed the term to 'client-centred', to emphasise his view that clients should play a key role in the self-direction of their own therapeutic work. He further altered the term to 'person-centred' when his approach became popular outside the counselling arena, for example in nursing and education.

In person-centred therapy, the quality of the counsellor and client relationship is considered paramount. Roger's believed that to build a therapeutic alliance and growth-promoting climate, three 'core conditions' must be demonstrated by the therapist.

1. Unconditional Positive Regard (UPR). The therapist believes that people are essentially good and displays this conviction to the client. Accepting the client as intrinsically worthwhile however, does not mean that the therapist necessarily agrees with all aspects of the client's behaviour – rather the client is respected for the person she is, not judged by what she does. Acceptance recognises the potential of the client for self-help, and encourages promotion of growth in the client.
2. Congruence, also known as genuineness, transparency and authenticity, means not hiding behind a façade, acting out a role, putting up a front or trying to make a good impression. The congruent therapist strives to be 'real' and integrated in

the relationship. Congruence by the counsellor encourages genuineness, openness and realism by the client.

3. Empathic understanding. The empathic therapist strives to enter the client's world (his frame of reference) with the aim of perceiving the client's world as he sees it and by communicating that understanding cautiously, caringly and sensitively. Demonstrating empathic understanding means standing back far enough to remain objective (*as if* I was that person), without losing the *as if* quality, which runs the risk of becoming too enmeshed in the client's world and loss of objectivity.

Cognitive Behavioural Therapy (CBT)

CBT is a short-term problem-focused psychological treatment; the average number of sessions is normally 8–20. It too deals with 'here and now' issues as opposed to unconscious conflicts originating from childhood. The relationship between therapist and client is similar to that of tutor and student, both working collaboratively to identify thoughts and behavioural patterns that are causing difficulties, and to plan a structured way ahead with agreed realistic goals. Homework tasks formulated by the client with the therapist are a key component of the treatment. These may include challenging self-defeating beliefs, thought stopping, graded exposure, assertiveness training, social skills training, and developing relaxation techniques.

CBT is essentially a structured programme of self-help with the therapist acting as the guide. It has been found helpful in treating depression, anxiety and panic attacks, obsessive–compulsive disorder, drug or alcohol problems, phobias and eating difficulties.

Dialectical Behaviour Therapy (DBT)

DBT, a psychosocial treatment, developed by Marsha Linehan, was originally designed to treat patients with Borderline Personality Disorder (BPD). It is now used in a variety of inpatient and outpatient settings. Reports suggest that the treatment has proved effective for some clients that self-injure. DBT is a systematic cognitive-behavioural approach that teaches clients four skills:

- *Core Mindfulness:* Developing increased awareness of one's experience, and mastering the ability to stay in the moment.
- *Interpersonal Effectiveness Skills:* Similar to skills taught in assertiveness and interpersonal problem-solving classes (e.g., saying no, and dealing with interpersonal conflict).
- *Emotion Regulation Skills:* Learning to identify and regulate emotions, identifying obstacles to changing emotions, reducing vulnerability to 'emotion mind', increasing positive emotional events; increasing mindfulness to current emotions, taking opposite action, and applying distress tolerance techniques.
- *Distress Tolerance*: Learning to accept and tolerate distress proficiently.

The focus of DBT is communication and relationship; therefore, in addition to attending weekly skills training classes, clients are required to be in individual therapy. Marsha Linehan's book *Skills Training Manual for Treating Borderline Personality Disorder* (1993) is an excellent systematic guide for teaching clients the four skills.

Eye Movement Desensitisation and Reprocessing (EMDR)

EMDR is a comparatively recent therapeutic procedure developed by Francine Shapiro, which is being increasingly used by therapists to relieve symptoms of post-traumatic stress disorder (PTSD), disorders of extreme stress not otherwise specified (DESNOS), also referred to as complex or chronic post-traumatic stress disorder (CPTSD), and a wide range of other psychological disorders. See Appendix 2 for DSM-IV-TR diagnostic criteria for PTSD, and proposed criteria for DESNOS.

EMDR is a controversial treatment approach (sceptics question the legitimacy that the 'eye movement' part of the procedure works, as there are no concrete facts to explain it). It is a complex, powerful and often rapid treatment intervention, which 'uses an eight phase approach' to alleviate traumatic memories, and includes rudiments of 'psychodynamic, cognitive behavioral, interpersonal, experiential, and body-centered therapies.' (EMDR Institute, 2004).

In short, clients receive instructions to bring to mind an image of a traumatic experience that is causing distress, and to hold the image for as long as possible, while following the therapist's fingers moving back and forth in front of their eyes. Then the therapist will usually invite the client to talk through whatever the experience brings up (bodily sensations, thoughts, emotions, and any imagery connected with the traumatic event), which in turn is believed to reduce the intensity of emotions and relieve other distressing symptoms.

The eight-phases of EMDR are:

1. History-taking
2. Assessing the client's coping skills
3. Assessing a traumatic memory that results in anxiety and how to reduce the anxiety
4. Desensitisation, through visualisation and discussion
5. Installation. Increasing the strength of positive thinking
6. Visualisation. The client visualises the traumatic event to identify any bodily tension states
7. Closure. The client keeps a journal
8. Re-evaluation. Should be implemented at the beginning of each new session.

Does EMDR work?

A study to establish the therapeutic advantages of EMDR (Edmond, T. & Rubin, A. 2004) for adult female survivors of childhood sexual abuse provided initial confirmation that the benefits can be sustainable over a period of 18 months. Additionally, the study lent support to the notion that EMDR 'did so more efficiently and provided a greater sense of trauma resolution than did routine individual therapy.'

To the contrary, a meta-analysis of 34 studies that investigated

EMDR treatment (Davidson, P. & Parker K. 2001) found that the model was no more efficient than other exposure techniques. The authors conclude, 'evidence suggests that the eye movements integral to the treatment, and to its name, are unnecessary.'

Shapiro's book, *Eye Movement Desensitisation and Reprocessing: Basic Principles, Protocols, and Procedures* (2001) provides instructions on how to conduct the therapy.

Case study 12.2: Linelle

Retraumatised by EMDR

I recovered memories of abuse when I was 34 and became very depressed and suicidal but didn't self injure. I recanted the memories and buried them again when my mother reacted to my disclosure by getting seriously ill. I was on antidepressants briefly. For the next ten years I think I was functioning in survival mode, just getting through each day and staying as busy as possible so I wouldn't have to think.

I started having PTSD [post-traumatic stress disorder] symptoms including flashbacks when I was 45. After about 3 sessions of EMDR I started cutting myself to cope with the extreme distress I went through after my therapy sessions. I also banged my head to stop flashbacks and memories from coming.

EMDR works with the major trauma first. In fact, you are encouraged to pick the most traumatic memory to work with. It's supposed to bring complete relief when that memory is processed and resolved (didn't happen but I did recover pretty much all the memories). The therapist who performed EMDR on me was trained in it. The procedure was explained to me but the risk wasn't. I don't think my therapist was aware that EMDR could cause self-harm or make it worse but I hadn't told him about the self-injury I engaged in as a child or young adult either. I haven't found anyone else anywhere in the literature that I've read who started cutting after EMDR. I have since heard from others who have used EMDR that it is usually done in a two-hour session. I had only one-hour sessions. Even without

EMDR I frequently found myself leaving my therapist's office in a very agitated and unsafe state. And I think my therapist should have spent more time helping me to feel safe with him and his office before tackling anything. I think he saw my attempts to create safety (small talk, less upsetting issues) as stalling or avoiding the problem. I know he got very frustrated with me. One reason I think the EMDR was retraumatising for me was the way it was done. My therapist would pull his chair up next to mine so that I was trapped in my chair with no way to get out (I had a wall on the other side). I don't think he understood the significance of that. And he shouldn't have used his fingers to perform the EMDR. Picture an animal who has only experienced the human hand as something that injures and now you corner that animal and wave your hands in front of its face. I know that EMDR is performed with light boxes and with headphones and tones. That would have been better. But even if he had been farther away from me and used an object such as a pen it would have been better. I do think the EMDR worked. It took about a week for me to process the particular trauma issue each time. Maybe I'm better off for having done it. I seem to be in better shape than some people I know who had childhood trauma and have spent years in therapy. But the experience was so traumatic in itself that I would never attempt it again.

I don't think my therapist was experienced with self injury and that became a major problem for the two of us. He was very angry when I first told him about the cutting. I don't think we ever got past that. I also think he underestimated how suicidal I was in 2003. Maybe we should have spent more time talking about that. I felt very alone with it.

Observations from Linelle's case study

The therapist did not explain the risks associated with EMDR. Furthermore, it appears as if time and consideration to history gathering, creating a safe environment, building trust, checking out Linelle's coping capacity, and discussing her concerns around touch and closeness, didn't receive adequate attention in the early phase of therapy. Nor does it seem as if the therapist enquired about suicidal thoughts or self-harm (essential when working with trauma survivors).

There seems little doubt that the EMDR procedure worked effectively in bringing to mind an image of a traumatic experience. The problem was Linelle had to cope alone with the aftermath – the intense emotional arousal, flashbacks, and memories that flooded her outside the sessions. As a way of coping with the acute anguish generated by the treatment, she started self-injuring, and when she disclosed she was cutting the therapist got angry, and therapy became stuck.

While Linelle's experience of EMDR is hopefully an isolated case, it highlights the need for extreme caution and a high degree of professional training when adopting this approach with trauma survivors.

Did you notice that Linelle's abuse memories returned at age 34? Moreover, how she retracted the memories, not because they were 'false' but because her disclosure caused her mother to become very ill. Did you observe too that she managed to keep the memories at bay for a further ten years by keeping herself busy, but started getting posttraumatic symptoms including flashbacks at the age of 45? The important topic of therapeutic precautions to help prevent false memory allegations is discussed later in this chapter.

The trauma model

In *Trauma and Recovery* (1998), Judith Herman devotes three chapters to outlining a three-stage framework for recovering from trauma – the three stages are explained briefly below.

1. The establishment of safety

The therapist aims to provide a safe haven for the acutely traumatised client and to establish a strong therapeutic alliance. Within this secure and trusting relationship, the client is empowered to develop the capacity for self-protection, self-soothing and self-care outside of the therapy environment. According to Herman, the first stage of recovery can be difficult, challenging and cannot be rushed.

2. **Remembrance and mourning**

Reconstructing and integrating the traumatic experience is an important aspect of the second stage of recovery. However, early exploratory work should be avoided until the foundations of safety are firmly erected, cautions Herman. In the second stage, the therapist's task is one of spectator and helper, enabling the client to tell the untold. Telling the traumatic story may be pieced together through verbal communication by the client, or conveyed through non-verbal methods such as drawings, paintings or writings. For a therapeutic outcome though, explains Herman, the eventual goal is to put the traumatic experience into words (including describing any painful emotions, haunting images and bodily sensations associated with the trauma). Through the process of narrating the traumatic story, feeling the feelings associated with it, and being heard, the client is able to move forward and reconnect with life, rather than being shackled by the pain of the past.

Another essential facet of the second stage is mourning the inevitable losses that result from trauma. For example, in the case of abuse survivors, this involves grieving the loss of childhood, the loss of innocence, the loss of safety and trust, and letting go of the belief that a parent was kind, caring and considerate, etc. The second stage of recovery can be a protracted, painstaking, and intricate process, advises Herman.

3. **Reconnection with ordinary life**

The third phase of recovery is about developing a new sense of self, building a new future and forming new relationships, taking tangible steps to build up strategies for self-protection against possible future perils, enhancing one's sense of power, control and self-esteem, strengthening associations with people that can be trusted, and perhaps revitalising previous life aims and goals.

To quote Herman 'No single course of recovery follows these stages through a straightforward linear sequence.' (p.154)

She also assigns a chapter to discussing the dynamics of her concept of complex post-traumatic stress disorder, used to discern symptoms and circumstances of CPTSD from those of PTSD, as well as presenting the diagnostic criteria for the theory.

Helpful aspects of therapy

Helpful aspects identified by the sample group who completed the survey for *Healing the Hurt Within*, 1st edition (Sutton, 1999) included:

- Being trusted to take care of one's own wounds.
- Unconditional acceptance.
- Feeling valued and respected.
- Exploring unresolved issues from the past.
- Being assured feelings are normal.
- Being able to talk openly and honestly about issues.
- Feeling understood in spite of self-injury.
- Space to explore why self-injury happens.
- Regular time set aside, and privacy.
- Feeling safe to cry.
- Being taken seriously.
- Revealing scars for the first time.
- Speaking to a non-judgmental person.
- Being treated with firmness and gentleness.
- Learning to understand thought processes more.
- Working out how to cope with difficult situations.
- Keeping a journal/diary.
- Drawing painful and shameful experiences.

- Setting small targets and goals.
- Monitoring self-injury and working out the triggers.
- No pressures to stop self-injury until other coping strategies are firmly in place.
- Learning assertiveness, anger management, and stress management techniques.

> 'Therapy helped me change the way I behave insofar as my impulsivity by relating present-day feelings with past occurrences and childhood trauma. Once realising what the stimulus is for behaviour, it is easier to say, that was then, this is now, and to not engage in the impulsive behaviour. To tell myself that I don't have to hurt myself any more because I have feelings, that feelings are OK, they are real, but they will not hurt me or kill me no matter how bad it feels at the time. My behaviour will hurt me and kill me as a reaction to the feelings, but the feelings will not. Learning to have feelings was the hardest thing to learn, and is the hardest thing to live with.'

Unhelpful aspects included:
- Personal prejudices, preconceived ideas, and stereotyping.
- Lack of continuity.
- Lack of empathy.
- Not feeling heard.
- A dictatorial, arrogant, and judgemental approach.
- Self-injury not recognised as a problem.
- Deeply-ingrained issues not being addressed.
- Ban on self-injury.
- Left alone to cope with the aftermath.
- The traditional 50-minute hour (considered sacrosanct by some therapists).

'The particular therapist I went to did not specialise in self-injury. When I told her that SI was the problem, it seemed that she pushed it to the side because she was uncomfortable or uneducated and she wanted to talk about other issues, like my relationships, etc. I was totally disheartened by this and mentally closed down. I lost my will to get better.'

'You can have a therapist with the type of orientation that you would like to work with, however, if the therapist rubs you the wrong way or you don't "gel" together, things just don't work out.'

'I think that there are probably many routes to take which are equally valid, but you need a good person who knows the way! You have to like, trust and respect your therapist. I think that finding the right person is perhaps the most important part of therapy, followed closely by being ready to commit to the process.'

Summary

The foregoing emphasises the importance of the client and counsellor relationship, as well as suggesting that the presence of Roger's 'core conditions' are necessary to achieve a successful therapeutic outcome. The need to explore past unresolved issues indicates that psychodynamic counselling has a key place in the healing process; further that cognitive behavioural techniques can also play a valuable role in assisting clients to challenge self-defeating or unrealistic thinking, goal setting, monitoring thoughts, feelings, actions and self-injury triggers, learning to become more assertive, and developing constructive anger management strategies and the art of relaxation. Moreover, as previously mentioned, it appears as if expressive therapies such as art therapy for example, can also be helpful.

The overall picture suggests that an eclectic approach (combining useful therapeutic techniques that already exist) or an integrative approach (integrating therapies or helpful aspects of therapy to create a new model [DBT and EMDR are examples]) is needed.

Dissociation

Rosemary Bray

Dissociation is a continuum, something we all experience at some level, a response to the fact that we 'have other things on our mind'. All of us have experienced times when we 'don't feel like ourselves', 'were daydreaming' or realise, in retrospect that we have been functioning on 'automatic pilot'. This can be viewed as normal or simple dissociation.

Dissociation is a means of survival

For some children however, who are subjected to abuse, neglect, chaos or other stressful childhood experience, dissociation is more than a normal defence mechanism. It is a means of survival, a coping technique in a situation that is intolerable, a creative and highly effective learned response born of the child's self-hypnotic statement (made originally during experienced danger) 'I am not here'. It involves both denial of and detachment from the trauma whether the experience is current, real, threatened or remembered. It enables the child to escape, to *not know, not feel and not be.*

How dissociation is experienced

Dissociation may be experienced by the child as observing oneself from outside the body as if 'floating on the ceiling while watching one's other self being abused in the room below'. It is often said 'It wasn't me it happened to, it was a dream', and described as 'a feeling of everything being unreal even though recognised'.

As the degree of dissociation increases (this appears in general to be relative to the extent and frequency of the trauma) the individual may experience dissociative amnesia and dissociative fugue. This is a trance-like state, which provides 'escape' during the traumatic experience after which there is usually total amnesia both regarding events and the passage of time. The same trance state is often witnessed by the therapist as a client accesses the memory of the traumatic experience.

At the extreme end of the continuum of dissociation is Dissociative Identity Disorder (DID). The primary criteria for DID (DSM-IV-TR, 2000, p 529) is 'the presence of two or more distinct identities or personality states (each with its own relatively enduring pattern of perceiving, relating to, and thinking about the environment and self)'.

Dissociation can become a habitual trigger response

For the child under threat of actual or perceived danger, internal or external, to dissociate may become a habitual trigger response; thus dissociation can occur frequently even when actual danger is not present. As with the 'fight or flight' response to trauma, when an individual dissociates, physiological and psychological processing is shut down to a minimum and bodily and mental functioning suspended. Recovery starts as soon as the danger is past and processing of the traumatic event can then take place.

The effects of repeated trauma

When an individual is subjected to repeated traumatic events, which keeps them in a state of dissociation or denial concerning the experience, processing of the trauma is unable to take place. This results in the splitting off not only of the actual experience but also of part of the self. This is often experienced by the child as 'I went away and someone else came to take over'.

The role of the splits is to protect the host personality. This they do very effectively. However, the more parts that split off the greater the internal conflict and uncertainty, and the smaller and less cohesive the sense of self is (identity confusion). The very nature of dissociation requires the core person to be 'missing' and therefore means that it becomes impossible for the individual to maintain the consistent and continuous sense of self and time that is fundamental to the normal development of the psyche. This results in a 'vertical' splitting. Instead of the sense of self being continuous and connected through the passage of time, dissociation creates a pattern of separate, unconnected 'snapshots' of different selves.

This vertical splitting of the self differs from the horizontal splitting Freud described as repression in that with DID we become aware that the unconscious is actually easy to access in a safe therapeutic relationship.

Dissociation provides a means to separate the abused and non-abused child

Attachment is an innate response. A fundamental problem with dissociation is attachment to the perpetrator. For a child who is offered abuse and caring, good and bad, life and death inseparably from the same source, dissociation provides a means to separate the abused and the non-abused child and to live in the 'now' in isolation from either past or future.

For abused and neglected children it is within an environment where others are cruel, uncaring or helpless and there is pleasure in pain that they must develop a sense of self in relation to others; where intimate relationships are corrupt and the child itself defined as 'a thing', 'a slave', or 'a whore', they develop their capacity for intimacy. In a world where their body is at the disposal of others and there is no solace they are required to develop a capacity for body self regulation and self soothing. In this environment where absolute conformity to the mind of the abuser ensures the child's survival the child has to develop a capacity for initiative.

Although the core self may be separated from the splits by a total amnesiac barrier, and there is likely to be some amnesia between groups of splits (normal world and abusive world, victim and perpetrator) there is some degree of awareness between splits of the existence of each other; particularly between those who hold similar memories.

Expression of the splits

The split-off parts of the self seek opportunity of expression in a response to the blocked-off part of the psyche's attempts to process the trauma. These different identity states compete for control of the body resulting in the individual often presenting as completely different people. Each split has one way of being. Mood, speech, skills, age and name may change dramatically as different splits take over. Each split has a life experience only of their personal existence and, although they may observe from their inner place, their personal truth, and life view may come from a very brief window of time. A central paradox of dissociative identity disorder is that the splits are not 'real', as in being a whole person with an independent mind and body, but they are experienced by the self and others as real.

Dissociative Identity Disorder is frequently misdiagnosed

Frequently clinically misdiagnosed, frequently judged as mad within the community the dissociative individual has in fact developed a life saving technique. However, with changing circumstances and environment, the very response that has been the solution often becomes a problem.

Dissociative Identity Disorder in relation to self-harm

Self-harm features very frequently in the history of dissociative individuals, often in extreme forms. Many of the issues in relation to this mirror those already discussed in this book; the reliving, addictive effect, toxic shame, expression of rage and self-loathing.

There are however some issues more specific to the dissociative client one of which is that self-harm is sometimes used as a tool to 'get back' from a period of dissociation into the here and now, rather like an extreme grounding technique.

Self-destructive inner voices can be held not only by the core personality but by some of the splits (each of the splits has a specific function within the system). Until some level of integration has taken place, each identity believes themselves to have, on one level, an independent existence, thus there is an absence of understanding that harm to the self, equals harm to the whole system.

Another issue specific to dissociative individuals is that of hypnosis. If we understand dissociation as a type of highly effective self-hypnosis we can understand the ease with which a perpetrator could both sow seeds of self-harm in an existing split or create a split expressly for this purpose.

Working with dissociative clients

Undeniably the complex concepts of dissociation hold a fascination for those working in this area, not to mention the privilege of a therapeutic partnership with individuals of such immense courage and resourcefulness. However, no counsellor should lightly undertake a commitment to work with a client with DID. Inevitably the work will be long term, intense and demanding and the subject matter of disclosures often extreme and perverted. A background of sound practice including specialist supervision and a stable and supportive personal life is essential.

Boundary issues are constantly challenged by dissociative clients who are highly skilled at manipulation and have the resources of a whole range of splits (identities) to draw from. In many ways the dynamics of working with DID are similar to those encountered in group work.

It is impossible within the limitations of a few hundred words to give more than the smallest insight into this complex subject, and indeed into the issues of and approaches to working with DID clients. A relationship of trust between the client and counsellor is however the single most important feature.

Distorted cognitive thinking, double binds and attachment to the perpetrator are all major issues in this work. Working with abreaction and controlled regression can be beneficial to the individual as can painting, writing, and other alternative forms of expression and healing. The client may experience flashbacks and body memories. These are splinters of traumatic memory, which filter through the amnesiac wall.

Often they re-trigger the dissociative state thus providing some kind of containment for the memory.

Dissociation allows the knowledge, bodily sensations, affect, and behaviour associated with the event, which would normally be integrated, to be separated. The bringing together of these in therapy allows the individual **to know, feel, process and integrate the experience**.

© 1999 Rosemary Bray
Used with permission

Therapeutic precautions to help prevent false memory allegations

George F. Rhoades, Jr., Ph.D., Clinical Psychologist

There is never a guarantee that one will not be sued for 'implanting false memories' within the context of one's therapeutic work. The following twenty precautions were developed subsequent to the review of False Memory Syndrome Foundation (FMSF) literature and court cases wherein therapists were sued for the reported 'implantation' of false memories.

1. Don't accuse an individual of sexual abuse, but comply with the abuse reporting laws in your jurisdiction.
2. Don't over estimate the accuracy of 'recovered' memories.
    (a) Be aware of the process of memory.
    (b) Be aware of possible contamination effects on memory.
    (c) Be willing to educate your client regarding memory.
3. Don't tell your clients that you 'know' that their memories are true.
    (a) Unless you were physically present or had confirmed corroborating evidence at the time of the abuse, you cannot verify that abuse.
    (b) You may give your opinion regarding diagnostic impressions of the client, the process of the patient's memory recovery, and the relation of his/her account to current research and/or knowledge of memory and abuse.

4. Don't tell your clients to 'cut off' their reported abusers/families. The therapeutic environment may be used to discuss the possible implications of major life changes, before choosing and acting on said changes.
5. Don't lead your client in the recovery of his or her memories.
    (a) Some clients may embellish memories to please your quest for more details.
    (b) Don't suggest types of abuse or possible perpetrators.
    (c) Don't jump to conclusions; allow the client to recover their own memories.
    (d) Don't push a client to discover and process memories too quickly.
    (e) Don't tell your client that he/she has the characteristics of an abuse victim.
6. Don't recommend books, support groups to your clients that you are unfamiliar with.
7. Don't breach confidentiality.
    (a) Adult clients have the right of confidentiality (given the limits of abuse reporting laws). Don't speak to family members without written permission.
    (b) Written permission obtained, inform concerned parties regarding the therapeutic process and therapist's limits in disclosure.
8. Don't encourage the confrontation of reported abusers.
9. Don't encourage legal action/retribution of clients against reported abusers.
10. Don't look at your client(s) as a possible 'good article', subject for a 'good book', and/or to be interviewed by the media.
11. Don't search for 'dissociated' memories.
12. Remember your role, that of a therapist not a police officer, investigator, etc.
13. Document the history of the recall of the 'recovered' memories.
14. Document treatment process.
    (a) Treatment goals and progress towards goals.

(b) Therapeutic interventions.

(c) Patient's statements regarding progress and interventions.

15. Obtain records of previous therapists.

16. Don't utilise hypnosis without adequate training and supervision.

17. Be a reality check for your client.

18. Seek supervision/consultation.

19. Obtain Informed Consent.

(a) Hypnosis

(b) Innovative techniques

(c) Working in the area of 'recovered memories'.

20. Be willing to refer a client.

© 1998 George F. Rhoades
Used with permission

Key points

- Don't be afraid to enquire about self-injury — it gives the client permission to talk about it (if not at that moment, later on).
- Typically, counselling with people that self-injure is long-term.
- There is no blueprint for working with people that self-injure. The overall picture suggests an eclectic or an integrative approach is needed.
- Addressing the underlying issues that are motivating self-injury is a primary goal of therapy.
- Don't expect self-injury to stop straight away — giving up self-injury can be a slow process.
- Exploring difficult feelings or traumatic experiences may lead to a short-term increase in the client's self-injury.
- Typically, individuals who self-injure are sensitive to other people's reactions, and trust is often a key issue. Building trust takes time — it cannot be rushed. It's also vital to be genuine with clients about your reactions to their self-injury; otherwise trust can be easily broken.
- 'No self-injury contracts' invariably do not work and can be counterproductive.

- If a client is self-injuring at an unsafe level and is at risk of becoming a danger to herself/himself, then hospitalisation may be necessary, but in general hospitalisation is not recommended for the majority of people that self-injure.
- Working with trauma survivors who self-injure can be taxing, and the risk of vicarious traumatisation (VT) should not be underestimated.
- Self-harm frequently features in the lives of individuals with a history of dissociation.
- A further risk of working with trauma survivors is the prospect of being sued for 'implanting false memories'.
- Regular supervision, support and therapist self-care are crucial for therapists working in the area of self-injury and trauma.

About the contributors

Tracy Alderman, Ph.D. Tracy is a licensed clinical psychologist, leading expert in the field of self-injury, and author of *The Scarred Soul: Understanding and Ending Self-Inflicted Violence* (New Harbinger Publications, 1997), co-author of *Amongst Ourselves: A Self-Help Guide for Living with Dissociative Identity Disorder* (New Harbinger Publications, 1998), and numerous articles on the topic of self-injury. She provides training, workshops, and consultations nationwide and internationally.

Karen Marshall, LCSW. Karen is currently in private practice in San Diego where she specialises in treatment of self-injury, dissociative disorders, trauma, and sexual identity issues. She has been in private practice since 1991. Karen has consulted and presented on these topics nationally for over a decade. She is co-author (with Tracy Alderman) of *Amongst Ourselves: A Self-Help Guide for Living with Dissociative Identity Disorder* (New Harbinger Publications, 1998).

George F. Rhoades, Jr., Ph.D., Clinical Psychologist, is Chair of the International Society for Study of Dissociation World (ISSDWorld) and an International Speaker and Author on Trauma and Dissociation.

Rosemary Bray is an independent therapist. She lives in the UK, and has considerable experience of working with dissociative clients.

Useful resources
The following web pages were all retrievable at June 04, 2007.

Dialectical Behaviour Therapy (DBT)
Dialectical Behaviour Therapy
Behavioral Tech, LLC
Founded by Dr. Marsha Linehan
DBT resources, products and training
http://www.behavioraltech.com/

Dialectical Behaviour Therapy: An Overview of Dialectical Behaviour Therapy in the Treatment of Borderline Personality Disorder
Barry Kiehn and Michaela Swales
http://www.priory.com/dbt.htm

Eye Movement Desensitisation and Reprocessing (EMDR)
EMDR Institute, Inc. http://www.emdr.com/

Flashbacks
Coping with flashbacks: goals and techniques for handling the memories
Mental Health Matters
by Sean Bennick
http://www.mental-health-matters.com/articles/
article.php?artID=154

Ideas for coping with flashbacks
Bristol Crisis Service for Women
http://www.users.zetnet.co.uk/bcsw/leaflets/flashbacks.htm

Vicarious traumatisation/secondary stress/traps for therapists
A Phenomenological Study of Vicarious Traumatisation Amongst Psychologists and Professional Counsellors Working in the Field of Sexual Abuse/Assault
Lyndall G Steed and Robyn Downing, School of Psychology, Curtin University of Technology, Perth, Western Australia.
http://www.massey.ac.nz/~trauma/issues/1998-2/steed.htm

Chu, J.A. (1988). Ten Traps for Therapists in the Treatment of Trauma Survivors. Dissociation, Vol. 1, No. 4.
https://scholarsbank.uoregon.edu/dspace/bitstream/1794/1393/1/Diss_1_4_5_OCR.pdf

Special Considerations in the Treatment of Traumatised Patients
http://www.psychiatrictimes.com/p020292.html

Secondary Stress and the Professional Helper
http://www.ctsn-rcst.ca/Secondary.html

Vicarious Trauma: Bearing Witness to Another's Trauma
http://www.uic.edu/orgs/convening/vicariou.htm

Therapy
British Association for Counselling and Psychotherapy (BACP)
Explanation of theoretical approaches
http://www.bacp.co.uk/seeking_therapist/theoretical_approaches.html

Chapter 13

Creative works by contributors

Fig. 13.1: Dignity by Sheelah.

Fig. 13.2: 'What I see' by Rachel J.

Fig. 13.3: Untitled by Sheelah.

Fig. 13.4: Untitled by Sheelah.

With trepidation
I approach myself.
with a glinting slide
I divide myself.
With this scarlet solace
I become myself.

—*Kate*

Messages for staff working in accident and emergency

A plea to A & E staff

Listen to me, won't you,
Please don't close your mind,
Look beyond the injury
To the person here inside.

Please don't condemn or judge me:
I see that look upon your face,
I know your time is precious,
But I'm not a 'waste of space'.

Don't whisper to your colleagues
Behind the curtained door,
I'm not a diagnosis,
I'm a casualty of war.

Just treat me with some dignity,
Respect me as I am,
I don't ask for special treatment,
But please try to understand.

The way I cope may seem bizarre,
How can you comprehend?
When your own life experiences
Have been so different.

And please don't hurt me further,
By discounting how I feel,
'cos though you cannot see them,
My inside wounds are real.

So, please listen to me, won't you,
Don't be cruel or curt,
I need compassion and acceptance,
To heal the inside hurt.

—*Anon.*

A plea on behalf of those who self-injure

This person's known great suffering,
This person's in great pain,
She needs words of reassurance,
Not telling to refrain.

She doesn't need rejecting;
Punishing to calm her down,
She needs your respect and your acceptance,
A smile — not a frown.

She may struggle to communicate
What's hurting her within,
But if you're prepared to listen,
Her healing will begin.

I appreciate your time is precious,
And understanding her is hard,
But I make my plea on her behalf,
Look beyond the scars.

You don't need to know the answers;
tell her what she should do,
some warmth and reassurance,
are all she asks of you.

She is fighting a great battle;
her wounds are deep and raw,
so please treat her with some tenderness,
and help her win the war.

—Jan

Saviour in disguise

Trusted Friend

I'd like to introduce my friend
No need to be afraid
Just be careful how you shake his hand
When you greet my friend the blade.

Some say that he's a cut throat
With murder in his eyes
Though much maligned by others
He's my saviour in disguise.

And made of steel and sharp of wit
He always understands
My knight in shining armour
He never makes demands.

He cuts right through the chaos
That runs riot through my brain
He knows just how to soothe me
And chase away my pain.

Many people fear him
But there's no reason why they should
My silver suited friend the blade
Is oft misunderstood.

Life giver, not life taker
He keeps suicide at bay
Both protector and Samaritan
He's a friend in every way.

I often wonder how I'd cope
Without the blade, and yet
I'd like to have the courage
To say goodbye without regret.

The time will come I'm certain
When our relationship will end
But until that day he will remain
My good and trusted friend.

—Sinead

Relief

My razorblade,
my best friend.
You make me bleed
to ease my pain.
You keep me alive
when there is no hope.
My best friend,
thank you for you are
the reason I am alive.

—Jenny

Controlling emotions

Fire Fighter

Emergency situation
Systems overload
Tension mounting, pressure builds
Threatening to explode.

Volcanic lava rising
Vesuvius run amok
Imminent eruption
How do I make it stop?

Forest fire engulfing
Searing heat inside
Panic overwhelming
Nowhere safe to hide.

Flames are growing steadily
A raging funeral pyre
Survival instinct override
I'll fight this fire with fire.

A lighted cigarette
A glowing magic wand
Takes me where I feel no pain
To safety and beyond.

And as the fire's extinguished
on the outside and within
The only evidence of battle
Are the scars upon my skin.

—*Sinead*

Thermostat

Ever suffered with a boil?
Filled with anguish, threatening to erupt
An invasion of your body
Its purpose, to poison and corrupt.

Ever feared to even touch it?
Lest you might spread its vengeful seed
Cautiously avoiding contact
A victim of it's power and greed.

Ever felt it throb with anger?
Raging mindlessly
Growing stronger by the hour
Pulsating furiously.

Ever wanted to destroy it?
To slice right through its core
To give relief and ease the pressure
To anaesthetise the sore.

Imagine all this angst inside you
Straining to be free
Feeling disempowered and helpless
Filled with pain and misery.

What would you do to escape it?
How would you survive?
When to take a blade and cut it
Could help you stay alive.

Cutting is my safety valve
Never failing me
Controlling painful pressure
Thermostatically.

—*Sinead*

Childhood betrayed

Crumpled paper

Virgin white, unlined A4, blemish free
That was my paper when I was born.
And as I grew
So my paper turned a gentle shade of grey,
Awaiting the words I had yet to write
To make it mine.

But then you came, and you took my paper,
And you used it as your own.
You filled it with words, not of my choosing.
Your words, written by your hand,
Covered my paper.

And when you were done,
You screwed up my paper
And threw it crumpled on the floor.
And for so long
I didn't care that it had gone.

But now I mourn the loss of my paper,
And the words I would have written upon it,
And though I cannot take away
What once was done,
I can unravel my crumpled paper
And gently ease away the creases.

I can run my fingers over its imperfection
And admire it for its strength,
For though it may have been battered and used
Still it has survived.
And I am proud to claim it as my own.

—Stephanie

Princess / Mistress

You called me your princess.
I was really your mistress.
Sleeping with you
Through age 17.
Feeling totally responsible
For your happiness.
You called me your princess.
I was really your mistress.
You showing me pornography
To show me I'm not fat.
Then telling me to drop a few pounds
Even as I was a size four.
You called me your princess.

I was really your mistress.
You told me to run
Through the sprinklers naked,
And had me take a bath
And looked in on me.
You called me your princess.
I was really your mistress.
I don't know if you touched me,
Don't know if you entered me.
You did touch me . . .
Tickling me when you shouldn't have.
You called me your princess.
I was really your mistress.
Well, I don't want to be your damn princess,
Your fucking mistress.
All I wanted
Was to be a child
Safe in Daddy's arms.
Well, I don't need that anymore.
I am strong and will survive

—*Paige*

The legacy of child abuse

Ugly is my body
Ugly is my mind
Ugly are the memories
For so long undefined.

Ugly is the fearfulness
Ugly is the pain
Ugly is the loneliness
Ugly is the shame.

Ugly is the child's belief
That 'I'm not good enough'
Ugly is the knowing
'I'm not worthy of their love'.

Ugly was his gift to me
The day he stole my trust
The taking of my innocence
The ugliness of lust.

Ugly is the enemy
I must fight to stay alive
My self-inflicted injuries
Are the way that I survive.

Ugly is the legacy
From which I cannot hide
The battle scars of war
Depict the ugliness inside.

—A client

Traumatic memories

My terror

I'm learning to understand why I fear
the things I do.
Yet still I feel
the panic.

Building up inside,
A knot growing bigger and tighter
trying to force out
in a spasm, a jerk
under pressure
like a volcano bursting forth.
My body, though, resists . . .
chest and throat constricting
pushing back the terror of
physical feelings,
or trying to.

Think, concentrate – it's not real
or so I'm told.
Tell myself that there is
nothing now that can hurt me.
But there is.
Memories that still tear me apart,
hurt inside that still
throbs, gnaws, grinds into me,
reducing me to that same pitiful heap.

Say he's not there, look he's not there –
but reality blurs with memories,
then he is there
looming large, powerful, threatening.
Just his look, those eyes
make me want to cringe,
cower and run
away for ever.

Not his look now, but yet it is
because at times I am not aware that it is not him
Hurting me, abusing me,
doing things I cannot understand
other than they are sick, ghastly, horrid, abhorrent,
sore, agony, terrifying.

Just as then
I think I am dying
choking, unable to swallow, breathe
or cry out in fear.
His huge body overwhelms me, pins me down
so that I cannot even try
to push that awfulness away.

Still it is the same
the torture, rhythmic pumping
tearing my insides apart,
pushing me down and down into
hell or oblivion.

Surely, there will be an end one day.

—*Jill 2*

Memories
(but not the nice ones)

There were no memories
one should have.
Of good and happy times
when young.
No warm memories, no cuddles, kisses
No feeling safe or happy.

Now memories are in abundance
but not nice.
Coming from the buried depths of my tortured mind.
Fear, dismissiveness, mockery, ridicule and ignorance.
Dominance, strictness, power and danger.
No questions, no feelings allowed,
no mind of my own.

I tried so hard to please,
to be good, to gain his respect,
Always finding, though, that his opinion was the only one
  allowed.
Even Mum passed over to Dad
for him to deal out the verdict and punishment.

Yet for all his show of morality,
his male chauvinistic views and regime,
What lay beneath it all? …
A monster
that lurked day and night
waiting to pounce,
on me the timid, little one.

Now memories in abundance
Fear, shame, disgust, horror,
I felt then, and still do.
Rape, buggery, choking, dying
not once, or twice
but many, many awful times.
Day and night; night and day.
At home, away . . . anywhere.

That little girl of four or five
tried running – miles, even then.
Run and escape.
But there was no escape,
just back
to the same horrors,
again and again . . .

As my body grew, my mind could not
leave those memories behind.
It fought to suppress by
fainting, running away
in panic, nightmares and flashbacks.
Burying it all deep in insecurity,
depression, anxiety
that grew and grew until
the battle became too much.

Despair overwhelmed.

—Jill 2

Toxic shame

I feel guilty and full of shame,
Yes, I have cut again.
As the blood flows my soul is clean,
And I can pretend it was all a dream.
The pain I feel makes me good,
Makes me feel the way I should.
I feel clean and pure within,
I've washed away all my sin.
I know this sin will build again,
But for now, it takes away my shame.

—Vanessa

Burned

Sunshine, the rays burn through my skin.
Blisters and swells, red rash.
Insides are contaminated,
Poison seeps through.
Locked away in my dark hole,
I can't get out.
Shakes and tears.
I swim through my blurriness
And find a way out.
Bright, silver and shiny,
It's a beautiful piece of art.
Slice, slice, slice.
The poison is released . . . .

Oh no, here comes the sun again.

—Crystal

Dissociation and depersonalisation

Succumbing
(printed as written by request)

something's unconnecte.........d
something's gone astra.........y
looking down on something I'm not part of;
wondering if i ever will be again.

"Sorry did you say something?" i ask,
but don't hear the reply.

something's unconnecte.........d
am i stuck in this fragile trance?
my mind escapes
when my body can't.

"What did this person just ask me?"
i'm just skipping through time again!

something's unconnecte.........d
my life seems reflected in fragments;
my body aches with tension,
taut with grievance, and I try to hide it.

"Sorry i was miles away then"...
if only you knew it was a step too far!

something's unconnecte.........d
but how do i reconnect?
head spinning, mind racing
can't slow it down!

skin to blade? blade to skin?
too weak to fight . . .
"i give in!"

—*Erin*

Fragmented by Erin

Fig. 13.5: Fragmented by Erin.

The fragments are the pieces that make up the whole of me. The woman self-harming represents the girl inside me who feels broken and shattered.

Outsider

Memories of a forgotten childhood
Spent forever on the outside,
Looking in at what might have been.
Not knowing what it felt like
To be special in the eyes of those she loved.

They, taking their rightful place upon that pedestal,
She, afraid to be seen, or to be heard
Or to just . . . be,
Lest that pedestal should rock
And the foundations crumble.

Knowing that deep void of emptiness
Never to be filled,
And hungering and yearning for a fullness
Never quite discovered.

Swallowing whatever it
Took to take away the empty.
Food, the surrogate mother
Hugging from the inside.

And, ever searching for a way
Not to feel the pain.
Floating above the streets,
Out of body,
Out of mind,
Out of sight,
The invisible child.

The taste of loneliness bitter on her tongue,
Turning to acid in her throat,
And
Mingling with her unshed tears to
Slowly and painfully, erode away her insides.

And in that awful moment of despair,
When unable to end it all,
(The blade too blunt to do its deed)
She runs away,
Knowing that her passing will go unnoticed.

The oily taste that clings to her tongue,
A reminder of what she was,
And what she is,
And what she fears she'll always be.

Too worthless to matter,
Too ugly to be loved,
Too empty to ever be enough.
A lonely child,
Forever on the outside
Looking in.

—*Stephanie*

Feelings
(A lesson in control)

That
'crazy' feeling
that
'too much pain' feeling
that
'can't breathe, panicky, mind-fucked' feeling.
That
'gotta do it' feeling
that
'one last time' feeling
that
'scared, excited, totally mine' feeling.
That
'in control' feeling
that
'powerful' feeling
that

'overwhelming, do it or die' feeling.
That 'just released' feeling
that
'sense of peace' feeling
that
'hazy, switched off, mind-numbed' feeling.
That
'safe and familiar',
'nothing' feeling.

—Stephanie

My child

She appears
ghostlike,
a child,
lost and alone,
fearful to cry
lest someone should hear her pain.

And though I try to keep her from me,
she touches me
somehow,
and I sense her need of me,
and I of her.

Yet, I dare not comfort her
though she needs me to,
I dare not mourn her loss of innocence,
or share the bitter taste of her sorrow,
or give voice to her pain,
lest I should hear it as my own.

And though I feel the strength of her anger,
I fear the power of her tears,
and so she remains a prisoner,
locked within the stone walls of my heart,
waiting for that moment when I can set her free,
to be the child that is her, to be the child that is me.

—Sian

A storm in the eye by Linelle

Fig. 13.6: A storm in the eye by Linelle.

There is a storm within the eye. That's how I feel a lot – as if there is a storm inside me. The blades are turned towards the eye because the anger that I feel is all directed inward.

I suppose the obvious reason for the tears of blood [*note: the tears are red in the original drawing*] is that self-injury is a way of expressing emotion for people who are unable to express emotion in other ways. But I do cry too and often am crying when I self-injure.

When I made my picture I was thinking of the eye as a window on the soul. Quite often I can be feeling a mix of strong emotions on the inside and still remain perfectly calm on the outside. No one looking at me would see anything amiss. I was brought up with the idea that emotional displays were inappropriate and a sign of weakness. I was taught to always appear to be in control. And I do use self-injury to keep myself in control.

I also use self-injury to display, to myself at least, the times that I feel I've been hurt by someone else. So in that sense, the tears of blood are wounds I've received on the inside. Maybe there's a bit of "Do you see that I've been hurt?" even though I never show the self-injury to anyone. I think too, that there is a sense of the need to have visible wounds that match the pain and suffering caused by the sexual abuse. I feel absolutely tormented by it but there is nothing to show for it. It's almost as if for me there has to be a scar.

Finally, I was taught to be unaware of the abuse as it was happening. The times I told, I was told that it never happened, that my abuser would never do that, and that I was either making it up or dreaming it. I was even told that I remembered it wrong and was punished for what I said. As a small child, the only option I had was to believe the adults that it wasn't happening and I was a bad girl for thinking it. But a part of me remained aware; did see it happening and does remember. I think for me that part is represented by the eye in my picture.

Invalidation and crimson tears

(don't speak, don't feel, don't cry, don't get angry, don't be you, be strong)

Be Quiet

"Be quiet", he said,
"It doesn't matter.
Those words of yours
Are mindless chatter."

"Be silent", he said,
"Don't flap your jaws.
My words are important
Your words have flaws."

"Who cares", he said,
"You're not so bright.
Who are you?
I'm always right."

"Not valid", he said,
"Your thoughts and voice.
I'm in control;
You have no choice."

"Don't cry", he said,
As tears poured forth.
"Keeping them in
Shows your true worth."

"Be brave", he said,
"When feeling pain . . .
My highest value
You will attain."

"No anger", he said.
Bad feelings rifled.
Obediently quelled;
Finally . . . stifled.

So . . .
Be quiet,
Be silent,
Not valid,
Don't cry,
Be brave,
No anger.

"Be quiet", I say,
When it all matters.
These words of mine
In blood now splatters.

"Be silent", I say,
"Won't flap my jaws."
My words aren't important
Wrapped up in gauze.

"Don't care", I say.
Just stupid and dumb;
I am nothing;
No pain, now numb.

"Not valid", I say.
Thoughts, voice, not real.
"Who'll believe you?"
Sharp pain to feel.

"Don't cry", I say.
Tears well inside.
My true worth shown,
Marred skin to hide.

"Be brave", I say.
Pain old and new.
Retrieving my value;
Streaked bright red hue.

"No anger", I say,
As the feelings abate . . .
Into nothing.
With blood . . . sedate.

—Tacita

Don't cry

Don't cry, didn't cry
Won't cry, wouldn't
Both of them were told
That they mustn't and they shouldn't.

Don't cry, didn't cry
Locked her tears away
Never to be free
To see the light of day.

Now they both are starting
To let other people see
Just what it is they're feeling
And their vulnerability.

Don't cry, didn't cry
won't cry, wouldn't
both of them now asking
why they mustn't or they shouldn't?

—Sian

Crying

My tears aren't empty.

My tears are full of broken dreams, of hopes that one day everything will be "all right" but knowing that they won't be.

My tears are full of grief for innocence that it lost.

My tears are full of secrets. Of monsters in my night that only I can see, of secret words that only I can hear, of things I must not say.

My tears are full of cleansing oil to take away the slime that clings to me all over, that overflows from inside out; the dirt that no amount of soap or scrubbing can ever take away.

My tears are full of shame.

Only, my tears aren't made of salty water that flows away without a trace. My tears are made of blood.

—Charis

The hurt child inside

There are two people inside of me
Both are bound, but long to be free
One is adult, the other a child
But people around seem easily beguiled.

They see the adult and want to look no deeper
But it's the child that needs help, needs some kind of keeper
She's frightened, ashamed but can raise no alarm,
So in desperation, she turns to self-harm.

Who wants to listen . . .
I mean really **wants** to care
For the child who is hurt
Bruised, perhaps beyond repair.

The child is the one who rules me day-to-day
But I'm hoping and praying in that role she'll not stay,
Meanwhile I'm coping as best as I can,
And searching for someone who wants to understand.

And I know that one day the child who's been abused
Will be more peaceful, and not so confused
Secure in the knowledge that it's okay to be just me
and that no matter what happens, my spirit can always be free.

—Juliet

Hollow Girl

Hollow girl, nothing left inside
empty soul, too much left to hide
tired mind, standing at the edge
pain filled eyes, wonder why I tried.

Hollow girl, fighting through the day
lying words, although the scars betray
salty cheeks, all the times I cried
tired life, wonder why I stay.

Hollow girl, crying though the night
quiet tears, only out of sight
bloody hands, there has to be another way
waiting game, will it ever be alright?

Hollow girl, crippled by the pain
hurting child, see her in the blood stain
groping arms, reaching for the light
broken bits, wanting to be whole again.

Hollow girl, could you understand?
slipping feet, searching for the land
future gone, drowning in the rain
begging now, please come hold my hand

Hollow girl, wanting to be dead
endless thoughts, racing through my head
will to try, slipping through like sand
Hollow girl, will I bleed instead?

—Laurel

Be quiet inside
(printed as written by request)

"be still" i say
noisy beast inside
craving attention
talking too loud
too fast
too much
racing
running
"be quiet" i say

"please not today" i say
noisy beast inside
screaming for attention
shaking me within
too loud
too constant
unyielding
unfeeling
"not now" i say

"just leave" i say
noisy beast inside
pressing for attention
shouting and bawling
too mean
too keen
using
refusing
"just go" i say

"very well" i say
noisy beast inside
demanding attention
incessant chatter
too harsh
too hard
cutting
bleeding
....
silence

—Erin

Be kind to your child inside

She lives in your heart; she dwells in your soul,
She wants to be part of you – to be complete and whole.
She yearns for your love; longs to be held near,
but she holds on to her pain, because she's known only fear.

She reverberates around your mind,
Desperate to be heard,
She appears in your memories, your thoughts, your dreams,
Screaming her silent words.

You carry her around with you,
She's heavy; she leaves you weak,
You try to drown out her emotions,
But your child deserves to speak.

She wishes you could trust her to join you,
To accept her and you as one,
Because without you she's lonely,
without you she's sad,
without you, your child has no fun.

The grief that she causes you is too much to bear,
Yet perhaps by hearing her and showing you care,
You could help her break free from the pain of the past,
And it would bring you and her some peace at last.

So please be kind to your 'Child'; please give her a voice,
She's been silenced too long, please give her a choice.
She may need to rant, but in time she'll feel calm,
And perhaps it she's cherished, she won't speak through self-harm.

—*Jan*

The hurt child speaks

There's no need to shout,
I can hear you know,
I'm not fucking stupid,
just 'cos you say so.

I can do things right,
and I have got a voice,
what you do and what you say,
they're not the only choice.

Don't take your anger out on me,
make my life a misery,
Fuck off and let me be,
you can't deny my reality.

—*Anon.*

Father

I hate you for the physical abuse you forced upon me.
I hate you for using me, giving me to your friends,
standing, watching, then laughing,
every time I screamed out in pain.

You never saw me as a child,
only as an object in your mind,
which you could use whenever you felt the need
to quench your thirst for sex and violence,
also to regain your power and authority over me.

As I have grown I dare not remember you consciously,
I buried you in my brain,
but your image was reflected
in every man who looked at me,
every man that wanted me was you.

You lay in my bed night after night,
in my fantasies . . . in my dreams you were there,
always in disguise, but the terror was all the same.
Terror was real, your cruelty has reached my children,
you hurt them through me.

I feel I want revenge,
but rarely is it possible to take direct revenge,
it gets twisted, distorted, disguised,
put on to the wrong people
causing new ripples of pain to spread.

**If you were alive today,
it would give me the greatest pleasure to kill you.**

—Linda

Therapy: contrasting views

Take my advice (Why don't you?)

Go and get a life I say
just tell your hurt to go away.
I don't like it when you're low,
I want the 'old you' back, you know.

It's not healthy to be depressed,
you're getting really self-obsessed,
get out of bed and face the day,
put on a smile; it's better that way.

There, there, dear, I know how you feel,
but it's all in the past so what's the big deal?
Go find a job: you could learn how to knit,
I think that you should stop dwelling on it.

Aunt Maud says that her neighbour Miss Wood,
thinks all this counselling really does you no good,
And my friend Beryl (her sister's a nurse),
says she's read in the paper that they just make you worse.

And I'm not being nasty, but can you not see
how your nervous breakdown is worrying me?
You know that I love you, you know that I care,
but I really do think that you're being unfair.

And then there's the children, they still need their mum,
so pull up your socks and get off your bum.
I know what you're thinking, I'm nobody's fool,
emotional blackmail's a powerful tool.

So take my advice and block out the past,
live for today and put on your mask,
try not to cry, try not to feel,
who really cares if you're not being real?

What does it matter, what small price to pay,
to take who you are and lock it away?
So please stop this nonsense, do it for me,
I know that you're hurting, but I don't want to see.

—*Stephanie*

Words

Words, thoughts and feelings
for so long repressed,
have very slowly, carefully
been eased out of my tortured mind
through therapy.

Looking back one sees
the years and years
that I was not allowed to feel
or think for myself.
What thoughts I had could not escape
for fear of mockery, ridicule and
the slamming of the door.
Time after time.

Occasionally a feeling would escape
to derision and the putting down
of a 'very vivid imagination'.
How I believed it all,
hating myself
for not controlling my own body and mind.

Then spasmodically the feelings
would erupt
into a chaos of self-torment, shame and hatred
of myself.
Plunging me into recrimination, mental torture
and despair.

That was my mind 'playing tricks'
or so I was told.
Then my body too
would play the 'game'
by putting on 'pretence'.
Fainting, hypochondria –
an over active mind
attention – seeking.

Or so they told me so.

From childhood to my teens,
through early adulthood
to my forties.
The same scenarios
reared their ugly heads,
each time destroying me
more and more.

Then when despair became
that tangled mess of
suicidal thoughts and deeds.
My life was taken over
to be pointed in the right direction
of my therapist.

How soon and fast then
did the feelings emerge,
pour forth.
Like a torrent, volcano
spilling out.
Yet still as feelings –
the words tied up inside.

Slowly though, my thoughts and feelings
were recognised and understood.
No dismissiveness or humiliation now
No suggestion that I was making it up.
Just a kind, thoughtful, listening ear.
Someone who cared
and gave me the time.

Tentatively the words crept forth
on paper first,
then spoken reluctantly, unsurely
in case the door was slammed shut again.

Yet no, I was believed at last.
Slowly too, I believed myself,
my feelings, thoughts and memories.

No rebuffs or cruel denials
from my therapist,
just encouragement to speak out more.

Now I find
the words pour forth
fast, furiously, never ending.
In black and white
horrid, dirty facets of my mind,
secrets once.

Now why hide
my words, thoughts and feelings.
Why be ashamed of
Being me?

—Jill 2

A message for helpers

Be with me (please)

Can I trust you with my pain?
To treat it with kindness and respect?
To listen to it,
so I can speak the unspoken?

Will you help me catch my tears
as the floodgates open?
Swim with me into the unknown?
Save me from drowning in my sorrow?

If I entrust you with my grief,
will you help me take care of it?
Console it? Soothe it? Make it feel safe?
Will you accept it as a gift to be protected?

If I take the risk and end the drought,
will you leave me alone and sodden after the storm?
Will you reach for your umbrella,
and just walk away?

I feel my need and I fear it,
as I fear all that I do not understand,
yet I ask you to be with me,
for I am tired of walking alone.

—A request from a client

And finally, a message for everyone

Let the children speak

Welcome to the Channel 5 news
the death of a child
found battered and bruised.
Oh, dear me, poor little mite,
wonder what's on TV tonight?

Small child playing,
her eyes on the door,
Uncle John enters
to molest her some more.

Who's there to help her?
Who's there to care?
Society's answer –
pretend it's not there!

Why show our outrage?
Why rock the boat?
They're just little children,
not people who vote.

Don't look at what's happening,
just close your eyes,
ask them no questions,
they'll tell you no lies.

But if children whisper
then give them a voice,
let them speak loud –
it's society's choice.

They're just little people,
and they have rights too,
they need to be heard,
by me and by you.

—Stephanie

Table of acronyms and colloquialisms

. . . .

Description	Acronym/Colloquialism
Accident & Emergency	A&E
Body Dysmorphic Disorder	BDD
Body modification	Bod-mod
Borderline Personality Disorder	BPD
British False Memory Syndrome Foundation	BFMS
Child Sexual Abuse	CSA
Cognitive Behavioural Therapy	CBT
Complex/Chronic Post Traumatic Stress Disorder	CPTSD
Community Psychiatric Nurse	CPN
Compulsive Skin-Picking	CSP
Dialectical Behaviour Therapy	DBT
Diagnostic and Statistical Manual of Mental Disorders	DSM-IV-TR
Disorders of Extreme Stress Not Otherwise Specified	DESNOS
Dissociative Identity Disorder	DID
Dissociative Disorder Not Otherwise Specified	DDNOS
Deliberate Self-Harm	DSH
Deliberate self-harm without suicidal intent	Parasuicide
Direct Self-Injury	DSI
Eating Disorder	ED
Electroconvulsive Therapy	ECT
Eye Movement Desensitisation and Reprocessing	EMDR

False Memory Syndrome	FMS
False Memory Syndrome Foundation	FMSF
General Practitioner	GP
Multiple Personality Disorder	MPD
Non-direct Self-Harm	NDSH
Obsessive Compulsive Disorder	OCD
Person who uses self-injury	'Cutter'
Post Traumatic Stress Disorder	PTSD
Repetitive Self-Mutilation	RSM
Sadomasochism	S&M
Selective Serotonin Reuptake Inhibitors	SSRIs
Self-Harm	SH
Self-Injury	SI
Self Injury And Related Issues	SIARI
Self-Injurer	SI'er/SI-er
Self-Injuring	SI'ing
Self-Injurious Behaviours	SIBs
Self-Inflicted Violence	SIV
Self-Mutilation	SM
Self-Mutilating Behaviour	SMB
Self-Poisoning (overdosing)	SP
Tattoos	Tats
Trauma Reenactment Syndrome	TRS
Trichotillomania	TTM/trich
Tricyclic Antidepressants	TCAs
Vicarious Traumatisation	VT

Appendix 2

DSM-IV-TR criteria for:
Post-traumatic Stress Disorder (PTSD)
Depersonalisation Disorder (DP)
Borderline Personality Disorder (BPD)
Disorders of Extreme Stress Not Otherwise
Specified (DESNOS): Proposed Criteria

. . . .

Diagnostic criteria for 309.81
Post-traumatic Stress Disorder

A. The person has been exposed to a traumatic event in which both of the following were present:

   (1) the person experienced, witnessed, or was confronted with an event or events that involved actual or threatened death or serious injury, or a threat to the physical integrity of self or others.

   (2) the person's response involved intense fear, helplessness, or horror. **Note:** In children, this may be expressed instead by disorganized or agitated behaviour.

B. The traumatic event is persistently reexperienced in one (or more) of the following ways:

   (1) recurrent and intrusive distressing recollections of the event, including images, thoughts, or perceptions. **Note:** In young children, repetitive play may occur in which themes or aspects of the trauma are expressed.

   (2) recurrent distressing dreams of the event. **Note:** In children, there may be frightening dreams without recognizable content.

(3) acting or feeling as if the traumatic event were recurring (includes a sense of reliving the experience, illusions, hallucinations, and dissociative flashback episodes, including those that occur on awakening or when intoxicated). **Note:** In young children, trauma-specific reenactment may occur.

(4) intense psychological distress at exposure to internal or external cues that symbolize or resemble an aspect of the traumatic event.

(5) physiological reactivity on exposure to internal or external cues that symbolize or resemble an aspect of the traumatic event.

C. Persistent avoidance of stimuli associated with the trauma and numbing of general responsiveness (not present before the trauma), as indicated by three (or more) of the following:

(1) efforts to avoid thoughts, feelings, or conversations associated with the trauma.

(2) efforts to avoid activities, places, or people that arouse recollections of the trauma.

(3) inability to recall an important aspect of the trauma.

(4) markedly diminished interest or participation in significant activities.

(5) feeling of detachment or estrangement from others.

(6) restricted range of affect (e.g., unable to have loving feelings).

(7) sense of a foreshortened future (e.g., does not expect to have a career, marriage, children, or a normal life span).

D. Persistent symptoms of increased arousal (not present before the trauma), as indicated by two (or more) of the following:

(1) difficulty falling or staying asleep

(2) irritability or outbursts of anger

(3) difficulty concentrating

(4) hypervigilance

(5) exaggerated startle response.

E. Duration of the disturbance (symptoms in Criteria B, C, and D) is more than 1 month.

F. The disturbance causes clinically significant distress or impairment in social, occupational, or other important areas of functioning.

Specify if:
   Acute: if duration of symptoms is less than 3 months
   Chronic: if duration of symptoms is 3 months or more
Specify if:
   With Delayed Onset: if onset of symptoms is at least 6 months after the stressor.

Reprinted with permission from the Diagnostic and Statistical Manual of Mental Disorders, Fourth Edition, Text Revision. Copyright 2000. American Psychiatric Association. (pp. 467-468)

Diagnostic criteria for 300.6 Depersonalization Disorder

A. Persistent or recurrent experiences of feeling detached from, and as if one is an outside observer of, one's mental processes or body (e.g., feeling like one is in dream).

B. During the depersonalization experience, reality testing remains intact.

C. The depersonalization causes clinically significant distress or impairment in social, occupational, or other important areas of functioning.

D. The depersonalization experience does not occur exclusively during the course of another mental disorder, such as Schizophrenia, Panic Disorder, Acute Stress Disorder, or another Dissociative Disorder, and is not due to the direct physiological effects of a substance (e.g., a drug of abuse, a medication) or a general medical condition (e.g., temporal lobe epilepsy).

Reprinted with permission from the Diagnostic and Statistical Manual of Mental Disorders, Fourth Edition, Text Revision. Copyright 2000. American Psychiatric Association. (p. 532)

Diagnostic criteria for 301.83 Borderline Personality Disorder

A pervasive pattern of instability of interpersonal relationships, self-image, and affects, and marked impulsivity beginning by early adulthood and present in a variety of contexts, as indicated by five (or more) of the following:

    (1) frantic efforts to avoid real or imagined abandonment. **Note:** Do not include suicidal or self-mutilating behavior covered in Criterion 5.

    (2) a pattern of unstable and intense interpersonal relationships characterized by alternating between extremes of idealization and devaluation

    (3) identity disturbance: markedly and persistently unstable self-image or sense of self

    (4) impulsivity in at least two areas that are potentially self-damaging (e.g., spending, sex, substance abuse, reckless driving, binge eating). **Note:** Do not include suicidal or self-mutilating behavior covered in Criterion 5.

    (5) recurrent suicidal behavior, gestures, or threats, or self-mutilating behavior

    (6) affective instability due to a marked reactivity of mood (e.g., intense episodic dysphoria, irritability, or anxiety usually lasting a few hours and only rarely more than a few days)

    (7) chronic feelings of emptiness

    (8) inappropriate, intense anger or difficulty controlling anger (e.g.,

frequent displays of temper, constant anger, recurrent physical fights)

(9) transient, stress-related paranoid ideation or severe dissociative symptoms.

Reprinted with permission from the Diagnostic and Statistical Manual of Mental Disorders, Fourth Edition, Text Revision. Copyright 2000. American Psychiatric Association. (p. 710)

Disorders of Extreme Stress Not Otherwise Specified (DESNOS): Proposed Criteria

A. Alterations in regulating affective arousal
    (1) chronic affect dysregulation
    (2) difficulty modulating anger
    (3) self-destructive and suicidal behaviour
    (4) difficulty modulating sexual involvement
    (5) impulsive and risk-taking behaviors

B. Alterations in attention and consciousness
    (1) amnesia
    (2) dissociation

C. Somatization

D. Chronic characterological changes
    (1) alterations in self-perception: chronic guilt and shame; feelings of self-blame, of ineffectiveness, and of being permanently damaged
    (2) alterations in perception of perpetrator: adopting distorted beliefs and idealizing the perpetrator
    (3) alterations in relations with others:
        (a) an inability to trust or maintain relationships with others
        (b) a tendency to be revictimized
        (c) a tendency to victimize others

E. Alterations in systems of meaning
  (1) despair and hopelessness
  (2) loss of previously sustaining beliefs.

Reprinted with permission from Guilford Press.

TABLE 9.2. Disorders of Extreme Stress Not Otherwise Specified (DESNOS): Proposed Criteria

van der Kolk, B. A., McFarlane, A.C., & Weisaeth, L (Eds.) (1996). *Traumatic Stress: The effects of overwhelming experience on mind, body, and society.* New York: The Guilford Press. (p. 203)

Questionnaires

· ·

These questionnaires formed the basis of my Internet research into self-injury. If you are a support person working with people that self-injure you might find them useful in your work. If you self-injure, they could serve as a constructive self-help instrument for providing insight into your behaviour, or as a valuable tool to use in conjunction with your support person. If you are a significant other of someone who self-injures (family member, friend, or partner) you could find Questionnaire 6 a useful tool for gauging your reactions towards the person who you are trying to support, and in considering your own needs. Typically, people who self-injure suffer from low self-esteem, high stress levels, and struggle to be assertive, hence the inclusion of Questionnaire 7, which focuses on these specific areas.

Self-injury: Questionnaire 1

About the first time you self-injured
What made you choose self-injury as a way of coping with your difficulties?

1. Did it happen accidentally?
2. Just seemed to happen?

Had you heard about self-injury?
1. Through a friend/colleague?
2. Through the media?
3. From someone else who self-injures?
4. Other?
5. If you had heard about it, do you think it influenced your decision to self-injure?

About your most recent episode of self-injury

1. Did you plan to self-injure?
2. Would you say the episode was: Deliberate? Compulsive? Impulsive? Other?
3. Are you aware of the events/situation that triggered the need to self-injure?
4. Can you explain the events/situation?
5. Were you experiencing racing or intrusive thoughts, traumatic memories or flashbacks before self-injury?
6. Are you aware of what you were thinking before self-injury?
7. Can you describe what you were thinking/saying to yourself?
8. Were you getting conflicting thoughts? Or hearing voices?
9. Did you try to talk yourself out of self-injuring? If you did, are you aware of what you were telling yourself?
10. Did you try any other strategies for distracting yourself from thoughts of self-injury? For example, ring a friend/therapist/support worker, focus on something else?

Establishing how you felt prior to self-injuring

1. Prior to self-injuring did you experience a feeling of numbness, detachment or spaciness (dissociation/depersonalisation), or a feeling of unreality (derealisation)? These are often described as 'feeling outside my body', 'detached from myself', or 'unreal' – like the world is fuzzy round the edges? If your answer is yes, can you please describe in your own words how it felt to you?
2. What other feelings/emotions did you experience? Feeling overwhelmed, out of control, angry, or frightened, are common feelings and emotions reported, but everyone's experience is different. Can you name the feelings or emotions you were experiencing?

Goals of self-injury

1. What was the purpose of your self-injury?
2. Can you explain in your own words what you hoped to achieve?

During self-injury

1. Did you experience any pain during self-injuring?
2. Did you experience a sense of detachment? (As if you were looking in on yourself injuring yourself).
3. Did you feel in control of what you were doing?
4. How did you know when to stop?

After self-injury

1. How did you feel after self-injuring? Common feelings reported are numb, calm, relieved, relaxed, more in control. Again, people's experiences are different. Can you name the feelings you experienced?
2. Were you surprised or shocked by the level of harm you had done to yourself?
3. Were you kind to yourself after self-injuring? (Some people describe it as an opportunity for self-soothing). Did you do anything that was self-nurturing?
4. Did you attend to your own wounds or was it necessary to seek treatment?

General questions

1. What do you see as the advantages of self-injury?
2. What do you see as the disadvantages of self-injury?
3. Would you like to stop self-injury?
4. What do you consider you would gain by stopping?
5. What do you consider you would lose by stopping?
6. Would you describe self-injury as addictive?
7. If you have stopped self-injury, were there any strategies/therapeutic approaches that particularly helped you?
8. What age were you when you started self-injuring?
9. How long have you been self-injuring?
10. How often do you self-injure?
11. What is your 'preferred method' of self-injury? (For example, cutting, burning, other).
12. Do you self-injure in private?

Self-injury: Questionnaire 2

Body modification as self-injury

1. What are your views on body modification? For example, what do you think motivates people to get their bodies altered? Do you think it is used as an alternative form of self-injury by some people? Why do you think it has become so popular?

Males vs. females that self-injure

2. Most research suggests that more women self-injure than men. What are your thoughts on this? Do you think men find it more difficult to admit they have a problem with self-injury? If yes, what makes you think this?
3. Research suggests that more women who self-injure seek treatment via psychological services than their male counterparts. Do you think this is the case? If yes, what makes you think this?

Self-injury among teenagers

4. A high percentage of people who have responded to the survey so far have been teenagers. Do you think this has anything to do with the Internet? For example, could it be that more teenagers use the Internet (or are more confident using the Internet) than older people? Any other thoughts on why this might be the case?

Self-injury: Questionnaire 3

Scars, rituals and wound care

1. Can you explain what your scars mean to you?
2. Research suggests that some people who self-injure engage in rituals prior to hurting themselves. Do you have any particular rituals? If so, can you elaborate?
3. Wound care. If a friend disclosed to you that he or she was self-injuring:
   — what advice would you give him or her about looking after the wounds?

— what items would you recommend she or he kept in a first aid kit?

Self-Injury: Questionnaire 4

Diagnoses and medication

Self-injury is not classified as a disorder or syndrome in DSM-IV (American Psychiatric Association: *Diagnostic and Statistical Manual of Mental Disorders,* Fourth Edition, International Version. Washington, DC, American Psychiatric Association, 1995).

1. Would you like to see self-injury included as a distinct classification in DSM-IV? If yes, do you think it should be included as a disorder or syndrome?

Associated symptoms and disorders

Self-injury is often associated with a range of other symptoms and disorders such as:

- Borderline Personality Disorder (BPD)
- Impulse-control disorders not elsewhere classified
- Anxiety disorders
- Post-traumatic Stress Disorder (PTSD)
- Major depressive disorder
- Bipolar disorder (formerly manic depression)
- Obsessive Compulsive Disorder (OCD)
- Eating disorders (anorexia, bulimia)
- Substance use disorders (alcohol, drug abuse)
- Dissociative disorders: Depersonalisation disorder, Dissociative Identity Disorder (DID) (formerly Multiple Personality Disorder), Dissociative Disorder Not Otherwise Specified (DDNOS)

2. Have you received a diagnosis from those listed above? If yes, can you please specify which?
3. If you have received a diagnosis, was it explained to you?
4. How do you feel about the diagnosis you have received?

5. Have you received a diagnosis not listed above? If yes, can you please specify which?

A common triad of symptoms

Research has shown that self-injury often goes hand–in–hand with eating disorders and substance misuse.

Eating disorders

6. Have you/do you suffer from an eating disorder?
7. If you have/do, which came first the eating disorder or self-injury?
8. Are you aware of what function the eating disorder serves for you?

Substance misuse

9. Have you/do you misuse alcohol/drugs/other?
10. If you have/do, which came first the substance misuse or self-injury?
11. Are you aware of what function the substance misuse serves for you?

Medication

12. Are you taking medication? If yes, can you please specify which? (For example, major tranquillisers, anti-depressants, anti-anxiety drugs, sleeping tablets).
13. Have any medications been effective in reducing your self-injurious episodes?

Self-injury: Questionnaire 5

Areas of the body harmed

1. Please place an 'x' beside any areas of the body that you self-injure/or have self-injured in the past.

Scalp	Head	Face
Throat	Neck	Shoulders
Upper arms	Lower arms	Wrists
Hands/fingers	Chest/breast	Belly/stomach
Back	Hips	Buttocks
Vagina	Penis	Testicles
Anus	Thighs	Knees
Lower legs	Feet/toes	Soles of feet

other (please specify)

2. Which areas of your body do you/did you injure most frequently? Is there/was there a specific reason for choosing these areas?

Severity of self-injury
3. How would you describe your self-injury?
   (a) Superficial? (Little blood loss with minimal scarring)
   (b) Moderately severe? (More blood loss with permanent scars)
   (c) Other? (please specify).

4. Does the severity of your self-injury vary according to the trigger/ situation/level of stress/anxiety, etc?

5. How many times have you self-injured? Please place an 'x' beside the most appropriate answer:
   — a few times?
   — hundreds of times?
   — thousands of times?

Episodic or repetitive self-injury
6. Would you describe yourself as an episodic self-injurer? 'The term *episodic* refers to behaviors that occur every so often. Episodic self-mutilators do not brood about this behavior, nor

do they have a self-identity as a "cutter" or "burner."' (Favazza, 1996: *Bodies Under Siege*, p. 243).

7. Would you describe yourself as a repetitive self-injurer?
    'Episodic self-mutilation becomes repetitive when the behavior becomes an overwhelming preoccupation in those persons who may adopt an identity as a "cutter" or "burner" and who describe themselves as addicted to their self-harm.' (Favazza, 1996: *Bodies Under Siege*, pp. 250-251).

8. If neither of these descriptions fit, how would you describe your self-injury?

Items used to self-injure

9. Please place an 'x' beside any items you use to self-injure/have used to self-injure in the past.
    (a) Razor blades
    (b) Knives
    (c) Scissors
    (d) Shards of glass
    (e) Needles
    (f) Lighted cigarettes
    (g) Cigarette lighter
    (h) Other (please specify)

10. Do you have a 'preferred' item?

11. What happens if your 'preferred' item is not available to you when you need to self-injure?

Methods used to self-injure

1. Do you/have you used multiple methods to self-injure?

2. If you cut and burn, do they serve different functions for you? Can you explain?

Self-injury: Questionnaire 6

For family members/friends/partners of people who self-injure

1. When you heard/discovered that your family member/friend/partner was self-injuring how did it make you feel?
2. How did you become aware that your family member/friend/partner was self-injuring?
3. Has your family member's/friend's/partner's self-injury changed the relationship between you? If so, how?
4. What do you think your family member's/friend's/partner's self-injury communicates?
5. What advice would you give to other family member's/friend's/partner's of people who self-injure?
6. What would help you personally as a family member/friend/partner of someone who self-injures?

Questionnaire 7

Self-esteem/stress/assertiveness levels

Self-esteem levels

To assess your current level of self-esteem, rank yourself on a scale of 1-5 on the questions below, 5 being the highest score. There are no right or wrong answers.

- I believe I am a worthwhile person
- I believe I am as good as the next person
- I accept myself for who I am
- I praise myself on my achievements
- I have faith in my abilities
- I set myself realistic goals
- I achieve my goals
- I view myself in a positive light

- I accept that it's OK to make mistakes
- I see myself as confident
- I acknowledge my strengths
- I respect myself
- I reward myself for the good things I do
- I am not afraid to take risks
- I accept that not everyone will like me
- I give praise and encouragement to others
- I seek support when I need it
- I act rather than react
- I don't strive to be perfect
- I focus on my successes not my failures.

How did you get on? The higher the score, the higher your level of self-esteem. If your score is low, this suggests that you could benefit by taking action to build your self-esteem.

© Jan Sutton (Source: Thrive on Stress)
How To Books Ltd; 2nd Rev Ed edition (1 Jan 2000)

Assessing your stress levels

The following are a range of physical, emotional, behavioural and mental symptoms commonly associated with stress. Place an 'x' beside any symptoms you have experienced more frequently than you would like during the last three months. Also note whether you tick more symptoms in any particular group.

Note: These lists are not exhaustive, and it's important to bear in mind that some of the symptoms listed may not necessarily be stress-related – they can also be associated with other illnesses. The lists merely serve as a pointer to the level of stress you are currently experiencing, and are not a substitute for seeking professional medical advice or diagnosis.

Physical symptoms

1. heart palpitations
2. hypertension (high blood pressure)
3. frequent bouts of indigestion/heartburn
4. breathlessness
5. shallow breathing
6. panic attacks
7. unexplained dizzy spells
8. blurred vision (spots or zigzags in front of the eyes)
9. fuzzy/woolly head
10. frequent headaches or migraines
11. pain and tightness in the chest
12. aching neck or shoulder muscles
13. stomach feels "knotted"
14. mouth gets dry
15. eyes get sore and tired
16. nausea
17. muscle twitches
18. feel tired/exhausted most of the time
19. unexplained skin rashes or irritation
20. clenched fists or jaw
21. excessive sweating
22. need to pass urine frequently
23. constipation or diarrhoea
24. susceptible to viruses and allergies
25. ringing in the ears (tinnitus)
26. changes in menstrual pattern in women.

Emotional symptoms

1. bursting into tears easily/tears close to the surface for no apparent reason
2. mood swings
3. increased worrying
4. feeling more tense/irritable/wound-up than usual

5. getting more angry than usual
6. loss of energy/motivation (no sparkle/enthusiasm/get up and go)
7. more cynical than usual
8. loss of self-confidence
9. reduced self-esteem
10. feeling more vulnerable than usual
11. feeling apprehensive, nervous, anxious
12. feeling worthless
13. feeling helpless
14. feeling hopeless
15. feeling depressed or gloomy
16. feeling as if something dreadful is about to happen
17. feeling overwrought
18. hyper-sensitive to criticism
19. a shut down of emotions (except anger/irritation/frustration)
20. feeling unable to cope.

Behavioural symptoms

1. find it impossible to relax/too busy to relax
2. no time for leisure/fun activities
3. more accident prone than usual
4. making more mistakes than usual
5. disturbed sleep pattern – difficulty getting to sleep, staying asleep, waking early, waking tired, sleeping more than usual
6. increased dependence on alcohol/cigarettes/drugs (prescribed/non-prescribed), self-injury
7. loss of appetite
8. comfort eating
9. neglecting self
10. sexual difficulties
11. poor time management
12. taking work home more/overworking
13. hyperactivity
14. procrastination (putting things off)

15. perfectionism
16. obsessive/compulsive behaviour (cleaning/checking/going on shopping sprees even though finances are tight)
17. less sensitive and caring than usual
18. agoraphobia/situational anxiety (fear of going out, crowded places)
19. withdrawal from friends and supportive relationships.

Mental symptoms
1. loss of former concentration/difficulty thinking straight
2. unable to switch off (thoughts keep racing)
3. loss of former ability to make decisions
4. loss of former reliable memory/keep forgetting things
5. impaired speech (talking faster than normal, missing words out of sentences, losing the thread)
6. worrying about everything
7. missing letters out of words when writing
8. persistent negative or irrational thoughts.

How did you get on? Have you ticked many symptoms? If you have, it may be wise to seek help from a medical professional, or stress counsellor.

Assessing your assertiveness levels
To establish how assertive you are, answer the following questions with a Yes or No. Again, there are no right or wrong answers. Note as you carry out the activity whether you tend to be more/less assertive with particular people, or in particular situations.

- I can state my views in a discussion or debate, even if they differ from other people?
- I take responsibility for my thoughts and feelings by using 'I' statements? For example, 'I think', 'I feel', 'I would like' rather than

'You' (blaming statements) for example, 'You've made me feel', 'Look what you've made me do'?
- I can stand up for my rights, without violating the rights of other people?
- I am willing to compromise or negotiate in conflict situations?
- I feel relaxed and confident with other people?
- I can maintain good eye contact with other people?
- I keep trying even when things get difficult?
- I can accept responsibility for my own decisions?
- I can allow other people to make their own decisions without stepping in, or telling them what they should/must do?
- I know when other people are trying to manipulate me?
- I can say 'no' without feeling guilty?
- I can complain if someone jumps ahead of me in a queue?
- I can express my feelings and emotions openly and honestly?
- I can handle other people's feelings and emotions?
- I can express my anger constructively?
- I can handle other people's anger?
- I can express love and affection easily?
- I can give constructive criticism when warranted?
- I can accept constructive criticism?
- I can reject non-constructive criticism?
- I can give compliments?
- I can receive compliments?
- I can ask for what I want or need?
- I can refuse unreasonable requests?
- I work with other people as equals?
- I can admit my mistakes?
- I can accept that other people make mistakes?
- I can listen to other people's opinions, without cutting them off, or jumping in with my own opinion?
- If someone has borrowed something, and has forgotten/failed to return it, I can ask for it back without feeling anxious?

- I can return faulty goods without getting aggressive, feeling anxious or embarrassed?
- I can refuse persistent sales people?

How did you get on? If you answered **yes** to all/most of the questions, you have no difficulty in being assertive. If you have answered **no** to many of the questions you could benefit from training to develop your assertiveness skills.

Self-injury monitoring charts

· ·

Designed principally for use by people that self-injure, the charts in this section may also be helpful to practitioners and voluntary workers to use in their work with clients that self-injure.

A word of caution to those who self-injure

While the aim of the charts is to help you, there is a possibility that you might find them too daunting to complete, especially if you are in the early stages of your recovery, or if you don't feel in the right place. If this proves the case, an alternative way of gaining benefit from them might be to complete them with support from your therapist, CPN, or a trusted partner, friend or family member. In any event, **please keep yourself safe.**

Chart 1: Feelings and emotions identified before and after self-injury

Chart 1 provides an overview of the feelings and emotions identified by respondents before and after self-injury The primary emotions recognised beforehand were anger, fear, and self-hatred, and after, numbness, relief, calm, relaxed, and feeling 'more in control'.

Chart 2: Before and after self-injury: feelings and emotions monitoring chart

The intention of Chart 2 is to help you to monitor your own feelings and emotions prior to and after self-injury. In the immediacy of the situation, however, you may not be aware of exactly how you are feeling, or in the right frame of mind to record your feelings. Nonetheless, later when you are feeling calmer it can still be useful to complete this activity – it can help you identify if there is a pattern to your self-injury, for example, what specific emotions or situation triggered it, and what self-injury achieved for you.

Chart 3: The cycle of self-injury monitoring chart
Chart 3 is based on Figure 7.1 (Chapter 7). You may wish to refer to this to help you complete the chart. Designed for completion following an episode of self-injury, it will help you:

- Identify the precipitating event (what triggered self-injury).
- Identify the emotions you experienced because of the precipitating event.
- Identify what action you took because of these emotions (form of self-injury).
- Identify the function self-injury served for you.
- Identify how you felt later (when the effect wore off).
- Reflect on what you have learned about your pattern of self-injury by completing the activity.

Chart 4: Self-injury trigger and alternatives monitoring chart
Chart 4 is based on the activities by Cheryl Rainfield included in chapter 10 (see Figures 10.1 and 10.2). You may find it helpful to refer to these for guidance before filling in the chart. This chart is particularly useful for considering how to get your needs met without self-injury, and encouraging you to explore alternatives to self-injury.

Chart 5: Sample monthly self-injury monitoring chart
Some people that self-injure find it helpful to count the number of days when they don't self-injure – it gives them confidence to keep going. You may want to design a chart similar to chart five to help you monitor your progress. Adding some smiley faces for self-injury free days and sad faces for days when self-injury occurs gives you an instant visual picture of how things are going. The chart is also designed to

assist you to identify any specific days of the week/month that are particularly problematic.

'A journey of a thousand miles begins with a single step.'

Lao-tzu, *The Way of Lao-tzu*

Chinese philosopher (604 BC– 531 BC)

Keep safe on your healing journey

FEELINGS AND EMOTIONS IDENTIFIED BEFORE AND AFTER SELF-INJURY

Feelings and emotions before self-injury

Anger	Rage	Frustrated	Frightened	Scared
Out of control	Overwhelmed	Sad	Unloved	Spaced out
Unwanted	Unlovable	Alone	Lonely	Numb
Calm	Hopeless	Self-hate	Self-loathing	Trapped
Abandoned	Agitated	Anxious	Depressed	Confused
Evil	Bad	Hurt	Panicky	Excited
Pressured	Upset	Rejected	Anticipation	Apathetic
Desperate	Disappointed	Concerned	Euphoric	Failure
Happy	Helpless	Lost	In control	Manipulated
Nervous	Pathetic	Poisoned	Unique	Special
Violated	Worthless	Stressed	Unsafe	Ugly
Waste of space	Bored	Dissociated	Detached	Unconnected
Shame	Unreal	Dirty	Stupid	Invisible
Contaminated	Alienated	Small	Different	Weird

Feelings and emotions after self-injury

Calmer	Contented	Numb	Relaxed	Relieved
Happy	High	In control	Rational	Euphoric
Grounded	Stronger	Superior	Triumphant	Tired/sleepy
Angry	Ashamed	Guilty	Depressed	Embarrassed
Stupid	Remorseful	Scared	Sad	Self-hate
Self-loathing	Stressed	Failure	Uneasy	Upset
Useless	Weak	Real	Connected	Alive
Safe	Secure	At peace	Strong	Clear-headed

Chart 1: Feelings and emotions identified before and after self-injury.

BEFORE AND AFTER SELF-INJURY:
FEELINGS AND EMOTIONS MONITORING CHART

Feelings and emotions before self-injury

Feelings and emotions after self-injury

Chart 2: Before and after self-injury: feelings and emotions monitoring chart.

The cycle of self-injury monitoring chart

Point A:
Mental anguish

The precipitating event. Identify what triggered your need to self-injure (thoughts, images, etc.).

_____
_____
_____

Point B:
Emotional engulfment

Identify the emotions you experienced because of the thoughts, images, etc.
See feelings chart for guidance

_____
_____
_____

Point F:
Grief reaction

Identify the feelings you experienced when the effect wore off?

_____

What have you learned about your pattern of self-injury by completing this chart?

_____
_____

Point C:
Panic stations

Identify the most powerful emotion(s) you were experiencing?
See feelings chart for guidance

_____
_____
_____
_____

Point E:
Feel better/different

Identify how you felt after self-injury?
See feelings chart for guidance

_____
_____
_____
_____
_____

How long did the effect last?

Seconds?
Minutes?
Hours?
Days?
Weeks?
Other?

Point D:
Action stations

Identify the action you took because of these powerful emotions, i.e., what form did your self-injury take?

_____
_____

Consider the following questions:
Were you:
Fully aware of your actions?
Partially aware of your actions?
Unaware of your actions?

What motivated you to self-injure?
A need to self-punish?
A need to shut down emotionally?
A need to feel more in control?
A need to feel alive, more real, more grounded in reality?
Other?

Chart 3: The cycle of self-injury monitoring chart.

SELF-INJURY TRIGGERS AND ALTERNATIVES MONITORING CHART

Trigger event/situation	
Thoughts/Images/Memories	
Feelings and emotions	
Link to past experience Can I see any connection with the past?	
Goal of self-injury What function did it serve?	

Alternatives to self-injury
If/when I get the urge to self-injure again, what can I do instead?

Alternative 1	
Alternative 2	
Alternative 3	
Alternative 4	
Alternative 5	
Alternative 6	
Start at the beginning again if you need to.	

Chart 4: Self-injury triggers and alternatives monitoring chart.

Sample monthly self-injury monitoring chart							Total self-injury free days per week
Wk comm. ____	Sunday ✔☺	Monday ✔☺	Tuesday ✔☺	Wednesday ✔☺	Thursday ✔☺	Friday ✗☹	Saturday ✔☺	6
Wk comm. ____	Sunday ✔☺	Monday ✔☺	Tuesday ✔☺	Wednesday ✔☺	Thursday ✔☺	Friday ✔☺	Saturday ✗☹	6
Wk comm. ____	Sunday ✗☹	Monday ✔☺	Tuesday ✔☺	Wednesday ✔☺	Thursday ✔☺	Friday ✔☺	Saturday ✔☺	6
Wk comm. ____	Sunday ✔☺	Monday ✔☺	Tuesday ✔☺	Wednesday ✔☺	Thursday ✔☺	Friday ✔☺	Saturday ✔☺	7
Wk comm. ____	Sunday ✗☹	Monday ✗☹	Tuesday ✔☺					1
Days self-injured this month = 5 ☹	✗ 2 Sundays	✗ 1 Mondays	✗ 0 Tuesdays	✗ 0 Wednesday	✗ 0 Thursdays	✗ 1 Fridays	✗ 1 Saturdays	Self-injury free days this month = 26 ☺

Chart 5: Sample monthly self-injury monitoring chart.

CIS'*ters*: Member Code of Contact

· ·

CIS'*ters*:

an experience in learning, sharing, growing – individually and together.

Core/workshop/conference (group) participation
Member Code of Contact

Each member is asked to agree to the following:

1. **What ever is said in the group is confidential** and should not go outside the group (*see additional paragraph below on confidentiality*).
2. On the basis of the belief that the resources for **healing lie within ourselves**, we ask each member to take responsibility for their own progress.
3. Much of the work undertaken in the group concerns releasing anger. **CIS'*ters*** wishes it to be known that it **does not condone violence in any form against any person.**
4. Some women may come to the group with a long established habit of **self-abuse**. We understand why this is so and how it has come about. However, we ask that they work towards overcoming this and refrain from abusing themselves whilst on premises used by the group. In addition we ask members not to drink alcohol or abuse any drugs before a meeting.

5. Members should **listen** to each other and **be non-judgmental.**
6. There should be **equal opportunity to talk**. In addition if members wish to **speak**, it should be **one at a time**.
7. To be **sensitive to the feelings** of other members.
8. **Not** to be **disruptive**.
9. **Not to discuss absent members** of the group.
10. Remember to provide **care and support** for themselves as well as for other members of the group.
11. **Placement in the** *Core* **Group.** We require these **members to make a commitment to attendance on a regular basis**. This is very important if the survivor is to get as much as they can out of the *Core* Group – and to provide continuity for both the survivor and other *Core* Group Members. Length of stay within the *Core* Group is dependent upon a number of factors which include measure of progress and ability to develop coping strategies. If the survivor does not attend regularly we will need to discuss with them whether or not they are ready to participate in a group environment. This can sometimes happen and, subject to individual circumstances, we can suggest that when they do feel ready to make a commitment they can seek a new placement in the *Core* Group.
12. **Confidentiality**. CIS*'ters* operates a confidentiality policy which is designed to protect all users of its services. This policy is strictly adhered to and only in the event of threat to life or a child being at risk will it be broken. Even in those circumstances, agreement will be sought whenever possible and **CIS***'ters* would wish to continue to support any woman involved.

What is the underlying philosophy of CIS'*ters*?
• healing from incest is possible. Women who suffered childhood sexual abuse are seen as strong survivors, not helpless victims;
• each survivor is the expert in her own healing and knows her own needs best ie there is no 'right' path to healing;
• the resources for healing lie within each survivor;

- all human beings are responsible for their own thoughts, feelings and behaviour. As such, survivors are responsible for their own progress in healing;
- no child is ever to blame for their abuse;
- the abuser is solely responsible for the abuse;
- it is not how 'severe' or prolonged the abuse is that is important, but rather the perceived impact on the survivor's life;
- forgiveness is not essential to healing;
- we honour and respect each survivor's personal belief system and world view. As such, we will not impose our belief system or judgements on anyone, but rather will support and encourage an individual to make her own decisions;
- sexual preference is not the result of sexual abuse;
- sexual abuse occurs across boundaries of class, race, religion and gender; and
- membership is open to all women survivors: regardless of race, class and sexual orientation provided that the member is committed to honouring the group code of contact and process.

What methods are used in the group?

The structure is very much determined by group members in consultation with the facilitator(s) within the philosophy of the organisation and according to agreed guidelines. The facilitator(s) clarify the skills and resources available to the group, help survivors become acquainted and answer queries. Survivors focus on realistic and achievable personal and collective goals, which are shared or remain private as desired.

Survivors are supported in:	Survivors experience growth in:
• sharing personal stories/experiences	• being believed and heard
• integrating memories with feelings	• being listened to with empathy & compassion
• expressed feelings	• sharing resources, coping strategies & insights

- exploring options and choices
- making their own decisions
- letting go of shame

- seeing new possibilities and options
- being inspired by others' progress and hope
- no longer feeling isolated
- gaining in confidence and self esteem
- no longer keeping the secret
- laughing as well as crying together

CIS'ters, c/o PO Box 119, Eastleigh, Hampshire SO50 9ZF

Helpline: (02380) 3380080 – Saturdays 10am – 12 noon

Description: Provides support for adult females who were sexually abused as children by a member of their immediate or extended family, a quarterly newsletter; group meetings (including workshops for survivor) and training for people working with survivors.

Case studies: training resource

- -

This resource is provided as a learning tool to assist those wishing to examine their attitudes to self-injury and to develop further insight into the behaviour. It is not intended as a research instrument. Single copies may be photocopied for non-commercial educational purposes provided the source is credited. Beyond that, permission to copy should be sought from the publishers.

The case studies presented are composites – they are not based on any particular people. They are designed to stimulate thinking and discussion, rather than considering the rights or wrongs, thus no answers are provided. Each case study is followed by questions to reflect on.

Examining your reactions to self-injury

Read Case study 1, and note your immediate reactions. When you have finished, consider the questions at the end of the case study. Repeat the same process with Case study 2.

Case study 1: Della

Della is a nurse. She works in a hospice. She loves her job, is efficient at it, and is popular with the staff and patients. Della lives alone. At the weekends, and sometimes during the evenings, she cuts her legs, arms or stomach with a razor blade. Della keeps her self-inflicted injuries a secret. She is always very careful about where she cuts herself, ensuring that she will be able to hide her wounds beneath her clothes. She dresses her own wounds, thus avoiding drawing attention to her behaviour.

Questions
1. Did you find yourself being judgemental about Della's behaviour?
2. Did you feel any compassion towards her?
3. Did you wonder why Della needs to hurt herself?

Case study 2: Karen

Karen works as a prostitute. When not selling her body, she often sits at home burning her arms with cigarettes. Occasionally, she goes to Accident & Emergency when her wounds are bad and need medical attention.

Questions
1. Did you find yourself being critical of Karen's behaviour?
2. Did you think the purpose behind Karen's behaviour might be to get attention?
3. Did you feel any sympathy towards her?
4. Did you wonder what motivated Karen to become a prostitute?

Case study 3: Selina

Read the following case study thoughtfully, focusing specifically on the following:
1. The various forms of self-harm Selina has engaged in.
2. The age that Selina started self-harming.
3. The circumstances that might have motivated Selina to self-harm.
Selina is aged sixteen. She is an only child. Her parents divorced when she was four, and since then she has only seen her biological father on a handful of occasions. Shortly after her father left, she started biting her hand and picking at her skin. Selina's mother, Kerry, remarried a divorcee when she was eight and they both moved in with Tom, Kerry's new husband, and his two teenage daughters from his previous marriage.

Selina didn't get on with Tom – he was always finding fault with how she looked, comparing her to her stepsisters, or accusing her of being a 'greedy guts'. Selina started dieting at age ten and lost some weight, which elicited the only praise she ever received from her stepfather. This bolstered her self-esteem, and lead to her becoming obsessed with her weight – her determination to reach a size zero driving a continuous struggle of dieting, self-starvation, and a rigid exercise regimen. After being severely bullied at school at the age of fourteen, Selina finally snapped. On arriving home from school one day, she grabbed a kitchen knife and dragged it across her left forearm. Discovering that this made her 'feel better' she has continued cutting herself in secret ever since.

Questions

1. How many different forms of self-harm has Selina engaged in?
2. What in your opinion is the most dangerous method of self-harm she has practised? What makes you think this?
3. At what age did Selina first start hurting herself?
4. What circumstances do you think might have lead to Selina self-harming?

Case study 4: Emily

Read the following case study thoughtfully, focusing particularly on the following:

1. The age that Emily started self-injuring.
2. The length of time Emily has been self-injuring.
3. The two distinct forms of self-injury that Emily practises.
4. The circumstances that might have motivated Emily to self-injure.

Emily is aged 25. Throughout her childhood, Emily's mother worked full-time, and she was left in the care of a nanny. Emily's father is a highly respected pillar of society. Between the ages of 6 and 14, Emily was sexually abused by her father. He told her that it was their 'special secret', and that bad things would happen to her if she ever told anyone what he did to her. He also lavished her with expensive gifts, informing her that she was his 'precious princess'. When Emily was nine, she could not hold on to the awful secret any longer. She told her mother what her daddy was doing to her, but was accused of being a 'filthy little liar', and an evil and wicked child for saying such a thing about her father. She also warned Emily to **never** say such a dreadful thing about her father again.

Between the ages of 10 and 14, Emily ran away from home on several occasions. Each time she was picked up by the police, who escorted her back. Nobody ever asked her why she had run away and often she was chastised for wasting police time or causing her parents so much worry. Emily left home when she was 16. She could not get a job and lived a hand to mouth existence, eventually drifting into a life of drug abuse and petty crime to fund her drug habit. When Emily was 17 she started cutting herself externally and internally. She has been doing this for eight years – she has told no one.

Questions
1. At what age did Emily start self-injuring?
2. How many years has Emily been self-injuring?
3. What are the two distinct forms of self-injury that Emily practises?
4. What circumstances do you think lead to Emily self-injure?
5. What function do you think self-injury serves for Emily?

Case study 5: Lucia
Read the following case study attentively, concentrating principally on the following:
1. Lucia's predominant form of self-harm during her teenage years.
2. How Lucia felt as a child.
3. The circumstances that lead Lucia to self-harm.
4. Her relationship with her father and her husband.

Until the age of 5, Lucia lived with her parents at her aunt's house. She was devoted to her aunt, who looked after her while her parents were at work. When Lucia started school her parents bought a house, quite a distance away from her much loved auntie. Lucia's parents didn't get on – they were at loggerheads much of the time. Her father drank heavily, and her mother was frequently depressed. On several occasions she threatened to leave Lucia and her father, and twice she took an overdose and was admitted to psychiatric care. Neither parent ever showed Lucia any affection – she felt invisible and unwanted. When Lucia was 12, her much loved auntie was killed in a car accident. She was devastated, and wept profusely, only to be chastised by her father who insisted she 'stop being such a cry baby'. Lucia was not allowed to go to her aunt's funeral because her parents thought she was too young. She has never cried since.

When Lucia was 13, she started having eating difficulties. She secretly stashed huge amounts of food in her bedroom, and would binge in the evenings, later taking laxatives or sticking her fingers down her throat and making herself sick to dispose of the food. Her parents didn't notice anything was amiss because Lucia's weight remained stable; also they were preoccupied with assaulting each other physically and verbally, often within earshot of Lucia.

Lucia left home at 18 to get married. Initially, her husband was kind and loving towards her, but after about a year into their marriage he started drinking heavily. He also became cold, distant and physically and verbally abusive towards her. The marriage ended after 2 years. Lucia got extremely depressed and her eating difficulties became life-threatening. She was admitted to hospital where she was 'force-fed'. From there she was transferred to a psychiatric unit. Two weeks into her stay, she started cutting her arms and legs with a razor blade.

Questions
1. At what age did Lucia start self-harming?
2. What forms of self-harm has Lucia practised?

3. What circumstances do you think lead to Lucia's eating difficulties and self-injury?
4. What characteristics do Lucia's father and her husband share in common?
5. Did you notice any similar patterns between Lucia's mother's mental health issues and Lucia's own?

Case study 6: Nathan

Read the following case study attentively, concentrating chiefly on the circumstances that might have lead to Nathan self-injuring.

Nathan is an only child. His father is unemployed and spends most of his time at the pub or at the betting shop. While his father is elsewhere drowning his sorrows, or banking on that 'big win' that will bring a blissful existence, his emotionally needy mother has a constant string of affairs, bringing men home when Nathan's father is seeking solace in a few pints of beer with his mates, or is getting excited at the thought of becoming an instant millionaire should his luck come up on the horses. Nathan's mother manipulated him into keeping her indiscretions secret from his father with bribes of money or treats.

Nathan was a small lad for his age and he got picked on at school. He found it difficult to make friends, was not allowed to invite anyone home, and spent most of his spare time in his bedroom playing games on his computer, or chatting to 'anonymous' friends via Internet chat rooms. Often the sound of breaking glass or crockery could be heard downstairs, and he would attempt to shut his ears to his mother's screams and his father's profanities.

On one occasion, however, which Nathan remembers vividly, he heard his mother yelling at his father: 'you know I never wanted children. He's ruined my life and my figure, and let's face it he's such a wimp ... it's all your fault ... I should never have let you talk me into having a baby.' In response, his father shouted back: 'you aren't the only one who's disappointed ... you knew I wanted a girl ...'

When Nathan was 18 he left home, and got himself a job. Soon after, he embarked on a relationship with a man almost twice his age.

They rented a flat together, and with some coaxing from his partner, Nathan visited his parents, albeit it reluctantly, to tell them that he had found happiness and to 'come out' that he was gay.

On hearing the news that their son was gay, his parents went berserk, accusing him of being perverted and sick in the head. His father's parting shot was 'you are no son of mine . . . don't you ever darken our doorstep again . . .' Nathan made a hasty retreat, headed straight for the nearest off licence, purchased a half bottle of whisky, took it to a secluded spot in a nearby forest, downed the whisky, smashed the bottle, grabbed a sliver of glass and made several crimson slashes across his chest.

Questions

1. What events in Nathan's life do you think lead to him self-injuring?
2. What effect do you think Nathan's mother's manipulation might have had on him?
3. How might the overheard argument between his parents have affected Nathan's feelings about himself?
4. What was the final straw that broke the camel's back?
5. Would you say Nathan's self-injury was compulsive or impulsive?

References

Ainscough, C. & Toon, K. (2000). *Breaking Free: Help for Survivors of Child Sexual Abuse.* London: Sheldon Press.

Alderman, T. and Marshall, K. (2006) 'Working with Self-Injuring Clients', paper presented at the conference 'Understanding Self-Injury and Responding Appropriately'. University of Southampton, Hampshire, UK, April 08.

Alderman, T. (1997). *The Scarred Soul: Understanding and Ending Self-Inflicted Violence.* Oakland, CA: New Harbinger Publications.

American Psychiatric Association (2000). *Diagnostic and Statistical Manual of Mental Disorders,* Fourth Edition, Text Revision. Washington, DC, American Psychiatric Association.

Arnold, L. (1995). *Women and Self-Injury: A survey of 76 Women.* Bristol: Bristol Crisis Service for Women.

Arnold, R. (1994). *My Lives.* New York: Ballantine Books.

Babiker, G., & Arnold L. (1997). *The Language of Injury: Comprehending Self-mutilation.* Leicester: BPS Books.

BACP (2003, June). *CPJ.* Cover page. Retrieved April 25, 2007, from, http://www.bacp.co.uk/cpj/june2003/editorial.htm

BBC (1997) Diana Remembered. The Panorama Interview: Transcript of the BBC1 Panorama interview with the Princess of Wales, broadcast in November 1995. Retrieved June 16, 2005 from http://www.bbc.co.uk/politics97/diana/panorama.html

BCSW (1998). Helpful responses to self-injury. Retrieved April 27, 2007, from http://www.users.zetnet.co.uk/BCSW/leaflets/helpresp.htm

BFMS (British False Memory Society) website. (Updated June 11, 2007). Retrieved June 15, 2007, from http://www.bfms.org.uk/

BMJ (2005, February 19). Repetition of self harm is not predicted well. *BMJ,* 330, Retrieved April 25, 2007, from, http://bmj.bmjjournals.com/cgi/content/full/330/7488/0-c

BMJ (2002). Self harm is not reduced by a letter. *BMJ.* Retrieved April 25, 2007, from, http://bmj.bmjjournals.com/cgi/content/full/324/7348/0

Braun, B. G. (1988a). The BASK Model of Dissociation. Part I. *Dissociation,* 1(1) 4-23.

Braun, B. G. (1988b). The BASK Model of Dissociation. Part II-Treatment, *Dissociation* 1(2) 16-23.

Calthorpe, B. and Choong, S. (2004). The coroner's court and the psychiatrist. *Advances in Psychiatric Treatment,* 10, 146-152. Retrieved May 01, 2007, from, http://apt.rcpsych.org/cgi/content/full/10/2/146

Camelot Foundation & Mental Health Foundation (2006). *Truth Hurts: Report of the National Inquiry into Self-harm among Young People.* Retrieved May 01, 2007, from, www.selfharmuk.org

Cameron, J. (1998). *The Right to Write: An Invitation and Initiation into the Writing Life. New York:* Tarcher/Putnam.

Cardeña, E. (1994). The Domain of Dissociation. In *Dissociation: Clinical and theoretical perspectives,* Lynn, S. J., & Rhue, J. W. (eds.), New York: The Guilford Press.

Conterio, K., & Lader, W. (1998). *Bodily Harm: The Breakthrough Healing Program for Self-Injurers.* New York: Hyperion.

Daily Mail (2006, March 22). Hospital allows patients to harm themselves. Retrieved June 12, 2007, from, http://www.dailymail.co.uk/pages/live/articles/health/healthmain.html?in_article_id=380718&in_page_id=1774

Davidson, P. & Parker K. (2001). Eye movement desensitisation and reprocessing (EMDR): A meta-analysis. *Journal of Consulting & Clinical Psychology,* 69(2): 305-316.

Davies, S. C. (2002). Self-harm: An examination of Antecedent and Maintenance Factors. Unpublished study. Masters Degree in Forensic Behavioural Science, Liverpool University.

Deacon, D. (2005, February 24). Children in Idaho Following a National Trend of

Slashing Themselves. [Electronic edition]. *Newswatch 3.* Retrieved March 07, 2005, from, http://www.kidktv.com/x18258.xml?ParentPageID=x3963&ContentID=x62758&Layout=kidk.xsl&AdGroupID=x18258

De Leo, D. and Heller, T.S. (2004). Who are the kids who self-harm? An Australian self-report school survey. *Medical Journal of Australia* 181, 140-144. Retrieved May 01, 2007, from, http://www.mja.com.au/public/issues/181_03_020804/del10634_fm.html

Devlin, A. (1998). *Invisible Women,* Winchester: Waterside Press.

Edmond, T. & Rubin, A. (2004). Assessing the long-term effects of EMDR: results from an 18-month follow-up study with adult female survivors of CSA. *Journal of Child Sex Abuse,* 13(1):69-86.

EMDR Institute, Inc. (2004). A Brief Description of EMDR. Retrieved May 27, 2007, from http://www.emdr.com/briefdes.htm

Fagin, L. (2006, May). Repeated self-injury: perspectives from general psychiatry. Advances in Psychiatric Treatment *12:* 193–201. Retrieved May 22, 2007, from http://apt.rcpsych.org/cgi/content/full/12/3/193

Favazza, A. R. (1996). *Bodies Under Siege: Self-Mutilation and Body Modification in Culture and Psychiatry,* 2nd ed. Baltimore: The Johns Hopkins University Press.

Favazza A, Rosenthal R. (1993). Diagnostic issues in self-mutilation. *Hospital Community Psychiatry,* 44, 134–140.

Favazza, A.R., & Conterio, K. (1989). Female habitual self-mutilators. *Acta Psychiatrica Scandinavica,* 79, 283-289.

False Memory Syndrome Foundation Website (1998-2007). FMSF. Retrieved June 15, 2007, from http://www.fmsfonline.org

Frean, A. (2004, March 31). Britain worst in Europe as self-harm increases. [Electronic edition]. *Times Online.* Retrieved April 25, 2007, from http://www.timesonline.co.uk/article/0,,8122-1057677,00.html

Freyd, J. J. (1996). *Betrayal Trauma: The Logic of Forgetting Childhood Abuse.* Cambridge, MA: Harvard University Press.

Gabrielle. (1999-2007). Self-Injury: A Struggle. Famous Self-injurers. Retrieved May 01, 2007, from http://www.self-injury.net/doyousi/famous/

Greenspan, G.S. & Samuel, S.E. (1989). Self-cutting after rape. *American Journal of Psychiatry,* 146, 789-790.

Gunnell D.J., Brooks, J., & Peters, T.J. Epidemiology and patterns of hospital use after parasuicide in the south west of England. (1996). *Journal of Epidemiology and Community Health,* 50, 24–29.

Hacking, I. (1995). *Rewriting the Soul: Multiple Personality and the Sciences of Memory.* Princeton, NJ: Princeton University Press.

Hawton, K., Rodham, K. with Evans, E. (2006). *By Their Own Young Hand: Deliberate Self Harm and Suicidal Ideas in Adolescents.* Jessica Kingsley Publishers: London.

Hawton, K., Rodham, K., Evans, E. and Weatherall, R. (2002). Deliberate self-harm in adolescents: self-report survey in schools in England. *British Medical Journal* 325, 1207-1211. Retrieved May 01, 2007, from, http://www.bmj.com/cgi/content/full/325/7374/1207

HealthyPlace.com (1999-2007). A Possible New Name For Borderline Personality Disorder. Heller, L. Retrieved June 10, 2007, from (http:

//www.healthyplace.com/Communities/personality_disorders/
biounhappiness/bpd/21a.htm)

Heller, L. (1991). *Life at the Border, Understanding and Recovering from the Borderline Personality Disorder.* Okeechobee, FL: Dyslimbia Press, Inc; 3rd edition.

Herman, J. L. (1998). *Trauma and Recovery: From Domestic Abuse to Political Violence.* London: Pandora.

Herman, J.L. (1994). *Trauma and Recovery: From Domestic Abuse to Political Terror.* London: Pandora.

Herman, J.L. (1992). *Trauma and Recovery: From Domestic Abuse to Political Terror.* New York: Basic Books.

Horrocks, J., Price, S., House, A., and Owens, D. (2003). Self-injury attendances in the accident and emergency department: a clinical database study. *British Journal of Psychiatry, 183*:34-39. Retrieved April 25, 2007, from, http://bjp.rcpsych.org/cgi/content/full/183/1/34

Horrocks, J, & House, A. (2002). Self-poisoning and self-injury in adults. *Clinical Medicine, 2* (6), 509-12.

James A. (2004, August 26) Psychiatrists rebuke colleagues over remarks on self harming patients. *Psychminded.co.uk.* Retrieved June 12, 2007, from http://www.psychminded.co.uk/news/news2004/august04/Psychiatrists %20criticise%20colleagues%20who%20describe%20self%20harming%20 patients%20as%20wilfully%20immature.htm

James, R. (2004, August 03). Cut it out, please. [Electronic edition]. *SocietyGuardian.co.uk.* Retrieved June 01, 2007, from, http:// society.guardian.co.uk/mentalhealth/comment/0,8146,1274966,00.html

Kihlstrom, J. (1996). False Memory Syndrome, Philadelphia. Frequently Asked Questions. Retrieved May 23, 2007 from http://www.fmsonline.org/ fmsffaq.html#WhatIsFMS

Kirby, J. (2006, April 26). Nurses want to help self-harm patients. *icBirmingham.* Retrieved June 12, 2007, from, http://icbirmingham.icnet work.co.uk/0100news/0100localnews/tm_objectid=16994348&method =full&siteid=50002&headline=nurses-want-to-help-self-harm-patients-name_page.html

Kreitman N. (ed) (1977). *Parasuicide.* London: John Wiley & Sons.

Lader, W. (2006, Winter). A Look at the Increase in Body Focused Behaviors. *Paradigm,* 14–18. Retrieved May 22, 2007, from http://www.crpsib.com/ documents/W06-ReprintLader.pdf

Linehan, M. (1993). *Skills Training Manual for Treating Borderline Personality Disorder.* New York: Guilford Press.

Lister, S. (2006, March 22). Hospitals to allow self-harm. *Times Online.* Retrieved June 12, 2007, from, http://www.timesonline.co.uk/tol/news/uk/health/article743872.ece

Malkin, M. (2005, February 25). 'Cutting Trend.' [Electronic edition]. *The Sun News.* Retrieved March 07, 2005, from, http://www.myrtlebeachonline.com/mld/sunnews/news/opinion/10987796.htm

Martinson, D. (2002). Common Myths about Self-Injury, The American Self-Harm Clearinghouse. Retrieved June 01 2005, from http://www.selfinjury.org/

Martinson, D. (1996-2007). Therapeutic approaches. Secret Shame Website. Retrieved April 27, 2007, from http://www.palace.net/~llama/psych/ther.html

Mazelis, R. (1998). The Cutting Edge, A Newsletter for Women Living With Self-Inflicted Violence, Volume 9, Issue 3 (35).

McKinstry, L. (2004, August 01). This 'epidemic' is all selfishness. [Electronic edition]. *Telegraph.co.uk.* Retrieved June 01, 2007, from, http://www.telegraph.co.uk/opinion/main.jhtml?xml=/opinion/2004/08/01/do0104.xml&sSheet=/opinion/2004/08/01/ixop.html

Mental Health Foundation (1997). MHFoundation Briefing No 1: Suicide and Deliberate Self-Harm, The Fundamental Facts. Retrieved March 04, 2005, from http://www.mentalhealth.org.uk/html/content/brief001.cfm

Miller, D. (1994). *Women who Hurt Themselves: A Book of Hope and Understanding.* NY: Basic Books.

Mills, S. (2005, May 08). On a knife edge. [Electronic edition]. *Times Online.* Retrieved April 25, 2007, from, http://www.timesonline.co.uk/article/0,,2104-1590809,00.html

Mitchell, J.M, & Morse, J. (1998). *From Victims to Survivors: Reclaimed Voices of Women Sexually Abused in Childhood by Females.* Bristol, PA: Accelerated Development.

Mollon, P. (1996). *Multiple Selves, Multiple Voices: Working with Trauma, Violation and Dissociation,* Chichester: John Wiley & Sons Ltd.

Morgan, H.G. (1979). *Death Wishes?,* Chichester: Wiley.

Myall, S. (2006, March 26). Self harm on the NHS. *The People.co.uk.* Retrieved June 12, 2007, from, http://www.people.co.uk/news/tm_objectid=16865221&method=full&siteid=93463&headline=self-harm-on-the-nhs--name_page.html

National Institute for Clinical Excellence (2002). *Self-harm scope.* Retrieved

April 25, 2007, from http://www.nice.org.uk/pdf/Self-HarmScopeFinal V3140502.pdf

National Collaborating Centre for Mental Health (2004). *Self-harm: the short-term physical and psychological management and secondary prevention of self-harm in primary and secondary care.* London: Gaskell & BPS.

NICE (2002, May 15) *Self-Harm Scope.* National Institute for Health and Clinical Excellence. Retrieved May 01, 2007, from http://www.nice.org.uk/pdf/Self-HarmScopeFinalV3140502.pdf

Nicholas, C. (2006, March 26). Hospital lets its patients self-harm in pilot scheme. *Scotsman.com.* Retrieved June 12, 2007, from, http://news.scotsman.com/health.cfm?id=468552006

Nijenhuis, E.R.S., Spinhoven, P., Van Dyck, R., Van der Hart, O., & Vanderlinden, J. (1996). The development and the psychometric characteristics of the Somatoform Dissociation Questionnaire (SDQ-20). *Journal of Nervous and Mental Disease,* 184, 688-694.

Nixon, M.K., Cloutier, P.F., & Aggarwal, S. (2002). Affect regulation and addictive aspects of repetitive self-injury in hospitalized adolescents, *Journal of the American Academy of Child and Adolescent Psychiatry,* 41(11): 1333-1341.

Owens, D., Horrocks, J., & House, A. (2002). Fatal and non-fatal repetition of self-harm: Systematic review, *British Journal of Psychiatry,* 181, 193-199. Retrieved April 25, 2007, from, http://bjp.rcpsych.org/cgi/content/full/181/3/193

Pattison, E. & Kahan, J. (1983). The deliberate self-harm syndrome. *American Journal of Psychiatry.* 140, 867-872. Abstract retrieved May 01, 2007, from, http://ajp.psychiatryonline.org/cgi/content/abstract/140/7/867

Pearlman, L.A., & Saakvitne, K.W. (1995). *Trauma and the therapist: Countertransference and Vicarious Traumatisation in Psychotherapy with Incest Survivors.* New York: W.W. Norton.

Pembroke (2007). Chapter 11: Harm Minimisation: Limiting the Damage of Self-injury. In Beyond Fear and Control, Spandler, M., and Warner, S. (eds.). Ross-on-Wye: PCCS Books.

Pembroke, L.R. (ed.) (2004). *Self-Harm: Perspectives from Personal Experience,* Chipmunka/Survivors Speak Out. Available for purchase from: www.chipmunkapublishing.com Retrieved April 25, 2007.

Penumbra (2001). No Harm in Listening. Retrieved May 07, 2007 from http://www.penumbra.org.uk/young_people/No_Harm.html
Full report: http://www.layc.org.uk/Pdfstore/Penumbra_Report.pdf

Revill, J. (2005, June 5). Self-harm epidemic now starts at age eight. [Electronic edition]. *The Observer.* Retrieved May 01, 2007, from, http://observer.guardian.co.uk/uk_news/story/0,6903,1499582,00.html

Rhoades, G.F. (1998-2007). Therapeutic precautions to help prevent false memory allegations, Trauma & Dissociation (TAD), Trauma & Dissociation Newsletter,Vol.1, No. 1. Retrieved April 27, 2007, from http://www.pixi.com/~grhoades/TAD1198.htm#5

Rhoades, G.F. (1998-2007). Trauma. Retrieved May 14, 2007 from http://www.anger-management.net/trauma.htm

Rothschild, B. (2000). The Body Remembers: The Psychophysiology of Trauma and Trauma Treatment. New York: W.W. Norton.

Ross, C.A. (2000). *The Trauma Model: A Solution To The Problem of Comorbidity In Psychiatry,* Richardson, TX: Manitou Communications, Inc.

Royal College of Psychiatrists (2004). Deliberate self-harm in young people

Factsheet 26, for parents and teachers. Retrieved April 25, 2007, from, http://www.rcpsych.ac.uk/mentalhealthinformation/mentalhealthandgrowingup/26self-harminyoungpeople.aspx

Royal College of Psychiatrists (2004). *Assessment following self-harm in adults Council Report CR122.* London: Royal College of Psychiatrists. Retrieved April 25, 2007, from, http://www.rcpsych.ac.uk/files/pdfversion/cr122.pdf

Royal College of Physicians & Royal College of Psychiatrists (2003). CR108. The Psychological Care of Medical Patients: A practical guide (2nd edition). Royal College of Physicians of London, Royal College of Psychiatrists (pp. 65-76) Retrieved April 25, 2007, from, http://www.rcpsych.ac.uk/files/pdfversion/cr108.pdf

Sale, A.U. (2004, April 8-24). Life on the edge. *Community Care.* (pp 38-39).

Samaritans (2000). *Youth matters 2000: A cry for help.* Retrieved May 01, 2007, from, http://www.samaritans.org/know/pdf/youth_matters.pdf

Saxe G.N., Chawla, N., & van der Kolk B.A. (2002). Self-Destructive Behavior in Patients with Dissociative Disorders, *Suicide and Life-Threatening Behavior,* 32(3), 313-20.

Scheflin, A.W. (November, 1999). Ground Lost: The False Memory/Recovered Memory Therapy Debate, Psychiatric Times, Vol. XVI, Issue 11. [Electronic edition]. Retrieved June 15, 2007, from http://www.psychiatrictimes.com/p991137.html

Shapiro, F. (2001). *Eye Movement Desensitisation and Reprocessing, Basic Principles, Protocols and Procedures.* (2nd ed.) New York: The Guilford Press.

SIARI (2001-2007). Responses to Guardian Article. Retrieved June 10, 2007, from http://www.siari.co.uk/Teenage-Girls-and-Cutting-Responses-to-Guardian-Article-May2002-On-SIARI.htm

Simeon, D. & Favazza, A.R. (2001). Self-Injurious Behaviors: Phenomenology and Assessment. In Simeon, D. & Hollander, E. (ed.) *Self-injurious Behaviors: Assessment and treatment.* Washington, D.C.: American Psychiatric Publishing Inc.

Sinason, V. (ed) (2002). *Attachment, Trauma and Multiplicity: Working with Dissociative Identity Disorder.* Hove, USA, Canada: Brunner-Routledge.

Steinberg M. (1994). *Interviewers Guide to the Structured Clinical Interview for DSM-IV Dissociative Disorders* (SCID-D). Washington, DC, American Psychiatric Press.

Steinberg, M., & Schnall (2000). *The Stranger in the Mirror: Dissociation - The Hidden Epidemic.* New York: HarperCollins.

Strong, M. (2000). *A Bright Red Scream: Self-Mutilation and the Language of Pain.* London: Virago Press.

Sutton, J. (1999). *Healing the Hurt Within: Understand and relieve the suffering behind self-destructive behaviour.* 1st ed. Oxford: How to Books.

Sutton, J. (2005). *Healing the Hurt Within: Understand self-injury and self-harm, and heal the emotional wounds.* 2nd ed. Oxford: How to Books.

Sutton and Martinson (2003). Self-Injury and Related Issues. Retrieved May 10, 2007, from http://www.siari.co.uk/

Taylor, G.J., Bagby, R.M., & Parker, J.D.A. (1997). *Disorders of affect regulation: Alexithymia in medical and psychiatric illness.* Cambridge: Cambridge University Press.

Templeton, S.K. (2006, February 05). Self-harmers to be given clean blades. *TimesOnline.* Retrieved June 12, 2007, from, http://www.timesonline.co.uk/tol/news/uk/article727174.ece

The Observer (2002, May 19). Why are so many teenage girls cutting themselves? Retrieved June 10, 2007, from http://observer.guardian.co.uk/focus/story/0,6903,718183,00.html

Triggle, N. (2006, April 25). Nurses back supervised self-harm. *BBC News 24.* Retrieved June 12, 2007, from, http://news.bbc.co.uk/1/hi/health/4942834.stm

Turner, V.J. (2002). *Secret Scars: Uncovering and Understanding the Addiction of Self-injury.* Minnesota: Hazelden.

University of Oxford, Centre for Suicide Research (1998-2007). About us. Retrieved May 01, 2007, from, http://cebmh.warne.ox.ac.uk/csr/profile.html

Valentine, P. and Wickham, V. (2000). *Dancing With Demons: The authorised biography of Dusty Springfield*. London: Hodder & Stoughton.

van der Kolk, B., Perry, C. and Herman, J. (1991). Childhood Origins of Self-Destructive Behavior. *American Journal of Psychiatry*, 148:12, 1665-71.

van der Kolk, B.A. (1994). The Body Keeps The Score: Memory and the Evolving Psychobiology of Post Traumatic Stress. *Harvard Review of Psychiatry*, 1:253-265. Retrieved June, 05, 2007, from http://www.trauma-pages.com/a/vanderk4.php

van der Kolk, B. A., McFarlane, A.C., & Weisaeth, L (Eds.) (1996). *Traumatic Stress: The effects of overwhelming experience on mind, body, and society*. New York: The Guilford Press.

Walsh, B. W. & Rosen, P. M. (1988). *Self-Mutilation: Theory, Research, and Treatment*. New York: Guilford Press.

Walsh, B. W. (2006). *Treating Self-Injury: A Practical Guide*. New York: Guilford Press.

Williams, M. (1997). *Cry of Pain: Understanding Suicide and Self-Harm*. Harmondsworth: Penguin Books.

WOOD TV8 (2004, May 7) Students form 'cutting club' at local middle school [Electronic Edition] Retrieved April 25, 2007, from, http://www.woodtv.com/global/story.asp?s=1835675&ClientType=Print

World Health Organisation (1992). *The ICD-10 Classification of Mental and Behavioural Disorders: Clinical Descriptions and Diagnostic Guidelines*. Geneva: WHO.

Young people and self-harm: A National Inquiry (2004). Aims of the National Inquiry. Retrieved April 25, 2007, from http://www.selfharmuk.org/aims.asp

Young people and self-harm: A National Inquiry (2004a). Self-harm definition. Retrieved April 25, 2007, from, http://www.selfharmuk.org/defs.asp

Young people and self-harm: A National Inquiry (2004b). First Interim Inquiry Report: 'What do we already know? – prevalence, risk factors & models of intervention.' Retrieved April 25, 2007, from http://www.selfharmuk.org/docs/public%20report%20from%20mtgs%201and2_17-08-04_final.doc

Zlotnick, C., Shea, M.T., Pearlstein, T., Simpson, E., Costello, E. & Begin A. (1996). The relationship between dissociative symptoms, alexithymia, impulsivity, sexual abuse, and self-mutilation. *Comprehensive Psychiatry*, 37(1):12-6.

Zlotnick, C., Mattia, J.I., & Zimmerman, M. (2001). The relationship between posttraumatic stress disorder, childhood trauma and alexithymia in an outpatient sample. *Journal of Traumatic Stress*, 14,177–188.

Resources

. . . .

The following resources are provided for information only. Inclusion does not necessarily imply recommendation or endorsement. The list is not exhaustive.

Information included in this section features well established websites and organisations. All websites and individual pages listed were retrievable at the time of final preparation (September, 2007). For websites mentioned in the main text see index.

Self-Injury and Related Issues

UK based websites and pages

Self-Injury and Related Issues (SIARI)
Jan Sutton's website
http://www.siari.co.uk
Established in 2001, this comprehensive, regularly updated website provides information on self-injury/self-harm and related issues such as eating disorders, abuse, rape, trauma, dissociation, and other mental health issues. It also offers references, self-help strategies for overcoming self-injury, guidance for friends, family, and young people, details of training events, conferences, and research projects, links to the latest news on self-injury, a bookstore, and a moderated message board. With its extensive links and wide-ranging information, SIARI is an ideal place to start searching for information on self-injury and related issues.

Basement Project
http://www.basementproject.co.uk/
The Basement Project provides support groups for those who have been abused as children and people who self-harm. Also provides

training, consultation and supervision for workers in community and mental health services, and a range of publications. Current publications include:

- Making Sense of Self-Harm
- What's the Harm?
- The Self-Harm Help Book
- Working with Self-Injury
- New Strength in Numbers
- Hurting Inside
- Lifting the Lid
- Getting it Right
- Self-Harm – A Resource Pack
- Young People & Self-Harm – An Educational Resource

beat (beating eating disorders) – previously known as **The Eating Disorders Association**
http://www.b-eat.co.uk

Better Services for People who Self-Harm
www.rcpsych.ac.uk/cru/auditselfharm.htm
The Royal College of Psychiatrists is running a programme to improve services for people who self-harm. Its aim is to ensure that people who self-harm and use A&E, ambulance, or mental health services, receive appropriate and fair care and treatment. For more information, please visit their website or call a member of the team on 020 7977 6642. *See also* **The Royal College of Psychiatrists** below

Borderline UK
http://www.borderlineuk.co.uk
Borderline UK is a national user-led network of people within the United Kingdom who meet the criteria for or have been diagnosed with Borderline Personality Disorder (BPD).

BPD World
http://www.bpdworld.org
Information, advice and support on Borderline Personality Disorder, Depression & Schizophrenia.

Bristol Crisis Service for Women (BCSW)
http://www.users.zetnet.co.uk/bcsw
BCSW is a national voluntary organisation that provides support to women in emotional distress; e.g., women who have suffered sexual abuse or self-injure.

Publishes a range of leaflets and booklets on self-injury. Current booklets include:

- Understanding self-injury
- Self-help for self-injury
- For friends and family
- Self-injury, support and self-help groups
- Women from Black and Minority Ethnic Groups and Self-Injury

Also run a national helpline (see website for details), support self-injury self-help groups, offer talks and training courses to professionals, and carry out research. Further publications include:

- Women and self-injury: a survey of 76 women (1995)
- Working with People who Self-injure Training Pack (updated 2006).

British Association for Counselling and Psychotherapy (BACP)
(The leading professional body for counsellors and psychotherapists in the United Kingdom)
http://www.bacp.co.uk
The BACP website offers a wide range of information on counselling and therapy; including the BACP's *Ethical framework for good practice in counselling and psychotherapy'* and guidance on seeking a therapist

(explanation of theoretical approaches, information sheet and online search directory).

Crisis Recovery Unit
http://www.slam.nhs.uk/services/pages/detail.asp?id=432
A national unit for individuals who repeatedly harm themselves and engage in difficult relationships.

Depersonalisation Research Unit (The Institute of Psychiatry)
http://www.iop.kcl.ac.uk

First Person Plural
http://www.firstpersonplural.org.uk
UK Survivor-led Association for Dissociative Survivors of Abuse & Trauma and their allies.

Howard League for Penal Reform
http://www.howardleague.org
'The Howard League for Penal Reform is the oldest penal reform charity in the UK. It was established in 1866 and is named after John Howard, one of the first prison reformers. The Howard League for Penal Reform is entirely independent of government and is funded by voluntary donations.' Current publications include:

- Suicide and self-harm prevention: A strategy for Northern Ireland
- Suicide and self-harm prevention: The management of self-injury in prison
- Suicide and self harm prevention: Following release from prison
- Suicide and self-harm prevention: Repetitive self-harm among women and girls in prison
- Suicide and self-harm prevention: Court cells and prison vans

- Scratching the surface: The hidden problem of self-harm in prisons

LifeLink

http://www.lifelink.org.uk

Provides free support and advice to people in crisis who self-harm and are at risk of suicide in the North Glasgow area.

LifeSIGNS (Self-Injury Guidance & Network Support)

http://www.selfharm.org

LifeSIGNS is an online, user-lead charity founded in 2002 committed to raising awareness about self-injury, and to providing information and support to people of all ages affected by self-injury. Offers training, factsheets, guidance to family and friends of people who self-harm, information on 'coming out' about self-injury, a free newsletter (available via email), and a self-injury awareness booklet. For further information about LifeSIGNS *see main text* (pages 359–360).

MIND (The leading mental health charity in England and Wales)

http://www.mind.org.uk

Mind publishes a large range of booklets and factsheets giving the latest information on mental health issues. For information on self-harm, borderline personality disorder and dissociation, see booklets *Understanding self-harm, Understanding borderline personality disorder,* and *Understanding dissociative disorders* (available on their website). *See also* MindinfoLine below.

National Self-Harm Network (NSHN)

http://www.nshn.co.uk/

Survivor-led organisation committed to campaigning for the rights and understanding of people who self-harm.

Newham Asian Women's Project (NAWP)

http://www.nawp.org

NAWP provides advice and support to Asian women and children experiencing domestic violence. Also has qualified trainers to provide Applied Suicide Intervention Skills Training (ASIST). The course is a two-day first aid interactive workshop that provides practical training for caregivers seeking to prevent the immediate risk of suicide. Current resources available from NAWP include:

- Silent Scream – Young Asian Women and Self-Harm: A Practical Handbook for Professionals working with Asian women
- Young Asian Women and Self-Harm: A Mental Health Needs Assessment of Young Asian Women in Newham, East London (A Qualitative Study) 1998.
- Painful Secrets – A qualitative study into the reasons why young women self-harm (summarises the key findings of their year long study on self-harm with young women aged 11-25 from across five London boroughs).
- Training DVD on Young People and Self-Harm. 'This unique DVD is the result of extensive consultations in England, Scotland and Wales with young people and professionals on the issue of self-harm. The DVD addresses a number of issues including: what self-harm is, why people may self-harm, common myths and stereotypes, some of the key issues affecting young people who may be self-harming, the different ways that people can be supported, as well as how people could support themselves and a charter of recommendations produced by young people for caregivers/professionals and policy makers.'

Fore more information on ASIST or to purchase any of their resources, contact Gurpreet Virdee on gvirdee@nawp.org or 0208 519 9136.

Penumbra
http://www.penumbra.org.uk
One of Scotland's leading mental health organisations providing a wide range of support services for adults and young people.

RecoverYourLife.com
http://www.recoveryourlife.com
Self-harm support community.

S.A.S.H. Survivors of Abuse and Self-Harming Information Service (for adults)
http://www.freewebs.com/sashpen

The Centre for Suicide Research (University of Oxford)
http://cebmh.warne.ox.ac.uk/csr

The Pottergate Centre for Dissociation and Trauma
http://www.dissociation.co.uk/

The Royal College of Psychiatrists (The main professional body for psychiatrists in the UK and Ireland)
http://www.rcpsych.ac.uk/
The RCP publishes a variety of leaflets and factsheets on a range of common mental health problems for parents, teachers and young people. For information on self-harm, see their *Factsheet 26:* Deliberate self-harm in young people: For parents and teachers. *See also* **Better Services for People who Self-Harm** above.

Trauma and Abuse Group (TAG)
http://www.tag-uk.net/
A group studying and supporting work concerning trauma, abuse and dissociation.

United Kingdom Society for the Study of Dissociation (UKSSD)

http://www.ukssd.org

Visible Memories: A film about self-injury (Mind, Croydon)

(VHS or DVD format)

http://www.mindincroydon.org.uk/videos.asp

'Visible Memories allows people who self-injure to describe their experiences. They tell us some of the reasons why they self-injure and what approaches they find helpful or unhelpful. Setting self-injury in a more general context of self-harm, the film argues that such behaviour is a valid coping mechanism for dealing with internal emotional distress, and that consequently, the challenge for those who do not self-injure is to come to terms with their own feelings in relating to those who do.'

Cost: £40. Running time: 27 minutes

Young minds

http://www.youngminds.org.uk/selfharm

Self-harm information.

Young People and Self Harm

http://www.selfharm.org.uk

Information resource for young people who self-harm, their friends and families, and professionals working with them.

Young People and Self Harm: A National Inquiry

http://www.selfharmuk.org

The National Inquiry website includes facts and figures about self-harm, links, interim reports, legal guidance, training resources, and information for families and professionals supporting people that self-harm. Downloadable publications include:

- The Truth About Self-Harm (young people's report)

- Truth Hurts – Full Report
- Truth Hurts – Executive Summary

For further information about the National Inquiry *see main text* (pages 95-96).

United Kingdom Society for the Study of Dissociation (UKSSD)

http://www.ukssd.org

UK helplines

ChildLine

http://www.childline.org.uk
ChildLine is a free helpline for children and young people in the UK. Children and young people can call them on 0800 1111 to talk about any problem – their counsellors are always available to help.

CIS'*ters*

Tel: (02380) 3380080 – Saturdays 10am–12 noon. *See* Organisations/ services supporting survivors of abuse, rape, and sexual violence and those who work with them for further information about CIS'*ters*.

MindinfoLine

http://www.mind.org.uk/About+Mind/Mindinfoline
Tel: 0845 766 0163 (Monday to Friday 9.15am to 5.15pm)
Confidential help offered on a range of mental health issues.

NSPCC Child Protection

http://www.nspcc.org.uk
Helpline: 0808 800 5000
Free confidential service open 24 hours.

Samaritans

http://www.samaritans.org.uk/

Samaritans provide confidential non-judgemental support, 24 hours a day for people experiencing feelings of distress or despair, including those which could lead to suicide.

UK organisations/services supporting survivors of abuse, rape, and sexual violence and those who work with them

Directory And Book Services (DABS)

http://www.dabsbooks.co.uk

Specialist book and information service for people who are overcoming childhood abuse, sexual abuse, or domestic violence, and for those who live or work with them.

CIS'*ters*

PO Box 119, Eastleigh, Hampshire SO50 9ZF

Helpline: (02380) 3380080 – Saturdays 10am–12 noon

CIS'*ters* provides support for adult females who were sexually abused as children by a member of their immediate or extended family, a quarterly newsletter, group meetings (including workshops for survivors), and training for people working with survivors. See *main text pages* 298-300, *and* Appendix 5 (pages 435-438) for further information provided by CIS'*ters*.

The Survivors Trust

http://www.thesurvivorstrust.org

The Survivors Trust is a national umbrella agency for specialist voluntary sector services working with survivors of rape, sexual violence and childhood sexual abuse. Includes information for survivors.

Self-Injury and Related Issues

US based websites and pages

American Self-Harm Information Clearinghouse

http://www.selfinjury.org

Includes a bill of rights for those who self-injure, Armando Favazza's comments on the bill of rights for people who self-harm, self-help ideas, self-injury fact sheet, and tips for emergency workers who encounter self-harm.

Babette Rothschild's website

http://home.webuniverse.net/babette

Babette Rothschild is author of:

- *The Body Remembers: The Psychophysiology of Trauma and Trauma Treatment*
- *The Body Remembers CASEBOOK: Unifying Methods and Models in the Treatment of Trauma and PTSD*
- *Help for the Helper: The Psychophysiology of Compassion Fatigue and Vicarious Trauma* (with Marjorie Rand)

Babette's website provides an introduction to her treatment of trauma and post-traumatic stress disorder (PTSD) plus an overview of her work through numerous articles. A schedule of her workshops is also provided.

BPD Today

http://www.borderlinepersonalitytoday.com

Child abuse statistics, research and resources

(By Jim Hopper, Ph.D.)

http://www.jimhopper.com

David Baldwin's Trauma Information
http://www.trauma-pages.com

HealthyPlace.com
http://www.healthyplace.com/Communities/Self_Injury/
healingtouch
Self-injury community.

Gift From Within
http://giftfromwithin.org
An international nonprofit organisation for survivors of trauma and
victimisation.

**International Society for the Study of Trauma and
Dissociation (ISSTD)**
http://www.isst-d.org

**National Center for Posttraumatic Stress Disorder
(NCPTSD)**
http://www.ncptsd.org

S.A.F.E. Alternatives®
800-DONTCUT®
www.selfinjury.com

'S.A.F.E. Alternatives ® is a world-renowned treatment program that
in its more than twenty years of operation has helped thousands of
people successfully end self-injurious behaviour. A treatment team of
experts uses therapy, education, and support to empower clients to
identify healthier ways to cope with emotional distress. The S.A.F.E.
Alternatives ® philosophy and model of treatment focus on shifting
control to the client, empowering them to make healthy choices,
including the choice to not self-injure.'

Secret Shame (self-injury information and support)
http://www.palace.net/~llama/psych/injury.html
Run by Deb Martinson, this long established website offers information on diagnoses associated with self-injury, etiology (history and causes), first aid for self-injury, help for families and friends, living with self-injury, quotes from personal stories, references, self-help, therapeutic approaches, trauma, what self-injury is, who self-injures, and why people deliberately injure themselves. Additional features include the popular bus (bodies under siege) online community and bus web board.

Self-Injury: A Struggle
http://self-injury.net

The Cutting Edge: A Newsletter for People Living With Self-Inflicted Violence
http://www.sidran.org
By Ruta Mazelis and published by the Sidran Institute.

The Healing House
http://www.thehealinghousela.org
A private therapeutic treatment centre for self-injury.

The Trauma Center (Founder: Dr. Bessel van der Kolk)
http://www.traumacenter.org

The Sidran Institute
http://www.sidran.org
Traumatic stress education and advocacy.

European website

European Society for Trauma and Dissociation (based in The Netherlands)
http://www.estd.org/

Further reading

. . . .

Although comprehensive, the following list of books is not exhaustive. Moreover, regrettably, space does not permit a detailed description of the books listed. Most can be ordered via Amazon (http://www.amazon.co.uk or http://amazon.com) or at other major online and offline bookstores. For a synopsis, or to view editorial or readers' reviews of a particular book, Amazon is a good starting point. To search for all books, use the Amazon book search facilities, keying in the terms self-harm, self-injury, self-inflicted violence, self-mutilation, etc.

Non-fiction

Alderman, T. (1997). *The Scarred Soul: Understanding and Ending Self-Inflicted Violence*. Oakland, CA: New Harbinger Publications.

Babiker, G., & Arnold, L. (1997). *The Language of Injury: Comprehending Self-Mutilation*. Leicester: BPS Books.

Bhugra, D. (2004). *Culture and Self-Harm: Attempted Suicide in South Asians in London*. Hove: Psychology Press.

Brophy, M. (2006). *Truth Hurts: Report of the National Inquiry into Self-Harm Among Young People*. London: Mental Health Foundation.

Clarke, A. (1999). *Coping With Self-Mutilation: A Helping Book for Teens Who Hurt Themselves*. New York: Rosen Publishing Group.

Connors, R.E. (2001). *Self Injury: Psychotherapy with People Who Engage in Self-Inflicted Violence*. Northvale, NJ: Jason Aronson.

Conterio, K., & Lader, W. (1999). *Bodily Harm: The Breakthrough Healing Program for Self-Injurers*. New York: Hyperion.

D'Onofrio, A.A. (2007). *Adolescent Self-Injury: A Comprehensive Guide for Counselors and Healthcare Professionals*. New York: Springer Publishing Company.

Farber, S. K. (2000). *When the Body Is the Target: Self-Harm, Pain and Traumatic Attachments*. Northvale, NJ: Jason Aronson.

Favazza, A. R. (1987). *Bodies Under Siege: Self-Mutilation in Culture and Psychiatry.* Baltimore: The Johns Hopkins University Press.

Favazza, A. R. (1996*). Bodies Under Siege: Self-Mutilation and Body Modification in Culture and Psychiatry*, 2nd ed. Baltimore: Johns Hopkins University Press.

Fox, C., & Hawton, K. (2004). *Deliberate Self-Harm in Adolescence.* London: Jessica Kingsley Publishers.

Gardner, F. (2001). *Self-Harm: A Psychotherapeutic Approach.* Hove: Brunner-Routledge.

Harrison, D. (1995). *Vicious Circles: An Exploration of Women and Self-Harm in Society.* London: Good Practices in Mental Health.

Hawton, K. et al (2006). *By Their Own Young Hand: Deliberate Self-Harm and Suicidal Ideas in Adolescents.* London: Jessica Kingsley Publishers.

Hyman, J.W. (1999). *Women Living with Self-Injury.* Philadelphia, PA: Temple University Press.

Kreitman, N. (Ed.). (1977). *Parasuicide.* Chichester, UK: Wiley.

Levitt, J.L., Sansone, R.A., & Cohn, L. (Eds.). (2004). *Self-Harm Behaviors and Eating Disorders: Dynamics, Assessment, and Treatment.* New York: Brunner-Routledge.

McVey-Noble, M.E., Khemlani-Patel, S., & Neziroglu, F. (2006). *When Your Child Is Cutting: A Parent's Guide to Helping Children Overcome Self-Injury.* Oakland, CA: New Harbinger Publications.

Menninger, K. A. (1985). *Man Against Himself.* New York: Harcourt, Brace Jovanovich.

Milia, D. (2000). *Self-Mutilation and Art Therapy: Violent Creation.* London: Jessica Kingsley Publishers.

Morgan, H. (1979). *Death Wishes? The Understanding and Management of Deliberate Self-Harm.* New York: Wiley.

National Collaborating Centre for Mental Health (2004). *Self-Harm: The Short-Term Physical and Psychological Management and Secondary Prevention of Self-Harm in Primary and Secondary Care.* National Clinical Practice Guideline 16. Leicester and London: British Psychological Society and Royal College of Psychiatrists.

Ng, G. (1998). *Everything You Need to Know about Self-Mutilation: A Helping Book for Teens Who Hurt Themselves.* New York: Rosen Publishing Group.

Pembroke, L. R. (Ed.). (1994). *Self-harm: Perspectives from Personal Experience.* London: Survivors Speak Out.

Levenkron, S. (1999). *Cutting: Understanding and Overcoming Self-Mutilation*. New York: W.W. Norton.

Miller, D. (2005). *Women Who Hurt Themselves: A Book of Hope and Understanding* 10th Ann Ed. New York: Basic Books.

Plante, L.G. (2007). *Bleeding to Ease the Pain: Cutting, Self-Injury, and the Adolescent Search for Self*. CT: Praeger Publishers.

Selekman, M.D. (2006). *Working with Self-Harming Adolescents: A Collaborative, Strengths-Based Therapy Approach*. New York: W.W. Norton.

Simeon, D., & Hollander, E. (Eds.). (2001). *Self-Injurious Behaviors: Assessment and Treatment*. Washington, DC: American Psychiatric Press.

Spandler, H. (1996). *Who's Hurting Who? Young People, Self-Harm, and Suicide*. Manchester. 42nd Street.

Spandler, H., & Warner, S. (Eds.). (2007). *Beyond Fear and Control: Working with Young People Who Self-Harm*. Ross-on-Wye: PCCS Books.

Smith, G., Cox, D. & Saradjian, J. (1998). *Women and Self-Harm*. London: Women's Press.

Strong, M. (1999). *A Bright Red Scream: Self-Mutilation and the Language of Pain*. London: Virago.

Turner, V.J. (2002). *Secret Scars: Uncovering and Understanding the Addiction of Self-Injury*. Minesota: Hazelden.

Turp, M. (2003). *Hidden Self-Harm: Narratives from Psychotherapy*. London: Jessica Kingsley Publishers.

Walsh, B.W., & Rosen, P.M. (1988). *Self-Mutilation: Theory, Research and Treatment*. New York: The Guilford Press.

Walsh, B.W. (2005). *Treating Self-Injury: A Practical Guide*. New York: The Guilford Press.

Williams, M. (1997). *Cry of Pain: Understanding Suicide and Self-Harm*. Harmondsworth: Penguin Books.

Winkler, K. (2003). *Cutting and Understanding Self-Mutilation: When Teens Injure Themselves*. NJ: Enslow Publishers.

Memoirs/novels/autobiographical/stories

Brecht, S. J., & Redheffer, J. (2005). *Beyond The Razor's Edge: Journey of Healing and Hope Beyond Self-Injury*. Lincoln, NE: iUniverse, Inc.

Duffy, V. F. (2004). *No More Pain!: Breaking the Silence of Self-Injury*. Longwood, FL: Xulon Press.

Kenrick, J. (2007). *Red Tears.* London: Faber and Faber.

Kettlewell, C. (2000). *Skin Game: A Cutter's Memoir.* New York: St. Martin's Griffin.

Leatham, V. (2006). *Bloodletting: A Memoir of Secrets, Self-Harm & Survival.* Oakland, CA: New Harbinger Publications.

Robson, A. (2007). *Secret Scars: One Woman's Story of Overcoming Self-Harm.* Carlisle: Authentic.

Smith, C.M. (2005). *Cutting It Out: A Journey Through Psychotherapy and Self-Harm.* London: Jessica Kingsley.

Vega, V. (2007). *Comes the Darkness, Comes the Light: A Memoir of Cutting, Healing, and Hope.* New York: AMACOM Books.

Training packs

Arnold, L. (1997). *Working With People Who Self-Injure.* Bristol: Bristol Crisis Centre for Women.

Williams, D., & Wildgoose, A. (2007). *Managing Self-Harm: A Training Pack for People Working with Individuals Who Self-Harm.* Brighton: Pavilion Publishing.

Workbooks

Bowman, S., & Randall, K. (2004). *See My Pain! Creative Strategies and Activities for Helping Young People Who Self-Injure.* Chapin, SC: YouthLight, Inc.

Connors, R., & Trautmann, K. (1994). *Understanding Self-Injury: A Workbook for Adults.* Pittsburgh, PA: Pittsburgh Action Against Rape.

Dace, E. et al. (1998). *The Hurt Yourself Less Workbook.* London: National Self-Harm Network.

Index